CONTACT

CONTACT

ART AND THE
PULL OF PRINT

JENNIFER L. ROBERTS

PRINCETON UNIVERSITY PRESS
Princeton and Oxford

THE A.W. MELLON LECTURES IN THE FINE ARTS
National Gallery of Art, Washington
Center for Advanced Study in the Visual Arts

BOLLINGEN SERIES XXXV: 70

CONTACT

ART AND THE
PULL OF PRINT

JENNIFER L. ROBERTS

PRINCETON UNIVERSITY PRESS
Princeton and Oxford

THE A.W. MELLON LECTURES IN THE FINE ARTS
National Gallery of Art, Washington
Center for Advanced Study in the Visual Arts

BOLLINGEN SERIES XXXV: 70

Published by Princeton University Press, 41 William Street, Princeton, New Jersey 08540

In the United Kingdom: Princeton University Press, 99 Banbury Road, Oxford OX2 6JX

press.princeton.edu

Cover image: Jennifer L. Roberts (photographer). Detail of *Nordlicht—6:08 pm*, 2018, by Christiane Baumgartner. Woodcut on Japanese paper. Harvard Art Museums/Fogg Museum, Cambridge, MA. Margaret Fisher 1986 Fund.

ISBN 978-0-691-25585-9
ISBN (ebook) 978-0-691-25586-6
Library of Congress Control Number: 2023948741

This is the seventieth volume of the A. W. Mellon Lectures in the Fine Arts, which are delivered annually at the National Gallery of Art, Washington. This volume is based on lectures delivered in 2021. The volumes of lectures constitute Number XXXV in the Bollingen Series, supported by the Bollingen Foundation.

British Library Cataloging-in-Publication Data is available

Designed by Roy Brooks, Fold Four, Inc. This book has been composed in Adobe Caslon and Motor

Printed in China

10 9 8 7 6 5 4 3 2 1

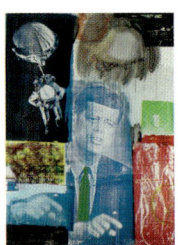

Inside covers: Detail from Robert Rauschenberg, *Retroactive I*, 1963. Oil and silkscreen ink on canvas, 84 × 60 in. Wadsworth Atheneum Museum of Art, Hartford, CT. Gift of Susan Morse Hilles, 1964.30

Photo credit: Allen Phillips/Wadsworth Atheneum

CONTENTS

For Lottie

PREFACE

Over a scattered series of weekday mornings in the winter and spring of 2021, I sat down alone in a small spare bedroom (really more of a closet) and delivered the 70th annual A. W. Mellon Lectures in the Fine Arts. Squinting into the glare of borrowed studio lights whose tangled cords ran through piles of laundry, backed up against a bank of shelving that had been designed for household storage rather than the tableau of printmaking books I'd arranged, I read my script into the built-in camera on my laptop and hoped that it would all turn out.

The pandemic marked those lectures in every way. Prior to the pandemic, I had already been planning to approach the lectures as a broad reframing of the meaning of print rather than a series of niche-focused research essays. The year of isolation leading up to their delivery cemented that idea: with the collapse of all my plans to visit print rooms and print studios for new research in 2020–21, I turned with renewed intensity to the prints that I already knew from my years of previous research and teaching (this, by the way, is why so many images in this book come from the collections of the Harvard Art Museums). I devoted myself to developing, reshaping, clarifying, and synthesizing ideas that I had begun to explore in classes, publications, exhibitions, and print studios over the previous ten years.

But if the pandemic reinforced some of my original inclinations for the lectures, it also changed them in fundamental ways. It changed them in content—in particular, they ended up centering on questions of touch and contact in ways that would have seemed unimaginable to me a year earlier. And it changed them in form. With the much wider viewership that was made possible by the video format, I had an opportunity to try to write the lectures in such a way that they would be as accessible as possible to the broadest range of audiences. The challenge I set myself was to try to make something that could somehow be interesting to art history professors, *and* first-year studio printmaking students, *and* doctoral students in early modern history, *and* painters, *and* graphic designers, *and* book historians, *and* museum curators, *and* old master print collectors, *and* casual museumgoers. And so forth. As tall an order as that was, and as impossible as it was to achieve it, I am glad that I made the effort.

As I began planning the book that would come out of the lectures, I briefly entertained the idea of a major overhaul, translating the scripts into a greatly expanded argument and remastering the prose until it adopted a more recognizably academic style. But it didn't take long to realize that pulling apart the lectures this way would irrevocably damage the peculiar coherence of the project. I realized that I could not—and did not want to—edit out the hard-fought sense of immediacy that I had invested in the language. I didn't want to dilute the sense of *invitation* that I was hoping to cultivate: an invitation to everyone to explore a field that can sometimes seem intimidating or obscure.

This book, then, attempts to preserve the spirit of the lectures *as* lectures. It is a moderately edited version of the original lecture scripts. I have tried to maintain the concision, clarity, and conversational cadence of the lectures as they were crafted for video. The original videos will remain available in perpetuity online; they have the advantage of including many more images than could be printed here, and they include some essential supporting video content.

I hope I have preserved something of the spirit of connection that I was trying to build in that tiny room, reaching out to an unknowable audience from a state of isolation. The history of printmaking is a history of connection, of making contact, across distance. It seems appropriate to me that this book might try to do the same.

CONTACT

CONTACT

INTRODUCTION

My goal in this book is to open up new ways of thinking about the significance of print and printmaking. I hope that it will serve as a compelling introduction to the profundity of the medium for anyone who has not (yet) studied it, and that it will serve as a provocative reintroduction to the potentials of the medium for anyone who has. It is not by any means a comprehensive history of printmaking, but it hopes to make printmaking recognizable to a wider audience across and beyond the arts, and thus, perhaps, to contribute to its future.

As it stands now, in the predominant narratives of the development of Western art, printmaking barely registers. It suffers from a weird form of double invisibility. It is somehow both too obscure and too familiar; both beyond and beneath notice. On the one hand, as a set of processes, printmaking can be so technically intricate as to verge on the arcane: from early modern etching to contemporary nanoprinting, the making of prints is complicated and nonintuitive. This has tended to push discussion about it into insular, hyperspecialized corners of art history that have been difficult to integrate with the rest of the discipline. The result is that the extensive (and wonderful) literature on the histories and techniques of printmaking has been walled off from the rest of the art world. With few exceptions, print is written about by print specialists who publish in print exhibition catalogs, print collectors' publications, and specialized print journals. Especially within the modern and contemporary fields, one would be hard pressed (as it were) to find a broad discussion or a theoretical manifesto about printmaking in a major peer-reviewed journal.[1]

On the other hand, as a class of art objects, prints tend to be devalued as overly common; they are (in a phrase I hear all the time) "just prints." Outside of the inner sanctum of the print world, the medium suffers from old prejudices about its marginal, secondary status in relation to painting, sculpture, and photography. It tends to be seen as a tool for unimaginative reproduction, or as a low-stakes territory for rehearsing ideas prior to deploying them in a higher-status medium. And now that print appears to be vanishing in the digital age, we seem to be letting it go quietly, as if its impending death were just a natural extension of its prior irrelevance. I hope to show that print is very much alive in its deep impact on art of all kinds, and to argue that printmaking is a much more strange and powerful affair than we have generally been led to believe.

In order to make this argument, I will need to take an unorthodox approach to the history and theory of printmaking. First, although I will often linger lovingly on historic prints and traditional printmaking techniques, I will focus my analysis primarily on modern and contemporary artists that work at the very edge of the medium and beyond. The chapter on pressure, for example, will feature printing presses being used to smash ironing boards, fires being set on press beds, and human bodies being used as printing plates. Such operations stretch printmaking almost beyond recognition (and they are often carried out by artists who do not strictly recognize themselves as printmakers), but in doing so they reveal some of the forgotten potentials that print has carried within itself all along. They also allow print to be recognized in a broader field of contemporary ideas and practices. Indeed, I hope to show that the seemingly provincial, esoteric operations of printmaking are, in fact, working at the very heart of some of the most prominent modern and contemporary art across mediums.

Second, I will focus relentlessly upon the "making" part of printmaking. I am interested in the unique ways that printmaking generates meaning at the level of fundamental physical operations. I want to get at the physics of print, and to explore the poetics and politics that might emerge from that physics. As I have learned by making prints and by watching others make them, technical matters are not "merely" technical (I am against all such "merelyisms" in art and art history). The act of making is its own form of intelligence, and when we recognize this, we can begin to explore the deep imbrication of the technical in the conceptual, the philosophical, the theoretical, and the political.[2]

So rather than organize this book around particular artists, or around chronological developments in print history, or around the standard workshop subdivisions of print media (etching, lithography, etc.), I'll organize it around a set of basic physical operations or maneuvers that cut across these traditional ways of arranging knowledge about print. The maneuvers I'll be tracing, one per chapter, are as follows: pressure; reversal; separation; strain; interference; and alienation. Each of these terms is designed to connect core materials and movements — the deep textures of printmaking — with the conceptual possibilities that those forces bring into being. So, for example: pressure is a basic physical force that transfers images in printmaking, but it also opens out onto social cognates like "impression" and "oppression." Each of these six terms denotes a form of intelligence and sensitivity that allows for specific kinds of intervention in social and political life. And each of these terms names a maneuver that emerges in printmaking but is not restricted to it — it can travel to and through other media.

These terms function for me as something like a primordial grammar of print, a grammar that has the potential to reveal new patterns of connection between balkanized areas of knowledge in and beyond print, and even in and beyond art history. They are a set of "receptors," as it were, that might allow print to be recognized across areas of focus and engagement where it is currently invisible. They are designed to be transitive: to open passages between the material and the social, and to create paths for thinking across different spheres of making—between print, painting, sculpture, and so on, but also between the fine arts and the industrial arts and the decorative arts and the domestic arts. This cross-sectional understanding of process means that although I will insist upon the meaningful specificity of printmaking (I will argue, for example, that due to the pressure involved in the printing process, the "picture plane" in a print, often taken to be a lite analog for a painting, is, in fact, entirely different than it is in painting), I am not interested in returning to restrictive twentieth-century models of medium specificity. Whereas these explored specificity in order to "entrench" each medium "more firmly in its area of competence" (to quote Clement Greenberg), I will propose something more like "medium generativity": a model of embedded material intelligence that assumes that specific ways of thinking arise in specific material operations but can then go on productively to perturb other spheres of activity.[3]

You may have noticed that my list of essential print operations does not include "replication" or "repetition" or "reproduction." This is intentional. To the extent that printmaking *has* found a place in the narratives of art history and other fields in the humanities, this has been by virtue of its replicative function. In 1953, the great print curator and scholar William Ivins published *Prints and Visual Communication*, which is still, seventy years later, the primary text on the meaning of printed images. Ivins saw the ultimate significance of print as its capacity to generate what he called "exactly repeatable pictorial statements."[4] In his writings and the writings of others who share his approach, print is taken to be fundamentally about replication, dissemination, and the visual public sphere that this does or does not produce.

Like everyone who studies prints, I am forever indebted to Ivins and his brilliant work, and I have happily immersed myself in the literature on print as replication. But I will be bracketing out the themes of reproduction and dissemination in the pages ahead. The theoretical focus on replicability has been remarkably productive as a way to explain the significance of print—so productive, in fact, that I am concerned that it has become monolithic, seemingly synonymous with print itself. The emphasis on "exactly repeatable pictorial statements," however valuable, has left many of the other qualities of print unexplored. And when we look for significance only to the downstream life of prints-as-copies—to what happens after they leave the press—we don't explore the ideas that can arise from and through the actual process of making them. In our focus on swarms of exact copies spreading through the world, we disregard everything that goes on in printmaking before the copy hits the streets.

Moreover, the emphasis on communicability that attends the study of replication can tend to normalize and familiarize print. The more effective and efficient print is seen to be as a tool of dissemination and communication, and the more it accords with the light of reason and discourse, the harder it is to see that a print is a rather bizarre thing—a thing that is born from a moment of dark and mysterious contact under intense pressure, in a drama full of inversion and reversal and blindness and uncertainty.[5] And without attending to this recalcitrance of print, its material-conceptual peculiarity, we will be unable to recognize some of the ways that print can matter most to contemporary art and life. I don't intend to devalue or disavow the centrality of reproduction to printmaking; I simply want to loosen its grip on interpretation long enough to establish footholds for other interpretive frameworks. And this is not a zero-sum operation: everything we might learn from a deep attention to things like reversal or pressure can be reintegrated into future studies of replication, to what I hope will be the ultimate benefit of the field.

As I trace out these maneuvers of print, I will focus primarily on art made in the United States and Europe after about 1960. My narrative could have been woven through any number of other artists and periods and places, and I hope that the book's approach will be widely applicable (or at least testable) well beyond this small sample. My decision to focus as I do is partially arbitrary: it just happens to be the field in which I am trained. But it is also a particularly productive period for rethinking print, because during this time, rich avenues of interchange were developing between print and the other arts. For example, let's look at three pivotal moments in the careers of three artists who have been central to the way we understand modern and contemporary art. In the later 1950s, Jasper Johns began using stencils to produce gridded paintings of numbers and alphabets (FIG. 0.1). In 1960, Robert Rauschenberg completed a series of drawings based on Dante's *Divine Comedy* that included solvent transfer images (FIG. 0.2). He had selected images from magazines, soaked them in lighter fluid, turned them face down, rubbed them with an empty ballpoint pen, and transferred them onto the paper in a kind of ghostly reverse. In 1962, Andy Warhol began using screenprinting to transfer photographic halftones of movie stars and car crashes onto large canvases (FIG. 0.3). In any canonical narrative of twentieth-century American art, these are transformative moments. Johns's number grids beget conceptual art, minimalism, and an entire range of systematic painting practices. Rauschenberg's transfers beget various strands of assemblage, intermediation, and performance. Warhol, of course, begets pop, and an enormous range of media-based art.

What I think has not been sufficiently recognized, and what these three events have in common, is that in each case the artist diverted a printmaking

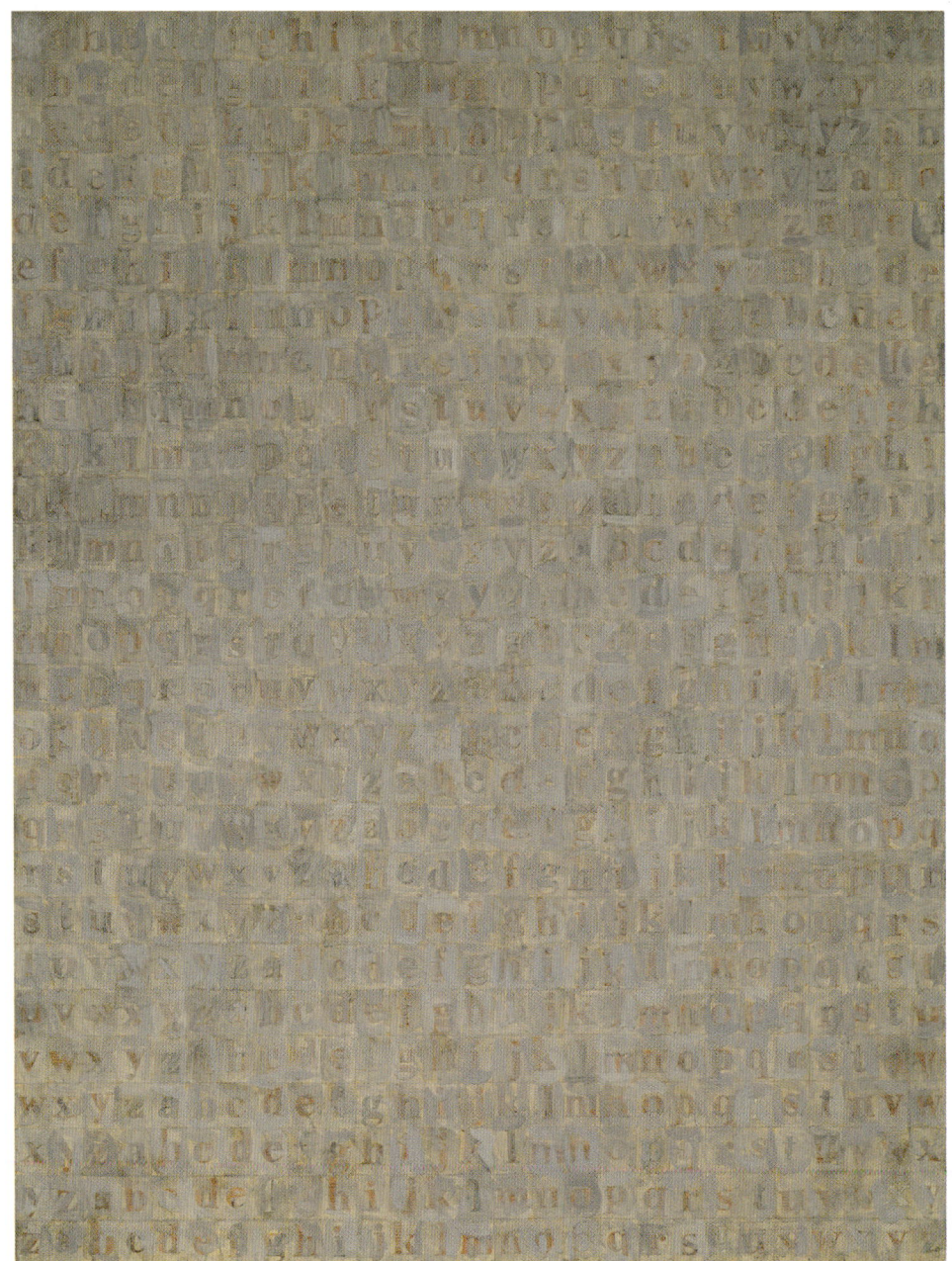

Jasper Johns, *Gray Alphabets*, 1956. Beeswax and oil on newspaper
and paper on canvas. The Menil Collection, Houston.

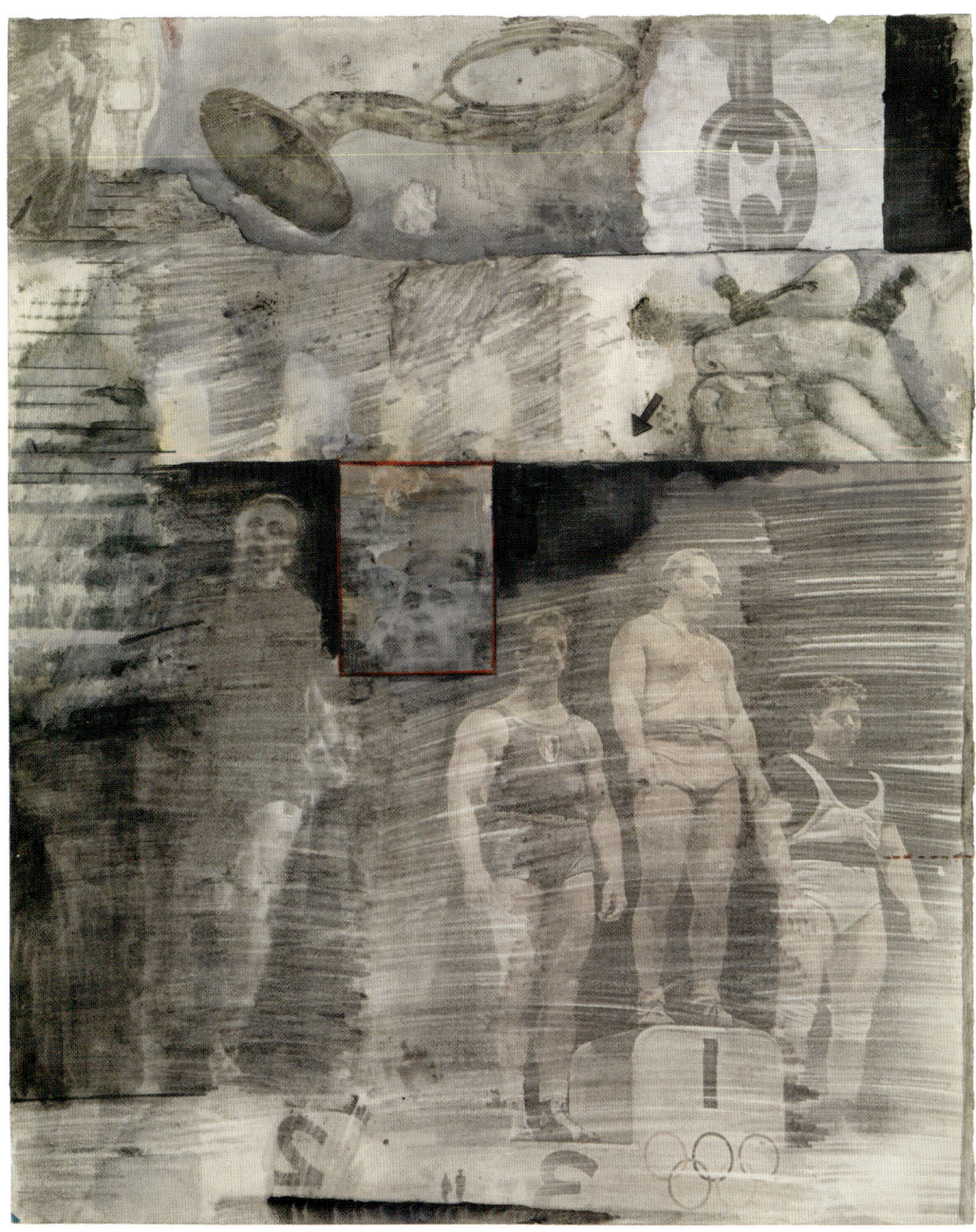

FIG. 0.2

Robert Rauschenberg, *Canto XXI: The Central Pit of Malebolge, The Giants*, from *Thirty-Four Illustrations for Dante's Inferno*, 1959–60. Solvent transfer drawing, gouache, cut-and-pasted paper, pencil, and colored pencil on paper. The Museum of Modern Art, New York. Given anonymously. 346.1963.31.

technique into another, higher-status medium (painting or drawing). The stencil is among the oldest of print technologies. Solvent transfer, moving ink from one surface to another, in reverse, under pressure, is blatantly a form of printing. And screenprinting is, of course, screenprinting.

At the same moment that this was happening, there were two major infusions of energy from print converging on painting and sculpture, one from the commercial side and one from the fine art side. First, new and more efficient commercial print techniques were transforming the visual landscape. The profusion of images in postwar culture was accelerated by the perfection of high-speed offset presses and the development of more precise and efficient color printing technology. And this world of commercial printing was becoming increasingly permeable to the fine arts, since so many notable artists (Warhol and Roy Lichtenstein among them) began their careers as commercial artists whose job was expressly to translate all kinds of images into this ebullient new language of print.

Second was the phenomenon known as the "Print Renaissance." The later twentieth century saw a surge of interest in older, traditional printmaking techniques like etching, engraving, woodcut, and stone lithography. In rapid succession, several legendary print studios were established to provide equipment, expertise, and training in these processes: Universal Limited Art Editions (ULAE) in Long Island in 1957, Tamarind Lithography Workshop in Los Angeles in 1960, Crown Point Press in the San Francisco Bay Area in 1962, and many more. I'll just briefly mention something about these studios that is worthy of extended further study: all three of these major workshops were founded and run by women.[6]

The standard operating model of these studios was to invite well-known artists to spend days or weeks in the workshop working with printers, learning and experimenting with print processes. They thus became another primary site for the crossover between printmaking and other art media. Artists like Johns and Rauschenberg spent enormous amounts of time in these environments, learning to make prints, and—crucially—learning to think and work like printers and printmakers (FIG. 0.4). And those experiences changed their work in painting and sculpture in fundamental ways.

These print studio residencies remain active today, and most of the contemporary artists featured in this book have spent weeks if not years working intensively with printers at Tamarind or Crown Point or ULAE or any number of other smaller but equally remarkable studios. There are as many different motivations for engaging with printmaking as there are artists who do so, but it is fair to say that mere reproducibility is not always or even often the primary goal of the endeavor. What else are these artists learning from print, and what can we learn in turn from them?

Andy Warhol, *Green Marilyn*, 1962. Acrylic and silkscreen ink on linen. National Gallery of Art, Washington, DC. Gift of William C. Seitz and Irma S. Seitz, in Honor of the 50th Anniversary of the National Gallery of Art.

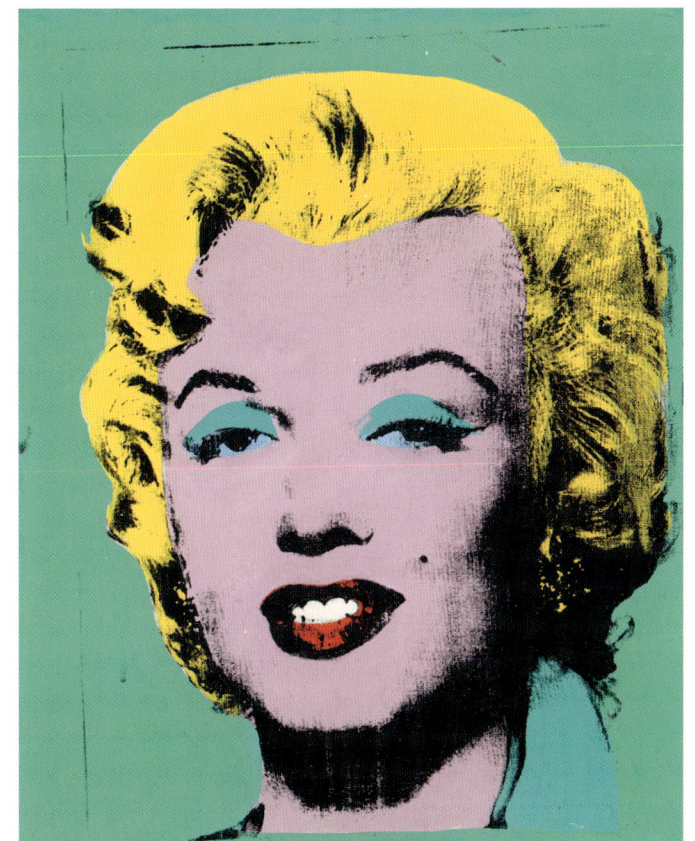

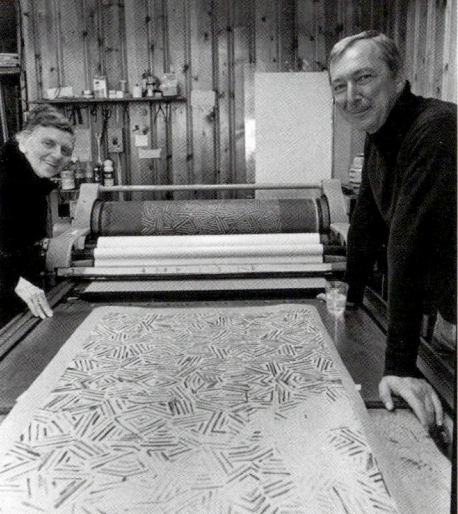

FIG. 0.4
Iris Schneider (photographer), Tatyana Grosman with Jasper Johns at the offset lithographic press at Universal Limited Art Editions, February 1976.

(overleaf)
FIG. 0.5
Common Printing Methods.

COMMON PRINTING METHODS WITH ASSOCIATED PROCESSES

RELIEF WOODCUT | WOOD ENGRAVING | LINOCUT | LETTERPRESS

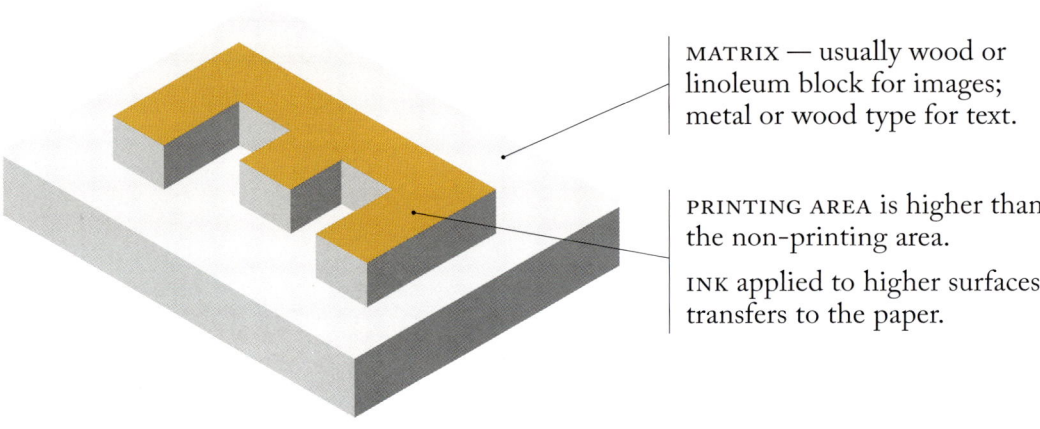

MATRIX — usually wood or linoleum block for images; metal or wood type for text.

PRINTING AREA is higher than the non-printing area.

INK applied to higher surfaces transfers to the paper.

PLANOGRAPHIC LITHOGRAPHY | OFFSET LITHOGRAPHY

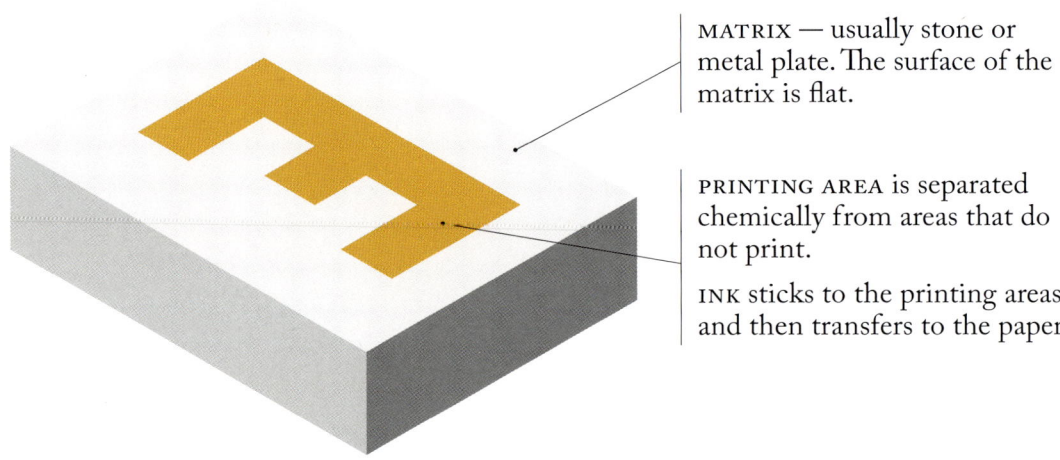

MATRIX — usually stone or metal plate. The surface of the matrix is flat.

PRINTING AREA is separated chemically from areas that do not print.

INK sticks to the printing areas and then transfers to the paper.

In OFFSET LITHOGRAPHY, ink from the matrix is picked up by a rubber roller, then transferred (offset) onto the paper. The image on the matrix is REVERSED on the roller, and REVERSED AGAIN on the paper.

These designations represent the four most common forms of matrix preparation and ink transfer in printing. These categories are fluid, however; many printmakers freely adapt and combine these methods.

INTAGLIO ENGRAVING | ETCHING | DRYPOINT | AQUATINT

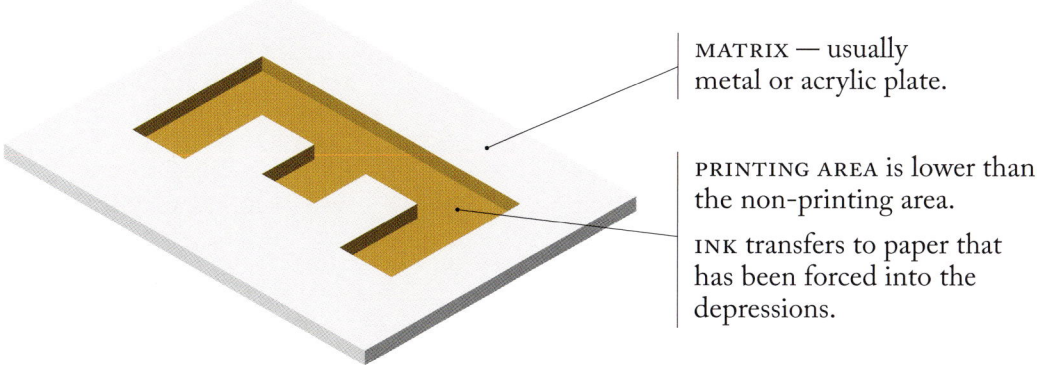

MATRIX — usually metal or acrylic plate.

PRINTING AREA is lower than the non-printing area.

INK transfers to paper that has been forced into the depressions.

STENCIL SCREENPRINTING | STENCIL

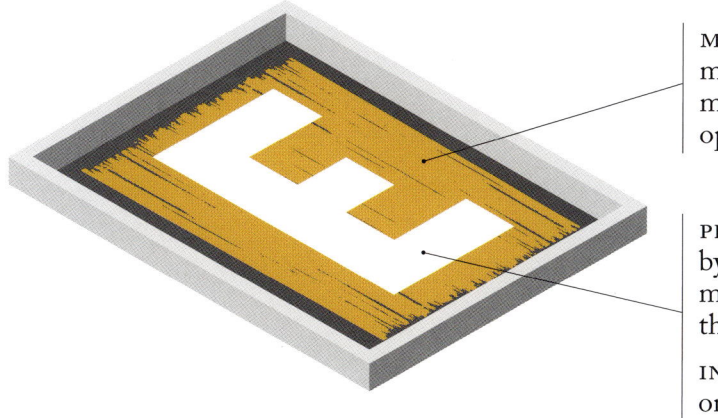

MATRIX — usually a screen mesh or a thin sheet of metal or paper, incorporating openings.

PRINTING AREA is composed by creating openings in the matrix, or by blocking off areas that should not print.

INK passes through open areas onto the paper below.

PRESSURE

The working definition of a print in this book will be as follows: *a print is an object that has been made by transferring an image between two surfaces in contact*. Every print is the result of a process of contact and release, which links it immediately to themes of touch, presence, and intimacy—but also to themes of loss, separation, and memory.

Most prints emerge from a combination of three basic elements. The *matrix* is the object—the plate or block or screen—that holds the image to be transferred (see fig. 0.5). The *support* is the surface that receives the image—usually but not always a sheet of paper. The *ink* is the substance transferred between the matrix and the support—with the proviso that you can still make an impression (as in embossing) without ink. What brings all these elements together, and makes the transfer possible, is *pressure*.

The earliest and most general meanings of the English noun "print" share this emphasis on direct contact and pressure. The first two definitions listed in the *Oxford English Dictionary* emphasize the act of impression or indentation, the preservation of a form left by the pressure of an object: "the impression or imprint made by the impact of a stamp, seal, die, or the like on a surface"; and "any indentation made in a surface preserving the form left by the pressure of some object coming into contact with it."[1]

Contact, then, is essential to the definition of print, especially as a means for usefully distinguishing printmaking from other reproductive media like photography. Like print, photography involves the precise transfer of information between surfaces, but, in the case of photography, the carrier of that transfer is light, which bounces from one surface to another at a distance. Photography does not require mechanical contact or pressure; print does. This has many implications; for example, print always happens at actual size while photography does not. Lens-based photography automatically rescales the image as it transfers it to the film, but because print involves touch, or contact, between the matrix and the support, the transfer between surfaces must happen at actual size. As art historian David Summers points out, "we can only touch things at the size they are."[2] As we will see in the chapters ahead, there is a close, codependent relationship between photography and print in modern and contemporary visual culture, but the criterion of contact is a useful way to distinguish them and to analyze more precisely the contributions of each.

Many of the earliest forms of printing, such as seals and stamps, drew their value from this guarantee of immediate physical contact. This ancient Mesopotamian cylinder seal (FIG. 1.1) is a cylindrical matrix of quartz into which a scene has been carved. When rolled out onto a pliable support, the cylindrical scene becomes a linear impression. Seals like this bore authority because of the direct contact required to produce them. If a particular king or official had

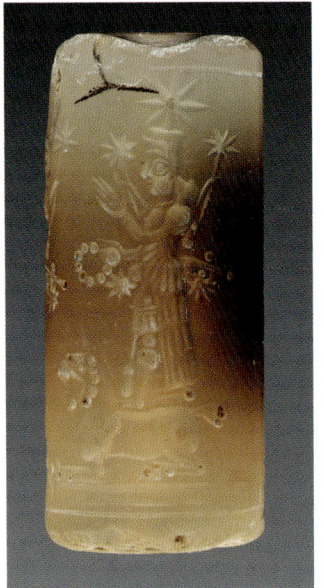
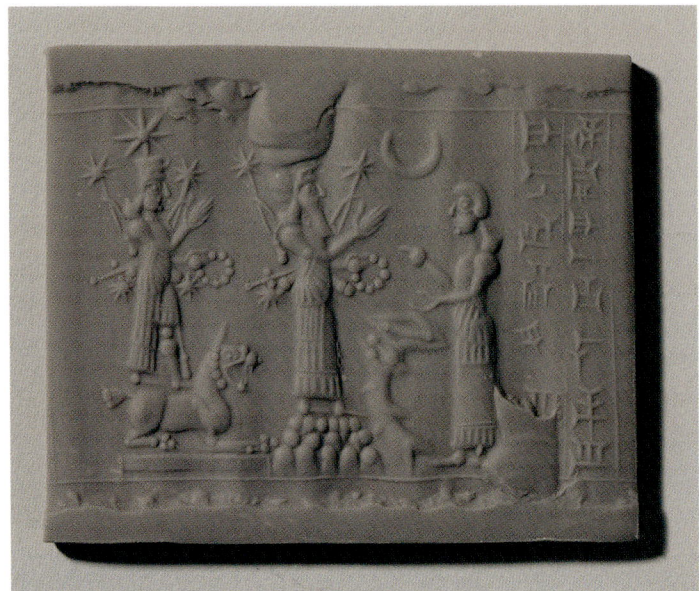

Cylinder Seal: Deities and Worshipper, c. 883–612 BCE. Mesopotamian. Quartz cylinder seal with impression. Harvard Art Museums/Arthur M. Sackler Museum, Cambridge, MA. Gift of Edward Waters.

such a seal, its imprint would authenticate a certain communication as having come from that office. It carried proof of fidelity through adjacency: it was the record of a contact event.

As records of contact events, prints also intersect with the history of contact relics, particularly imagistic relics like the Sudarium or "Veronica's Veil" (or simply "Veronica"), an iconic motif in Western Christianity since the Middle Ages. According to Christian tradition, when Saint Veronica stopped and used her veil to wipe the blood and sweat from the face of Christ as he made his way to be crucified, a miraculous image of the face remained on the cloth thereafter. The authority of this image derived from its direct contact with the face of Christ, and the transferred image was thus itself sacred. It is not surprising that early modern printmakers seized on the Sudarium as emblematic of their own work, which, after all, also involved transferring an image from one surface to another through contact. Here are Veronicas by two of the most brilliant and self-reflexive printmaking artists of the sixteenth and seventeenth centuries: Claude Mellan (FIG. 1.2) and Albrecht Dürer (FIG. 1.3).[3]

FIG. 1.2
Claude Mellan, *The Sudarium of Saint Veronica*, 1649. Engraving on laid paper. National Gallery of Art, Washington, DC. Rosenwald Collection.

FIG. 1.3
Albrecht Dürer, *The Sudarium Held by Two Angels*, 1513. Engraving. National Gallery of Art, Washington, DC. Rosenwald Collection.

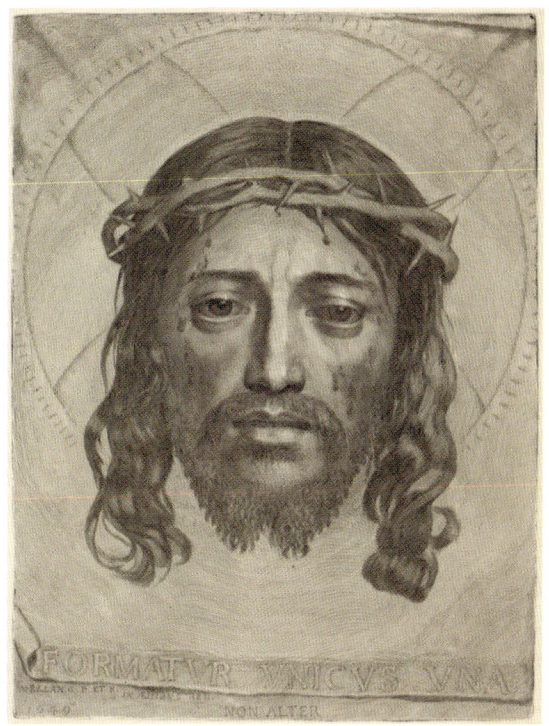

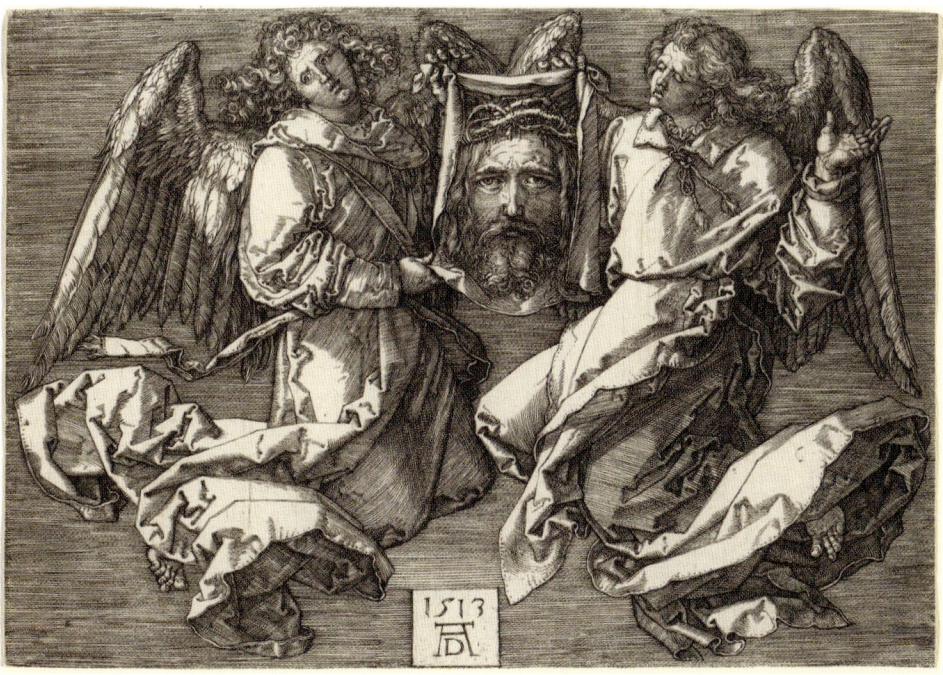

The Sudarium also evoked printmaking through its relationship to wounds and wounding. Like the veil absorbing Christ's thorn-gouged blood, prints are made by cutting and scratching into one body (such as a copperplate or woodblock) and transferring viscous matter (ink) from there onto another surface. Most prints are contact relics in this sense, inasmuch as they are essentially stains on one surface that attest to damage done to another surface.[4]

Because of their miraculous origins, relics like the Sudarium were *acheiropoetic*—meaning "made without hands." This, too, is a quality that is shared by prints in general. In printmaking, the print itself, in the last analysis, is made not by human hands but by the press or by whatever instrument is being used to apply pressure. The sensory implications of this nonhuman mode of image transfer are profound. Although it is not human, the printing press is a sensitive perceptual instrument: after all, it must sense the image on the matrix in order to print it. It does this by applying pressure to the matrix, which responds to that pressure according to the chemical or topographical qualities of its surface—the incisions on a copperplate, for example, or the greasy patterns on a lithographic stone. This is much closer to a tactile mode of perception than a visual one. Indeed, although the printing press is used for the production of visual art, it is not itself an optical instrument. If you want to print a visual image, you must first convert it into something that can be felt: the image must be translated into a pattern of grooves, ridges, or adhesions. The printmaking process is akin to an act of communication with an alien that has no eyes.

And printmaking is nonoptical in another sense: the moment of printing is radically invisible. The actual formation of the print occurs in a tight, unobservable space. The print is made darkly: what happens there happens between the matrix and the ink and the support; no one can watch it; no one can surveil it. This helps explain the mystique of the "pull" in printmaking: that moment when the image is peeled away from the matrix, revealing it to the eye and to the air for the first time (FIG. 1.4). Once the print is pulled, it enters the luminal world of the visual arts. It is released into the light, into space, into the range of the aerial and the optical. Now we can back up and get a look at it. But when we do, we should not forget that we are always looking at a recording of an event that occurred beyond the range of looking. We are looking at the fossilized traces of a hidden, sequestered act of material perception. No matter how airy or spatial the illusionary image on the print might be, it is first of all a remnant of blind, anaerobic contact.

Usually, this is forgotten as the print travels downstream and takes its place among other kinds of more blithely visible images. But contemporary artists have sometimes found ways to more fully acknowledge the conditions under which images come into being under pressure. John Cage's fire prints made at

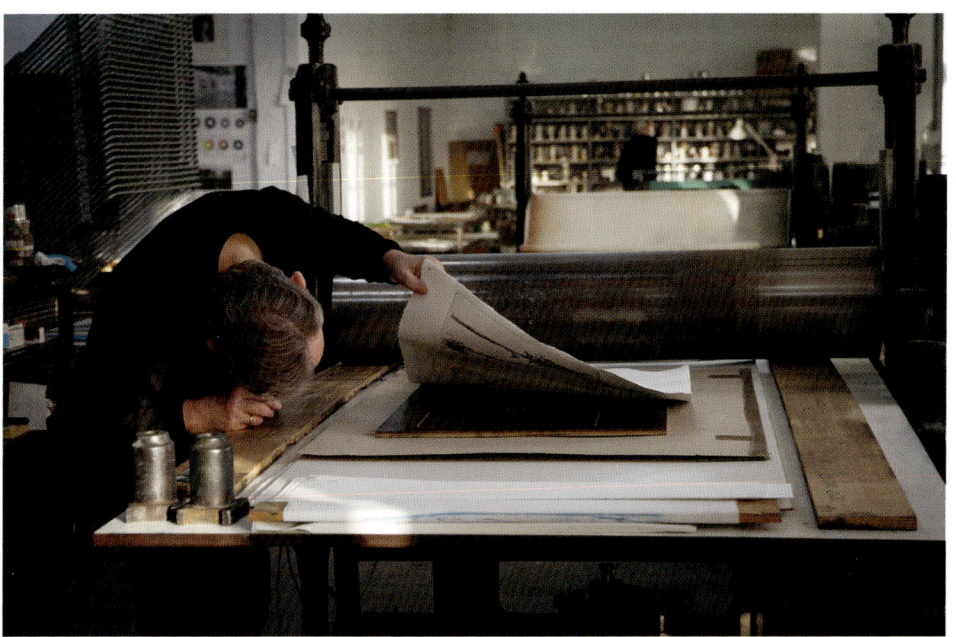

FIG. 1.4
Birgitte Rubæk (photographer), Niels Borch Jensen pulling a print.

Crown Point Press in the 1980s are a good example (FIG. 1.5). Throughout his work, Cage tried to avoid the imposition of his own artistic will or authority, preferring instead to make decisions based on chance operations, and to operate in an attitude of open receptivity rather than control. At Crown Point, he made a series of prints that were thoroughly open to the closed conditions of the press. He would start a small pile of crumpled newspapers on fire, cover it with a damp sheet of paper, let it smolder for a while, and then run the whole conflagration through a roller press (FIG. 1.6). The prints that result are, quite simply, extinguishments. The suffocating pressure and blindness of the press becomes the work itself—the image is literally composed by putting out the fire, putting out the light. Pressure is not an accessory to the creation of some other independent image. Pressure creates the image in total. Note that these prints, though born of destruction, also have a quality of delicacy and sensitivity to them. This paradoxical copresence of delicacy and pressure will be a continuing refrain in this chapter.[5]

Robert Rauschenberg also explored the generative qualities of pressure in the printing process. In the fall of 1974, he worked with the experimental Los Angeles print workshop Gemini G.E.L. on a series of works known as the

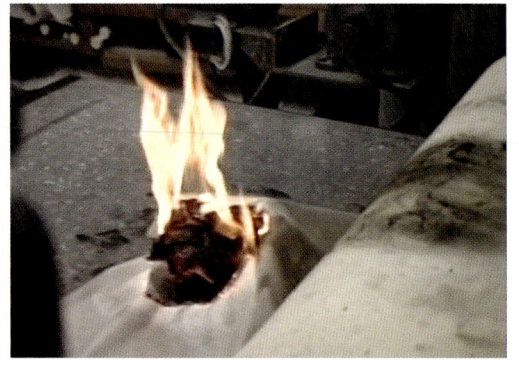

FIG. 1.5
John Cage, *Eninka No. 29*, 1986. Burned, smoked, and branded gampi paper mounted to Don Farnsworth handmade paper. National Gallery of Art, Washington, DC. Gift of Crown Point Press.

FIG. 1.6
Still from the film *Printing John Cage's "Eninka 29,"* 1986. National Gallery of Art, Washington, DC.

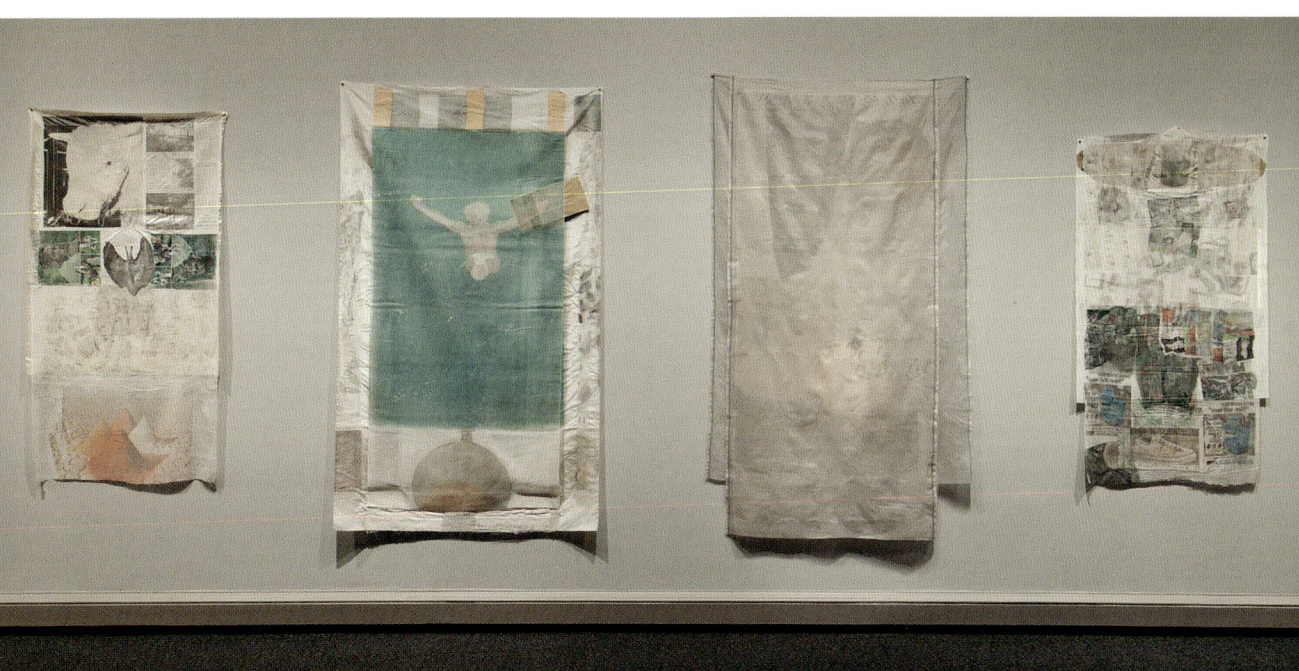

FIG. 1.7
Robert Rauschenberg, *Hoarfrost Editions*, 1974. Partial installation view. National Gallery of Art Archives, Washington, DC.

Hoarfrost Editions (FIG. 1.7). This was a group of prints made on multilayered fabric that emphasized veiling effects and fugitive, fragmentary imagery. They were made by spreading out fabric on the bed of a lithography press, then topping the fabric with pages torn from newspapers and magazines: some flat, some folded, some wrinkled, some balled up (FIG. 1.8). Rauschenberg frequently nestled empty paper bags, sometimes flat and sometimes folded, into the layers. Often there would be multiple layers of fabric and paper balancing on the bed in what I can only think to call a print sandwich. At various points in the construction of the sandwich the newspapers and printed matter would be sprayed with chemical solvents that would solubilize the ink so that it could be released onto the fabric.[6]

The layered assembly of paper bags, printed papers, fabrics, adhesives, and solvents then went through the press several times at pressures ranging from six hundred to one thousand pounds per square inch. After pressing, the materials were less than a centimeter thick. When the smashed strata were peeled apart and the newspapers removed, what remained were flattened paper bags nestled

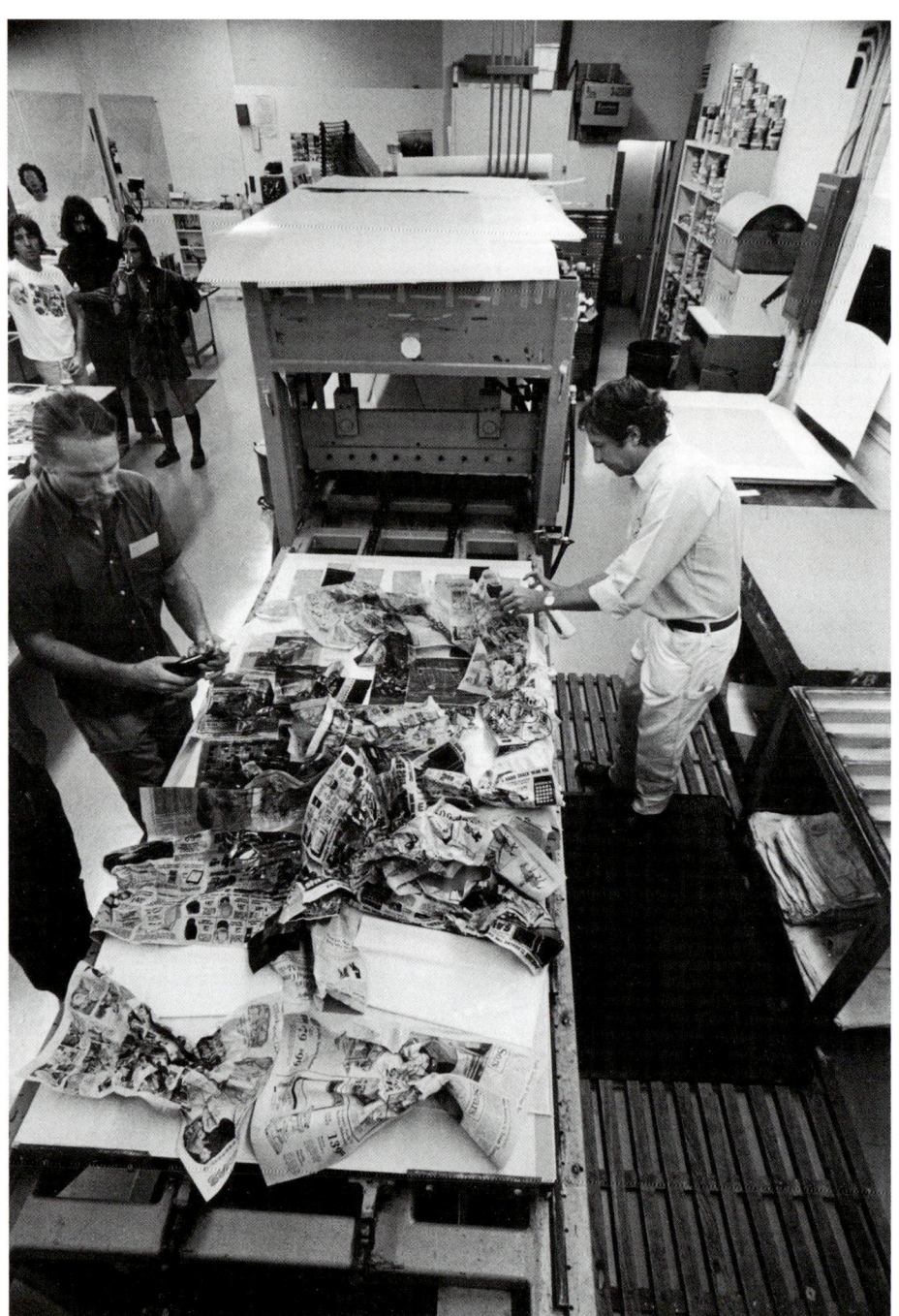

FIG. 1.8
Daniel B. Freeman (photographer), Robert Petersen (left) and
Robert Rauschenberg (right) arranging newspapers on the press,
September 1974.

between layers of diaphanous fabric imprinted with transferred newspaper ink. The chaotic and fragmentary quality of the transferred news made clear that this was, we might say, a pressure-cooked image. The images on the prints were not replicated by pressure but rather *composed* by it (FIG. 1.9). As the press crumpled and crushed the printed matter, it made a new print that disrupted the original images and rewrote the newspaper text, reversing, recombining, smudging, and offsetting the ink, announcing the creative role of pressure in the work.

The paper bags were left between the layers of fabric, demonstrating that they had also been reshaped by pressure as they were flattened into their interleaving forms. Through these flattened paper volumes, Rauschenberg was addressing serious questions about what it might mean to understand pressure as a means of dimensional translation, and thus as a mode of pictorial representation. One of the main problems to be worked out in pictorial art is: How do you get three dimensional objects onto a two-dimensional surface? The prevailing solution in the West, of course, is illusionism: perspectival projection, modeling, and so on. This is how an artist like Leonardo da Vinci gets a human head onto a flat plane. But another solution, as Rauschenberg implicitly points out, is literal: you do it by essentially running over the object, by smashing it down from a volume to a plane (FIG. 1.10).

There was a lot of talk of "modernist flatness" in postwar American art theory—more than I can possibly review here. Suffice it to say that Rauschenberg's smashed paper bags (along with the entire *Hoarfrost* project) give us a version of flatness that is not reflected in the prominent art criticism of the period. With the partial exception of the work of art historian Leo Steinberg (see note 7), the discussions and debates about modernist flatness took place almost entirely in the context of, and in reference to, painting. Yet the flatness of a painting is not the same as the flatness of a print. From a physical standpoint, the flatness of a stretched canvas is rather like the surface of a small trampoline: painters feel the tautness and tooth of the canvas as it responds, springily, to their gestures. No wonder that the images that come to rest on that plane can be seen to occupy it lightly; they can be seen as spatially elastic, bouncing in and out of the third dimension. Rauschenberg hints here at a different rubric, giving us a glimpse of other models that might have emerged if printing, with its crushing forces, were instead the medium driving art theory and criticism.[7]

What kind of picture plane is a picture plane under pressure? It is a picture plane upon which forces act bidirectionally, from both above and below. In printmaking, it is not only the application of pressure from above that creates the impression. It is also, and equally, the necessary grounding resistance of the print bed from below, offering an equal and opposite reaction. You need both pressure from above and counterpressure from below to make a print. Every act

Robert Rauschenberg, *Mule* (details), from *Hoarfrost Editions*, 1974. Offset lithograph and newsprint transferred to collage of paper bag, cheesecloth, muslin, silk, and satin. National Gallery of Art, Washington, DC. Gift of Gemini G.E.L. and the artist, 1991.

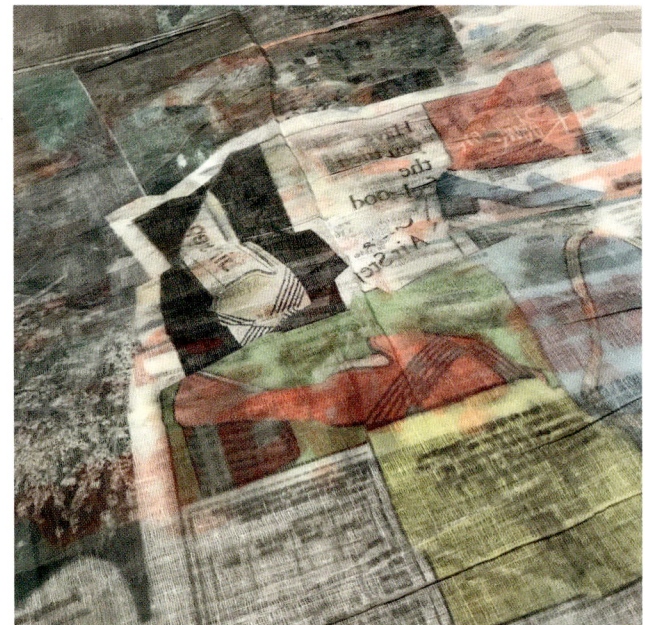

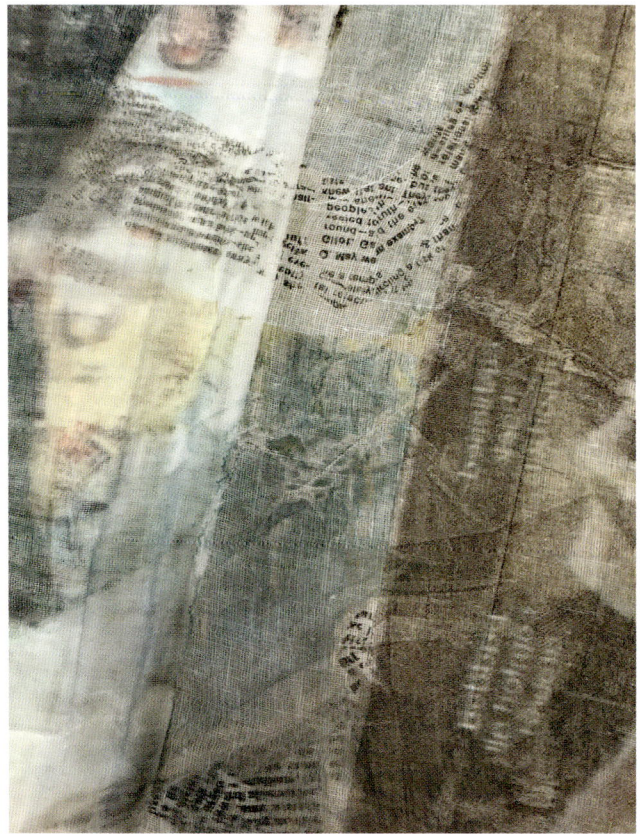

Leonardo da Vinci, *Head of Leda*,
c. 1504–6. Black chalk, pen, and
ink. Royal Collection Trust,
London.

Robert Rauschenberg, *Scent*
(detail of smashed bag), from
Hoarfrost Editions, 1974. Offset
lithograph and newsprint
transferred to collage of paper
bags, silkscreen fabric, and silk
chiffon. National Gallery of Art,
Washington, DC. Gift of Gemini
G.E.L. and the artist, 1991.

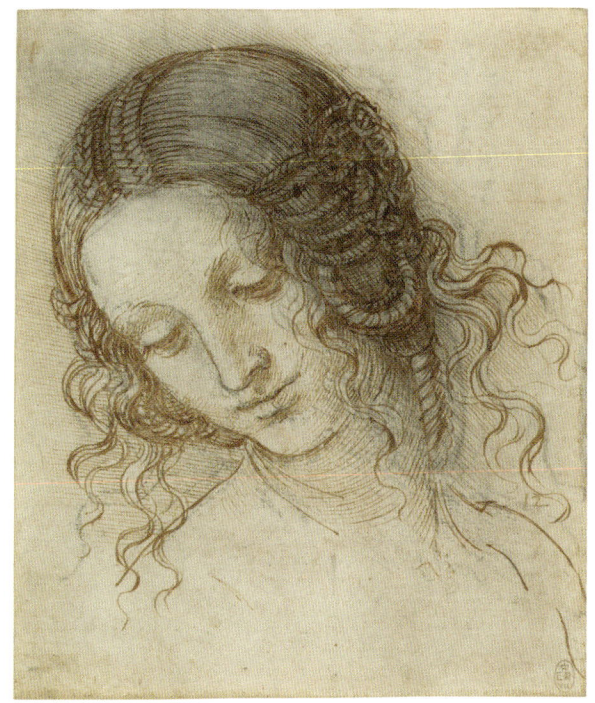

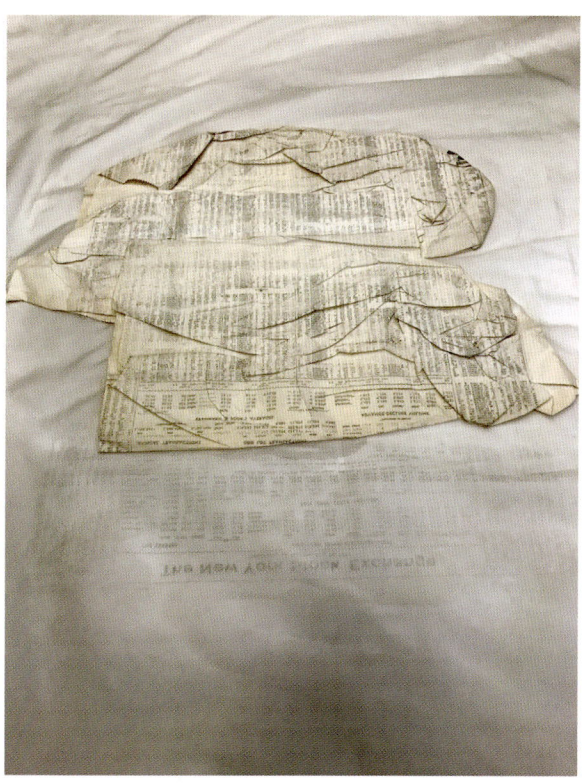

of printing is simultaneously a pressing down and a pressing up. Both pressure and resistance live in the print. A pictorial object born out of this kind of space is charged with these counterforces in ways that far exceed the standard painterly flatness. It is an object that has been pushed, and pushes back.

There are other forms of what we might call extreme printing that capture this sense of the image emerging by force from below or behind the picture plane. Consider the rubbing. In 2016, Jennifer Bornstein completed a complex project in which she made rubbings of her deceased father's belongings (FIG.1.11). For this print, she covered a pair of khakis with a sheet of paper and rubbed the image through in blue encaustic. The image is strange and haunting, particularly in the way the clothing appears to become partly transparent under the pressure of the rubbing tool. It is as if we are seeing through the top pant leg to the bottom pant leg; this is because Bornstein's application of pressure to the top of the paper also, automatically, registers counterpressure from beneath, essentially seeing through the object by rubbing it.

If the resulting image is visually nonsensical and slightly otherworldly, it is because rubbing, like all printing, shows us the world as "seen" by touch, and only later given over to the eye. Bornstein's work picks up on the history of Surrealist rubbings and frottage. And, given its memorial subject matter, it recalls even more directly the history of monument and gravestone rubbing. For example, a famous series of New England gravestone rubbings published in 1963 by Ann Parker and Avon Neal (FIG. 1.12) includes a resurrection scene, with an angel hovering over a tomb, sounding a call for the dead to rise. The act of making a gravestone rubbing is itself eerily like a form of resurrection, because rubbing the blank paper from above causes the image to appear before you as if lifted through it from the stone below. This contact image, made through pressure, somehow combines extreme tactility with a sense of phantomlike emergence.[8]

So both sides of the "picture plane" emerge together, in a play of pressure and counterpressure, in the printing process. The back of a print is made along with its front. The artist Matt Saunders explores these bilateral dynamics of printing in a slightly different way: by printing from both sides of a matrix that has undergone these forces. Saunders recently completed a series of complex etchings at Borch Editions in Copenhagen that register the impact of printmaking on both the front and the back of a copperplate. For his series *Ratlos (Indomitable)*, Saunders used enormous copperplates (over five feet high and three feet wide) for a series of images based on film stills. Each plate was etched and an edition of six was pulled from its "image" side according to the usual procedures. But then Saunders took each copperplate and printed another edition from its back side. While the prints from the front of the plate recorded Saunders's deliberate image-making activities on the matrix, the prints from the back, with

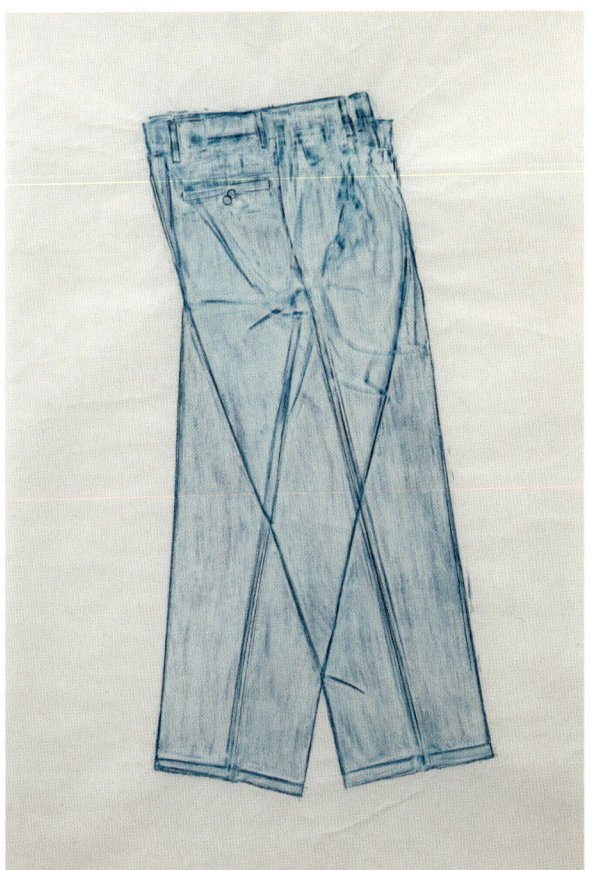

FIG. 1.11
Jennifer Bornstein, *Khakis*, 2016.
Rubbing. Encaustic and wax on
Kozo paper. Property of the artist.

FIG. 1.12
Ann Parker and Avon Neal,
Tombstone of Richard Holmes, 2nd,
Plymouth, Massachusetts, 1828,
1963. Rubbing on paper. Harvard
Art Museums/Fogg Museum,
Cambridge, MA. Gift of Mr. and
Mrs. Philip Hofer.

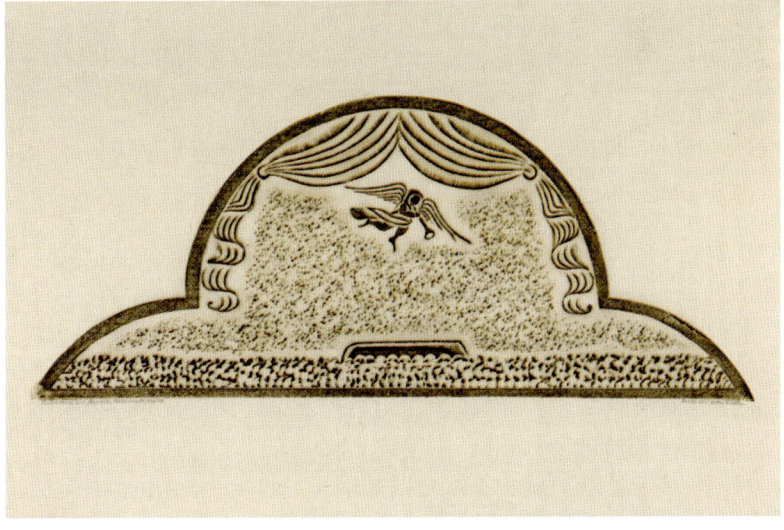

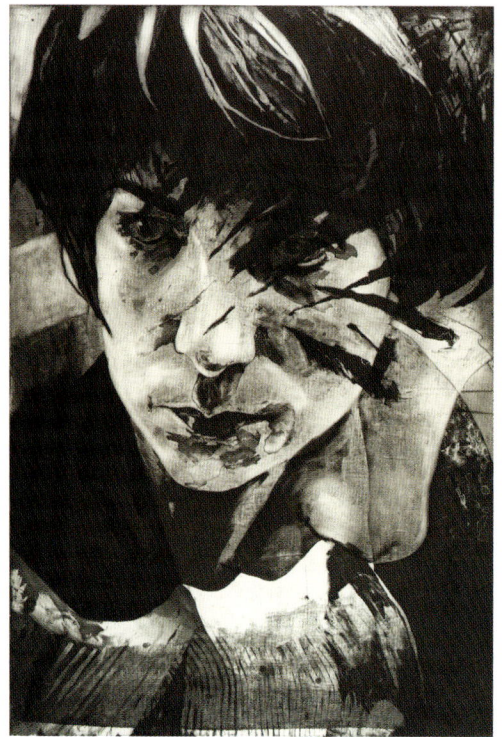
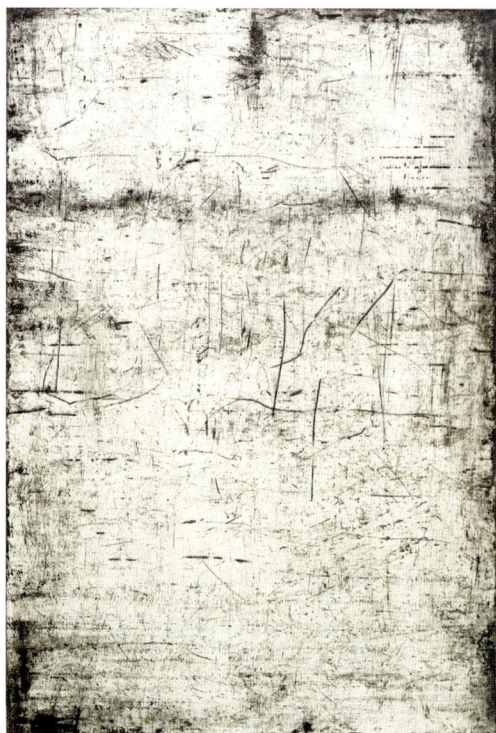

FIG. 1.13

Matt Saunders, Left: *Ratlos/Indomitable V*, 2017. Right: *Back (Ratlos/Indomitable V)*, 2017. Copperplate etching; soft ground etching, soap ground aquatint, spit bite aquatint, sugar lift aquatint, open bite on paper. Property of the artist.

their intricate networks of gouges and scratches, recorded what was happening to the back of the plate throughout the process. They recorded each nudge and turn of the plate on the table as Saunders worked, the adventures of the plates as they were dragged across tables, into acid baths, and through the press for each impression taken from the front (FIG. 1.13). In every printmaking operation, the material stresses of incision, transfer, and reproduction are felt by both sides of the matrix, but it is usually only on the front that the record of these stresses is enshrined as a print. Saunders, by printing the back as well, reveals that the printerly picture plane cannot be fully captured by any neat frontalities.[9]

 We've seen so far that printing, in its deployment of pressure, generates not just multiple images but multiple models of the image. These range from the revelatory or redemptive model that draws from the conversion between touch and vision, to the forceful model that is shot through with echoes of both violence and resistance. Why does this matter beyond the world of the print studio? What does this range of sensitivity and expression, born out of printerly pressure, make possible? For the remainder of this chapter, I want to explore these questions through the work of two African American contemporary artists: Willie Cole and David Hammons.

Both Cole and Hammons have dexterously harnessed the printerly language of pressure in order to negotiate the challenges of representing the Black body in a visual field that is always already structured by racism and racial violence. As Saidiya Hartman has asked, "how does one give expression" to the outrages of Black bodily pain and suffering without presenting it as a spectacle, without reenacting subjection, without submitting that body to repeated objecti-fication?[10] Cole and Hammons show how the language of pressure in print, with its tactile subtlety and sensitivity, and its tolerance of contradiction and ambiguity, can uniquely intervene in these questions.

Willie Cole's *Beauties* is a series of twenty-eight prints made from stripped, hammered, flattened, inked, and printed ironing boards. Each print bears a woman's name from the generation of Cole's grandmothers (FIG. 1.14). In multiple generations in Cole's family, the women worked as housekeepers; Cole remembers that as he was growing up they would often ask him to fix their steam irons. The whole series is a testament to the invisible labor of Black women in America. Each print is also a meta-print about pressure. The very process of making them with a *press* reiterates the acts of *pressing* from which they ultimately derive. And they are not only about pressure but all its conceptual and social con-notations—oppression, compression, impression.

For more than thirty years, Cole has been using irons and ironing boards as both tools and motifs, evoking the history of slavery and racist oppres-sion in America. He is known for his steam-iron scorch prints, which evoke the practice of branding. He has also explored the resemblance between the ironing board and the ship, particularly the iconic diagram of the slave ship.[11] The *Beauties* carry all of these associations forward in Cole's work, but they are not simply records of brutality. They do recall slave ships, as well as branding, but they also evoke full-length aristocratic portraits, African shields, X-rays, Gothic windows, and more. They have this complexity because Cole has engaged with the full range of associations that pressure can bring forth. The *Beauties* were made at the Highpoint Center for Printmaking in Minneapolis, where Cole had a residency in 2011–12. Cole and the printers at Highpoint took a set of vintage ironing boards, removed the covers, and battered them with hammers and sledges in a parking lot, creating a series of strike marks and scratches on the surface of the steel boards. The boards were then run through the press between sheets of

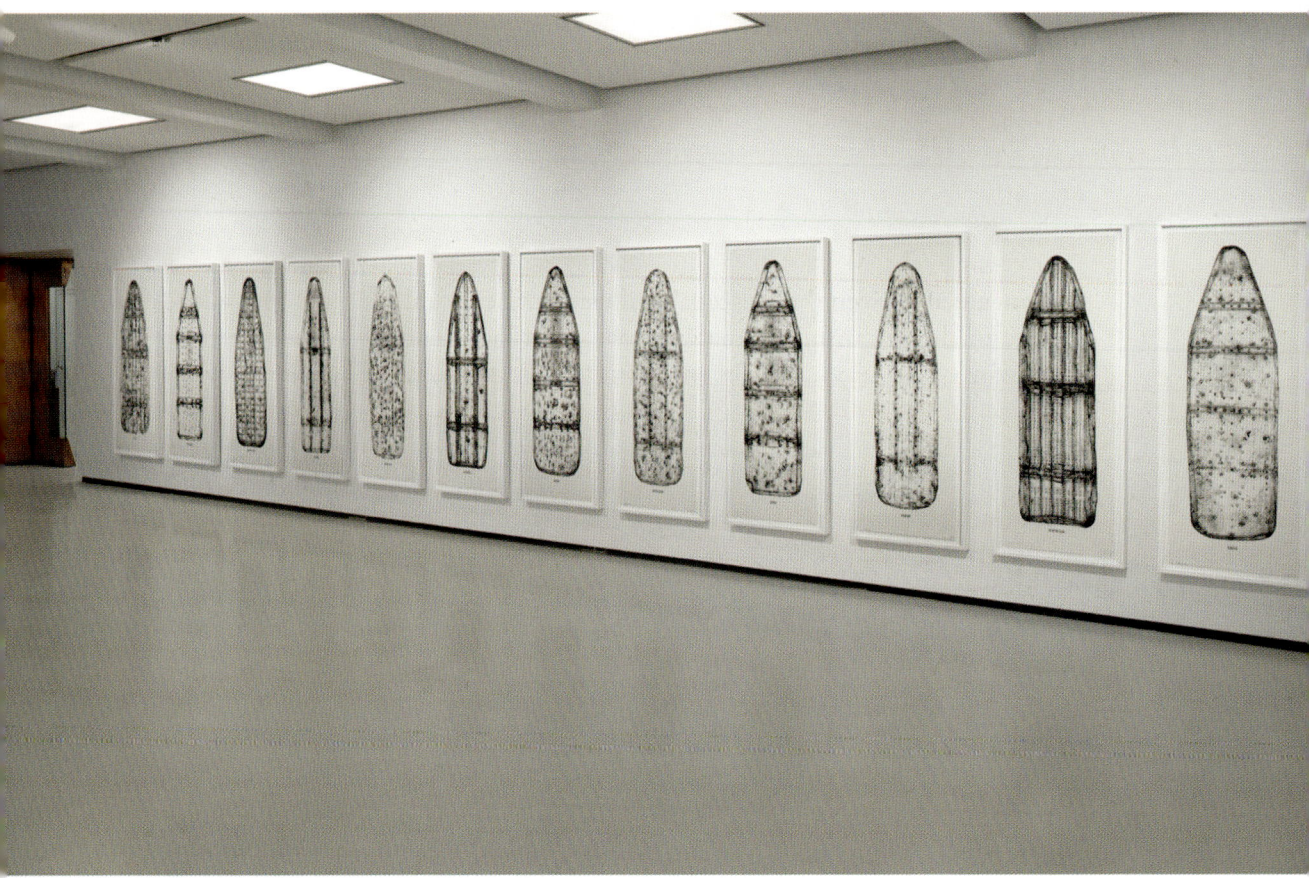

FIG. 1.14
Willie Cole, partial view of the *Beauties* series, 2012. Intaglio
prints from flattened ironing boards. 2019 installation view
from the Radcliffe Institute for Advanced Study, Harvard
University, Cambridge, MA.

Masonite. Each was reduced to about 4–5 mm thick. With its pattern of depressions and incisions, each board was then a matrix to be inked and printed in essentially the same way that a copper engraving or etching plate would be handled in a traditional print shop.[12]

The resulting prints embody the model of the image as a contact relic, particularly as a wound-image. There is a sacrificial quality that pervades every mark on the prints. The hammering, dragging, gouging, and crumpling of the original ironing boards produce physical evidence of violence that transfers directly to each print. Cole's work seizes the medieval model of the sacrificial

Veronica image and extends it to African American and women's history, fusing the sanctity of the wounded saint with that of the victim of racial and/or gendered violence (FIG. 1.15).

But it goes beyond this. As we have seen, applying pressure to a matrix transmits information about texture and topography that is not available to the eye, thus performing an act of revelation or transparency. Take *Dot*, for example (FIG. 1.16). Standing in front of it, you know that you are looking at an imprint taken from just one side—the top—of the board, which is a solid sheet of steel. Yet you are also given the inescapable illusion of being able to see through it as if it were made of translucent material: the print looks like an X-ray or a stained glass window. You can clearly perceive the pattern of struts and supports that occupy the *other* side of the board: two strong vertical lines and two horizontals, each darkening against the pattern of the facing front surface.

How is this possible? The printing press senses variations in the thickness of the boards; in this case, it "reads" the struts on the back because the board is thicker in those areas. The print *Queen*, too, reveals more to the eye than does the board or matrix itself (FIG. 1.17). The print is so full of exquisite incidental detail that it resembles a Rembrandt etching, with its wide variation in sharpness, tone, and scale of the incisions. And it clearly indicates the three horizontal struts behind the board. The matrix itself (the board) is surprisingly reticent in comparison.

The press, we might say, "sees" the topographical incidents of the ironing board far better than does the human eye. Like a tactile X-ray, it diagnoses hidden internal wounds or injuries. The press thus bears a strong forensic power in its ability to manifest or make visible the insignificant or invisible—its ability to expose what is hidden, whether we think of the skeletal underside of the board or the tiniest scratches and insults to its surface that might otherwise have gone unnoticed. There is a truth-telling quality about printing: no wonder the first prints pulled from a plate are called "proofs."

Considering that these prints are about revealing the overlooked in so many ways, Cole could not have chosen a more powerful medium of perception, memory, transfer, and testimony. But this is not just an act of forensic exposure; it also cultivates forces of resistance and creative agency born from pressure. Consider the dignity inherent in the vertical posture of the prints on the wall. The prints strongly recall full-length aristocratic portraiture in the West. *Queen*, for example, when standing tall with its flaring, folding contour and elaborately patterned surface, recalls any number of other queens in the history of aristocratic representation. If these had simply been paintings, their upright posture would have been uncomplicated: after all, full-length portrait paintings are made vertically in the first place. But here, the uprightness of the figures is all the more

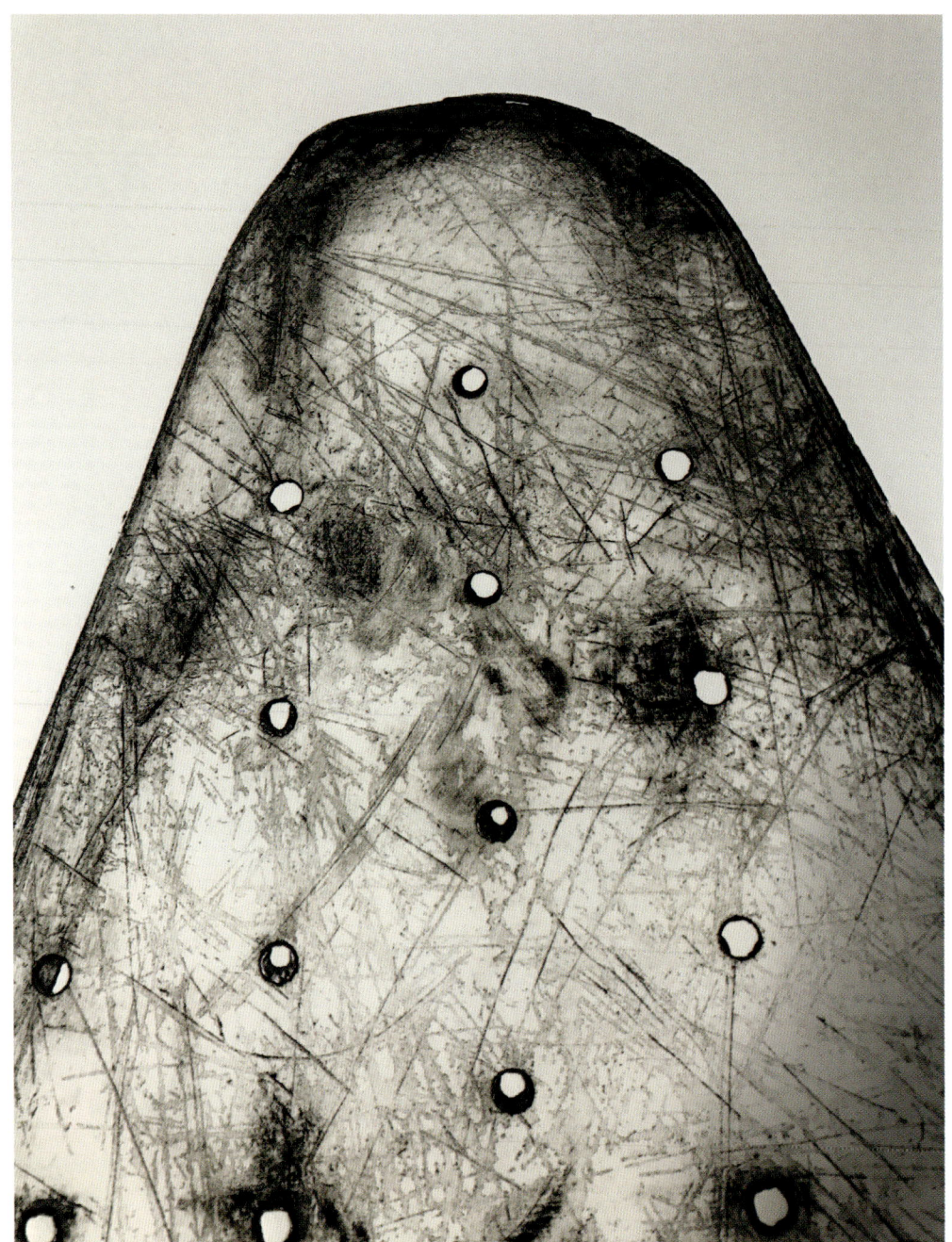

FIG. 1.15
Willie Cole, *Lilly* (detail), 2012. Intaglio and relief on paper.
Highpoint Center for Printmaking, Minneapolis.

FIG. 1.16
Willie Cole, *Five Beauties Rising (Dot)*, 2012. Intaglio and relief on paper. Harvard Art Museums/ Fogg Museum, Cambridge, MA. Margaret Fisher Fund.

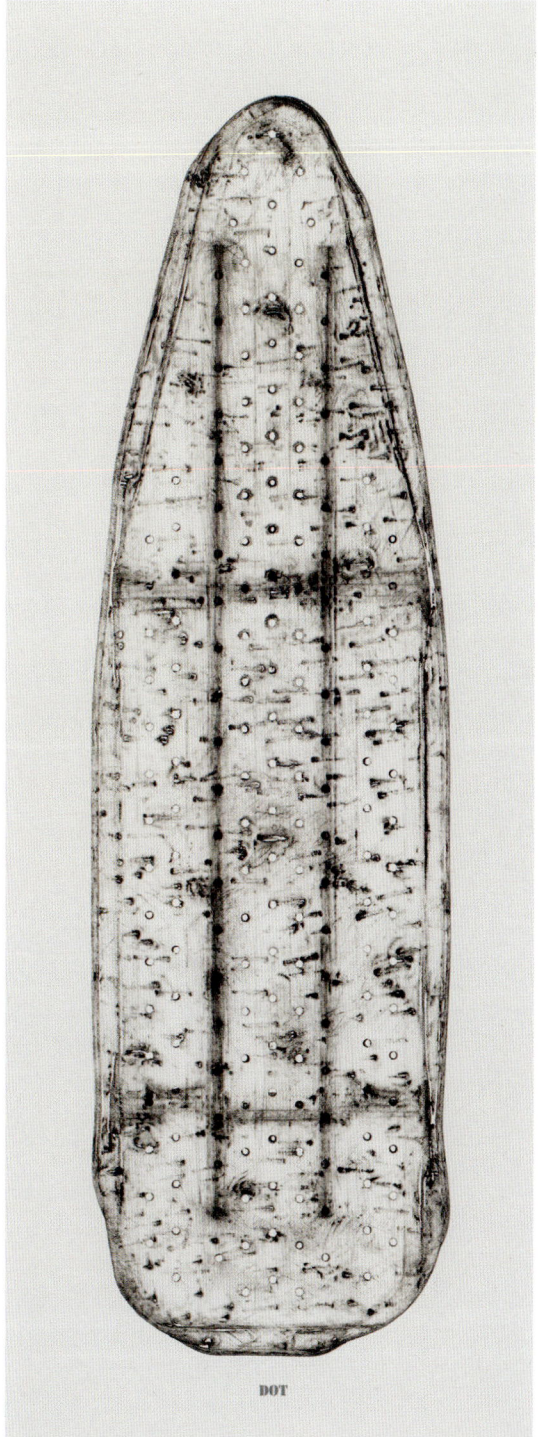

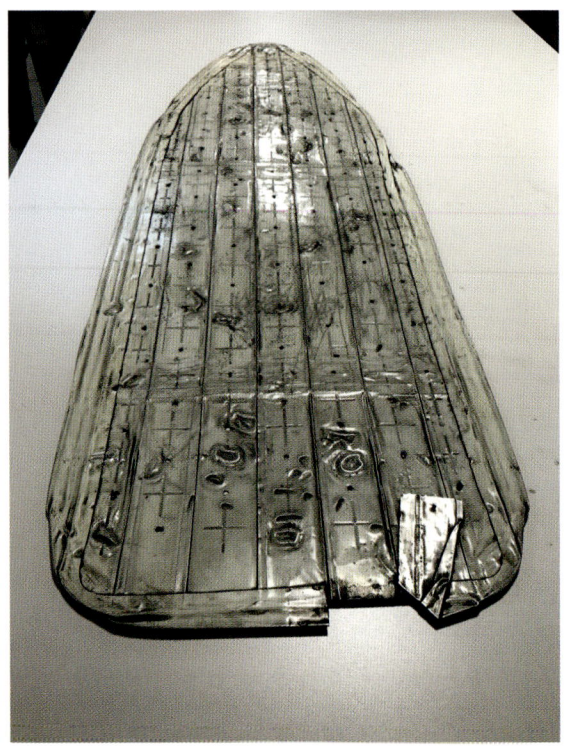
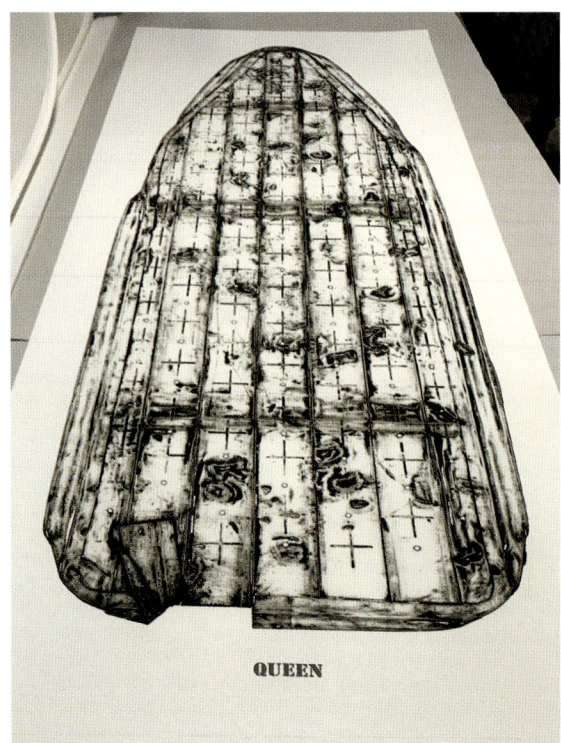

FIG. 1.17
Matrix for *Queen*, Highpoint Center for Printmaking. Willie Cole, *Queen*, 2012. Intaglio and relief on paper. Highpoint Center for Printmaking.

significant because we know that they have risen up, pivoted from a horizontal, pressurized scene of making. This emphasizes the endurance, resistance, and precarity behind their standing rather than any easy sense of self-possession: the *Beauties* don't just stand; they *withstand*.

This awareness is available even for a viewer who may not know the details of the intaglio printing process, because anyone who's used or seen an ironing board is aware of its horizontal posture and the scenes of pressure that accompany the act of ironing. And by attending to pressure as a fundamental determinant of print, we are able to see connections between Cole's work and the work of his grandmothers that might not otherwise have been available to us. Ironing resembles printmaking in many ways, and these prints reveal that both practices encourage unique forms of perception, sensitivity, and intelligence. To give just one example: ironing and printmaking both generate unorthodox forms of cognition and critical insight about bodies in space. Ironing the sleeve of a shirt is an act of multidimensional perception: seams and buttons on the back of the sleeve emboss the front as the two layers merge under the heat and pressure. Just as the printing press can generate transparency from pressure, the ironer "sees through" these front and back layers with the iron. Cole and his grandmothers, then, are linked by a direct legacy of pressure and perception. By harnessing pressure as a creative force, Cole makes visible the labor of Black domestic servants in a way that fully acknowledges the pressures under which they worked, but also acknowledges, and passes along, their knowledge and their artistry.

Before moving on to the work of David Hammons, it will be helpful to provide an overview of the qualities of pressure that are brought into play in each of the major printing processes. There are four basic kinds of printing: four essential mechanisms by which a printing matrix can be structured in order to generate an impression (see fig. 0.5). First, there's relief, as in woodcut and letterpress, in which the areas to be printed stand up from the level of the block and ink is pulled only from the high points. Then there's intaglio (engraving, etching, etc.), where the printing area is carved into the plate and ink is pulled out of those low areas. In planographic printing, the printing and non-printing areas are separated chemically into hydrophilic and hydrophobic areas, rather than topographically. Lithography is the major example here. And finally, there are stencil methods, in which the binary coding of the matrix is achieved by creating closed and open areas that do or do not allow ink to pass through. These include screenprinting, but also the most basic forms of stenciling, as in the letter-stencil painting technique used by Jasper Johns.

Most of the pressure I've discussed so far has been high pressure: the crushing, flattening pressure of structurally massive printing presses. In general, intaglio printing requires the highest pressure. Some rough numbers: to print a sheet of (relief) type on a common or platen press you need at least 175 pounds per square inch, multiplied over the entire area to be printed. Lithography presses (the kind Rauschenberg used for the *Hoarfrost Editions*) require eight hundred to one thousand pounds per square inch, multiplied along the length of the pressure bar. (By the way, if you've ever wondered why lithography stones are so thick, it's because they need to be able to withstand this enormous pressure. Stones can and do break—during the printing of one of Rauschenberg's most famous lithographs, *Accident*, the stone broke in the press. He decided to cobble it back together and print it as broken.) To print an intaglio etching or an engraving of about the same size on a roller press requires about 1,500 pounds per square inch, multiplied along the entire length of the cylinder roller. And then there are hydraulic presses—like the one at Two Palms Press in New York, which produced the intense deformation that you see in this print by Mel Bochner (FIG.1.18). Craig

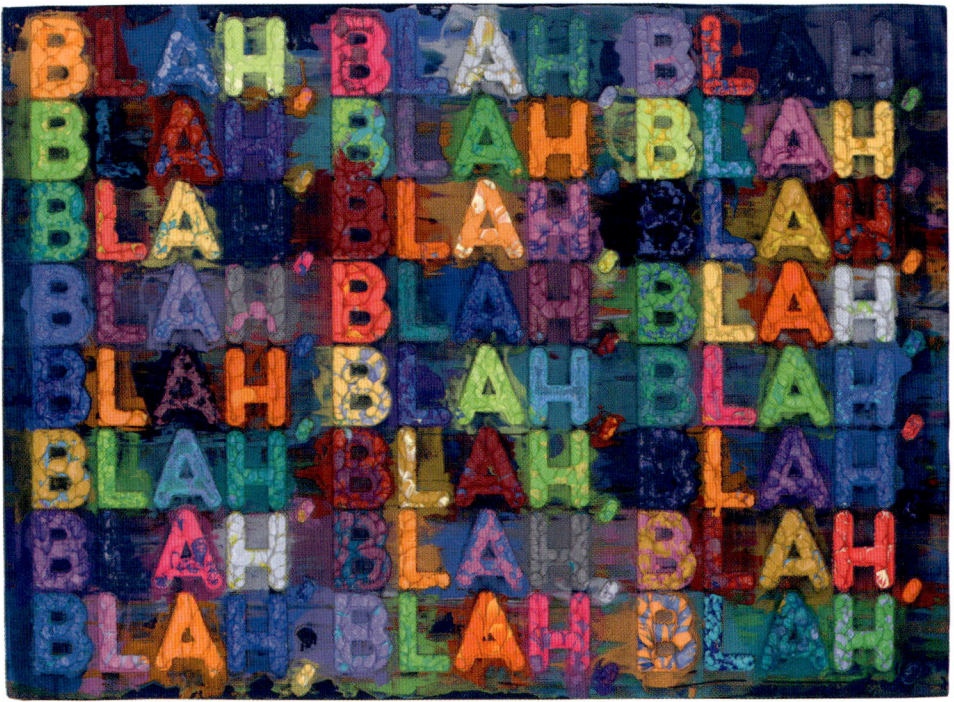

FIG. 1.18
Mel Bochner, *Blah, Blah, Blah*, 2023. Monoprint in oil with
collage, engraving, and embossment on handmade paper.

Zammiello, master printer at Two Palms, has said they usually run this press at a
million pounds per square inch.[13] Throughout his career as an artist, Bochner has
been interested in the way language (like other symbolic systems) can never provide full access to the world it purports to describe. Working at Two Palms,
Bochner uses the language of pressure to perform these vexations. At some level,
all language is just "Blah Blah Blah": sound that circles around reality but cannot
reach it. The deep embossing that a million-psi printing process makes possible
is perfectly suited for this conundrum: Bochner's words, printed from laser-cut
Plexiglas plates whose incisions have been filled with paint, seem as if they are
struggling mightily to be enunciated through the paper into the world, but ultimately, they cannot quite break that plane. Bochner's prints stage an extreme version of the ambivalent play between materiality and transparency that
high-pressure printmaking invites as a medium.[14]

　　All that said, there is plenty of printing that lies on the other end of the
pressure spectrum. Many modern printing technologies use rubber elements to

transfer ink softly. There's the squeegee in screenprinting. In offset lithography, the most common method of printing commercial images today, a rubber roller (called a "blanket roller") rolls over the matrix, picking up the ink from the plate, moves over to the paper, and rolls it back out again, depositing it on the paper. The blanket roller's pressure is referred to as a "kiss." In fact, several types of very light impressions, taken softly, are called "kiss impressions" in printing lingo.

Or think of paper marbling, which is also a form of printing (FIG.1.19). In marbling, a tray is filled with a mucilaginous substance or water treated with surfactants, and inks are floated and then manipulated on this surface. The image is then transferred by gently laying a sheet of paper on the surface and carefully lifting it away. This is a limit case of delicacy in printmaking: the matrix is the surface of the liquid, and pressure is provided by gravity and atmospheric pressure as the paper meets that surface.

Marbling may seem quaint and old fashioned, but many of the most advanced printing technologies today are actually closer to marbling than they are to something like copperplate engraving. They work by exploiting the very fine, often nanoscale, behavior of fluids and forces. The Wyss Institute at Harvard University, for example, has developed a form of acoustophoretic printing that uses sound waves to control the size of droplet formation in biopharmaceutical 3D printing applications.[15] The future of printing is based on the physics of bubbles and droplets and their own responses to tension and pressure. This is very light pressure, but still pressure, and it reminds us that the contact inherent in printing can link up both materially and metaphorically with a huge range of sensory associations: print can perform gentleness and intimacy as well as violence or stress.

In the late 1960s and early 1970s in Los Angeles, David Hammons made a series of body prints that show how this full range of sensory contact can operate within the racial politics of representation. To make his body prints, Hammons would first cover himself, including his clothing, with a greasy or oily substance (usually margarine), and press himself against a piece of blank paper or board on the floor. He would then sift powdered pigment onto the clear oily impression, letting it fall like a dust cloud onto the latent image below; it would adhere to the oily areas and thereby "ink" the print. These prints come across as records of an impact event between body and surface, and many of them not only suggest but even reenact racial violence. In order to make these prints, Hammons had to press his body onto the paper in awkward contortions, essentially assuming a series of stress positions on the ground. Imagine putting your own body in this position, and the traumatic connotations of this performance of pressure become unmistakable, not to mention horrifically familiar from countless scenes of police brutality. Printing, pressure, and pressing here are equated with blunt oppression.[16]

FIG. 1.19

Stills from film on marbling
made by Bedfordshire Record
Office of Cockerell, 1970.

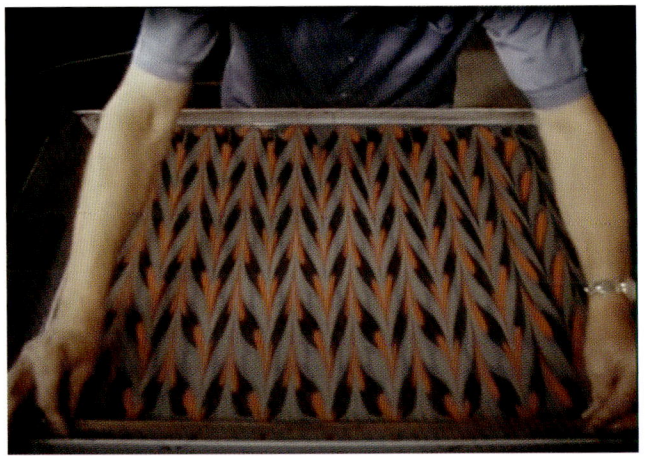

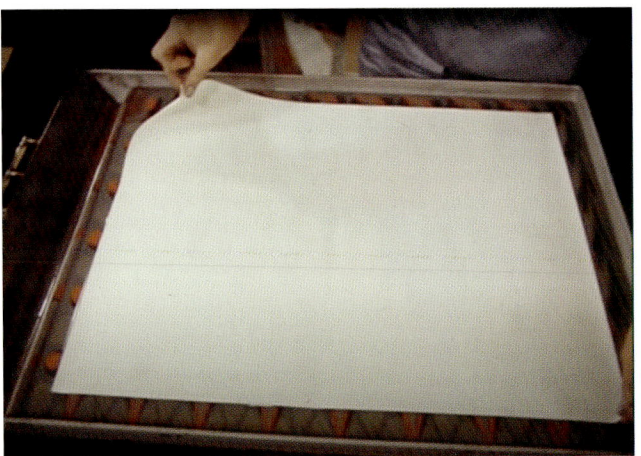

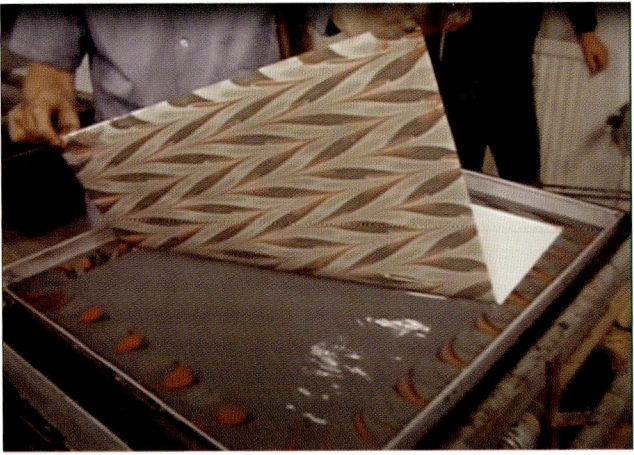

Within this context, Hammons might seem to be reducing his own body to an object of brutality, just another hypervisible trace of racist violence. But, as art historian Kellie Jones has said, "The gift of these works . . . is that the element of violence is seen not as an immobilizing force but as one in which black language can intervene."[17] How does this intervention actually work in Hammons's language of pressure and print?

First of all, built into the process of Hammons's self-pressing is a model of internally conscious representation, a model of the self-possessed image. In a 1971 interview, Hammons spoke about a key technical challenge in his work: namely, how to get up from the paper again:

> When I lie down on the paper which is first placed on the floor, I have to carefully decide how to get up after I have made the impression that I want. Sometimes I lie there for perhaps three minutes or even longer just figuring out how I can get off the paper without smudging the image that I'm trying to print.[18]

This is a remarkable statement. It means that his postures, while acknowledging a certain traumatic immobilization, are also about strategic, even artful, subjectivity. When we look at Hammons's body prints, we are looking at the trace of a figure that was thinking about being a figure at the moment of figuring itself, thinking about how to make the transition in and out of a state of representation. And the key point here is that Hammons does get up again; in fact, the print is only possible because of this, this successful act of pulling oneself up. We've already seen that print requires both contact and release; press and pull, and these works ensure that a certain release and even redemption are inherent to the very act of representation in print.

In most of his body prints, Hammons would repeat this process of press and release multiple times, responding to previous impressions with new impressions, either by himself or with others. He built up the prints according to a sequential process of returning to the imprinted body. There is a self-sedimentation at work here in both time and space. In his *Untitled (Body Print)* from the Harvard Art Museums collection, we see evidence of multiple different impressions (at least three) that have been rendered in several different colors (FIG. 1.20). One impression is a profile, arms folded, in a defiant position. But there is also a face impressed frontally, and a frontal torso. There are at least two different shirts—one a button-down and one a knit sweater—and two different pairs of pants.

If these prints acknowledge the impact of violence, then, they also record a practice of care for the victimized body, a practice based explicitly on

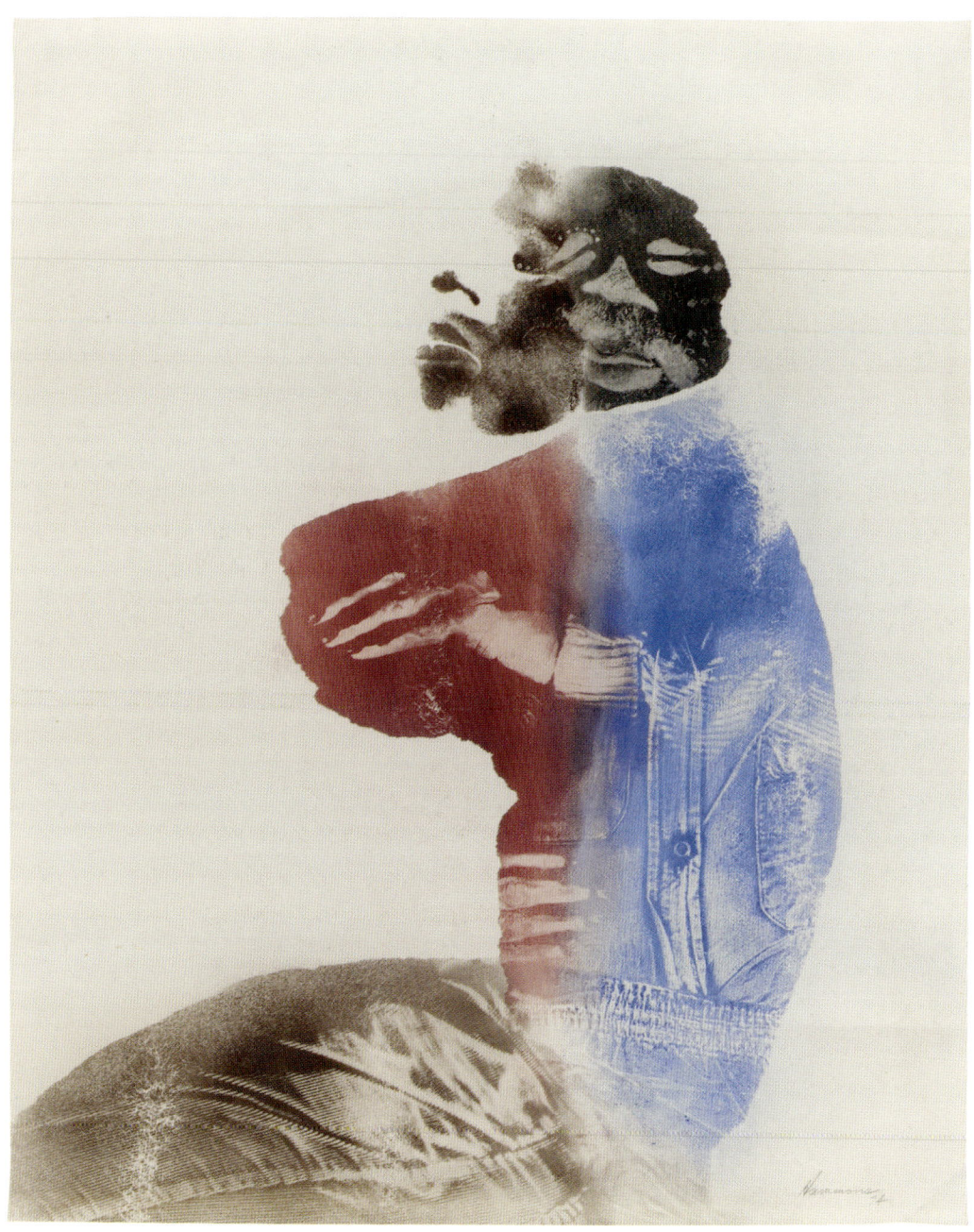

FIG. 1.20
David Hammons, *Untitled (Body Print)*, 1974. Five-color
monotype on white wove paper. Harvard Art Museums/
Fogg Museum, Cambridge, MA. Margaret Fisher Fund and
anonymous gift.

touch and intimacy. Hammons returns to each impression as he would to another body, laying his head on its chest, laying his cheek on its cheek, wrapping his hand around its waist, bringing eyelash to eyelash in a butterfly kiss. We might say that Hammons's body rolls over, even mourns over, previous bodily traces. This is an inherently careful and gentle operation, because he needed not to disturb or destroy the previous impressions with the new ones.

The delicacy and sensitivity of this operation cannot be overemphasized. This is not the record of a blunt impact. These are prints made by the softest, most sensitive parts of the body: prints made by lips, hair, eyelashes, and even the tiny reticulations of the surface of the skin: those finest networks of corporeal sensitivity. Making these prints must have required a remarkable blend of strength and gentleness; Hammons had to press himself to the paper, but only lightly, resisting the pull of gravity in order to capture a coherent imprint of such tenuous structures. Note that in doing so Hammons offers a gentle, and thus all the more powerful rebuke to the history of racist ideas about the Black body as immune to fine sensation. The hair is especially important here: it races through the print like a fine electrical discharge, a system of precarious but powerful energy.

Hammons insists on this delicacy as the last word, the last impression, of the print. Here, notice that a flurry of body hair appears to sit on the outside of a corduroy pant leg, a strange reshuffling of bodily integuments, an inversion of boundary layers. As in so many of the other rubbings and impressions in this chapter that create images of internal revelation, Hammons's prints use the subtleties and sensitivities of printerly pressure to create a new model of subtle and sensitive representation.

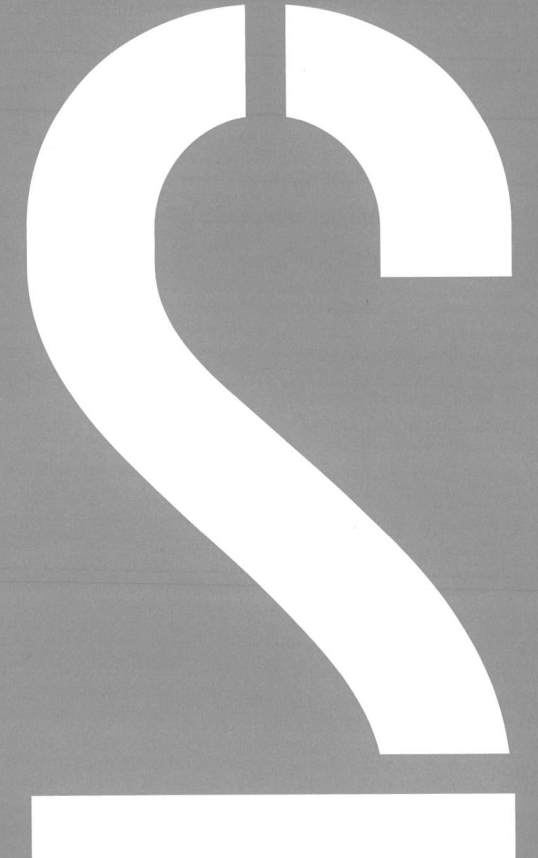

Most prints made prior to the digital age were born of an act of reversal. Everything that we evoke when we evoke the history of print culture or the print revolution—the reproduction of images, the dissemination of beliefs, the communication of knowledge, the very properties of modernity—ultimately depends upon the reversal of information. Although the exact manner of reversal differs across processes, traditions, and time, reversal is a fundamental maneuver in the history of printing (FIG. 2.1).

In most cases, the conspicuous and culminating act of reversal in printmaking happens at the moment the impression is made, as the image is transferred between the matrix and the support. (I will explore the main exception to this—stencil printing—later in this chapter and in chapters 4 and 5.) When the matrix is positioned face to face against the support—as in woodcut, engraving, lithography, and so on—the final print is a reversal of the matrix. To make a print face a certain way, you have to prepare the matrix so that it faces the other way. This mirror reversal is clearly evident when a print is juxtaposed with the matrix from which it was pulled, as in this famous 1642 etching by Rembrandt, *The Raising of Lazarus*, and its copperplate (FIG. 2.2). This pairing demonstrates not only the mechanics of reversal but also its mystery and its capacity for conceptual disruption. At the time this print was made, Rembrandt was castigated because he represented Christ resurrecting Lazarus with his left hand. This was theologically irritating, because all such divine errands were supposed to issue from the right hand. Still, one might argue that Rembrandt etched the scene properly on the plate itself. In the copper, where Rembrandt's own hand operated, Christ raises his right hand. One "side" of this print—matrix or impression—was going to be wrong no matter what. Which side holds the primordial truth of the directional image: the matrix or the print?[1]

Whatever his motivations, Rembrandt's flip offers us a glimpse into the profundity of reversal in print. Usually, prints give us little reason to think about their inverted origin. The reversals at the heart of printmaking do not usually reveal themselves out in the world where printed matter circulates. Once the print has been pulled from the press, it moves on and the matrix stays behind. The mirror-pair that it makes with its matrix at the moment of emergence from the contact event vanishes from the scene of print culture.

And so when we look at prints and books and newspapers and broadsides, it seems to me that we see only one side of them. The more I've thought about this, the stranger it's seemed. It is as if we were zoologists studying only the right sides of animal bodies. When we look only at the print but not at its originating reversals, we miss a lot. We miss the way print intersects with problems of symmetry and topology. We miss the way print engages with the (mostly) symmetrical structure of the human body—our corporeal organization around a

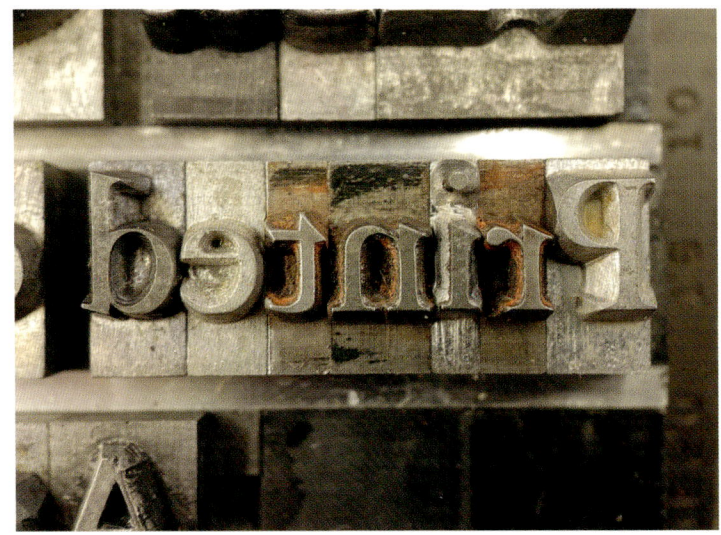

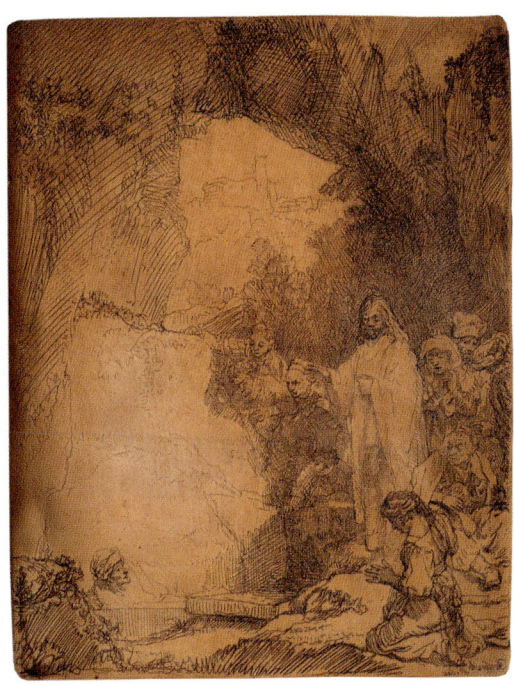

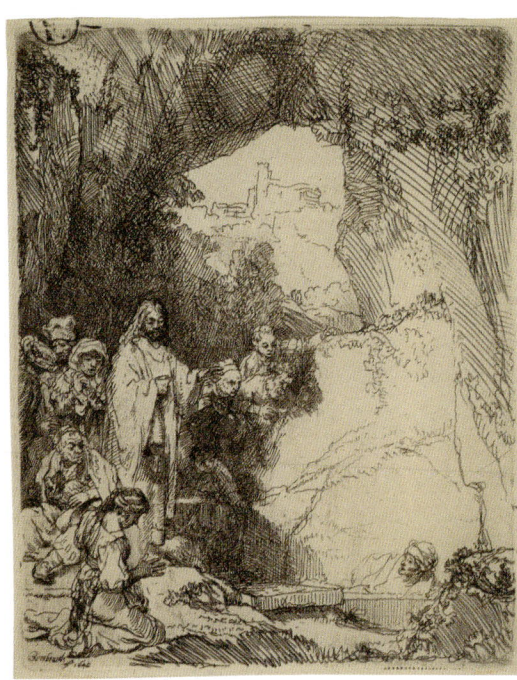

central seam—and the way we fold ourselves up around that seam. We miss the way print opens up hinges and folds and pleats (to call back to the ironing topic in the previous chapter) in spatial and social experience. We miss the way print orients us toward that experience. What would it look like to hold onto that deep awareness of reversal in printmaking and in art history? What would it look like to put it to work?

I first became interested in reversal through the work of Jasper Johns, an artist whose thinking in all media has been driven by printmaking. Johns allows the reversals inherent to printmaking to remain active and evident in his finished compositions. We might say that he refuses to leave the reversed matrix behind in his work. Indeed, throughout his work, what we might call the "reverse intelligence" of printmaking breaks through to the final image and breaks out of printmaking into other media.[2]

Johns made the lithograph *Corpse and Mirror* at Universal Limited Art Editions in 1976 (FIG. 2.3). This is a print that seems to be thinking about what it means to be printed. It's organized bilaterally, mirroring itself around a central seam as if it were composed of a print pulled away from its matrix. The "corpse" in the title is worth comment. It suggests the bodily quality of the composition, especially the way bilaterally symmetrical forms tend to evoke bodies in the round simply through the act of symmetry. More pointedly, however, it refers to the Surrealist drawing game known as the "exquisite corpse." To make an exquisite corpse, participants collectively complete a drawing on sections of a folded piece of paper. One person completes a section, then someone else picks up at the fold and draws another section without being able to see the previous drawing. Johns evokes this in the fold-like-divisions in the work, and in doing so also empha-sizes several other aspects of printing mentioned in the previous chapter, espe-cially its blindness. When making an exquisite corpse, no one sees the final image until it's unfolded at the end of the game. Same with printmaking—it's not until the pull, not until the final unfolding of the reversal, that the image emerges. Johns's evocation of the Surrealist game also highlights the collectivity of print-making: the way no print can ever be attributable to the mind or hand of a single artist. The mind of the print exists somewhere in the seams between all the peo-ple in the print studio, between materials, between dimensions, between the world and its mirror.

Johns has spoken extensively about the impact that printmaking has had on his other work:

> Just the process of printmaking allows you to do—not allows you to do things but makes your mind work in a different way than, say, painting with a brush does . . . And some of that feeds back into

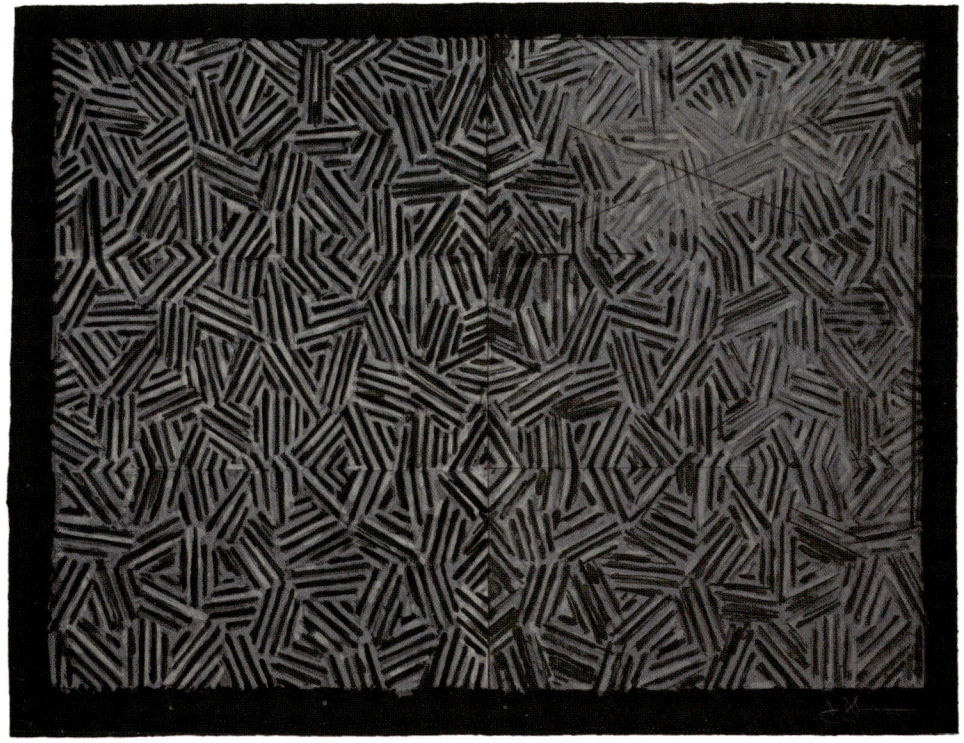

FIG. 2.3
Jasper Johns, *Corpse and Mirror*, 1976. Lithograph from twelve
aluminum plates on German Etching black wove paper. Harvard Art
Museums/Fogg Museum, Cambridge, MA. Margaret Fisher Fund.

> painting, because then you see, you find things which are necessary to
> printmaking that become interesting in themselves and can be used
> in painting where they're not necessary but become like ideas. And in
> that way printmaking has affected my painting a lot.[3]

And speaking in particular of reversal:

> The images in my early prints were such that I had to be very con-
> scious of drawing them backwards on the stone. That was a real
> concern to me. . . . I had to draw them backwards so that they would
> read correctly when they were printed. It's hard to know what the
> effect of this kind of activity has been, but it certainly rubbed off onto
> my painting.[4]

We can see Johns picking up on reversal "like an idea" throughout his work in painting. Consider *Field Painting*, which highlights reversal through the principle of the hinge (FIG. 2.4). In a cascade of text traveling along a vertical seam, Johns allows each letter to face forward and backward simultaneously. He also conveniently leaves the imprinting objects or matrices (wooden letter blocks) attached to the painting. Take special note of the way the wooden letters pivot into the third dimension. I'll return to this dimensional drama later in this chapter.

Robert Rauschenberg was also a student of reversal. Here we might return for a moment to the *Hoarfrost Editions*, which we explored in the last chapter in terms of pressure, to note the way they show an incredible sensitivity to the perpetual quiddities of reversal that beset print media. In details from *Mule*, it's possible to see that Rauschenberg's fields of wrinkled and fragmented text are oriented mostly backward. Because these are essentially transfer prints from newspapers (which, of course, originally read the "right" way), they read the wrong way when transferred (FIG. 2.5). Looking at passages like this, you realize that everything there that is now backward was once forward and vice versa. The backward advertisement was forward on the copy of the *Los Angeles Times* from which it was transferred, but it was backward on the printing plate that printed the newspapers and was forward on the original art. Rauschenberg captures here the switching of information in and out of reversal as it moves between generations of media — the somersaulting dynamism of reversal that delivers virtually all printed matter.

This chapter will focus on a group of contemporary artists who, like Johns and Rauschenberg, move fluently between printmaking and other media. All of them deploy reversal as a critical tool, and all of them feature text in their work. By using text, all of them make the act of reversal highly conspicuous while also connecting it to the realm of communication and dialogue. They show how the reversals that are native to printmaking can generate critical interventions in social space.

Printmakers and would-be printmakers need to be able to think and work backward as they work on the matrix. They need to be able to imagine source images in reverse and to anticipate the printed image in what we might call "pre-verse." Printmaker's statements are full of testimony about the mindset and body-set that this requires. "The engraver has to see everything reversed."[5] "You have to flip everything in your head."[6] Reversal is one of the fundamental ways that printmaking, to quote Johns again, "makes your mind work in a different way."[7] For highly skilled printmakers who have had years of practice, reversal often comes to feel automatic and natural. It becomes part of their tacit intelligence. But for everyone else, this flipping is not easy. Although we are beings with more or less symmetrical body plans, our experiential orientation to the world

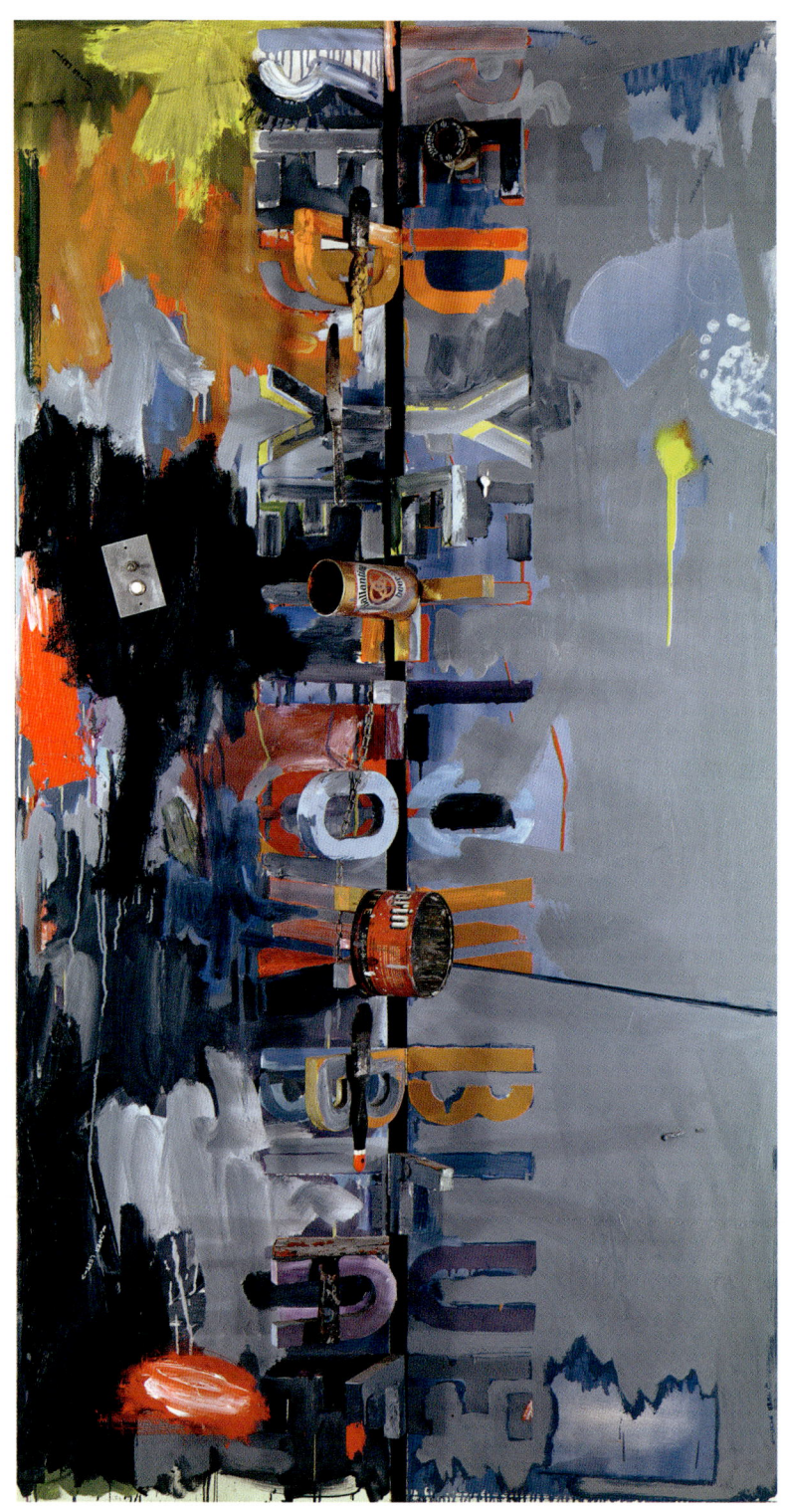

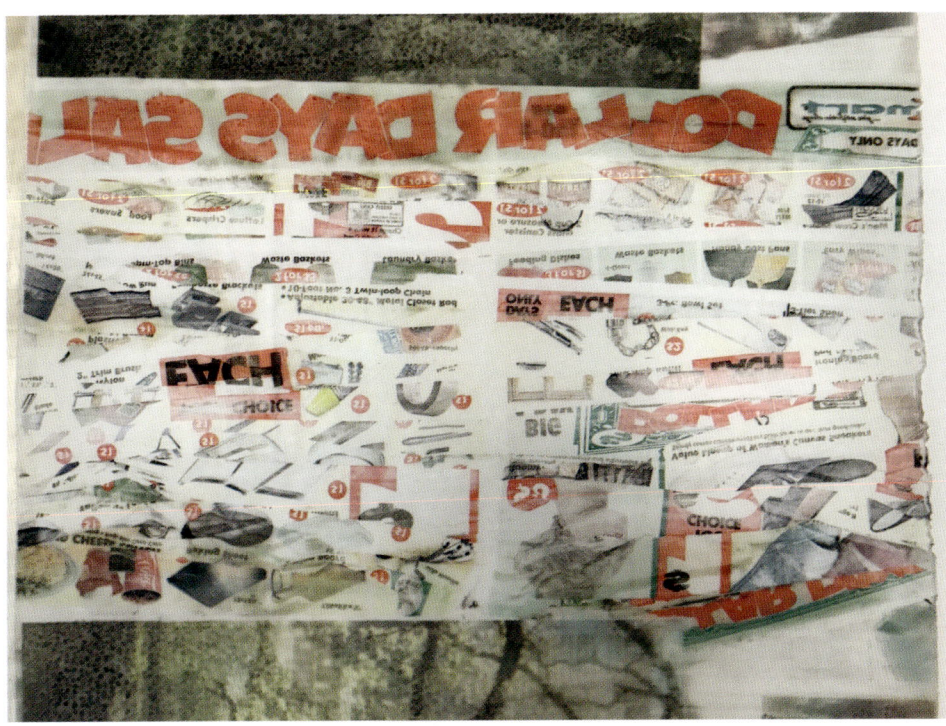

FIG. 2.5
Robert Rauschenberg, *Mule* (detail), 1974. Offset lithograph and newsprint
transferred to collage of paper bag and fabric. National Gallery of Art,
Washington, DC. Gift of Gemini G.E.L. and the artist, 1991.

tends to lean in one direction, to settle itself into handed or sided routines and
perceptions. Most of us are not ambidextrous.

In my own initiation to printmaking over the years, I have found that
working in reverse on a matrix is almost like an out-of-body experience; it pulls
you out of all of your habitual postures. It creates an experience of self-
estrangement that burrows into the spaces between intention and execution,
mind and body, similar to the deep disorientation that a left-hander feels with a
right-handed pair of scissors, or that an American feels when traveling in a
country where people drive on the left. I'm an amateur printmaker, but even the
most accomplished artists struggle with these reversals. Vija Celmins, who is
known for her intricate images featuring oceanscapes and starry skies, had this
to say in a 2011 oral history she gave for the Museum of Modern Art: "The
whole printmaking thing is the most irritating thing you can do. They're all
backward . . . because when you print it, it goes the other way. . . . I'm a real 'right

there' person, you know, so it's very hard for me to be right there, but upside down, inside out, whatever."[8]

One might well ask why, given this evident discomfort, Celmins has made so many prints over the course of her career. Or why any other contemporary artists have engaged so seriously with printmaking. For many, it is because this disorientation is precisely the point of the operation. Contemporary artists often seek out the destabilization of printmaking because it forces them out of the technical facility that they have attained in, say, drawing, painting, or sculpture. As they enter that mirror world of printing, they are taken out of the bodily and conceptual complacency that comes along with their own skills, out of the comfort of their internalized orientation to their work. This turn to printmaking as an experience of estrangement or difficulty became a common refrain as the Print Renaissance gained steam after the 1960s. The archives of the great print shops are full of accounts of artists discovering the value of printmaking as a way of interrupting mastery.[9] This is partly attributable to the imperative toward deskilling that took over contemporary art in the 1960s and 1970s. Making prints was a good way to refuse the kind of artisanal facility that was increasingly seen as bankrupt at the time. But it's more complicated than that, because this was not so much a refusal of artisanal skill as it was a decision to embrace an unfamiliar set of artisanal skills. We will return to the relationship between print and deskilling in chapter 4.

In turning to print, contemporary artists also tap into a centuries-old ethos of the critical power of reversal. The mythology of printmaking in the West has long flirted with the idea that reversal provides access to special forms of otherness and opposition. The ability to work and perceive in reverse evokes a seer-like divination of alternative dimensions and forms. It is often understood to be coincident with mystery or secrecy, inasmuch as the reverse lurks as the invisible "other side" of any form. As printmaker Kathryn Reeves writes of this critical history:

> Printmakers have the capability to see the dual nature of all images/texts/identities which exist always as themselves and always as their mirror images. But this experience of reversal is not shared with the rest of the art world nor with society; this experience further marks the printmaker and printmaking as other, as "eccentrics" . . . those who do not occupy the center.[10]

In the previous chapter, I evoked printmaking's association with critique, assessment, judgment, and justice in my discussion of the work of Willie Cole. All of these impulses are also attached to the process of reversal.

Let's think again about the concept of the "proof" in this context. In printmaking, the term proof is used to designate "a trial or preliminary impression . . . taken to be checked for errors and marked for correction before subsequent revision or final printing." It designates the production of a reversal as an act of testing and correction. The idea actually has a long history in painting: Renaissance theorist Leon Battista Alberti advised painters to examine their work in the mirror in order to check it for flaws or infelicities. Reversal lurks behind the broader concept of proof as the establishment or demonstration of truth or validity or authenticity. To reverse something is either to validate it or to expose its weaknesses—to prove or disprove it.[11]

A good example of these dynamics, inspired but not contained by the print medium, is Glenn Ligon's ongoing series of neon sculptures that subject the word "America" to various kinds of reversal. Although Ligon is not known primarily as a printmaker, his work is inseparable from the life of print: especially his signature paintings, which feature text made with stencils. In the neon sculptures, Ligon turns letters backward, upside down, and flips them front to back. We can see this as a kind of testing or proofing of America—looking at it from both sides and checking on whether the image of the nation is sound (hint: it isn't). In *Rückenfigur*, the word maintains its normal letter order, but each letter is reversed left to right (FIG. 2.6). However, because of the way some of the letters have internal symmetry planes ("A" looks the same in either direction), that reversal is only evident in the C, R, and E. The estrangement of the letters through reversal causes other words to insinuate themselves into the scene of reading. The suggestion of the word "crime" pops out, and "acrimony," as if they had been latent in "America" all along. In *Untitled (America)*, an upside-down "America" reads right way up only when it is seen as a wavering reflection, in blood red, on the floor (FIG. 2.7).

There is something sinister about this reflection. And indeed, the critical power of reversal has long carried shades of the sinister. The very term "sinister" derives from the traditional denomination of right and left as dexter and sinister. Book historians are familiar with the term "printer's devil"—slang for an apprentice in a print shop. The expression probably derived from an earlier belief that a devil haunted every print shop, causing various forms of mischief but especially inverting letters. Whether conceived of as sinister or merely mischievous, the point is that reversal engenders critique, a refusal to accept the status quo, and the insight that every form is accompanied by its reverse.

Notice that Ligon's work takes the act of reversal off of the page-like plane and puts it in space; each letter is suspended sightly away from the wall, and the light and reflections project into the architecture of the room. Ligon, in other words, treats these printerly reversals in an inherently sculptural way. But in doing

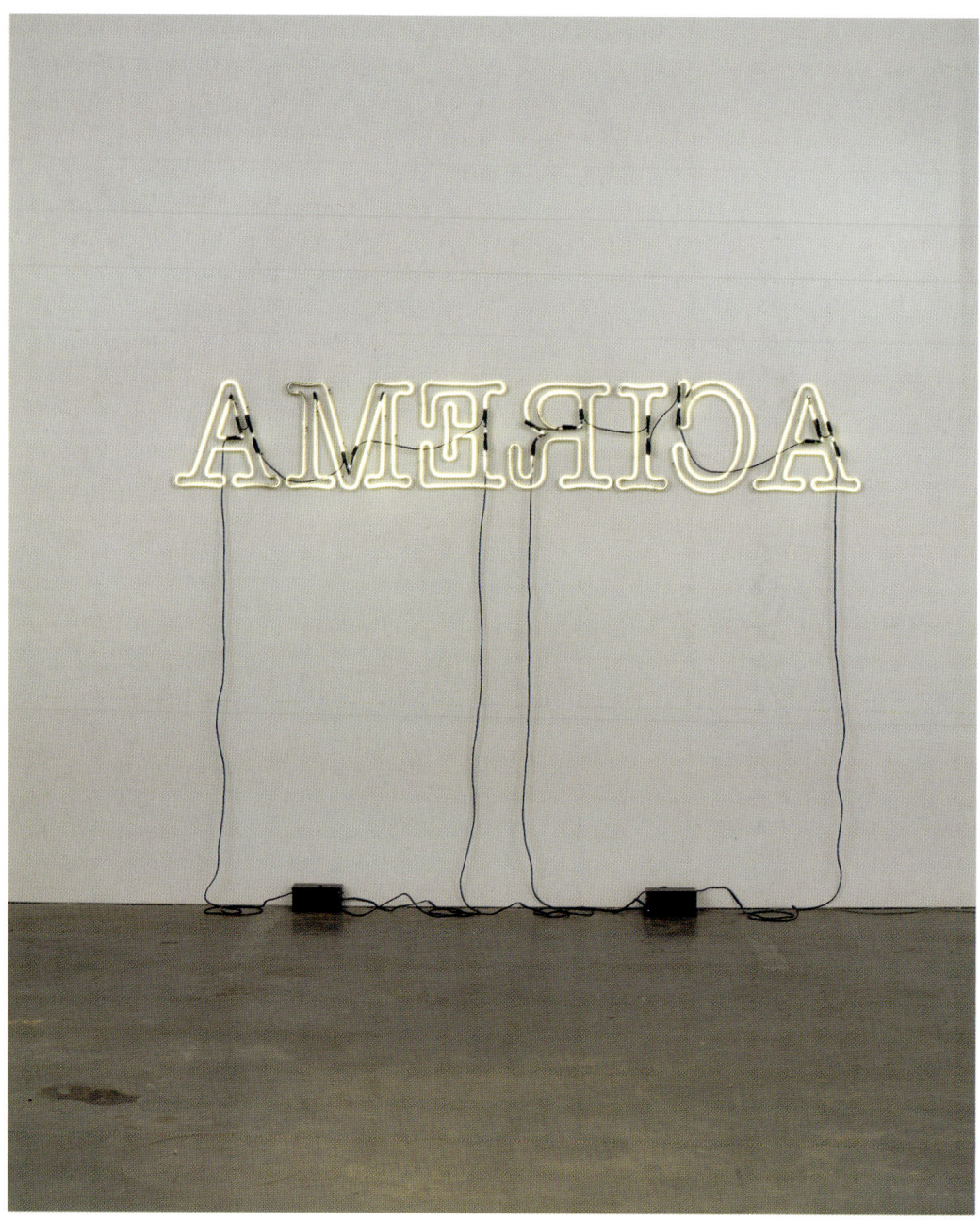

FIG. 2.6
Glenn Ligon, *Rückenfigur*, 2009. Neon and paint. Whitney
Museum of American Art, New York. Purchase, with funds
from the Painting and Sculpture Committee.

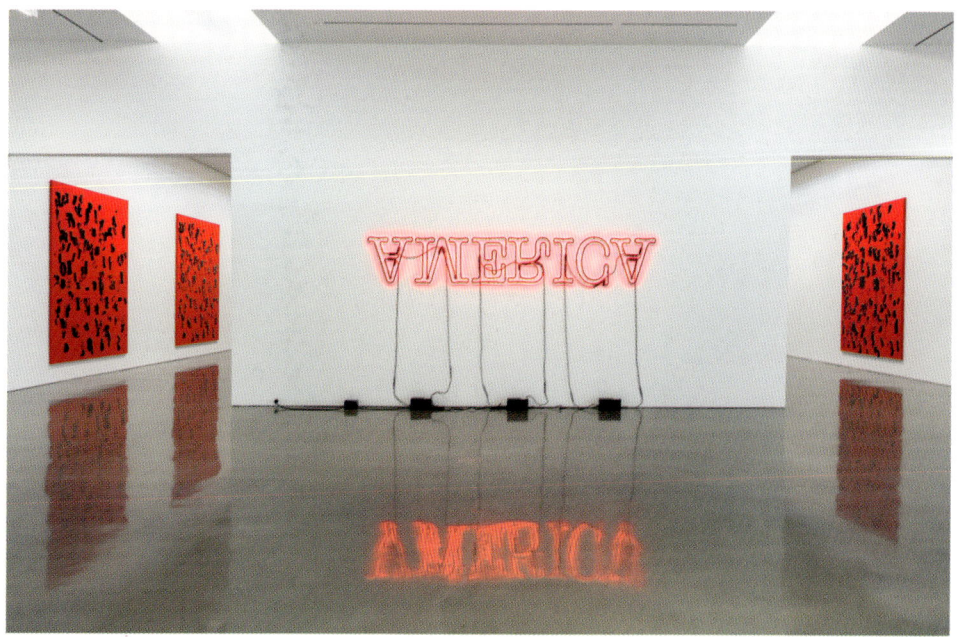

FIG. 2.7
Glenn Ligon, *Untitled (America)*, 2018. Neon and paint.
Installation view at Regen Projects, Los Angeles.

so he is not so much adding extra space to an inherently flat system as he is exploiting the way that the act of reversal always already generates expanded spatial effects. He is making visible something that is already latent deep in the work of print—namely, that reversal can be seen as a sculptural or architectural process.

Reversal can shape space, including social space. Take an asymmetrical form—let's say the lowercase letter "e"—and flip it over (FIG. 2.8). This mirror reversal is technically known as "chiral" reversal, and it is the same form of mirroring we encountered with Rembrandt at the beginning of this chapter (see fig. 2.2). The term chiral comes from the Greek word meaning "hand," and it is commonly used to refer to left- and right-handed forms throughout the natural world that lean or spiral in opposite directions: human hands, certain crystals and shells, certain stereoisomeric molecules, and so on. This mirroring may seem unremarkable at first, but what makes it interesting for us here is that it always implies an additional dimension. It evokes an activated space around itself.

This requires some elaboration. Even though it's obvious that these two e's are closely related to each other as they sit on this two-dimensional plane, they cannot be superimposed on each other, or brought together, while remaining in

FIG. 2.8
Mirror-reversal of the letter e.

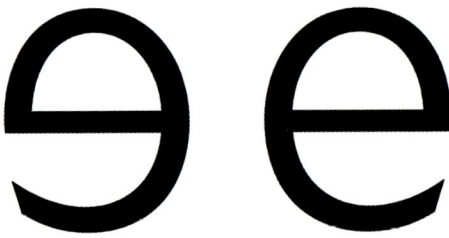

the plane. Take the e on the left: no matter how vigorously or creatively you scootch it around on the page, you cannot bring it into alignment with the e on the right. In order to do that, you have to flip it up and over, off the page and into three-dimensional space. You have to imagine it pivoting around, say, a hinge, into an extra dimension. Every "meeting" of forms that are chirally related in the n dimension takes place in the n+1 dimension. It gets weird quickly: if you want to superimpose three-dimensional chiral objects, such as a left-spiraling snail shell and a right-spiraling snail shell, you would need to rotate them in four-dimensional space. Unfortunately, there is no room here to pursue these mind-bending problems into the higher dimensions. What is most useful to remember is that chiral reversal evokes three-dimensional space on a two-dimensional plane in a way that is fundamentally different from linear perspective and similar methods of spatial suggestion common in Western representational painting. (This is one reason why Jasper Johns was so attracted to print in the early years of his career—its reversals gave him ways of evoking complex spatial experiences without resorting to optical illusionism.)[12]

Reversal can also trigger spatial activity across the picture plane from front to back. Johns, again, provides an excellent illustration. For the lithograph *Skin with O'Hara Poem* of 1965 (FIG. 2.9), he pressed and rolled his hands and face across the surface of a lithographic stone before printing. What is most conspicuous about this print is not the left-right reversal, but the implied reversal across the plane. In the process of making the face and handprints, Johns was always on *this* side of the stone. No matter how hard he smashed his face against it, he could never pass through it, and in fact, it is that very obdurate resistance of the surface (as we discussed in the last chapter) that makes the printed mark possible. But in the print that issued from this, his image suddenly seems to have leapt over to the other side of that impermeable barrier. The same pressing and pushing of the artist's body now appears to be coming from *that* side of the surface, and, as many commentators have noted, it appears to be locked there: as Kirk Varnedoe put it, it's "a figure trapped and desperately pushing forward from a space behind the surface."[13]

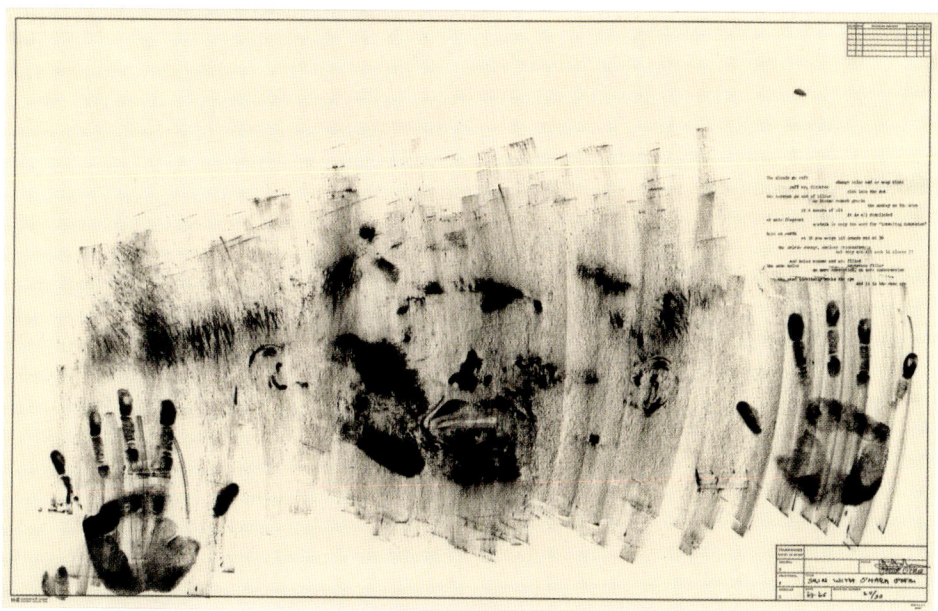

Jasper Johns, *Skin with O'Hara Poem*, 1963–65. Lithograph (stone) in two blacks on KE Albanene Engineer Standard Form paper. National Gallery of Art, Washington, DC. Gift of the Woodward Foundation, Washington, DC.

After going through the press, the image leaves the immediate sphere of the artist and returns in reversed form. The press takes the artist's gesture and bounces it back backward; the image returns to the artist from a different perspective, as if from a distant mirror on the other side of the universe. It is his mirror image, but it is not quite himself. The printed mark looks back from a space of hard ontological quarantine that is inescapably other.

This has had an immense appeal for Johns, who has spoken repeatedly of his desire to detach images from his own specific subject position: "I . . . want an object to be free from the way I see it."[14] As he has said, reversal accomplishes this: "Things become 'other' when you look at them backwards."[15] For Johns, then, the reversal generated by the press can serve as a device for the automatic generation of otherness: it splits apart the singular viewpoint of the artist and opens up a circuit with some "other side." It installs an alter ego through reversal and separation. It puts someone on the other side of the picture plane. This essentially activates both sides of the picture plane through reversal, and suggests a model for thinking of the print as a dynamic, dialogic surface that structures a particular kind of relationship with something beyond or behind it.

This simultaneous left/right and front/back reversal—one generates the other—holds enormous possibility for critical artistic exploration. The artist that has taught me the most about the social and dialogic potential of that splitting across the picture plane is Corita Kent.[16] Kent was a prodigious screenprint artist in Los Angeles in the 1960s and 1970s. She was also a Roman Catholic nun who was instrumental in running the famous art program at the Immaculate Heart College in Hollywood. In the mid-1960s, a strong progressive energy was running through world Catholicism, a wave of reforms attempting to modernize the faith and its practices. These included the use of vernacular languages (instead of solely Latin) for the liturgy, and encouragement of Catholics to become more involved in social causes. Inspired by this and by the first stirrings of Pop Art in New York and Los Angeles, Kent began a series of remarkable screenprints that fused the vernacular energies of Pop and progressive Catholicism.

Kent's prints, which focus on text, are full of double meanings—she borrowed slogans and brand names from advertisements, retaining their promotional graphic design and their commercial associations, but also insisting upon their spiritual and aesthetic resonances. In *a man you can lean on* (FIG. 2.10), the title phrase is borrowed from an advertising campaign for Klopman Mills, but it can also have a Christian spiritual meaning. Kent wrests these connotations of faith back from the corporate identity that had appropriated them for commercial gain. This doubling or turning back of language was also accomplished through reversal in her prints. She used many forms of reversal, but I'll focus here on chiral reversal. Many of the terms and phrases in her prints—such as "turn, turn" in this print—read backward, as if seen in a mirror. But Kent did not think about them in terms of mirrors and reflections. Instead, she claimed that looking at backward text is akin to seeing it from behind, from the other side of the letters. As she said on several occasions, "It is necessary to turn the words over to see what's on the other side."[17] This resembles the cross-plane reversal that we've just seen with the Johns print. Kent suggests that she is trying to evoke a flipping over of the print or page or screen in order to view or occupy it from the other side. "Turn, turn" indeed.

Before continuing, it's important to clarify that Kent's chosen medium of screenprinting is not like the other print media we've seen so far in its relation to reversal. Processes like etching, engraving, lithography, woodcut, and letterpress work by forcing ink to move from the face of an obdurate plate or stone onto the face of the paper. The screen matrix, by contrast, is a soft, transparent mesh through which ink is pushed with a rubber squeegee to the paper below. The mesh is impregnated with or adhered to a stencil, which acts as a negative, blocking the passage of ink through parts of the screen and thereby generating the image.

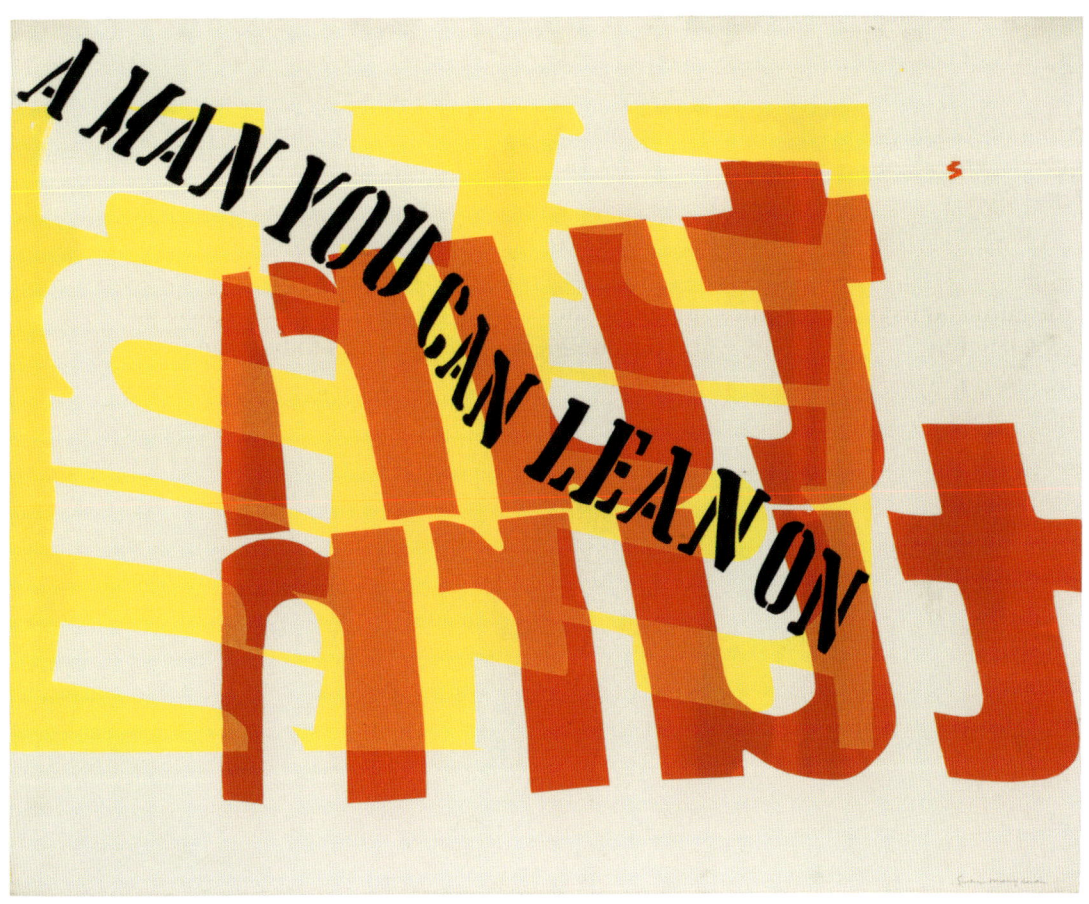

FIG. 2.10
Corita Kent, *a man you can lean on*, 1966. Screenprint on Pellon. Harvard
Art Museums/Fogg Museum, Cambridge, MA. Margaret Fisher Fund.

I'll talk a lot more about screenprinting in the coming chapters. But
the implication for now is that the image is *not* reversed as it passes through the
matrix to the paper or support. This is why screenprinting is usually categorized
as a non-reversing print medium. But just because there is no reversal at the scene
of transfer does not mean that reversal does not inhabit the process. In fact, as
Kent was well aware, reversal is a prominent and inescapable part of screenprinting; it's just that it occurs at a different point in the process, in a different way.

Unlike traditional matrices of copper, stone, or wood, the silkscreen
matrix is transparent. Because the screen is transparent, the reverse side of the
screen (and thus the reverse side of the stencil) is always visible and available to

FIG. 2.11
Looking through a screenprint
matrix.

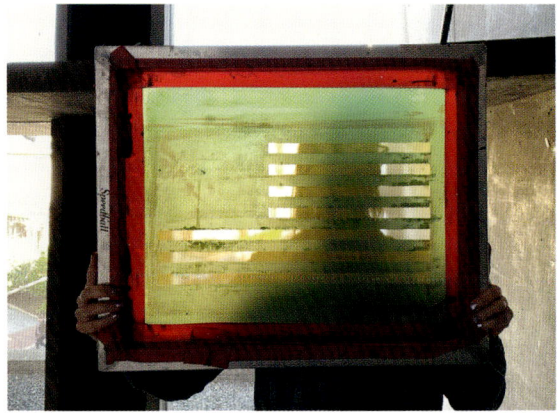

the artist. In fact, while working, the artist cannot help but confront the back side of images or texts (FIG. 2.11). With engraving, the right and reversed versions of the image are distributed across two objects: the matrix and the print. But in screenprinting, both of these forms have essentially been collapsed into the matrix alone. Through transparency, the screen matrix holds both the right and reversed versions in the same object—to make them switch from one to the other one need only look at the screen from one side or the other, or imagine doing so.

Screenprinting is essentially a twentieth-century invention. And while this magical doubleness of the transparent matrix may seem like a wholly new-fangled way of managing reversal, the fact is that it is not completely discon-nected from earlier printing methods. Historically, one of the fundamental challenges facing printmakers was the need to reverse original drawings during transfer so that the print would assume the proper orientation. For example: a common method of transferring a drawing to a copperplate for engraving was to coat the back of the drawing with chalk, place it on the plate, and trace the out-lines from above with a stylus so that a chalk version of the outline would be transferred to the plate below. But this would mean that the drawing would be right-facing on the plate (and thus wrong-facing on the print). Somehow the *reverse* of the drawing needed to be facing up to be traced by the stylus. But how do you reverse a drawing? You couldn't just flip it around in Photoshop. And it was not very efficient to laboriously redraw the entire drawing backward by squaring it off or eyeballing. It was difficult enough that printmakers often simply didn't bother. Take the beautiful drawing of fossil ammonites, or "snake shells" by the British artist Robert Hooke (FIG. 2.12). The printer of this drawing didn't reverse it before transfer to the plate, which is why in the print from this drawing (not shown) all of the shell fossils are facing the wrong way. Hooke had

FIG. 2.12
Robert Hooke, Drawing of
ammonites (snake stones), n.d.
Pen and ink with wash on
paper. British Library, London.
Ms Add. 5262, no. 152.

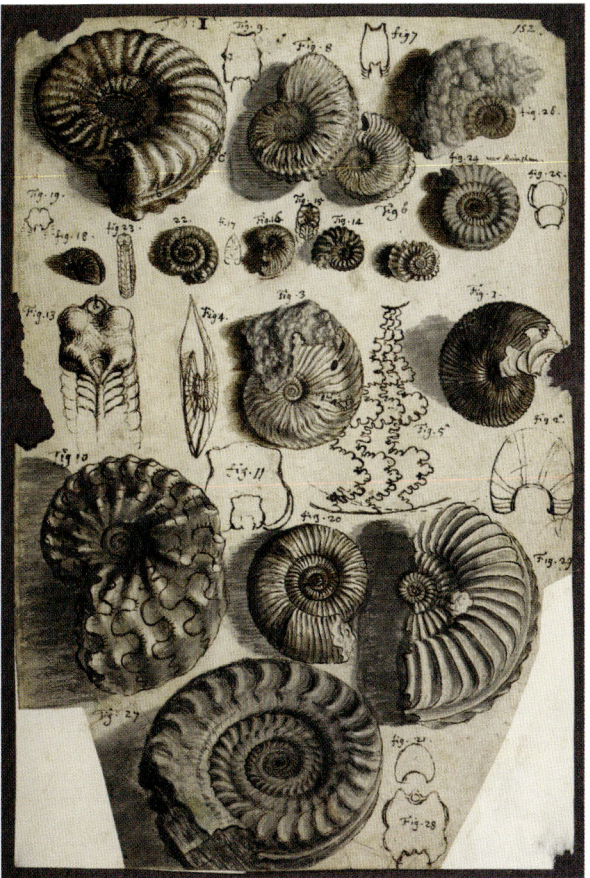

complained about the careless reversals of print: "In most of the heads that are
graved from Paintings or draughts made from the Life or from pictures the Right
side appears to be the Left & the Left the Right. This has caused all the pictures
of the shells in Bonnanis booke of shells . . . to be misrepresented and turned the
wrong way." Apparently, mis-reversal was a common fate befalling the illustration
of shells in the Age of Enlightenment. It's too bad, because while it may not matter to humans which way a shell is spiraling, it certainly matters to the shells.[18]

A common solution to the conundrum of reversing original drawings
was to find a way of rendering the paper transparent so that the drawing could
be placed face down and traced from behind. Paper could be made translucent by
soaking it in oil, turpentine, or naphtha; the drawing could then be held up to a
window and traced from the back. An image could be reversed, in other words,
by getting behind it: chiral and cross-plane reversal are equivalent. Another

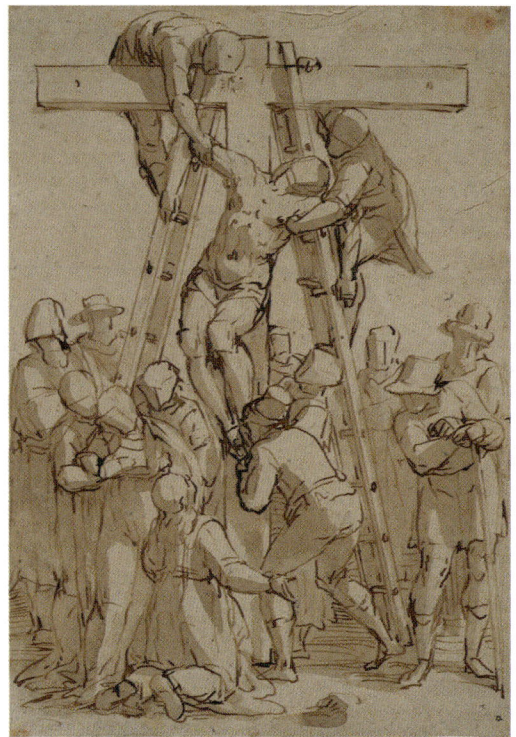
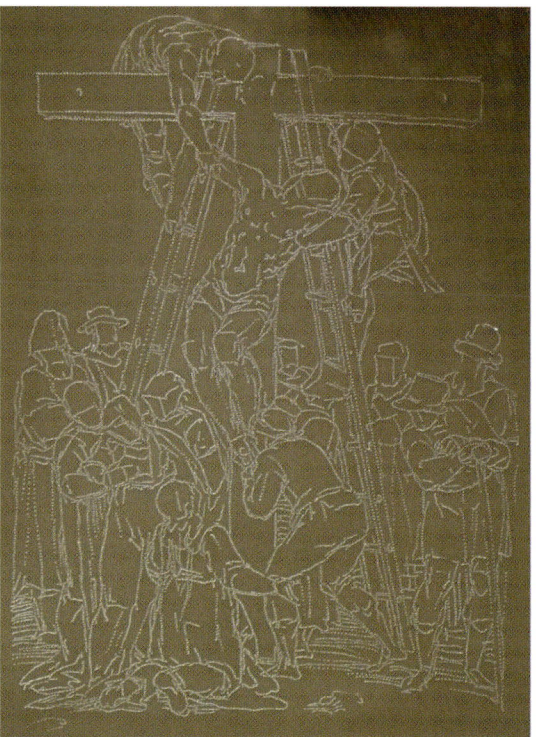

FIG. 2.13
Luca Cambiaso, *The Descent from the Cross*, c. 1570. Pen and brown ink on paper. RISD Museum, Providence, RI. Gift of Miss Ellen D. Sharpe.

Andrew Raftery, pouncing for *The Descent from the Cross*, 2013. RISD Museum, Providence, RI.

method of rendering an image transparent for reversal was *pouncing*: pricking tiny holes along the outlines, thus creating a perforated sheet where the basic contours of the reversed image could be had by simply flipping the sheet around (FIG. 2.13). On these oiled or pounced sheets, the drawing appears as both an image and its mirror, suspended simultaneously on a single surface. As the print historian Ad Stijnman has noted, from the seventeenth century onward, recipes for such transfer sheets commonly accompanied technical manuals for etching and engraving.[19]

As common transfer tools in every print shop, such sheets teach us something fundamental about print: any image that moves through a print studio implies, or derives from, or predicts, its own reversal. Transparent sheets embody the constant impulse for reversal in traditional printmaking processes, and this is what they have bequeathed to screenprinting. Screenprinting is a continuation of these practices, not a radical break from them. A useful way to think of screenprinting, then, is to imagine that these intermediary tissues, these delicate reversing interfacings, have simply migrated into the position of the matrix itself.

Corita Kent understood the conjunction of reversal and transparency. And she understood that it could be used as a way of creating critical social space. When we recognize the screen matrix as a form of reversing transparency, we are also able to see how closely it is related to other transparent image media of the twentieth century, many of which Kent used routinely in her work. One of these was, of course, film, with its transparent stock. Another was the 35 mm slide, which was ubiquitous in Kent's process. The Kodak Carousel projector was introduced in 1962; anyone who remembers using 35 mm slide projectors will remember how easy it was to misload a slide and have a backward image on the screen. Another was the grocery store window, the source of many of Kent's advertising-related compositions.

All of these media—screenprint, store window, film, 35 mm slide—are communications media that spatially organize communities. Kent's genius was to recognize that the transfer and transformation that is synonymous with reversal in print could be imagined in connection with these more spatial or architectural technologies. Like the store window or the slide, the screenprint matrix generates a relationship between inside and outside, before and behind. Although the screen matrix can only be seen from one side at a time, its transparency permits you to imagine taking a position on the other side or to visualize someone else in that position. This is especially true when approaching the backside of a screen on which text is suspended, because the act of attempting to read the words backward forces you to virtually inhabit the reversed position from which the words would read correctly. I would even go so far as to propose that the screen matrix inherently conjures the presence of another person viewing it from the other side, creating a dialogic milieu around itself in which it serves as a mediating surface.

Kent's prints carry this vision of a transparent dialogic screen through to the final print itself. Although in actuality the final print (on paper or fabric) made from the screen is opaque, the reversed words virtually perforate the picture plane and evoke a matrix of interchange—let's say, using the Catholic term, communion—between conversants facing each other. This does not correspond to an easy synthesis or merely palliative harmony. The printed texts, with their reversals, inherently split the community of readers even as they suggest their conjunction. Kent's surfaces retain the friction of difference and opposition even as they produce a congregation of viewpoints. The reversed texts conjure the "other," but the other is estranged, defamiliarized—backward. The other, like Johns's face, is over on the other side.

At the same time, the prints train us to imagine our own estrangement, our own reversal, from the other side of the page. If these are sites for communal understanding, they can produce that understanding only by first acknowledging "a moment of mutual nonidentification," to borrow a phrase from Claire Bishop.[20] As models of interaction occurring through and upon screens, Kent's prints have obvious resonances with our own contemporary lives, given that much of our social existence is now conducted through screens. But her reversals are more radical in their acknowledgment of difference and otherness than most anything in our contemporary screen experience.

We speak of interacting in social networks "through" our screens, but the disorienting reversals that Kent saw as inherent to the work of print have generally been expunged from our devices. When we exchange text messages, for example, our experience of the letters on the screen tends to absorb us into an illusion of shared orientation. After all, we all look at the letters the same way. But imagine what texting would be like if your friend's texts came to you with all of the letters and the speech bubbles reversed. Only then would you be participating in a spatial network that recognized otherness in anything like what Kent had imagined and what the reversals at the heart of print truly suggest. A reversed text, suspended on a veil between different parts of a social body, provides a shared plane of communication, an opportunity for dialogue, but does not assume or demand that both sides share precisely the same perspective.

So: reversal as otherness, critique, judgment, estrangement, displacement. These powers of reversal run, whether as a latent potential or a cultivated agency, through every print and every printmaking process. And a look around contemporary art will turn up several examples of artists who, like Kent, have used textual reversal to harness these dynamics.[21] I've already mentioned Ligon, but now that we have been talking about the relationship between transparency and reversal, we can better understand the way neon is working as an adjunct to print in his work. Think of the quintessential space for a neon sign: a window, suspended between inside and outside of a space, usually someplace like a bar or a restaurant, which evokes comfort and community and belonging. At least to those who feel like they belong there. At least to those who are not excluded.

A neon sign is like text on a silkscreen or trace paper: you can see it from the front or the back, and depending on which side of the window you're on, you see it differently. Ligon's neon pieces position the idea of America as something that has an inside and an outside. That tension, usually suppressed in our national fantasies of shared discourse and institutions, leaps into view through the critical power of reversal.

There are many other examples of the way these printerly reversals can speak to the problem of space, community, and belonging. In a recent exhibition,

Virgil Abloh showed a row of silkscreen matrices on the wall, oriented so that the viewer faced the back or the reversed side of the text. One screen included the words "watch your back" stenciled both forward and backward into the mesh. Not only does this create an exaggerated expression of the double-sided reversibility of all silkscreens, it also speaks to the way reversibility, when understood in the context of the body, can produce a feeling of spatial uncertainty. When the difference between front and back becomes ambiguous, which way are you to look when you "watch your back" (FIG. 2.14)?

Ed Ruscha has been famously working with palindromes and other reversal wordplay for decades. His work, which has always developed in and through print as well as painting, is incredibly canny in the connections it draws between reversibility and spatial experience. To give just one example: the

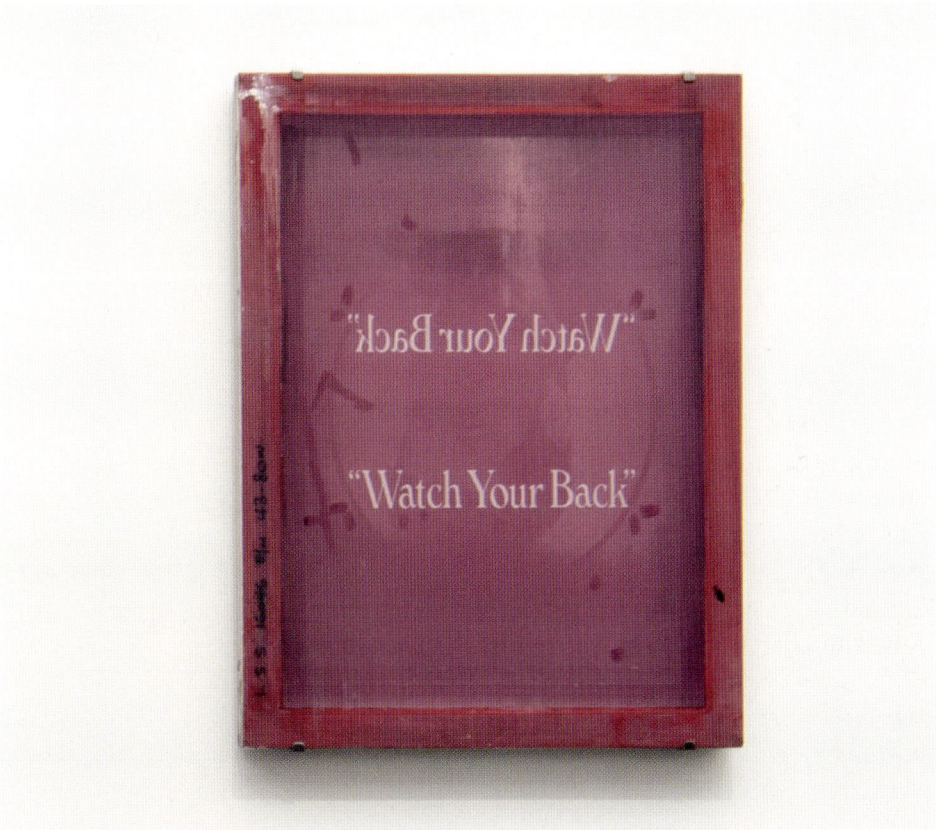

FIG. 2.14
Virgil Abloh, installation view of *Pyrex 2.0* (2018) at
Museum of Contemporary Art, Chicago, 2019.

drawing titled *Oh-Ho* might serve as a sort of mascot for this entire chapter, inasmuch as it explicitly interprets the act of word reversal as equivalent to rotation and inversion in space. Ruscha has signed along both the top and the bottom to indicate that it can be vertically reversed (FIG. 2.15). One day it can be HO, the next it can be OH. This seems playful, but there is a kind of terror lurking in it. It suggests vulnerability, because we realize here how thoroughly our experience of language — this supposedly stable space of sharing and communication — depends upon our specific spatial orientation. These words have no stable meaning apart from our perspective on them.

Or there is Deborah Kass's well-known sculpture *OY YO*. The sculpture consists of two giant yellow letters, an "O" and a "Y." The letters reverse their order when walked around, changing not only in sound but also in cultural referents and audiences — from OY to YO or YO to OY, from Spanish to Yiddish, from urban slang for a greeting to urban slang for dismay, and so on. This piece of freestanding typography both refers to and actively generates a community that coheres but retains its differences.

Bruce Nauman is another artist who is deeply invested in printmaking and its implications, especially reversal, although he tellingly calls it not reversal but "front back interplay."[22] In some cases these reversals are playful or punning, such as his screenprint *AH HA* (FIG. 2.16). But more generally his work plumbs the darker side of reversal (RAW-WAR is a flip that he commonly explored); we can think of him as a more pessimistic version of Corita Kent (FIG. 2.17). Like Ligon, his disorienting reversals of text are often pursued simultaneously in neon and in print, both of which, as the critic John Yau puts it, throw his words into a "continuously irritated condition," while also implying double perspectives and conflict.[23]

Nauman's interest in the profundity of reversal first developed in his sculptural practice in graduate school, where he found himself as interested in the molds and negative spaces of the objects he made as he was in the objects themselves. A work such as *A Cast of the Space under My Chair* demonstrates the eerie sense of disorientation that follows the reversal of positive and negative space (FIG. 2.18). It also inaugurates another of Nauman's longstanding motifs, the suspended and reversed chair. Like printmaking itself, these upside-down and inside-out chairs suggest displacement and a loss of security and stability. In much of his work, these chairs explicitly refer to torture and to the condition of the disappeared. Yau has said that, in observing these, "We learn about what it means to be deprived of gravity, orientation, and privacy."[24] This is not to equate printmaking with torture, but the process and its reversals do open out to these disorienting deprivations and estrangements, and make it a medium uniquely suited to working through these ideas.

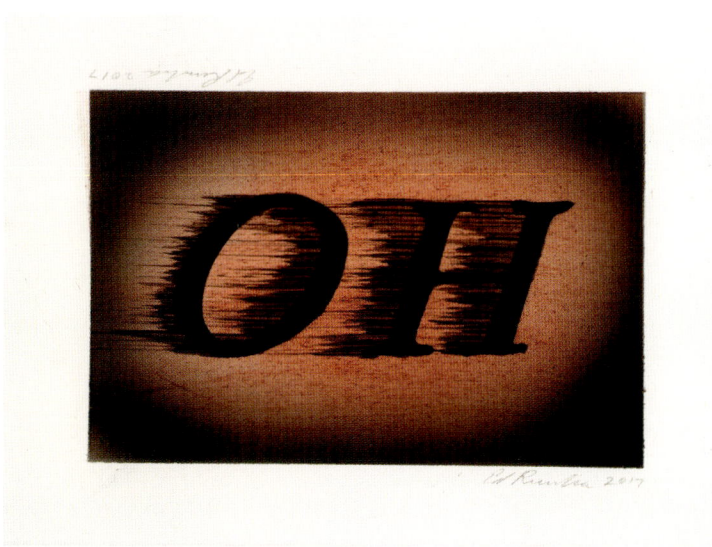

FIG. 2.15
Ed Ruscha, *Oh, Ho*, 2017. Dry pigment and acrylic on paper.
Peder Lund Gallery, Oslo.

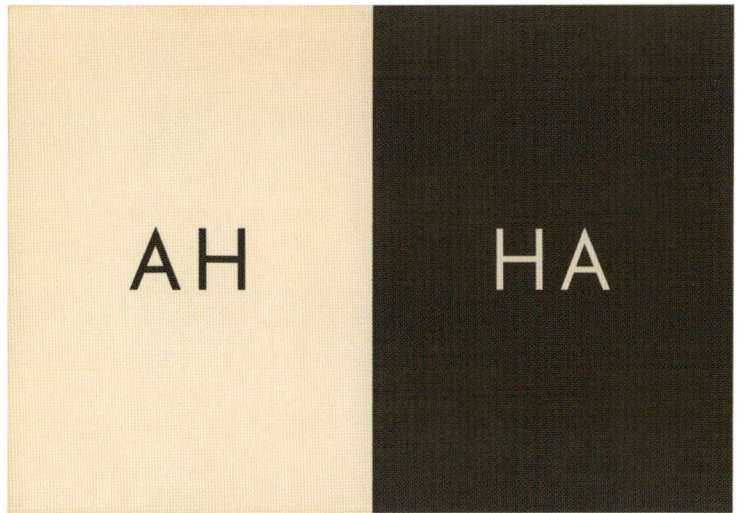

FIG. 2.16
Bruce Nauman, *Ah Ha*, 1975. Screenprint in black on Arches
wove paper. National Gallery of Art, Washington, DC. Gift of
Gemini G.E.L. and the artist.

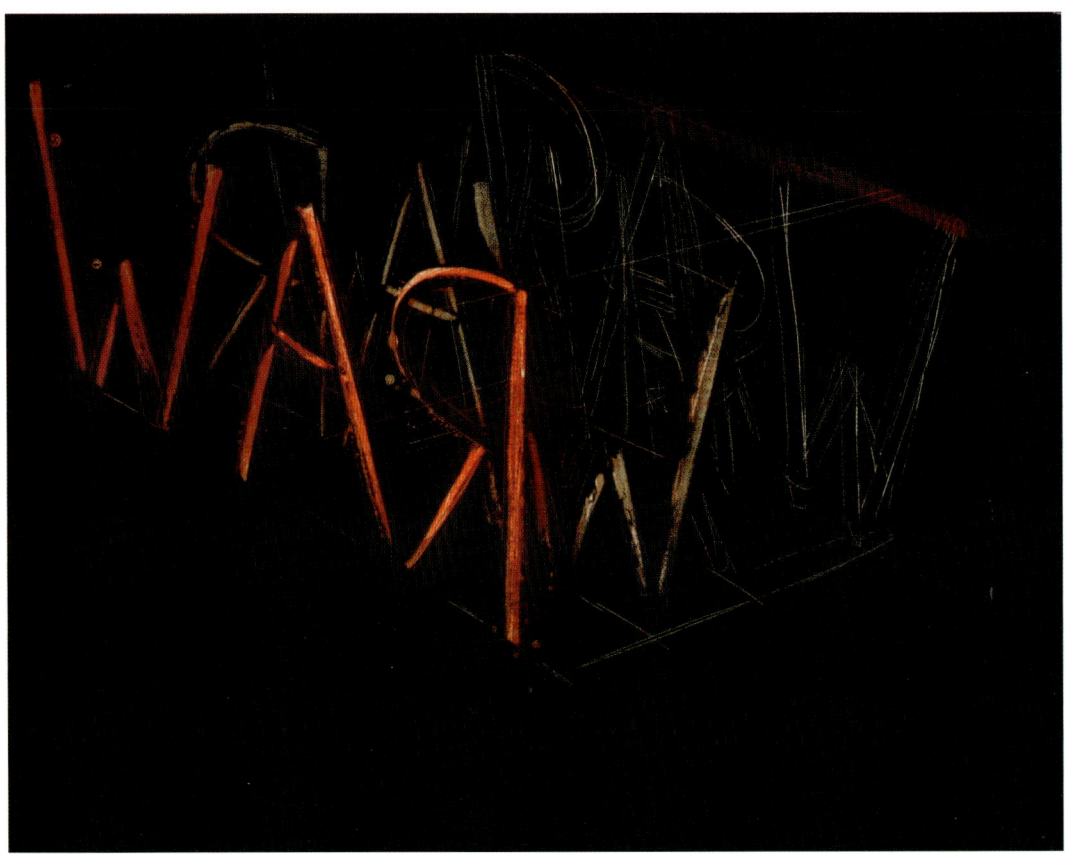

FIG. 2.17
Bruce Nauman, *Raw-War*, 1971. Three-color lithograph
on Arches paper, printed in three runs from three matrices
(stones and aluminum plates). Los Angeles County Museum
of Art. Cirrus Editions Archive. Purchased with funds
provided by the Director's Roundtable, and gift of Cirrus
Editions. M.86.2.678.

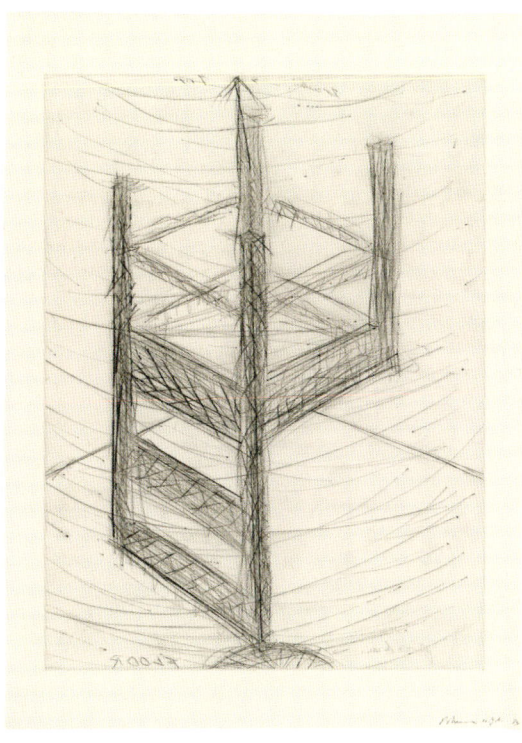

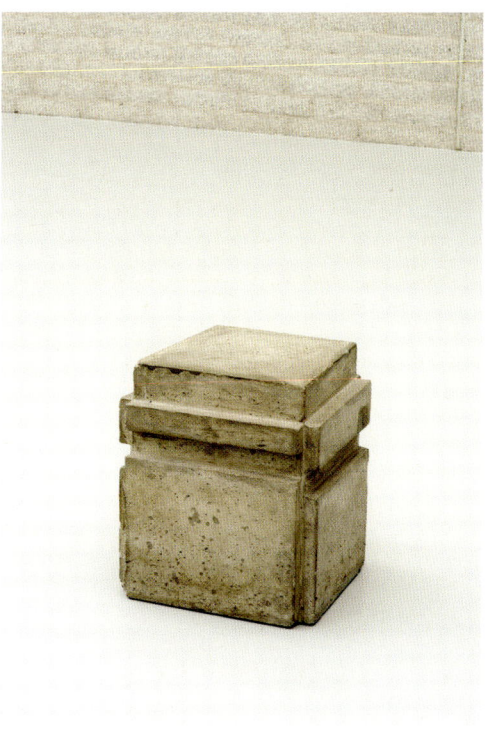

FIG. 2.18

Bruce Nauman, *Suspended Chair*, 1983. Drypoint in black
on Fabriano Rosaspina wove paper. National Gallery of Art,
Washington, DC. Gift of Gemini G.E.L. and the artist.

Bruce Nauman, *A Cast of the Space under My Chair*, 1965–68.
Concrete. Kröller-Müller Museum, Otterlo. Formerly in the
Visser collection, acquired with support from the Mondriaan
Foundation.

Finally, I want to linger on the work of Hock E Aye Vi Edgar Heap of Birds, a Cheyenne and Arapaho artist who lives and works in Oklahoma. He uses reversal extensively in his work, much of which is emphatically text-based. He recently designed the cover of *Art in America* (note the reversal of "America"), featuring one of a series of his monotype prints that contend with the destruction of Native American culture that haunts American history (FIG. 2.19). The texts he composes for the monotypes are brief, pointed poems that allude to state violence against Native communities.

Heap of Birds makes these prints by coating an acrylic plate with ink, then writing the text in reverse with his finger (the plate is then printed in only a single impression — this is what makes it a monotype) (FIG. 2.20). The text does not become legible in the correct orientation until the print is pulled from the plate. But meanwhile, by working in reverse, Heap of Birds engages in a form of communication in which he refuses to fully inhabit the space or orientation of the audience's language. His enunciation comes literally from an oppositional perspective, from the other side, from a space of critique and judgment. These monotypes are related to his series *Native Hosts*, which has been ongoing since the late 1980s. These are commercially printed signs that masquerade as official road signs. They are site-specific and all have the same structure (FIG. 2.21). For each sign, the English place-name of the site is printed in reverse, followed by the words "today your host is" and the name of an indigenous group that is native to that area. Heap of Birds claims, "The real mission of my art is to reset history."[25] It's the reversal of printed text in these works that allows that to happen. The history that needs resetting is the historical imaginary of American settler colonialism and its orientation toward the indigenous people who were removed in order to form the American state.

As codified around the nineteenth-century doctrines of manifest destiny, the march of Anglo-European civilization was presented as a progressive westward sweep before which the indigenous populations had no choice but to disappear. Indigenous people were imagined to be a "vanishing race," doomed to extinction. The violence of the settlement process was thus obscured under a romantic narrative of inevitable (rather than forced) decline. As this turn-of-the-century photograph by Edward S. Curtis suggests, the vanishing race ideology is already a kind of road sign, a directional indicator (FIG. 2.22). Curtis's Navajo are leaving the scene, back turned, retreating into a fuzzy pictorialist distance. The indigenous presence is receding. We are in the space of enunciation and vision, as if our perspective itself was driving the indigenous figures away. The photograph suggests that this is a one-way process.

Heap of Birds's reversed text, with startling efficiency, resets, repopulates, and unsettles this picture. This is partly due to the way his signs use

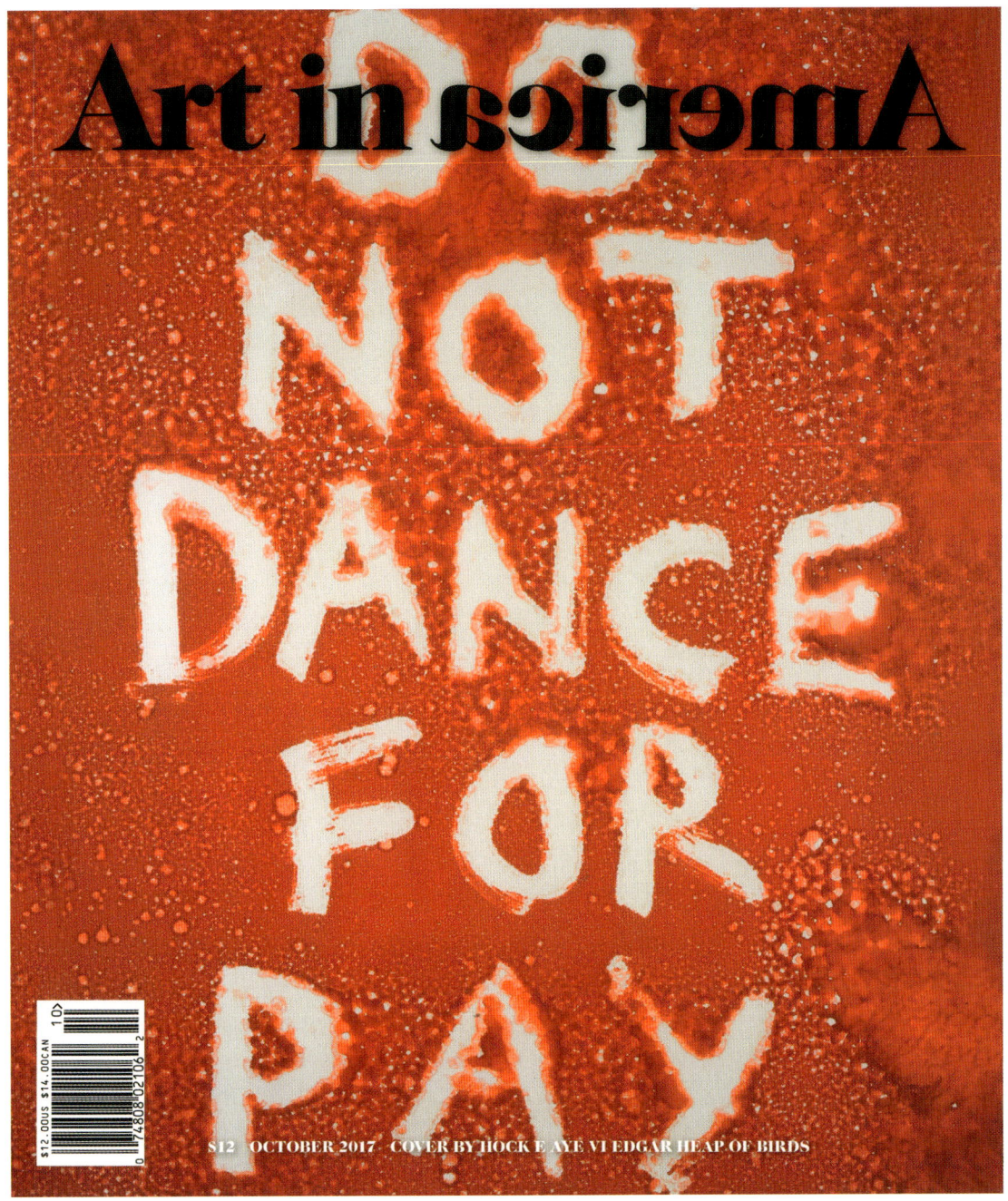

FIG. 2.19

Cover of *Art in America*, October 2017. Featuring Hock E Aye Vi Edgar Heap of Birds, *Do Not Dance for Pay* (detail), from *Surviving Active Shooter Custer*, 2018. Monoprint. The Museum of Modern Art, New York. Acquired through the generosity of Agnes Gund, Marlene Hess, and James D. Zirin, the Contemporary Arts Council of the Museum of Modern Art, Kathy and Richard S. Fuld, Jr., Linda Goldstein, Maud I. Welles and Marnie Pillsbury. 109.2019.a–vv.

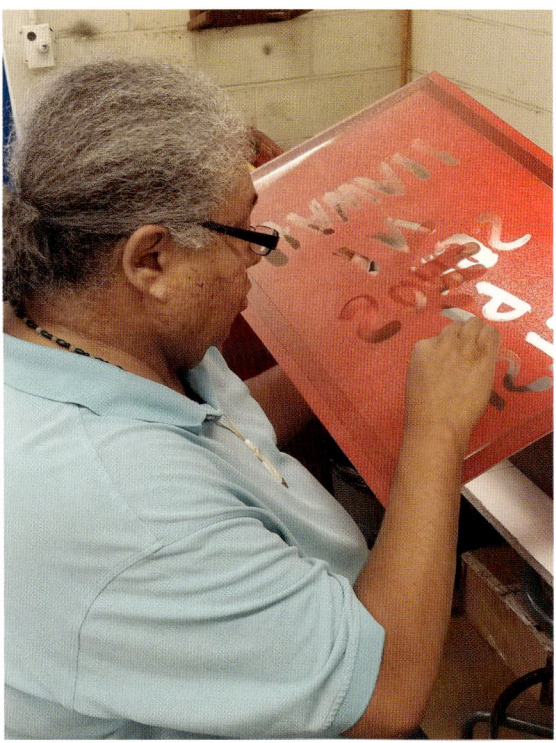

FIG. 2.20
Hock E Aye Vi Edgar Heap of Birds at work.

language to reinstall the indigenous groups in the present, for example by insisting on the word "Today." It also insists on the presence of indigenous voices anterior to the arrival of settlers, by presenting them as hosts for visitors. But the reversed text does all this even more pointedly, generating, as in Corita Kent's work, a double directionality that meets along the plane of the sign. This is a live and present encounter, a confrontation, with voices converging from two different directions. The settler finds her own place-name reversed, estranged, voiced from the other side by a presumably indigenous presence. Inasmuch as the threat to native sovereignty in American history was synonymous with the loss of land, this installation of a two-way dialogue also does something very important. The reversals, which open spaces on either side of the plane, give the indigenous speaker a place to stand. A location in the present, in active dialogue with the reader. Not retreating, but standing and speaking forward, through reversal.

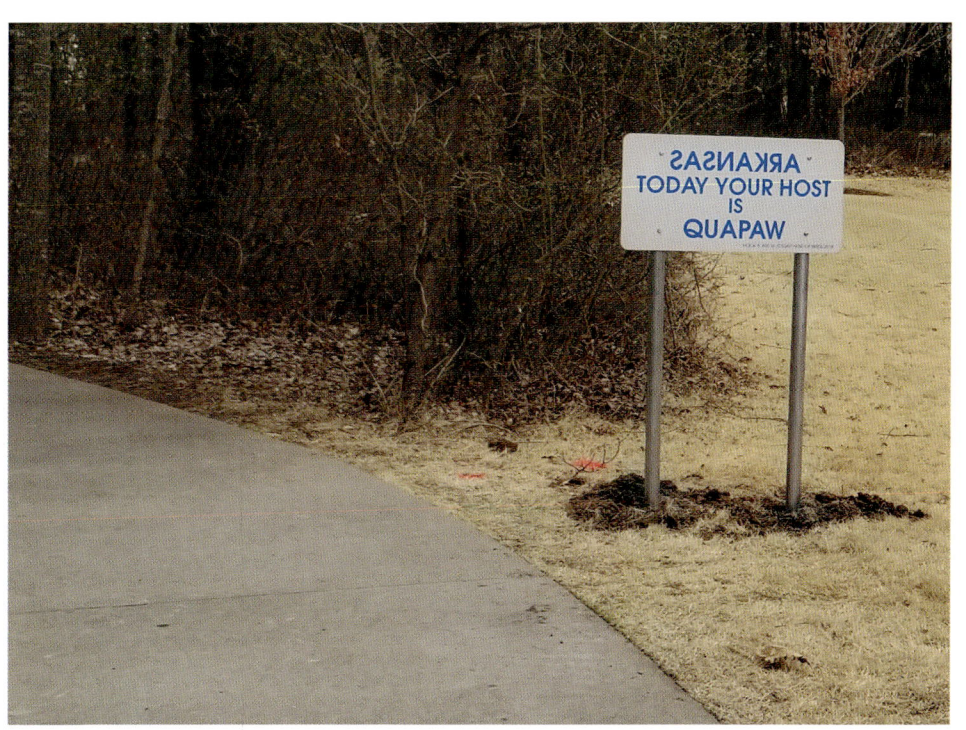

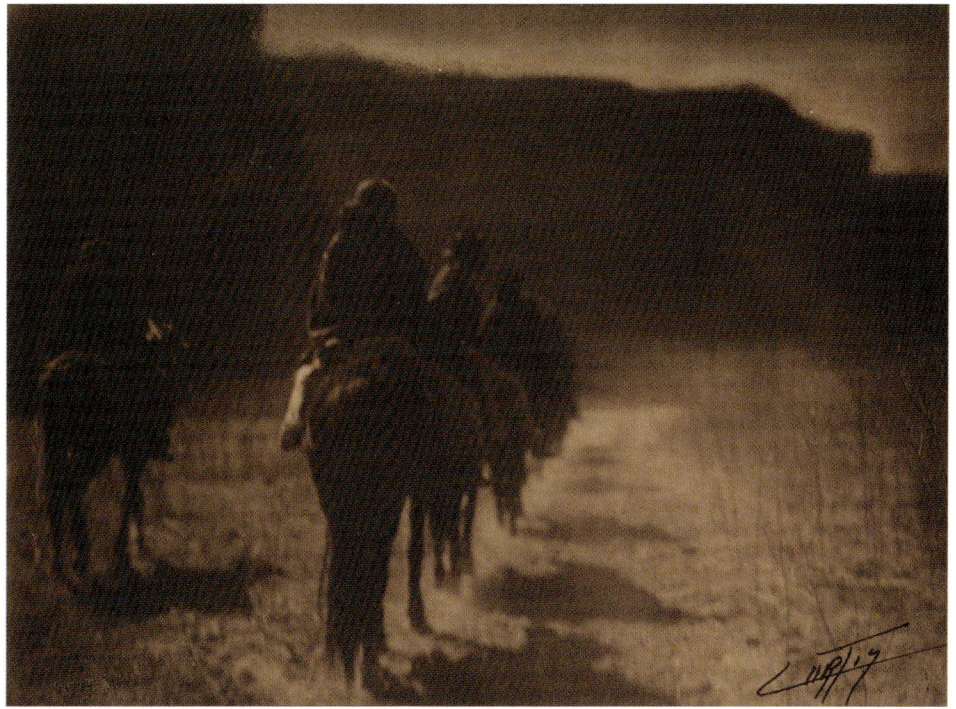

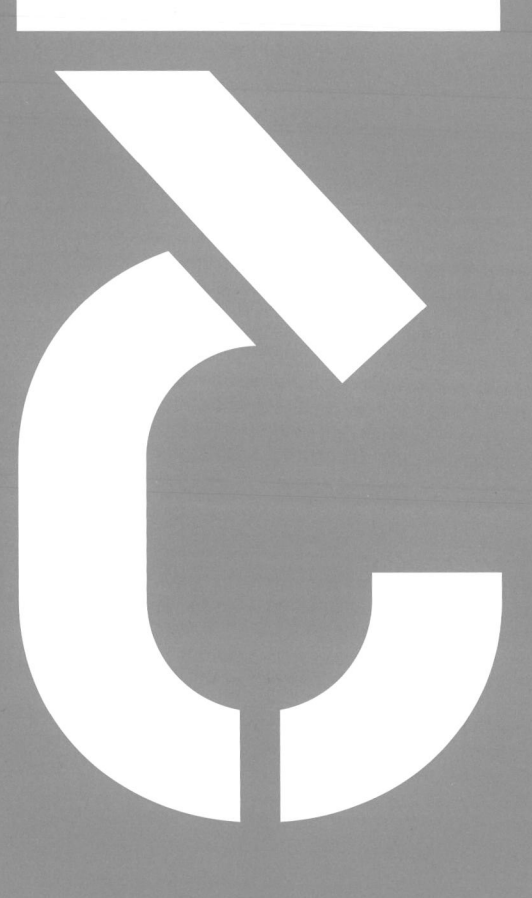

If I asked you to picture in your mind an artist in the process of creating a colorful image in the studio, you'd likely imagine someone standing at an easel with paintbrushes and a palette, or perhaps sitting at a table with paper and a collection of pastels or watercolors. The artist applies colors fluidly, spontaneously, and intuitively (a little blue here, a little green there), alternating colors at will and mixing new hues on the fly as the need arises. The colorwork develops pliably over time as the artist responds to the changing conditions of the painting or drawing. Although not all painters would fit this character study, the scene would be at least familiar to them. But no printmaker would recognize themselves in this scene. Color in printmaking is planned, assembled, sequenced, and selected in an entirely different way.

This is a chapter about the peculiar life of color in the printmaking process. The title—"Separation"—refers to the technical process of color separation that accompanies most color printing, and also opens out to the broader connotations of segregation, disjuncture, and difference suggested by the term. I'll be suggesting that modern and contemporary artists who explore the imperatives of color in printmaking have unique opportunities to grapple with these larger connotations as well. I'll start with a discussion of some of the essential qualities of printed color, and then turn to what this means for a contemporary art world that has been thoroughly, if inconspicuously, shaped by print technology.

What are some of the most significant qualities of printed color (see FIG. 3.1)? First: printed color is disjointed. Color must be broken down in order to be printed, and then it must be reassembled, usually in a series of layers. This reassembly is never complete, so for all intents and purposes printed color can be imagined as permanently fragmentary, even ruinous. A printed color image is like a stack of broken mosaics.

Second: printed color is conspicuously material. In the process of being printed, colors insist upon themselves as material substances with particular viscosities and textures. At the moment of printing, their status as optical phenomena that occupy different positions on the electromagnetic spectrum is irrelevant. Color in printing is not visual, immaterial, or ephemeral at heart; it is heavy, sticky, and squashy.

Third: printed color is only arbitrarily related to form. It has a fundamentally unstable relationship to the design that it delineates in a print project. The composition of any given print is encoded on the matrix, which is in itself "colorless": color joins the composition only in the moment of printing, and at that stage virtually any color can be used to delineate any area of the composition.

Fourth: printed color is methodical. It must be handled in an extremely meticulous and deliberate way. Printing is not a spontaneous or expressionistic medium for color.

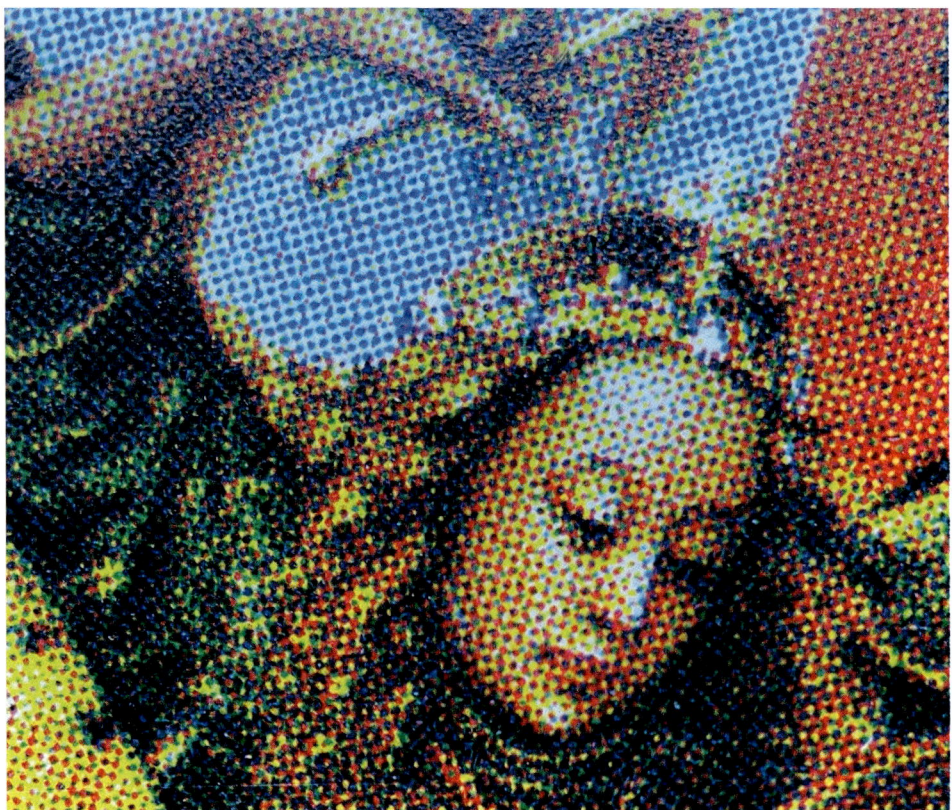

FIG. 3.1
Jennifer L. Roberts (photographer), macrophotographic detail of
The Crucifixion; The Last Judgment by Jan van Eyck, as printed in
History of Art by H. W. Janson (New York: Abrams, 1970), 2022.

For any printers and printmakers who might be reading this, these basic principles of printed color will undoubtedly seem painfully remedial. But what is second nature to them will likely be new to most everyone else, because this kind of knowledge does not travel very far beyond the inner sanctum of the print studio. Color in printing occupies one of the many yawning gaps between practical and theoretical knowledge that have, in my view, limited our range of critical imagination in the arts.

There is a fundamental difference, for example, between the way printers and art historians process color. Printers are always working to develop practical solutions to the problems that color introduces to the medium. Will this red ink tack properly to that yellow ink? How can I get these two color areas to register perfectly, without gaps, bleed, or overlap, on the same surface? Art historians, even in their most materially sensitive moments, tend to ask a different set of questions. How is color gendered? What symbolic associations have colors evoked across cultures? How do we think about color in its fugitivity, its resistance to language and memory? How did color theories develop across cultures and how did they intersect with the arts? What is the global or colonial biography of this or that pigment? It's tempting to imagine that the art historians are thinking more expansively, in a "higher" way, about color, but the practical ingenuity of printers is equally profound, and should be better integrated into the history of art. The historian of technology Davis Baird has coined the phrase "semantic ascent" to describe the way theoretical or symbolic intelligence has historically been understood as "higher" and better than material intelligence in the Western imagination.[1] One of my main goals in this book is to help flatten that hierarchy, making it more difficult to distinguish between practice and theory, and making it easier for makers and interpreters to communicate with each other.

This reminds me of the painter Amy Sillman's brilliant essay, "On Color." In the opening paragraphs of the essay, Sillman describes being surprised that an art historian she met didn't know that a tube of cadmium red paint is heavier in the hand than a tube of cobalt violet paint. She forgives the art historian, because this division of labor between practice and theory "is as old as the hills."[2] As she puts it, her job is to *hold* color; the art historian's job is to *behold* color. But, as an art historian, I'm not so sure that I can or should be forgiven for not knowing about things like the weight of color. One of the questions I ask myself every day is: How can I make my beholding more beholden to the holding?

There is a reason that when you walk into an exhibition of prints made before about 1800, most of what you see will be printed in ink of only one color (usually some version of black). Multicolor images were difficult to achieve in the most prominent early print techniques in the West—exponentially more difficult than achieving them in painting. Printing in a press is a binary process: it is based on the division of the matrix into printing and non-printing areas. The printing areas hold and transfer ink, the non-printing areas do not. The whole matrix goes through the press at once, and there is no way to adjust the action of the press to treat different areas of the matrix differently. This means that the press cannot print multiple colors at once; it can only print or not print the single layer of ink on a single matrix. Unless you engage in some fancy custom inking, the press can't put some red over here and some yellow over there in a single pass.

A general rule follows from this: if you want to print color with a press, you can only print one color at a time. So how to get multiple colors onto a print? Historically, the simplest method was to "cheat" and apply color by hand after the fact, often with wash or watercolor so that the printed lines would still be visible beneath. Hand coloring was practiced in the West almost as soon as printmaking was adopted, but it reached new levels of sophistication and scale in the nineteenth century.[3] Consider the immensely successful Currier and Ives firm in the United States, which marketed and distributed popular lithographic images—the example shown here was instrumental in disseminating the ideology of manifest destiny discussed at the end of the previous chapter (FIG. 3.2). Hundreds of thousands of impressions issued from the Currier and Ives operation every year, and they were often available to purchase in both black-and-white and color versions. When they were colored, they were colored by hand: the firm had "coloring rooms" staffed mostly by immigrant women who had previously worked in the European lithographic trade. Each colorist would be assigned a single color, with application often guided by stencils, and the print would come to life in an assembly line process.[4]

Consider the huge investment made in hand coloring here—Currier and Ives were essentially running a factory of hand coloring. Although lithography is one of the friendliest processes for color printing, in the mid-nineteenth century, it was still easier and cheaper to hire people to do all that color by hand than it was to integrate color into the printing process itself. It's worth pointing out that in hand coloring, color is always belated. It follows after printing, literally manifesting as a secondary quality, somehow less essential than form, which is carried by line. In this sense, it obeys the common hierarchical distinction between line and color that runs through Western art theory, in which line is thought to carry the essence of things—proportion, contour, balance—and color is a fugitive, inessential afterthought.[5] But as we will see throughout this chapter, those ideas about color as a secondary afterthought break down when you actually start printing systematically in color with a press. So how is this done—how can the press itself be made to manage color?

There are some transitional methods of color printing that involve hand-coloring the matrix rather than the printed sheet. One example is *à la poupée* printing, in which inks of two or more colors are applied directly to the plate or block before printing. This involves complicated and time-consuming inking procedures—especially in the areas where two colors meet. In these areas, inks need to be able to abut each other without mixing when the plate comes under pressure in the press. And the plate needs to be reinked this way for each and every impression. A more modular method is to break up the block or plate into pieces, ink different parts in different colors, and then reassemble the parts on the press bed. This is known as jigsaw plate printing. Edvard Munch's late nineteenth-century woodcuts made from sawn-up woodblocks are masterful examples of this process (FIG. 3.3).

Printing *à la poupée* and jigsaw printing are still practiced in specialized printmaking studios, but these methods are not efficient for reproducing large

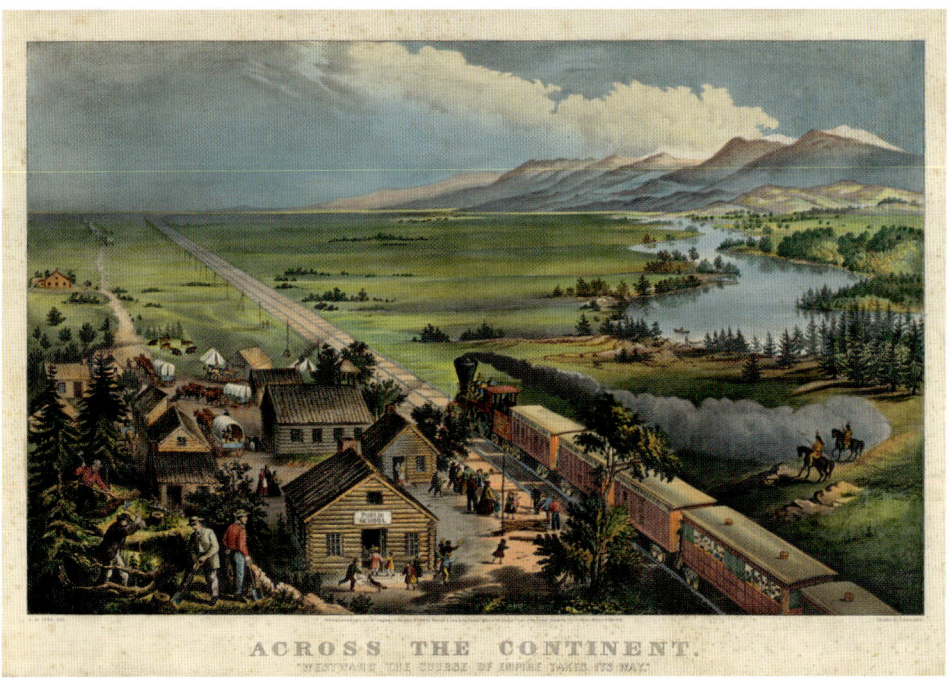

ACROSS THE CONTINENT.
"WESTWARD THE COURSE OF EMPIRE TAKES ITS WAY."

FIG. 3.2

Frances Flora Bond Palmer (artist); Currier and Ives (publisher), *Across the Continent: "Westward the Course of Empire Takes Its Way,"* 1868. Hand-colored lithograph, with touches of gum arabic, on wove paper. National Gallery of Art, Washington, DC. Collection of Mr. and Mrs. Paul Mellon.

numbers of impressions. Throughout the history of printmaking in the West, and especially after the later nineteenth century, the printing industry sought to develop mechanically generated printed color that would be compatible with existing print technology. This required stabilizing and automating the relationship between color and the matrix by separating different colors onto individual matrices, then printing them all on the same sheet of paper, one on top of the other. The same sheet of paper would go through the press multiple times, as the color from different matrices stacked up. This is known as printing *au repérage,* and although there were various forays into this method in earlier centuries (early modern chiaroscuro printing is one example), it did not become widespread until the late nineteenth century, when new modes of printing that were friendlier to color were developed and improvements in color separation technology made it easier to mechanize the process.[6]

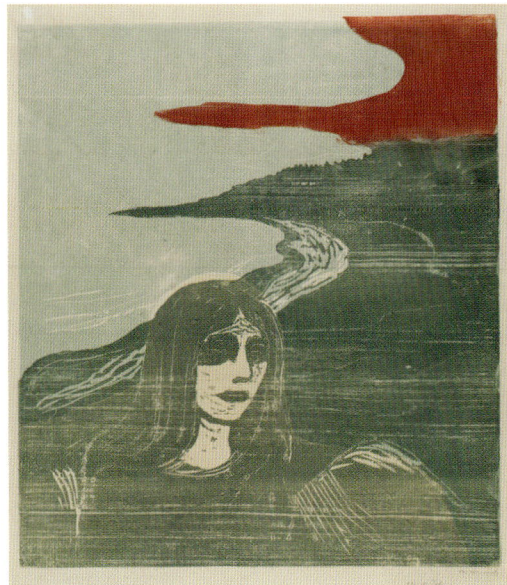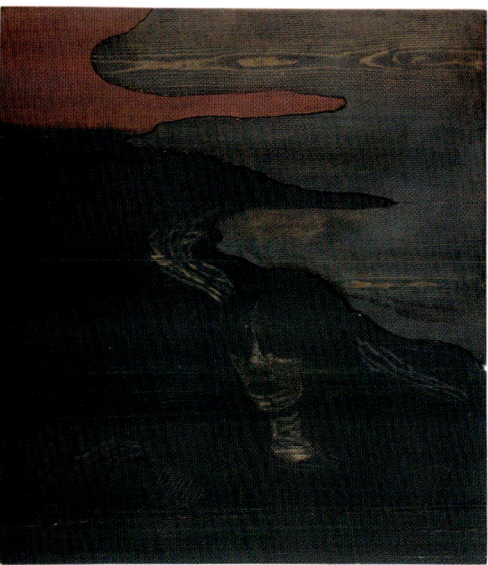

FIG. 3.3

Edvard Munch, *Woman's Head against the Shore*, 1899. Woodcut printed
in red and three different colors of green ink on tan wove paper. Harvard
Art Museums/Fogg Museum, Cambridge, MA. Gift of Lynn G. Straus in
memory of Philip A. Straus.

Edvard Munch, woodblock for *Woman's Head against the Shore*, 1899.
Spruce woodblock, sawn in two with fretsaw. Munchmuseet, Oslo.

Roy Lichtenstein's lithograph *Sunrise* provides a good basic tutorial in
color separation (FIG. 3.4). (Lichtenstein is always useful for exploring basic
print technology, because his entire practice as an artist was based on his experience with commercial printing; printing is the real subject matter of this work,
not the nominal sunrise referent.) *Sunrise* and its original color separations are in
the collection of the National Gallery of Art (FIG. 3.5). Each of these color separations was used to make a single matrix; each of those matrices printed a single
layer of ink on the paper. The color separation marked "blue," in other words,
became the matrix that printed the blue layer in the print.

The color separation process in studio printmaking is rarely as straightforward as it is in *Sunrise*. Consider *Entropia (review)* of 2004 by Julie Mehretu,
a prominent contemporary artist who has worked extensively in print as well as
painting (FIG. 3.6). The print is assembled from no fewer than thirty-two color
layers. Master printer Cole Rogers, who worked with Mehretu at Highpoint

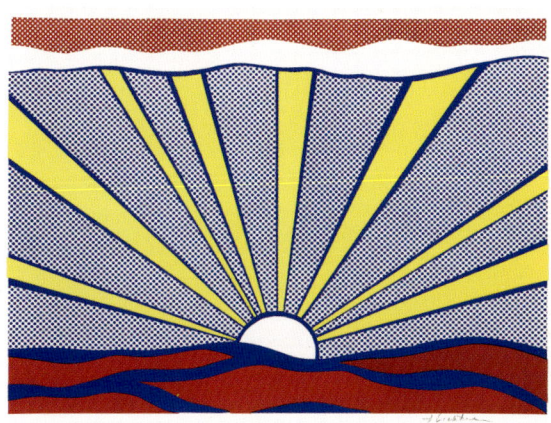

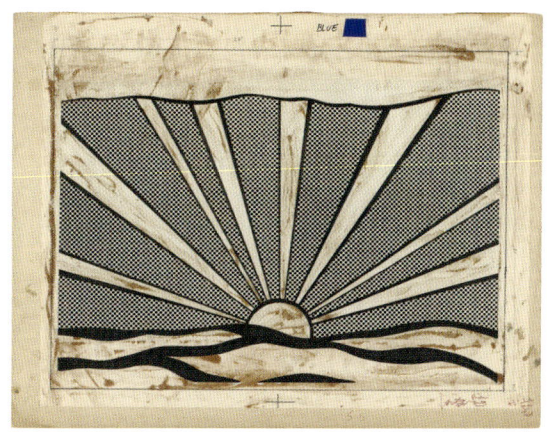

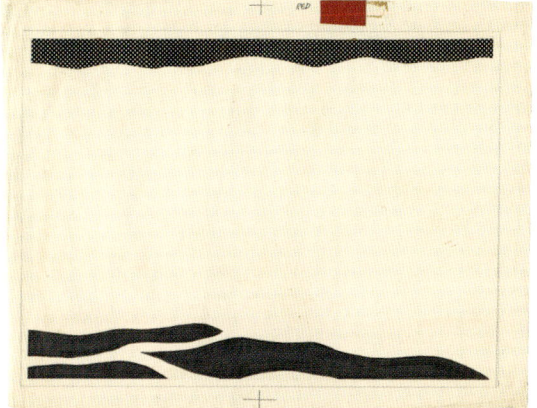

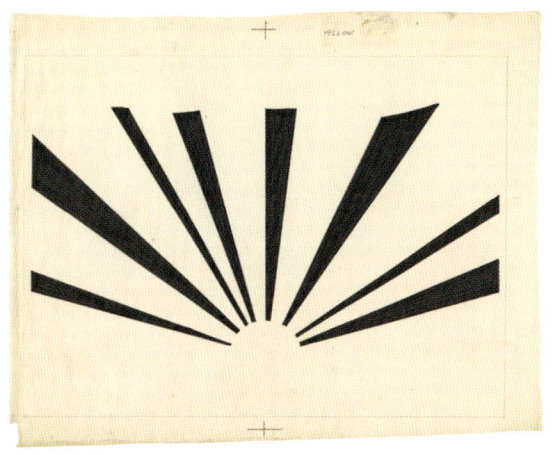

Roy Lichtenstein, *Sunrise*, 1965. Color offset lithograph on lightweight, white wove paper. National Gallery of Art, Washington, DC. Gift of Roy and Dorothy Lichtenstein.

Roy Lichtenstein, *Sunrise: Separation Drawing for Blue*, 1965. Collage of glossy gelatin silver print, felt-tip markers, and graphite, corrected with white gouache on paper with color chip, mounted on board. National Gallery of Art, Washington, DC. Director's Discretionary Fund.

Roy Lichtenstein, *Sunrise: Separation Drawing for Red*, 1965. Black felt-tip pen, collage, and graphite on paper. National Gallery of Art, Washington, DC. Director's Discretionary Fund.

Roy Lichtenstein, *Sunrise: Separation Drawing for Yellow*, 1965. Black felt-tip markers and graphite on paper. National Gallery of Art, Washington, DC. Director's Discretionary Fund.

Editions in Minneapolis, created an ingenious process book that he uses to show people how the different layers for this print came together. He printed each color layer on a separate sheet of mylar; then stacked and bound the mylars like a book, so that as you page through them you gain an intuitive understanding of the print's three-dimensional color stratification (FIG. 3.7).[7] Whenever you look at a color print, it's useful to imagine yourself looking into a sequential stack like this.

Color layers can also be deployed to produce effects beyond color per se. Jasper Johns's screenprint *The Dutch Wives* is twenty-nine screens deep (FIG. 3.8). You can be forgiven for wondering: Twenty-nine screens for that? It just looks gray. If you look very closely at the print you can begin to see the layers: newspaper text on one screen, a yellowish color on another screen, each subtle shade of gray on a separate screen, and so on. But color separations can do more than add different hues: Sometimes a layer will simply deliver a translucent white ink, an opacifier, to bring down the value of the color below it. Sometimes it will insert a film of opalescent or reflective ink to brighten the layers above it. Many of the layers in Johns's print are providing these sorts of oblique color effects. Most any effect of vibrance or brilliance, not to mention value or hue, requires depositing a discrete layer of ink that will function by intervening, in a particular position, in a series of stratified colors. The key lesson here is that every multicolor print, however flat it appears to be, has a three-dimensional structure. It is a stack of color layers, each interacting in different ways with those above and below. And the reorganization of these layers can create a nearly infinite set of possible outcomes.

An even more fundamental lesson to take from this process is that a multicolor image has to be separated—broken down, taken apart—in order to be printed. There is a kind of ruination in the very structure of color print. Mehretu's title—*Entropia*—is apt here. A precarious balance between structure and ruination is a hallmark of color printing, and Mehretu's work helps us see how this printerly suspension of color can inform an entire artistic practice. Mehretu's celebrated paintings explore complex systems—ecological, social, financial—that teeter on the line between construction and collapse (FIG. 3.9). Mehretu draws directly on her training in printmaking to evoke this uneasy balance. This is true at the literal level: her paintings include screenprinted layers interspersed between handmade marks. But it is also true broadly, in all the ways that printmaking has guided her imagination of layering, deconstruction, and depth in painting, as well as her invocation of social fragmentation, trauma, and reassembly. As she has said, for her "it is in printmaking that new things are invented, which I then want to bring into painting and drawing."[8] She's said that she's drawn to printmaking as a process of "taking apart and putting back together," and that is exactly what is at issue in each of her paintings of contemporary systems.[9]

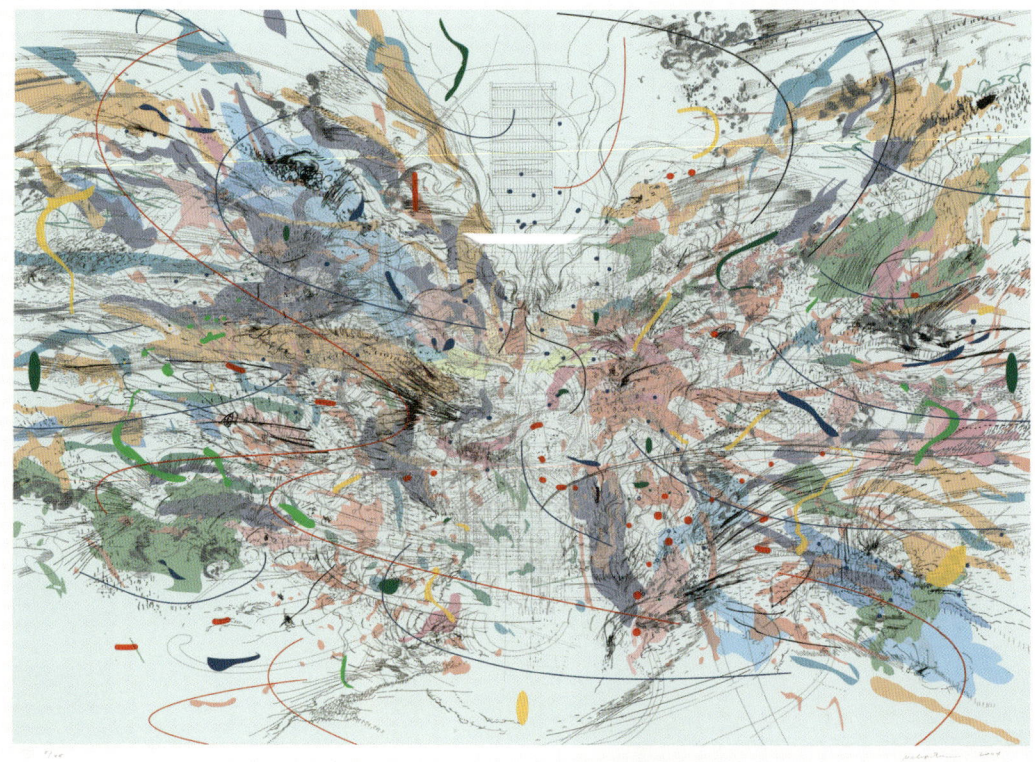

FIG. 3.6
Julie Mehretu, *Entropia (review)*, 2004. Color
screenprint and lithograph on Arches 88 paper.
National Gallery of Art, Washington, DC.
Thomas G. Klarner Collection. Gift of Neal
Turtell.

FIG. 3.7
Cole Rogers with the progression book
for *Entropia (review)*, Highpoint Center for
Printmaking, Minneapolis.

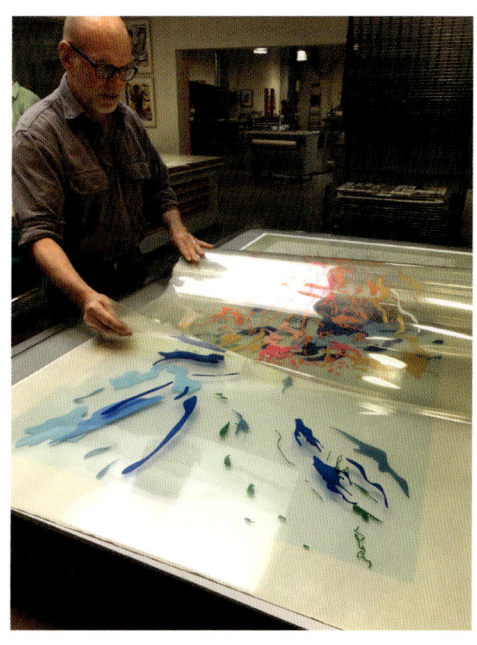

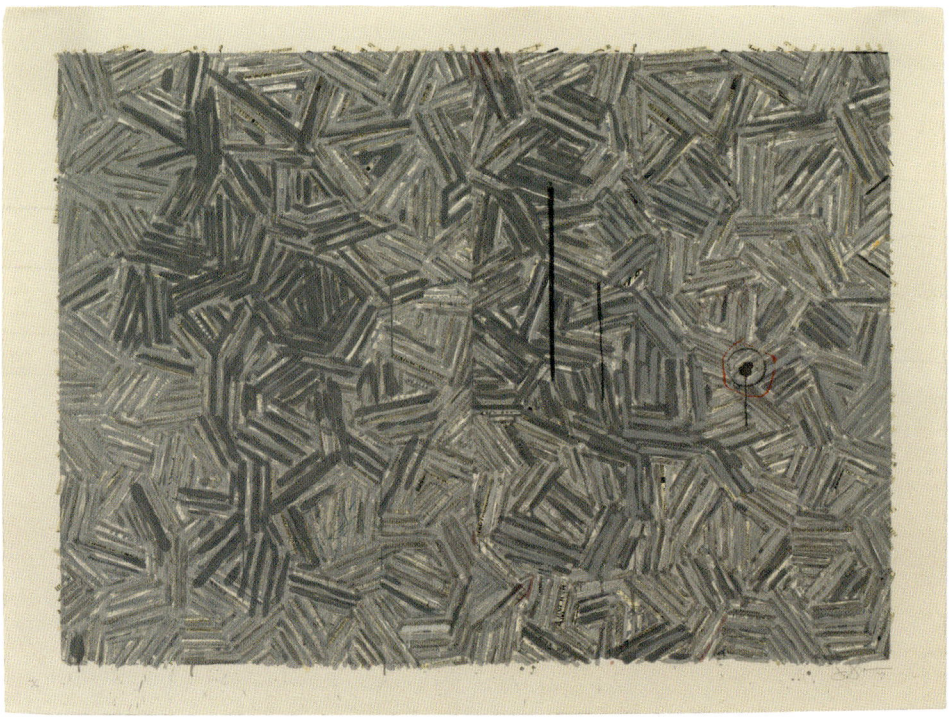

FIG. 3.8
Jasper Johns, *The Dutch Wives*, 1977. Screenprint from 29 screens on
Kurotani Kozo paper. Harvard Art Museums/Fogg Museum, Cambridge,
MA. Gift of Harry Kahn.

The Johns and Mehretu prints we've just seen are high-end print studio productions with custom designed color separations. Most commercial color printing works on the same principle of disjointed color assembly, but it breaks up the color in its images in a more efficient and automated way. I'm referring here to the 4-color CMYK printing process, which is the process used to make probably 99.99 percent of all the printed color images you have ever seen in your life — magazines, catalogs, art history books, newspaper photographs (FIG. 3.10). In this process, photography does the work of separating the color in the original images. An image is photographed using filters to separate it into cyan, magenta, yellow, and then black (K stands for black). Usually, the four color separations are also broken down into halftone dots — halftones will be discussed in chapters 4 and 5. Then these are each given a dedicated printing matrix and layered back up as a four-part stack in the printing process.

FIG. 3.9
Julie Mehretu, *Ghosthymn (After the Raft)*,
2019–21. Ink and acrylic on canvas.

Detail of *Ghosthymn (After the Raft)*.

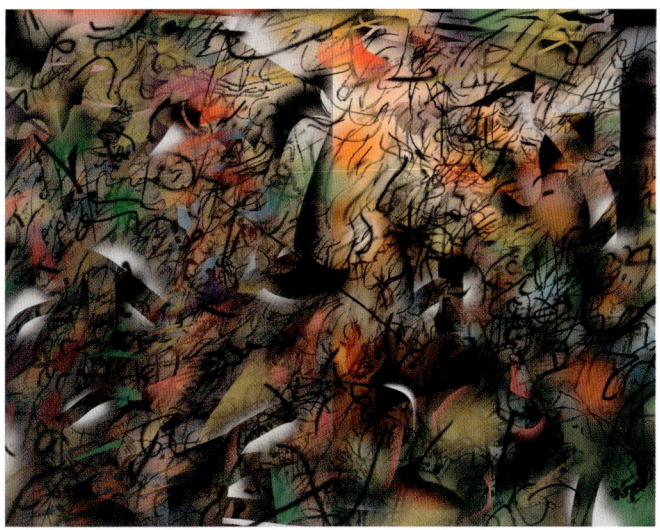

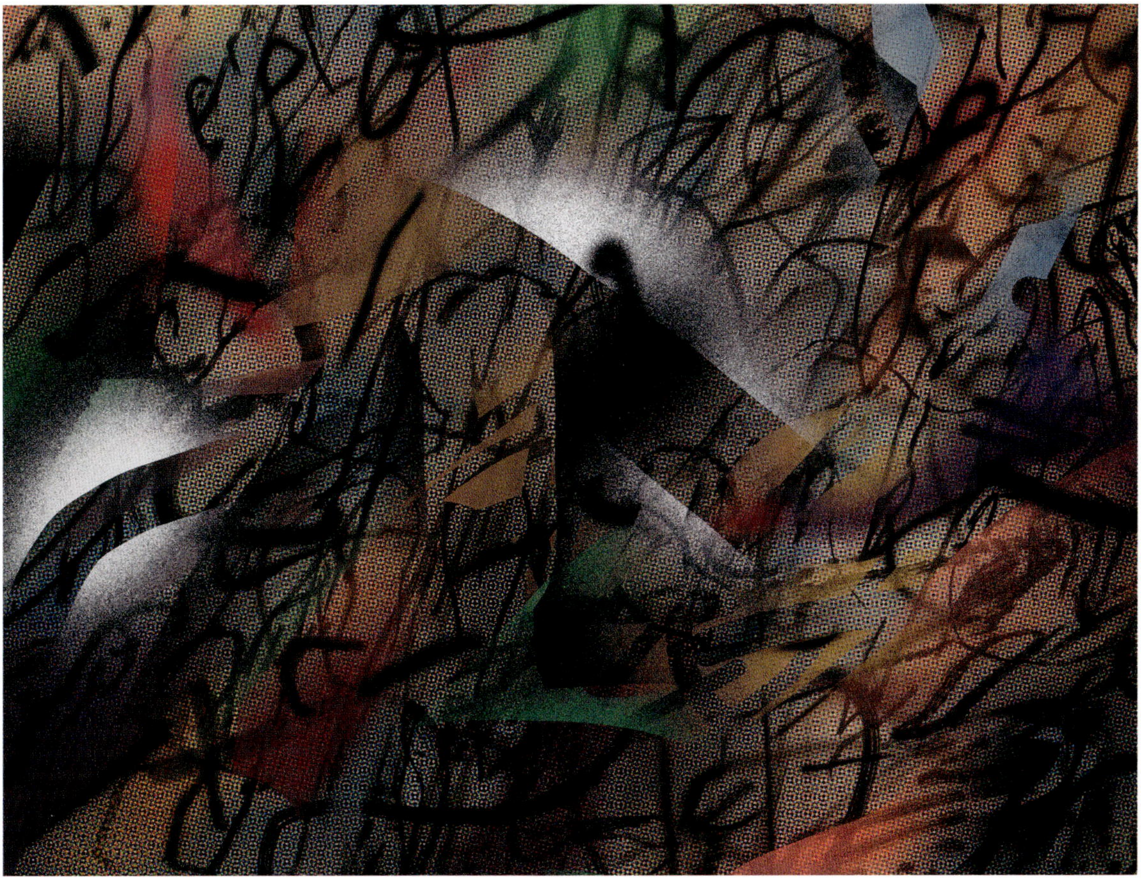

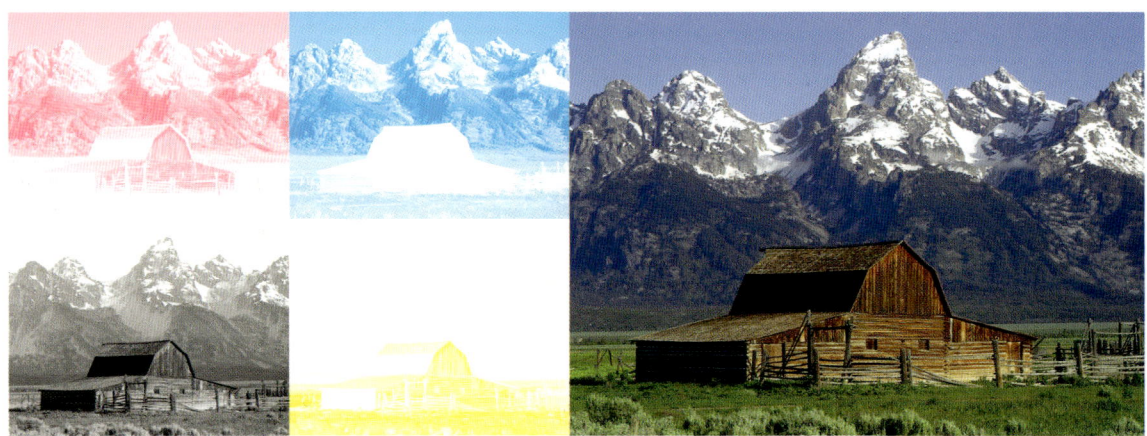

FIG. 3.10
The CMYK color separation process.

This is the wobbly color infrastructure of printed visual culture and visual knowledge—including art-historical knowledge. I say it's a wobbly infrastructure because while it can be difficult to break images down into color separations, it's even trickier to reassemble those separations in the final print. Once you've pulled the color apart, in other words, you've got to put it back together. You've got to stack it all back up again into a legible, cohesive structure on a single sheet of paper. The color layers need to be relaminated. And they need to come right back together in perfect juxtaposition, otherwise you get misregistration.

Color registration presents a material, physical challenge as well as a conceptual or an optical one. In order to convey a sense of the complexities involved, I'll focus here on what is probably the most difficult print medium for color registration: intaglio. Intaglio processes include engraving, etching, and related formats in which the matrix is prepared by gouging or incising the surface. Ink is then applied to the plate so that it sits inside these incisions: in the "valleys" on the plate, as it were (see fig. 0.5). This form of printing requires very high pressure because the ink needs to be pulled out of the grooves. Also—and this is the key issue for color—the paper has to be dampened before printing. This makes the paper more pliable so that it can be deformed into those grooves to pick up the ink.

Unfortunately, the same moisture that makes it possible to print the paper in the first place makes it incredibly difficult to print in color with any precision. The damp paper, as it is squeezed and pulled under the high-pressure roller of the press, stretches slightly. Paper stretch makes it impossible to regulate the scale relationship between the matrix and the paper. Normally, in single-pass black-and-white engraving, this doesn't really matter, although there are some places where it can have enormous, veritably epistemological consequences. In map printing, for example, paper stretch means that the scale of an engraved map becomes inaccurate as soon as it goes through the press. Historically, cartographic copperplates were engraved at a slightly smaller scale than required, so that the map would end up at the proper scale after the paper stretched in the press.[10]

But the place where scale inconsistency really becomes a problem is color registration. Say you've printed the first color in your color engraving. Now, as you go to print the second color on the same page, the paper is a little bit larger than it was before, and the second color does not line up with the first. And this keeps compounding with every color you want to add. One of the most innovative intaglio printmakers in the nineteenth century was Mary Cassatt. In 1891, she exhibited a groundbreaking group of color etchings that were inspired by Japanese woodblock printing. These have been recognized as the high point of color intaglio printing in nineteenth-century Europe, but even here, Cassatt handled some of the color with *à la poupée* techniques because the multiple plates she would need for the complex colors and patterns she wanted would be too difficult to register *au repérage* (FIG. 3.11).[11]

Another problem with color printing on wet paper is that with multiple passes through the press, the paper literally breaks down and begins wrinkling in the margins and the plate edges. The grain compresses to the point that the paper loses its absorbency, and cannot accept further color passes. At the legendary intaglio studio Crown Point Press, for example, the printers use a blank "pre-stretch plate" to take some of the stretch out of the paper before printing the first color, and have learned that color projects using more than six or seven plates are unfeasible.[12] Essentially, color printing is hampered by print processes that require moisture in the paper. The drier the paper and the lighter the pressure, the better. In relief methods, like woodcut, linocut, or letterpress, the ink sits on top of the surface of the matrix rather than in the grooves, on the mesas rather than in the valleys, so it does not require as much pressure to transfer the image, and moisture is not necessary. The spectacular color achieved in Japanese woodblock (relief) prints, developed over centuries into a precise system, inspired European printmakers like Cassatt to emulate them in intaglio. But Japanese color effects could never be perfectly translated to intaglio. The dry paper and lighter pressure used in Japanese woodblock printing allowed much more control over registration (FIG. 3.12).

The popular explosion of color printing in nineteenth-century Europe and the Americas derived at first from advances in color lithography. Lithography requires some moisture on the stone, but it uses a dry sheet of paper, so there is

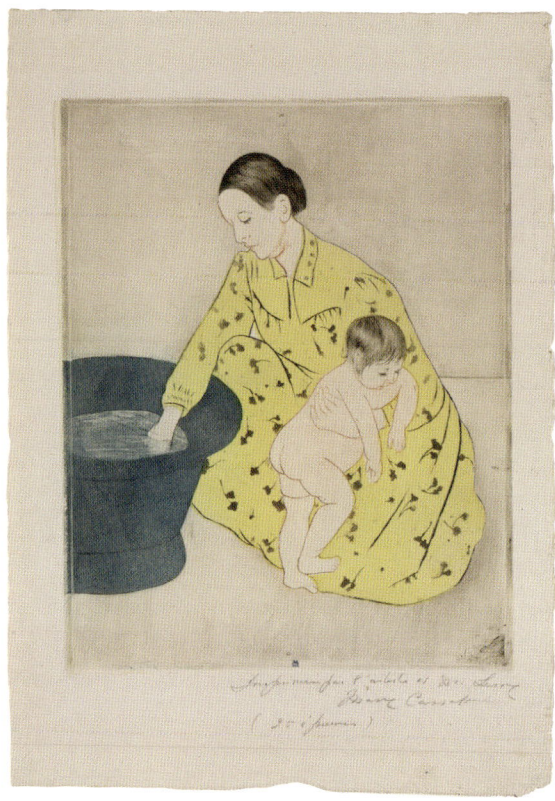

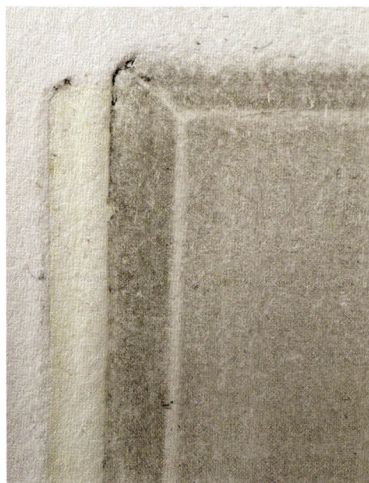

FIG. 3.11

Mary Cassatt, *The Bath*, 1890–91. Drypoint, soft-ground etching, and aquatint printed in yellow, black, blue, and light brown ink. Harvard Art Museums/Fogg Museum, Cambridge, MA. Gift of Dr. Ernest G. Stillman, class of 1907, by exchange.

Detail of plate-edge misregistration in *The Bath*.

less distortion and consequent danger of misregistration. Then, in the twentieth century, screenprinting became a primary color printmaking technology, again because it prints on dry paper. But even without paper stretch in these dry processes, all kinds of problems can pop up in the reassembly of color. In screenprinting, for example, the tensioning of the screen can be off from one color to the next; this will cause misregistration. Huge problems can arise when layering colors in halftone prints: interference patterns often erupt from the superimposition of color layers (this will be the subject of chapter 5). In essence, color in print is like Humpty Dumpty. It can never quite be put back together again.

The stratification in color printmaking has many other implications. For example, the stack of articulated color layers is a risk structure as well as a spatial structure. The printing process for a print like *Entropia (review)* (fig. 3.6) produces a dramatic escalation of risk as each subsequent color is added. The thirty-first layer in a thirty-two layer color screenprint is different from the fourth or fifth layer, because if you make a mistake printing that penultimate

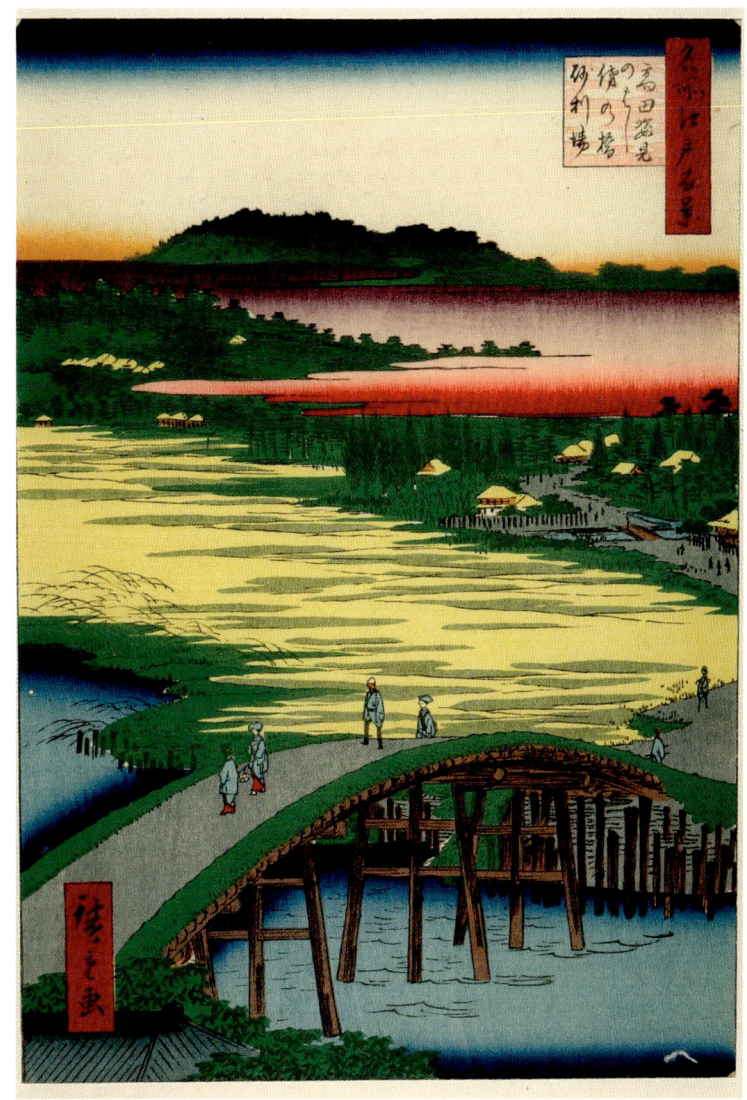

FIG. 3.12
Utagawa Hiroshige, *Sugatami Bridge, Omokage Bridge and Gravel Pit at Takata, No. 116*, from *One Hundred Famous Views of Edo*, 1857. Ukiyo-e woodblock print in "ōban" format; ink and color on paper. Harvard Art Museums/Arthur M. Sackler Museum, Cambridge, MA. Gift of the Friends of Arthur B. Duel.

plate or screen, you have to discard everything you've done below. Every additional layer of color on a print throws the colors below into an increasingly high risk ratio. The tiniest mistake in a later layer will neutralize all the perfections in the earlier layers.

This brings me to my second point about color in print as a material rather than an optical operation. The restacking of color separations has to happen on the press before any of the color reaches the viewer's eye. As explained in chapter 1, the press is not an optical instrument; it feels rather than sees the ink it transfers. It does distinguish between colored inks, but it distinguishes between them based on their material rather than their optical properties. Different colors might have different drying times, viscosities, adhesive properties, or responsiveness to solvents. This affects the way they interact under pressure. So when the press stacks up layers of color on the paper, those color relations have to succeed first at the physical level. They have to obey tactile laws of relation.[13]

One of those tactile considerations, for example, is the "tackiness" of ink. The layers of ink need to stick together, and this is affected by (among other things) the dryness or wetness of each ink. But colors often dry at variable rates, making it difficult to control the ability of the different layers to adhere to each other on the print. Sometimes, if the inks are drying unpredictably, they will actually resist each other rather than stick to each other. There is also the problem of the ordering of plates. Suppose you have, say, nine color layers to print. Which goes down first? Which comes second? Which comes last? Drastic variations in the final color profile of a print can emerge simply by changing the order of the layers. Red over blue looks different than blue over red. Opaque and transparent inks will obviously combine differently depending on which is above and which is below. It's daunting enough to manage the nearly infinite number of possible plate combinations. But the printer also has to think about the material way the different inks will respond to each other in that sequence. Red over blue may produce a satisfactory ink tack, while blue over red may not.[14]

To summarize where we are so far: every color print requires color separation and color reassembly. Although most color separations are initially achieved optically—through photographic filters—the reintegration of the color in the process of printing is a process that is strongly determined by material considerations even though its ultimate goal is to create an optical phenomenon, to "look" a certain way. Color may be pulled apart by wavelength, but it has to be reassembled by particle. No matter how much care is taken and no matter how much technical expertise goes into the registration and layering of printed color, it can never attain a perfect fusion or wholeness. It is always a more or less integrated aggregate of color pieces. A color print is an image made out of stratified, imperfectly laminated color rubble.

Another unusual aspect of printed color is that it is only arbitrarily related to form. Color has no organic or necessary relation to the design on the matrix. This is a drastic departure from the situation in painting: in painting, a brushstroke and its color are inseparably fused. You cannot make a yellow brushstroke without making a yellow brushstroke — the form and its color are one and the same. The brushstroke cannot exist without its yellowness. But in printmaking, the form or contour of the mark has its own independent existence apart from the color that ends up on the paper.

The American artist Louis J. Delsarte III was known as a brilliant colorist (FIG. 3.13). The Harvard Art Museums are lucky to have collected his lithograph *Unity* along with the full set of complex color separations that he drew to make the lithographic plates for it (FIG. 3.14). Notice that these color separation guides are not rendered in the colors that they would eventually take on in the lithograph; the separations are generally all made with black ink. Each drawing was transferred to a separate lithographic matrix, where it remained fundamentally colorless, existing only as a textural and chemical pattern on the surface that would attract and hold printing ink. It was not until just before printing, when the inks were applied separately to each matrix, that any given separation took on the color that it would transfer to the print. This is why we can say that color and design are only arbitrarily related in printmaking: the separations do not inherently demand that they be printed in any specific colors; they simply delineate a set of abstract areas that are to be inked in *a* single color. There's nothing to stop the printer from inking the color separation marked "green" in blue or yellow or red. The link between form and color is broken. Given the complexity of the color separations and Delsarte's deep understanding of the contingency of color in printmaking, the title of the print — *Unity* — signifies differently than it might otherwise. Unity isn't a given; it requires craft and intelligence to wrest it from a (color) world characterized by fragmentation, displacement, and delamination.

The inherent convertibility or interchangeability of color in relation to form in the modern pictorial arts has usually been discussed in terms of the history of painting. Impressionism and Fauvism, for example, are notable for having liberated color from the task of delineating objects and having relieved it of any obligation to naturalism. But is difficult to imagine that these innovations in turn-of-the-century color were not significantly impacted by the simultaneous developments in color printing, especially since color printing virtually forced its practitioners to develop an awareness of arbitrary, non-naturalistic color. The contribution of printmaking to these developments is a story that has yet to be fully told. One might begin with an artist like Arthur Wesley Dow, an American painter, printmaker, designer, educator, and theorist who mastered Japanese-style

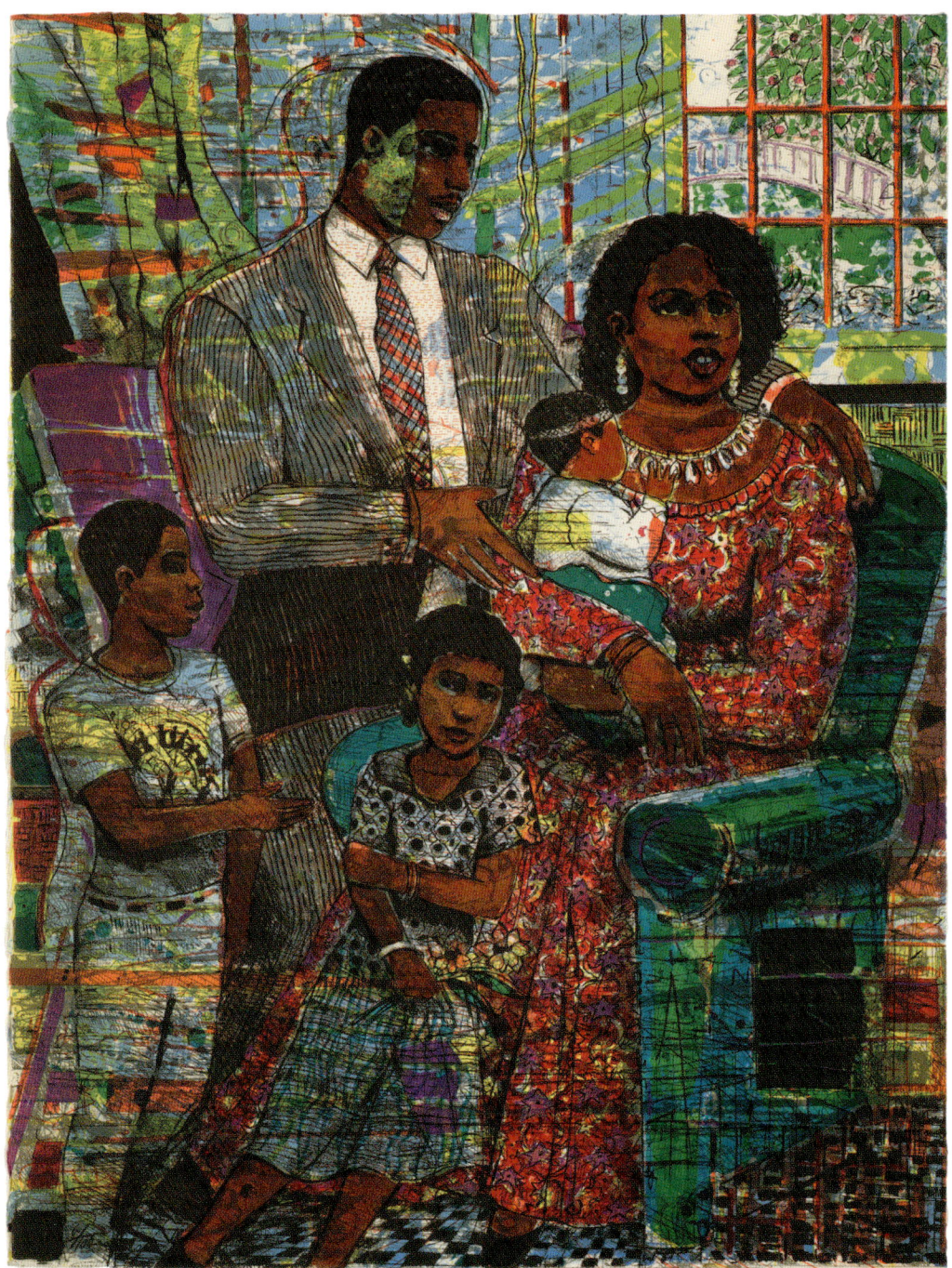

FIG. 3.13

Louis J. Delsarte III, *Unity*, 1995. Offset lithograph on white wove
paper. Printed by Brandywine Workshop, Philadelphia, PA. Harvard Art
Museums/Fogg Museum, Cambridge, MA. Margaret Fisher Fund.

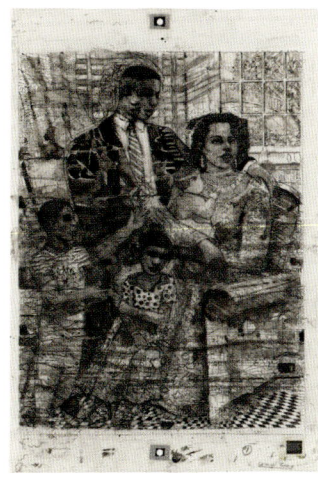

1

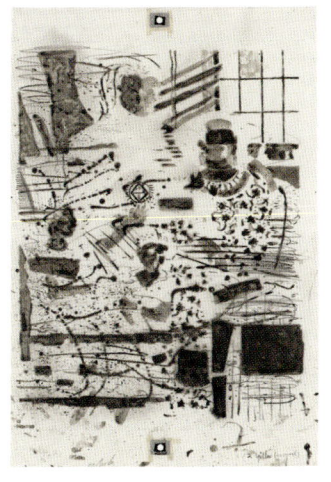

2

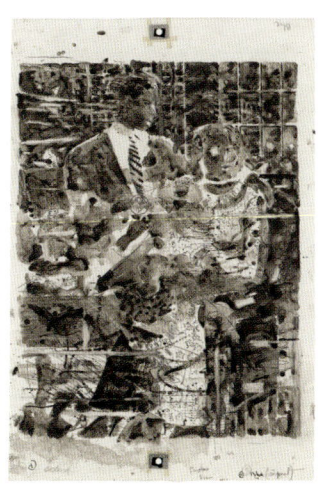

3

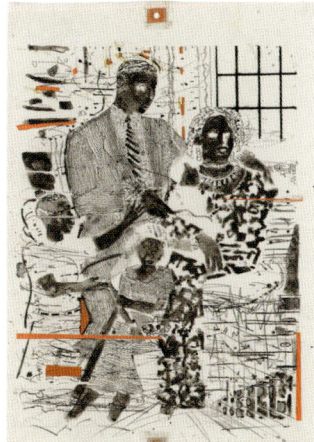

4

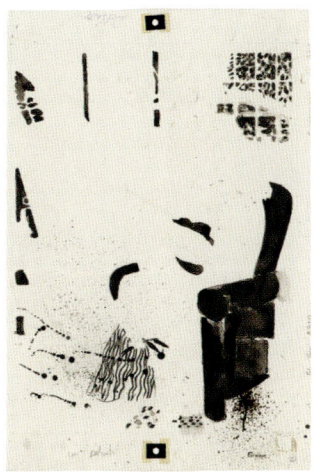

5

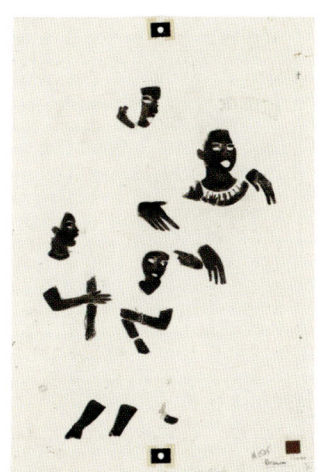

6

FIG. 3.14

Louis J. Delsarte III, color separation for *Unity*,
1995. Ink on Mylar. Harvard Art Museums/Fogg
Museum, Cambridge, MA. Gift of Brandywine
Workshop and Archives, Philadelphia, PA.

1 Gray.
2 Yellow.
3 Blue.
4 Red.
5 Bright Red.
6 Green.
7 Brown.

7

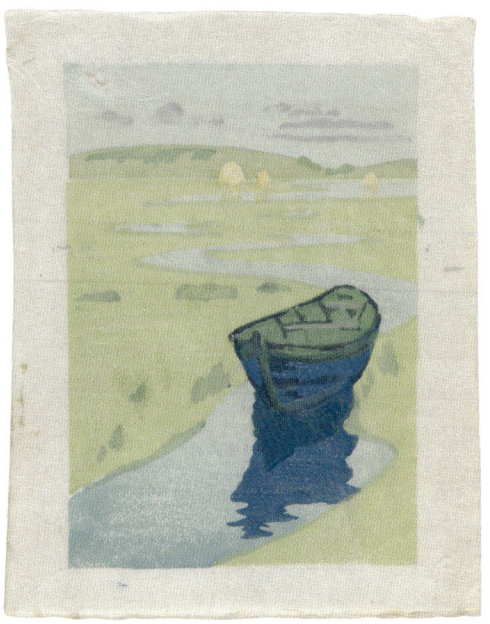
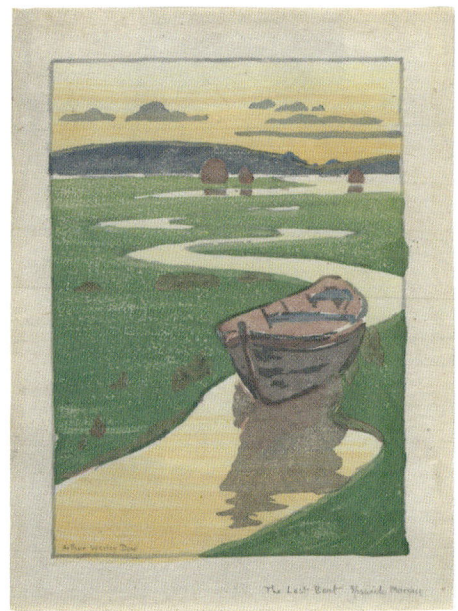

FIG. 3.15
Arthur Wesley Dow, *"The Derelict" or "The Lost Boat,"* 1916. Color woodcut; working proof. The Metropolitan Museum of Art, New York. Gift of the Dowd-Gallogly Family and Allan E. Dowd, 2016. 2016.406.1.

Arthur Wesley Dow, *"The Derelict" or "The Lost Boat,"* 1916. Color woodcut. The Metropolitan Museum of Art, New York. The Morse Family Foundation Fund, 2016. 2016.427.

woodblock printing. He would routinely print multiple variations of the same composition from the same matrices, each in a different color combination (FIG.3.15).[15] Releasing color from objects, denaturalizing it, and giving it its own expressive potential, Dow's work was a pioneering exploration of color-driven seriality later taken up by the likes of Warhol.

Jasper Johns was fascinated by this arbitrary relationship between color and form, and began exploring it as soon as he was exposed to printmaking. In his 1962 lithograph *False Start I*, Johns used stenciled letters to spell out the names of colors (FIG. 3.16). What was immediately perceived as radical about it was that the names of the colors and the colors of the ink used to print them were usually not the same. Sometimes blue ink was used for the word "blue," but more often "blue" would be printed in orange, or "orange" in white, or "blue" in yellow. Thus, the print forced a disjunction between referent and sign. As Douglas Druick put it, the image "occupies . . . the mind and eye discordantly."[16]

FIG. 3.16
Jasper Johns, *False Start I*, 1962.
Lithograph with pastel, pencil, and
printing ink on wove paper mounted
to a backing sheet. National Gallery
of Art, Washington, DC. Patrons'
Permanent Fund and Special Friends
of the National Gallery of Art.

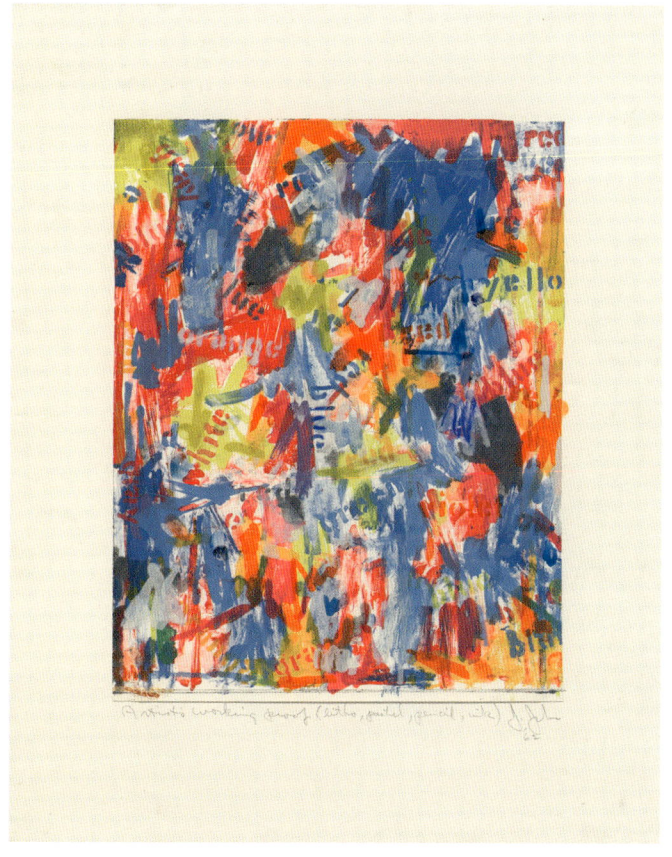

False Start was also made as a painting, and has rightly been interpreted as Johns's seminal contribution to the sea change in twentieth-century art toward a recognition of the arbitrariness of the sign. Johns's insight is often attributed to his exposure to structuralism, or his reading in Ludwig Wittgenstein. But Johns would also have come to this semiotic awareness through practice; through the actual making of prints. As he put it a few years later, "You never know exactly what a print is going to look like until it's printed, and then there is the possibility of changing: you can print it in any color."[17] So printing encourages, in fact requires, an understanding of color as nonlocal, nonintegral, nonobjective. Color is free from form. It's important to clarify that by "free" I don't mean that color becomes floaty or ephemeral in printmaking (this would only replicate its flighty reputation in Western art theory). Rather, it becomes materialized in a way that can take on its own, insistent logic in the print process—one that can be independent of a composition's design elements.

Finally, printed color is methodical, by which I mean that the process of producing a color print must be highly deliberate. This may seem to contradict my point that printed color is arbitrary, but by this I simply mean to emphasize that these elaborate color structures and all of their infinite possible combinations have to be meticulously planned and executed. The whole sequence of separations and layers needs to be programmed out and followed. Color is cerebral in print. This too, I might add, disrupts the old binaries between line and color, because it associates color not with chance or whim or ephemeral appearance, but rather with deliberation, intellection, and structure.

This explains why artists associated with conceptual art in the 1970s so often emulated printmaking when working with color. Conceptual artists were trying to control or eliminate spontaneity in their work, often by experimenting with methods of making that were systematic and contractual. Chuck Close was probably the best-known example of an artist associated with conceptualism whose approach to color was fundamentally printerly—he painted his enormous photo-based paintings, which established him as a major artist in the 1970s, by mimicking the color separation process (FIG. 3.17). He would create CMYK color separations from portrait photographs and then paint the final work by laying down one color at a time. This was his way of avoiding what he called the "lazy and slobby and indecisive" approach to spontaneous color in painting.[18]

Sol LeWitt, who also worked extensively in print, famously wrote that "the idea is the machine that makes the art," perhaps the primary motto or slogan of conceptual art.[19] He is known for the vibrant, gobsmacking color in his wall drawings (FIG. 3.18). Like any good conceptual work, the drawings exist as a series of instructions to be carried out in the process of site-specific installation. And those instructions indicate that the color is to be laid down in singular layers, one color at a time, as if it were being printed. An entire layer of one color is put down, followed by an entire layer of another. All of the color variations come about by different painting orders of a basic vocabulary of colors. This is an idea that is fundamentally printerly, and responds to the deliberation that color printing requires.

So printed color is disjointed, material, arbitrary, and methodical. But the true test of any such technical discussion is this: How does it help us see works of art more sensitively, to ask different or better questions, or to provide more robust interpretations? In the case of the early 1960s in the United States, a moment when artists began the wholesale importation of printing logic into painting, it means that we can better understand the role that color separation played in the destabilization and deconstruction of the image that has long been seen as a hallmark of postwar American art. Take the breakthrough silkscreen paintings of Robert Rauschenberg and Andy Warhol. Rauschenberg used

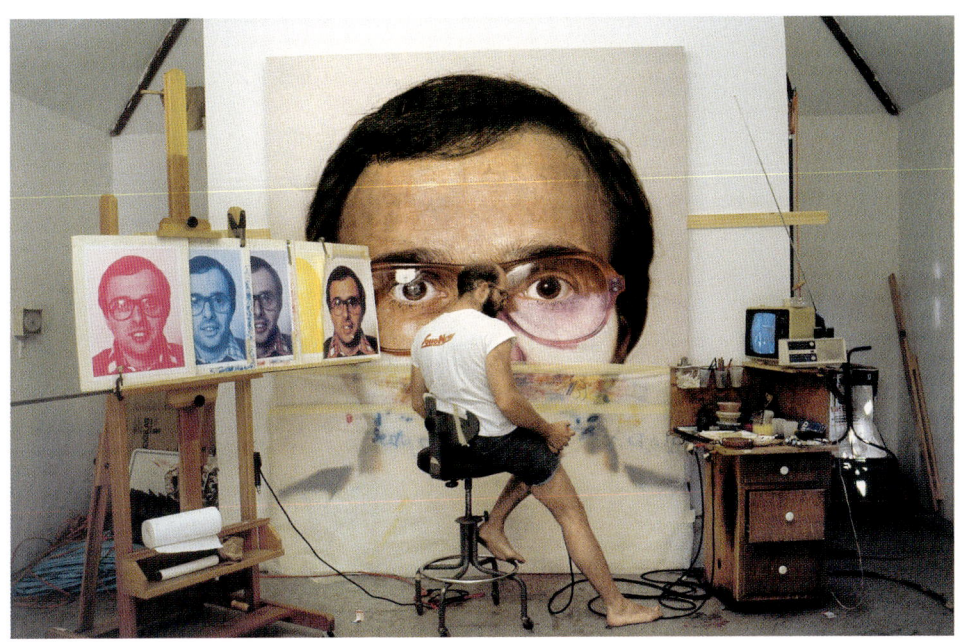

FIG. 3.17
Chuck Close working on *Mark*, 1978–79.

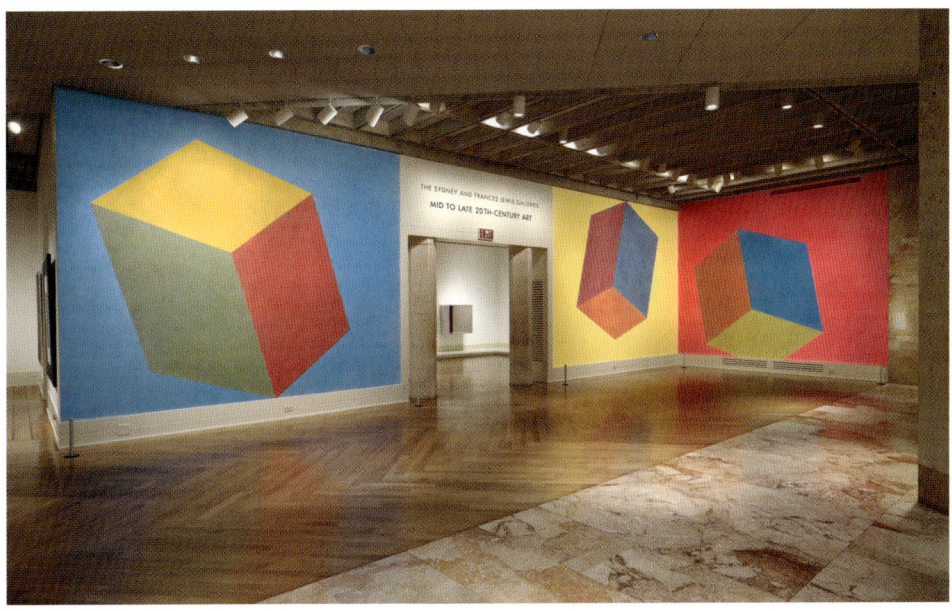

FIG. 3.18
Sol LeWitt, *Wall Drawing #541*, 1987. Acrylic wash on wall. Virginia Museum of
Fine Arts, Richmond. Sydney and Frances Lewis Endowment Fund.

screenprinting to import imagery from multiple sources onto his canvases. He made screen matrices of halftone photographs (often photographs taken of other, historical paintings), pressed the screens up against the painting, and squeegeed the image onto the canvas. This allowed him to "paint" a photograph onto a canvas surface in one fell swoop.

Rauschenberg's paintings are notable for their elaborate performance of the failure of color registration. Bright colors bleed out around the edges of image fields, showing the misalignment of their constitutive color separations. Images float into being with incomplete color profiles, made of only red and yellow, or blue and black. Printer's registration targets appear in the paintings, but only as if to call attention to the misregistration all around them (see inside covers). The imperfect reassembly of the image is the whole point. In Rauschenberg's hands, printing errors create an exuberant new world of color and light. Notice the way the source image in *Persimmon*—a detail of Peter-Paul Rubens's *Morning Toilet of Venus* (1612–15)—explodes into bright primary color through the breakdown of the color separations (FIG. 3.19). The misregistrations also impart an almost kinetic quality to the image. We perceive the image as a layered structure (something that more perfectly registered printing attempts to conceal from us). And because the layers fail to rejoin, the colors produce a choreography of shimmering, moving veils. Color separations shift and float, never locking into a rejoined whole. In the scholarly literature on Rauschenberg, these kinetic effects have primarily been related to a different image reproduction technology altogether: television. But these paintings were made before color television became standard. And besides: this is not really how televised color works. This is how printed color works. These are paintings of and about printing.

Or consider this portfolio of ten *Marilyn* screenprints by Andy Warhol. Each print in this series was made from the same five screens, but those screens were printed in different color combinations and variously dramatic levels of misregistration (FIG. 3.20). Warhol, of course, had been a commercial artist, intimately familiar with commercial printing techniques, before becoming a painter. In his work in advertising, he had apparently never been willing to make the effort to perform precise color registration.[20] Likewise, in his fine art work, registration was something he actively avoided. Misregistration was not just a glitch for Warhol; it was a fundamental philosophy of pictorial instability that derived from the printing process. Throughout this series, color separation conveys the suggestion of an image that is struggling to cohere. This precarity gives it a sense of dynamism both within the individual images and across the series. It's a disassembled image and a ten-part Homeric drama of a failed return to coherence.

The shocking, garish color of Marilyn's face seems unnatural. But, as we have already seen in the cascades of bright color in Rauschenberg's

FIG. 3.19
Robert Rauschenberg, *Persimmon*,
1963. Oil and silkscreen ink on
canvas. Private collection.

Detail of *Persimmon*.

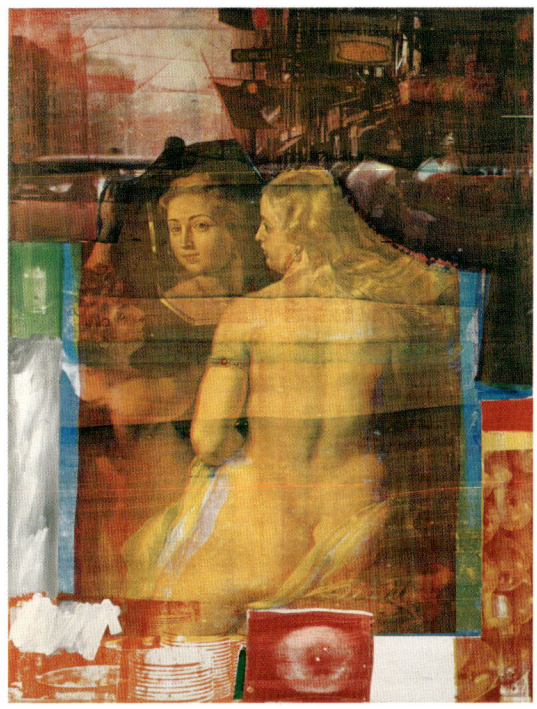

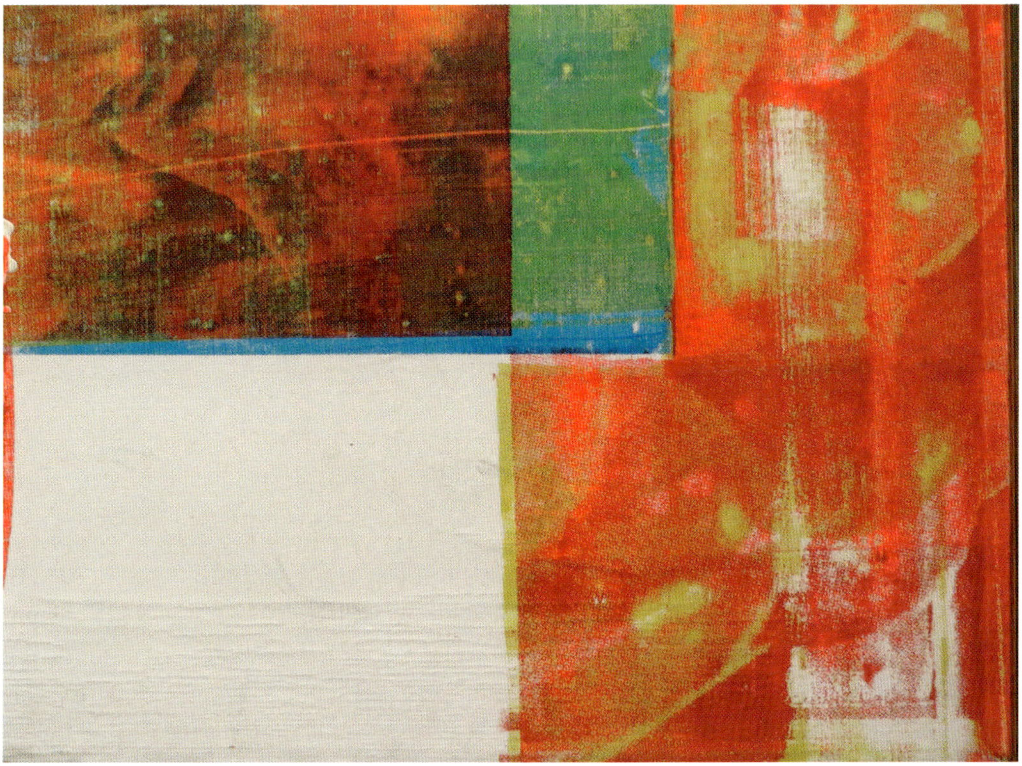

FIG. 3.20

FIG. 3.20
Andy Warhol, *Marilyn Portfolio*, 1967. Ten
screenprints on canvas. Harvard Art Museums/
Fogg Museum, Cambridge, MA. Gift of
Michael F. Marmor, AB '62, MD '66, and Jane B.
Marmor, MD '66.

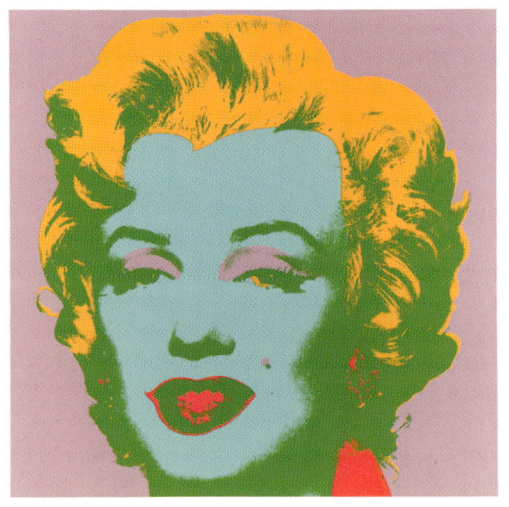
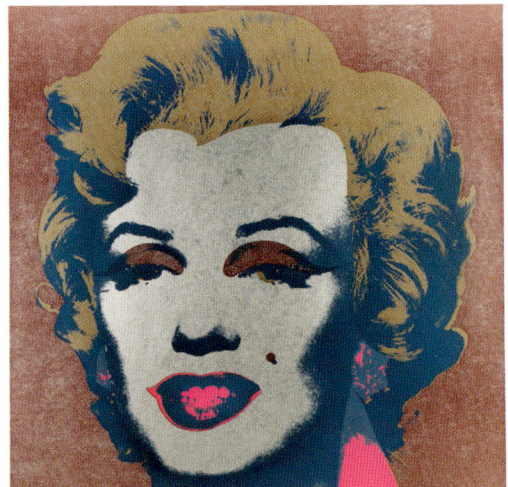
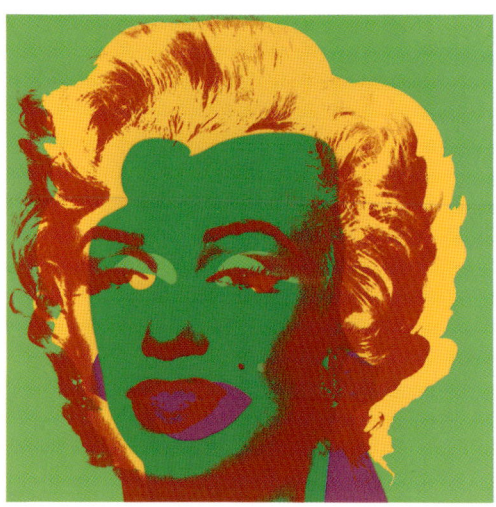
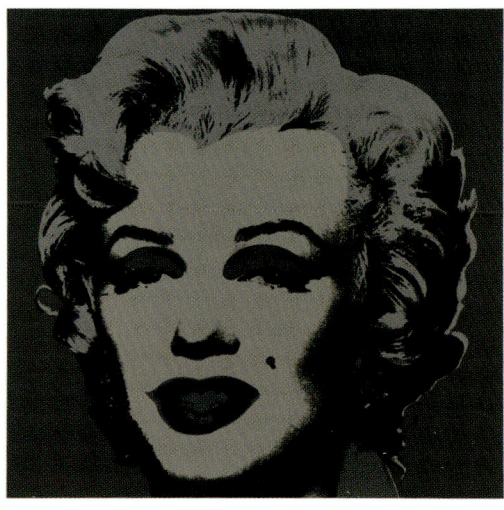

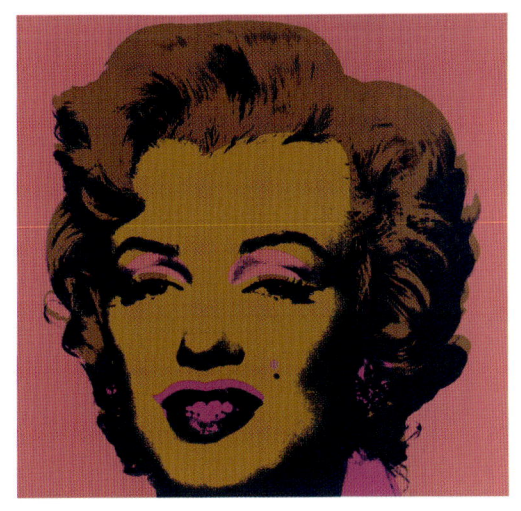
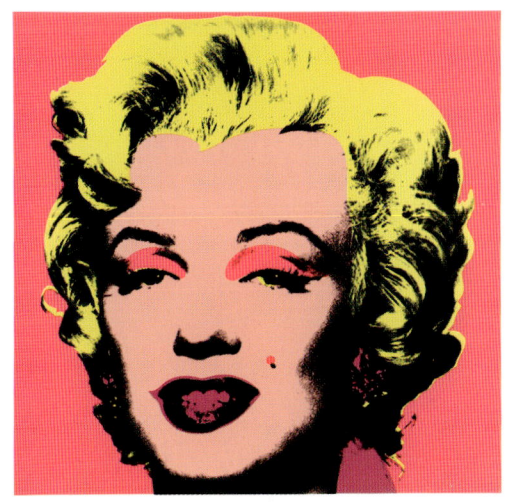
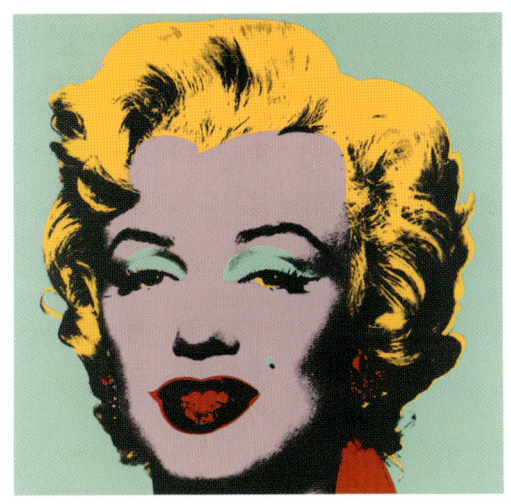
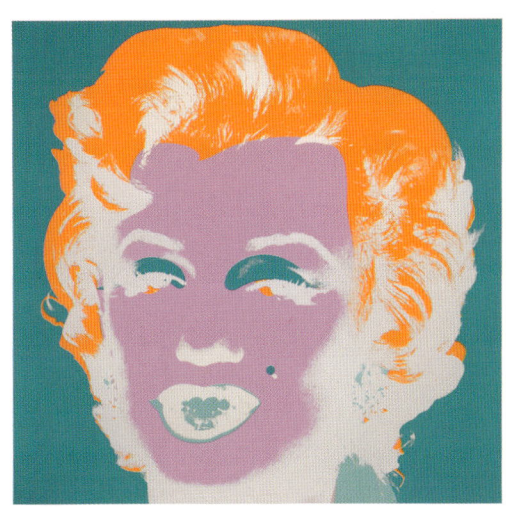
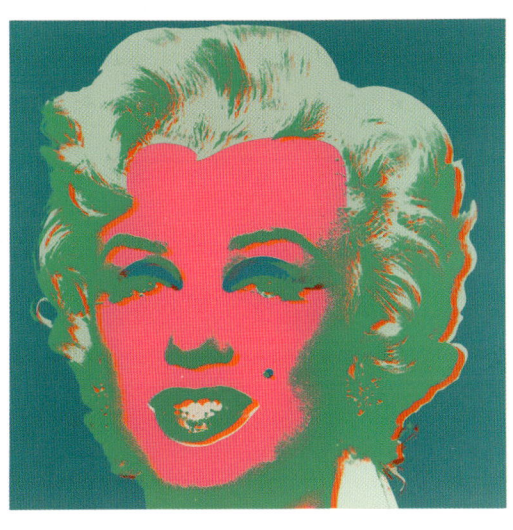
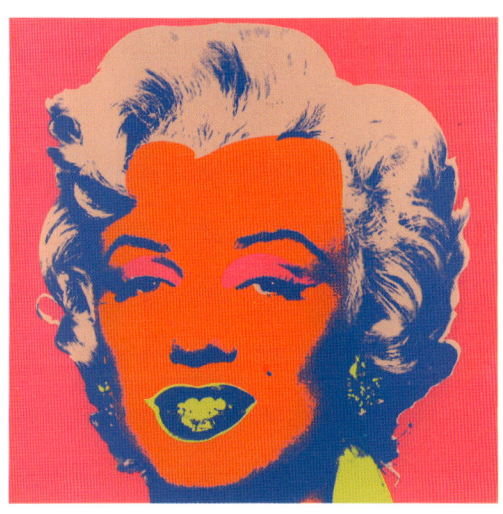

misregistered painting, this is a condition that is natural to color printing. Even the dullest beige or muddiest brown in four-color commercial printing is made up of bright, candylike CMYK elements. Warhol's clashing, garish color is the natural world of print. Of course, these prints are not just about technical printing matters; they are also about culture. They are about portraiture, about Marilyn Monroe, about the shape of subjectivity and identity in contemporary life. Warhol first began using this portrait, and the screenprint method, just after Monroe's death, so these are inevitably also about the tragedy of her death and the question of her identity—any celebrity's true identity—in a life lived in front of cameras, a life lived as an image.

Entire critical industries have been built around the models of subjectivity that Warhol's work suggested. Fredric Jameson's important book *Postmodernism, or, The Cultural Logic of Late Capitalism* relied heavily on Warhol's work—including the Marilyn screenprints—to theorize the evacuation of subjectivity in postmodernism. For Jameson, Warhol exemplified "a new kind of flatness or depthlessness, a new kind of superficiality" in late twentieth-century culture.[21] To Jameson, Warhol gives us a Marilyn who is merely a monolithic surface with no depth behind it, a Marilyn who lives only as image. Commodified, superficial, a simulacrum, a mask without a body. I can't dive all the way into Jameson and postmodern image theory here. I'll merely suggest that a reading of Warhol that was sufficiently attentive to the logic of color separation in printing would need to account for the fact that Warhol's color misregistrations do not quite line up with Jameson's claims. The shifting planes may not suggest some deep psychological interiority on the old humanist model (that much I agree with), but they do explicitly generate a certain kind of depth—a stratified, shifting depth structure that accords with the technical life of printed color. Where is Marilyn Monroe? Not hidden away in some imaginary interior world, but not fully exposed on the surface either. She exists somewhere between these separate surfaces, between layers of disassembled color that never quite cohere.

A few years ago, while doing a Google search for color separation diagrams, I came across an image by the graphic designer Michael Bancroft (FIG. 3.21). It shows our familiar commercial printing colors arranged in a line: Cyan, Yellow, Black, and Magenta. Yellow holds a protest sign that says "end color separation." Cyan makes a peace sign, Magenta holds up a lighter. Black bows its head and raises its fist, in a clear allusion to the Black Power salute by Olympians Tommie Smith and John Carlos in 1968. Bancroft's image is meant to be humorous, but it's uncomfortably so, because it also points to something that's dead serious. It raises a connection between color separation in printing and color separation in culture—segregation, race relations. Any account of color separation in contemporary art has to pick up where this illustration (maybe too quickly)

FIG. 3.21
Michael Bancroft, *End Color Separation*.

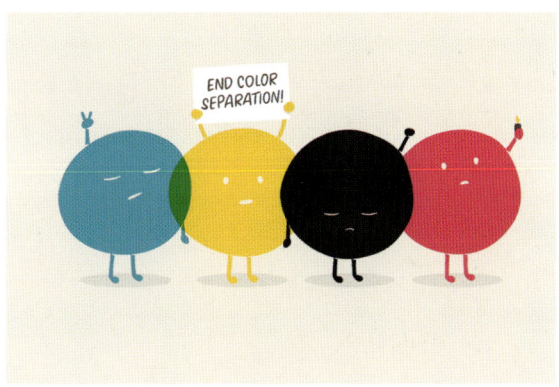

leaves off, and should be able to generate interpretive activity around the intersection of color printing and critical race theory.

I want to end with a short discussion of how such possibilities might unfold around the work of contemporary Los Angeles artist Mark Bradford. This is Bradford and his panoramic site-specific work *Pickett's Charge*, installed in 2017 along the circular inner gallery of the Hirshhorn Museum in Washington, DC (FIG. 3.22). The work follows the logic of color printing inasmuch as it is based on the notion of separation and precarious reassembly. The installation includes eight huge works, each forty-five to fifty feet long and twelve feet high. As with most of Bradford's work, these are usually identified as paintings. But that's a misleading characterization because they are essentially made of the materials of print.[22]

Bradford made this work in critical dialogue with an 1883 cycloramic painting that commemorated Pickett's Charge, the last bloody battle fought in Gettysburg, on July 3, 1863. That painting still exists, installed as a cyclorama, at the Gettysburg National Military Park in Pennsylvania. Pickett's Charge was seen as the turning point in the Civil War, in which the North pivoted to take the upper hand; in the prevailing narratives of US history, it symbolizes the eventual end of the war, the healing of the Union, and the reintegration and reconstruction of the nation. The painting installed in its rotunda is meant to take the viewer vividly and seamlessly back to that time and place, and to embody this narrative of a turning point toward unity. Bradford takes up this narrative today, in the twenty-first century, when the color lines over which the Civil War was fought are more persistent and intractable than ever. His *Pickett's Charge* is all about dissolution, deconstruction, disunity: a failure of unification. And that failure is performed by his reconstruction of the original painting in the medium of print.

Bradford had a full-size color print made of the painting (note its coarse halftone structure). He layered this huge print over multiple other layers of colored paper and printed matter and then peeled away portions of the halftone

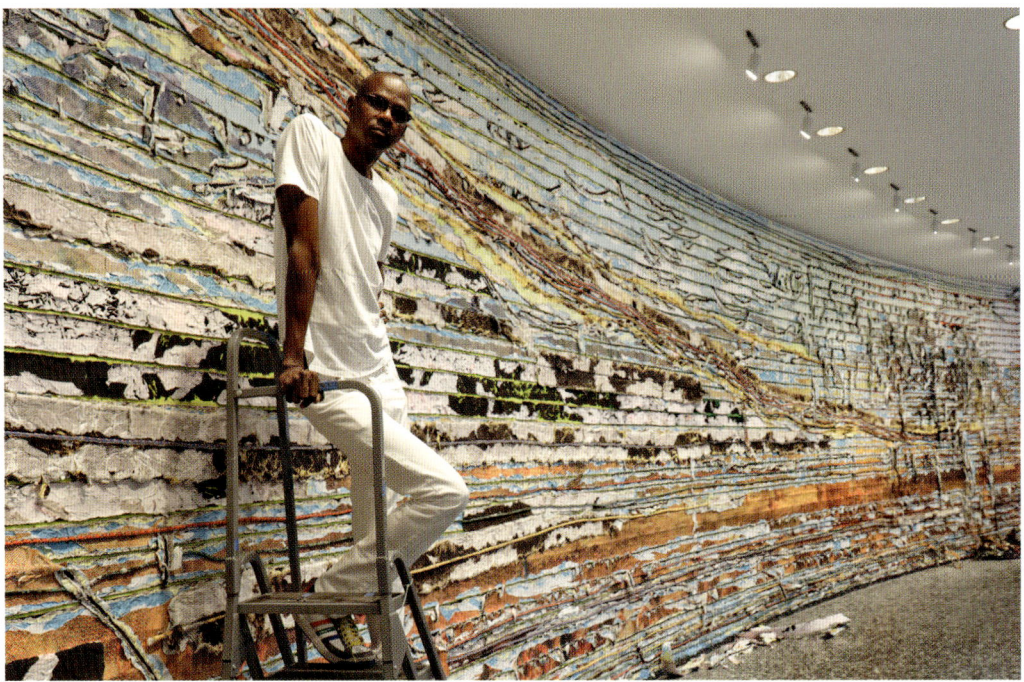

FIG. 3.22
Mark Bradford with *Pickett's Charge*, 2017, Hirshhorn Museum
and Sculpture Garden, Washington, DC.

to reveal layers below. *Pickett's Charge* picks up on Bradford's usual working methods. He works with printed matter—often flyers, street bills, and scrapped billboards from his South Central LA neighborhood. After collecting these printed sheets, he soaks them in water and layers them so that they stick together and form a kind of laminate surface of printed color and text. Meanwhile, he embeds string or rope at various depths. He then reveals the strata below through décollage, often by peeling or sanding away the top layers, or in this case by pulling out some of the rope-cord. For Bradford, an image is an archaeological or geological stratification of color as matter. He makes that block of layers evident by peeling and penetrating it, demonstrating its precarious construction (FIG. 3.23).

Bradford has spoken of his archaeological layers of printed paper in ways that mirror the structure of printing, with its discrete layers that create a kind of fusionless depth: "What fascinates me . . . is the way in which paper creates depth, but at the same time it still has its singular form. It's one complete thing on top of another."[23] Bradford speaks to the compressed energy of a structure that resists

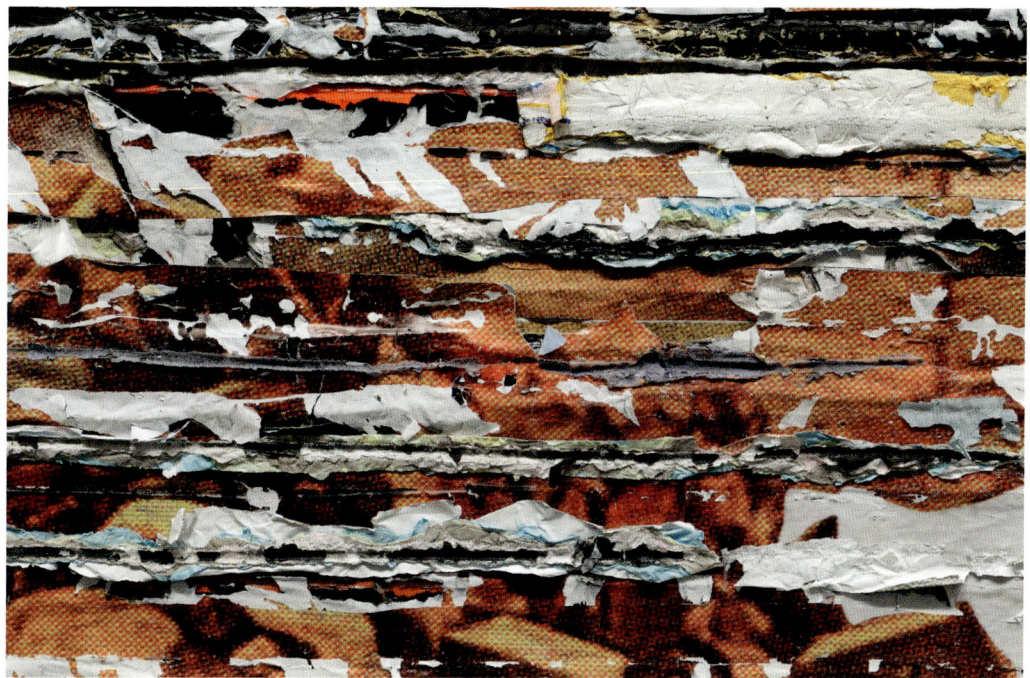

FIG. 3.23
Mark Bradford, *Pickett's Charge* (detail), 2016–17. Mixed media.
Hirshhorn Museum and Sculpture Garden, Washington, DC.

coherence—layers pressed together, crushed together, but still riven throughout by discontinuities. Having worked with printed color all his life, Bradford reiterates its structure here to disrupt the smooth and unified historical narrative of the cyclorama. The Civil War—and the racial politics it embodied—is still being fought. Its image is still raw. Its separations have not been seamlessly reassembled. This comes through not just in the disrupted layers, revealed in their failure to cohere, but also in the large-scale halftone color separations that constitute the image. Color here sits like an unstable aggregate, a kind of national-geological grit.

The closer you get to this *Pickett's Charge*, the less its picture coheres. A deeply critical image of historical reconstruction, it reveals itself as built on a ruin, a bunch of CMYK rubble. If the cyclorama was a kind of history painting that attempted the false reconciliation of a nation that was, in fact, still riven by racism and racial division, Bradford's work shows us what it might mean to create a kind of history *printing*. A history printing that would give form to the disjuncture and conflict that still serve as the precarious bedrock of American society.

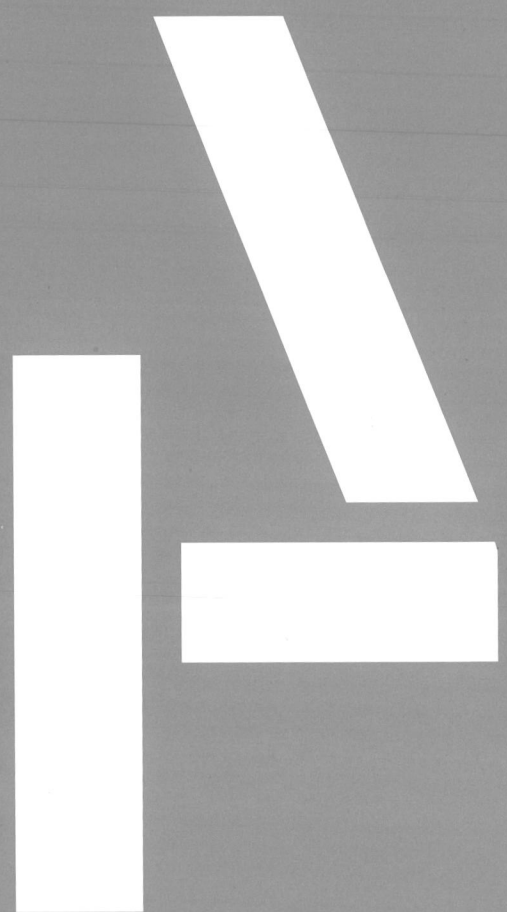

STRAIN

As with all of the chapter titles in this book, I'm asking the word "strain" to do a lot of work. I'm asking it to function simultaneously in the literal register and the metaphorical register, and thereby to reveal something about the way the material techniques of printing might signify beyond the print studio. But while the previous keywords like "reversal" and "pressure" had the virtue of being pretty self-evidently related to printmaking, "strain" might come as a bit of a surprise. It is not exactly a common printmaking term; it's not even really an art term. But it will, I hope, help us think differently about one of the most consequential print mediums in modern and contemporary art.

This chapter will explore works of art that are made or inspired by the stencil matrix, especially screenprinting (FIG. 4.1). Stenciling is one of the four main types of printing (see fig. 0.5); it differs from the others in that the image is printed by pushing ink through the matrix rather than pulling ink off of its face. In screenprinting, the stencil is suspended in or adhered to a fine mesh screen. Ink pushed through the screen by a squeegee is blocked by the stencil while being forced through the open areas of meshwork onto the support below. For the purposes of this chapter, I want to conceive of this action as *straining* rather than *screening*. There are three reasons for this: first, I want to emphasize the messy, material, mechanical realities of screenprinting. To do this, it's helpful to back away from the associations with film, television, and computing that accompany the word "screen" today. I want to get us thinking about the notion that making a screenprint is more like pouring soup into a strainer than it is like firing electrons at a cathode-ray tube or projecting light onto a movie screen. Second, in using the word "strain," I want to suggest something like the fatigue of the process. I want to emphasize the physical and conceptual consequences of the forcing action of the ink. Screenprinting brings images into being in a field of forces, forces that actively shape them rather than neutrally transmitting them. Screenprinting leaves its mark; it puts images under strain. Finally, I want to borrow the connotations of straining in order to connect these images to a longer history of sifting, selecting, and filtering in domestic, industrial, artisanal, and political realms beyond the art world.

I have already addressed screenprinting in some detail in previous chapters. After this chapter, and the next one, when I'll have even more to say about it, I will have devoted an inordinate amount of my time — and by extension your time — to a printing process that has not previously been thought to be worthy of so much attention by art historians. Despite its obvious centrality for modern and contemporary art through the work of Andy Warhol, Robert Rauschenberg, and others, the screenprinting process itself — its history, its specific operations, its conceptual implications — has been much less extensively studied than have the other major print processes. This is partially because of the general inattention to print processes in contemporary art history and criticism,

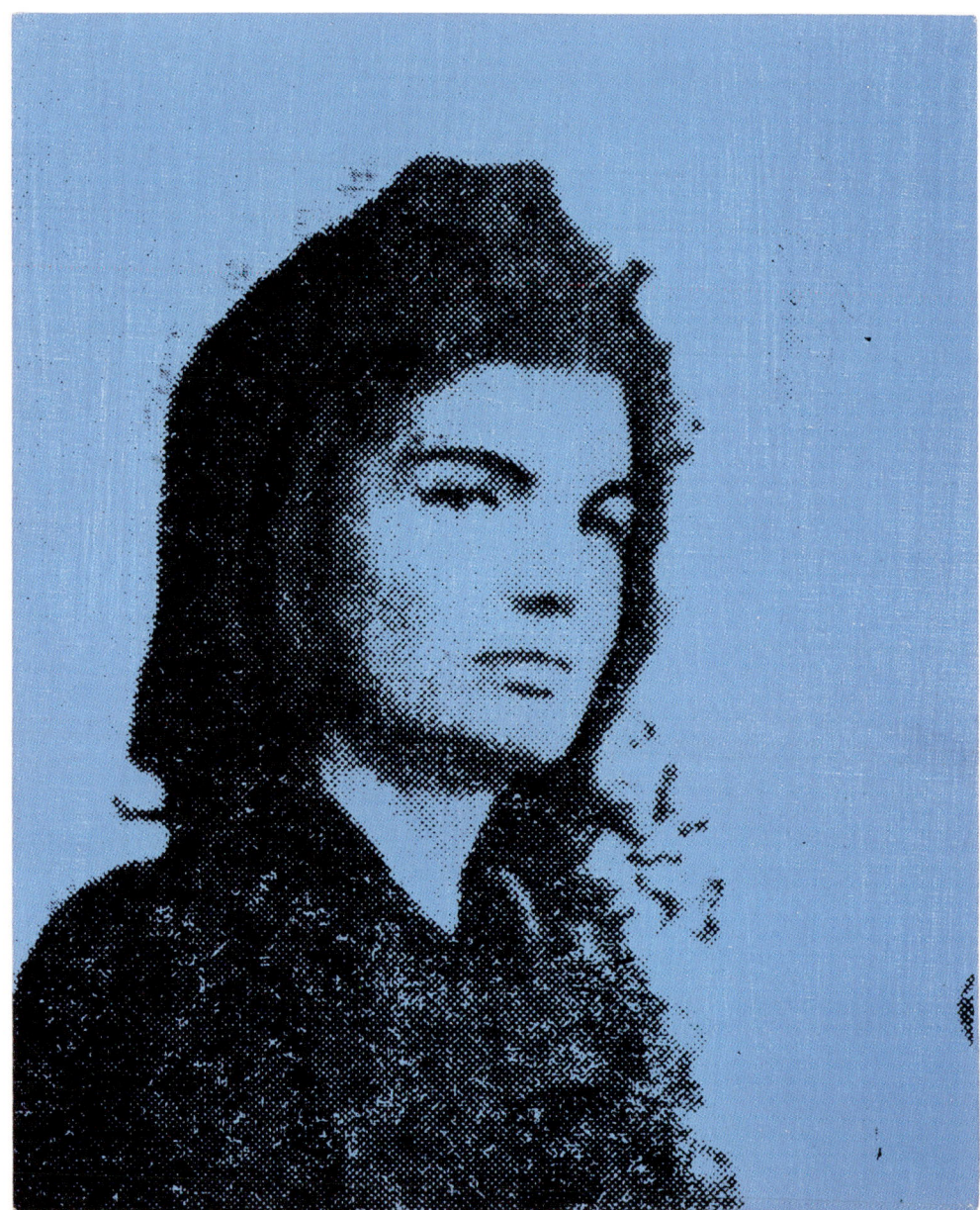

FIG. 4.1

Andy Warhol, *Jackie*, about 1964. Silkscreen ink on synthetic
polymer paint on canvas. Museum of Fine Arts, Boston.
Gift of The Andy Warhol Foundation for the Visual Arts,
Inc., with additional funds donated by the Catherine and Paul
Buttenwieser Fund and Barbara Fish Lee and Thomas H. Lee.
1994.87.

and partially because screenprinting and other so-called process printing methods are the ones whose reputations remain most tightly bound to commercial and industrial image-making. Even within the relatively specialized world of print studies, screenprinting is a low-status medium compared to more recognizably artisanal processes like etching.

Yet if we are going to understand the life of print in contemporary art, we need to do a much better job of incorporating commercial processes into our models of the field. We need to loosen up about the hierarchical distinctions we are prone to making between commercial and fine-art printmaking, and we need to bring all forms of printmaking into closer contact with critical and theoretical discussions of art. Which image-making processes get into serious art history? Which are kept out? These questions swirl around screenprinting in many ways, at many levels, not least because screenprinting itself—a process of straining images into being by letting some things through and holding some things back—recalls so many processes of cultural purification, hygiene, and refinement.

Screenprinting is the last of the major analog print processes to have been developed. Like many Western print processes, it has much older precedents in East Asia, where there is a long tradition of stencil making for dyeing textiles. This is a Japanese katagami stencil used for resist-dyeing openwork patterns on bolts of cotton or silk (FIG. 4.2). The stencil is comprised of handmade paper interpenetrated by a hand-threaded mesh made with single strands of human hair or silk. It anticipates screenprinting inasmuch as it is a complex stencil held together by a delicate mesh. But as an astonishingly fine tradition of hand craftsmanship, katagami developed in a completely different production context. In twentieth-century screenprinting proper, the screen mesh is much more finely spaced, and although it also has artisanal roots (it was woven of silk on hand looms until the 1960s), it was not, as it was in katagami, produced along with the stencil it supported. Screenprinting mesh was produced as a readymade material to which the stencil was added later.

Modern screenprinting was developed in a commercial context. Although there is some uncertainty about a single origination point, it likely took on its current form in the very early twentieth century in California. It was widely adopted for advertising and display, where it was prized for its ability to produce bold, flat, opaque color on virtually any surface (one of its earliest uses was for printing team names and logos on felt pennants). Screenprinting could print not only on paper, but also cardboard, wood, metal, textiles, cork, leather, fur, ceramics, and glass. Textile printing was one of its most common uses, since it was faster and cheaper than most other fabric printing methods, with better color (FIG. 4.3). From the outset, screenprinting was a form of ambient printing that could go anywhere. It could infiltrate the surfaces of the world.[1]

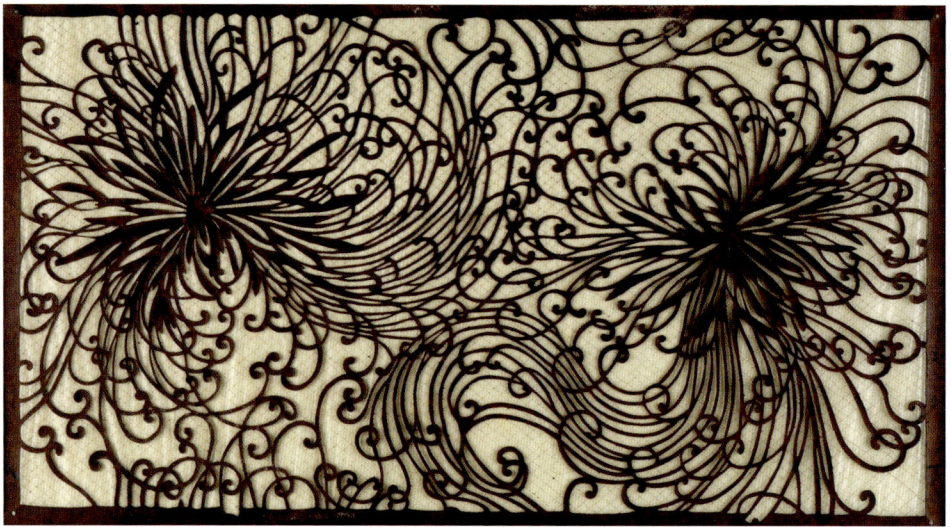

FIG. 4.2
*Textile Stencil (*Katagami*) with Chrysanthemum Design*, late Edo to
Meiji period, nineteenth to early twentieth century. Paper with silk-web
reinforcement. Harvard Art Museums/Arthur M. Sackler Museum,
Cambridge, MA. Gift of Dr. Denman W. Ross.

When Warhol began making his screened paintings in 1962, screen-printing was so thoroughly associated with commercial and institutional printing that it was essentially taboo in the realm of fine-art printmaking. Attempts had been made in the previous decades to establish fine-art credentials for it by masking or disavowing its commercial connotations; the print curator Carl Zigrosser invented the term serigraphy ("silk-writing") for this purpose. But the process had not been able to shake its original associations with propaganda, advertising and packaging: posters, calendars, signs, labels, boxes, cans. When the artists we associate with screenprinting in the 1960s adopted the technology, it was difficult to exaggerate just how debased it was as a form of image-making.[2]

Warhol took it up precisely for this reason. To make his paintings, he screenprinted images — usually photographic halftones — onto unstretched canvases that had been prepared with a single color of synthetic polymer paint. In *National Velvet*, for example, he repeatedly screenprinted an image of Liz Taylor (a still from the eponymous film) in black ink over silver paint (FIG. 4.4). Working with an assistant, Warhol moved across the canvas on the floor, setting the screen frame down to ink it with the squeegee, then picking it up, moving over, and

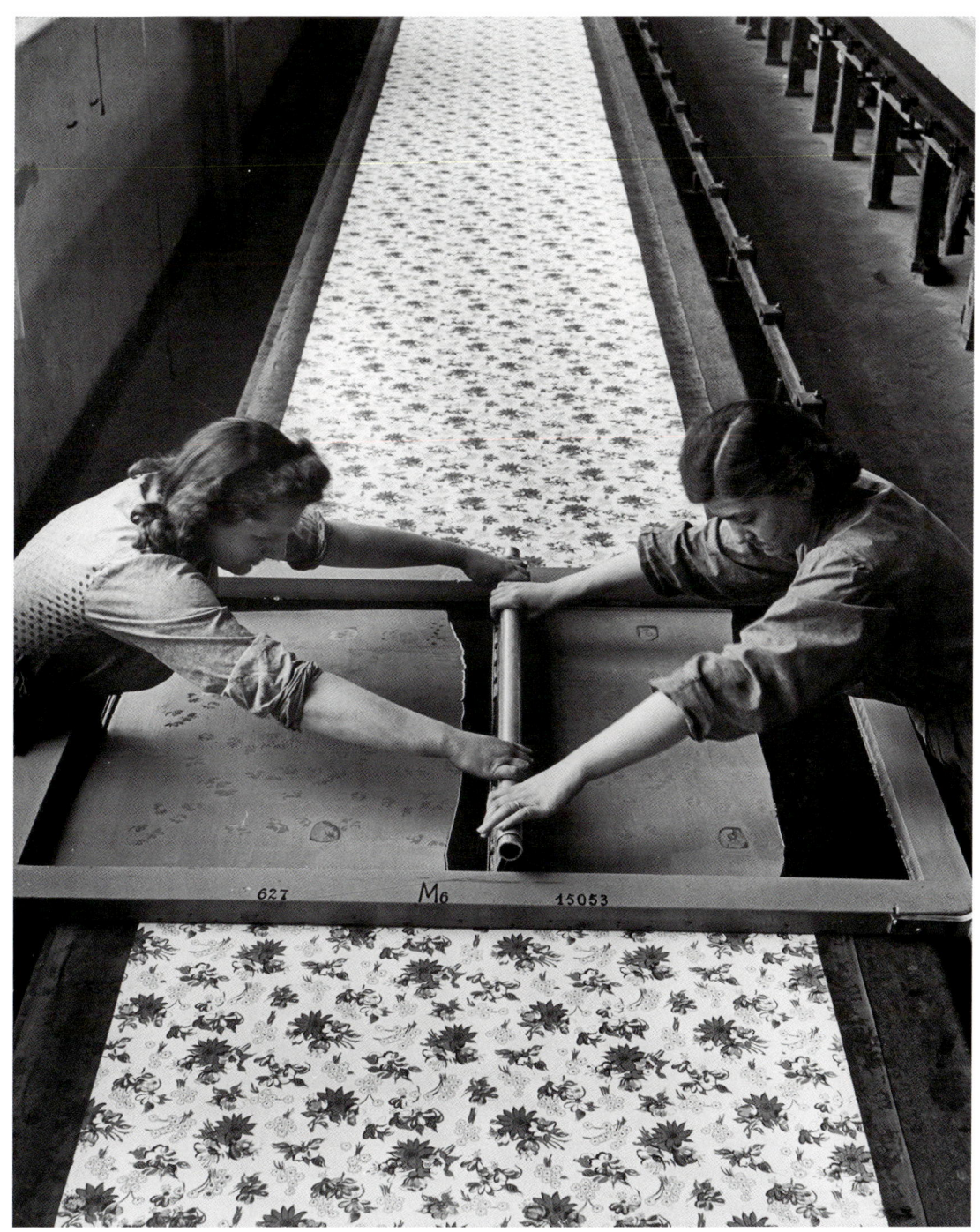

FIG. 4.3
Alfred Eisenstaedt, *Hand Printing Operation at the de Angeli–
Frua Plant, Milan, Italy*, n.d. Getty Images.

Andy Warhol, *National Velvet*, 1963. Silver paint, silkscreen ink, and graphite on linen. Collection SFMOMA. Accessions Committee Fund. Gift of Barbara and Gerson Bakar, Doris and Donald Fisher, Evelyn and Walter Haas, Jr., Mimi and Peter Haas, Byron R. Meyer, Helen and Charles Schwab, Danielle and Brooks Walker, Jr., and Judy C. Webb; Albert M. Bender Fund; Tishler Trust; Victor Bergeron Fund; Members' Accessions Fund; and gift of the Andy Warhol Foundation for the Visual Arts, Inc.

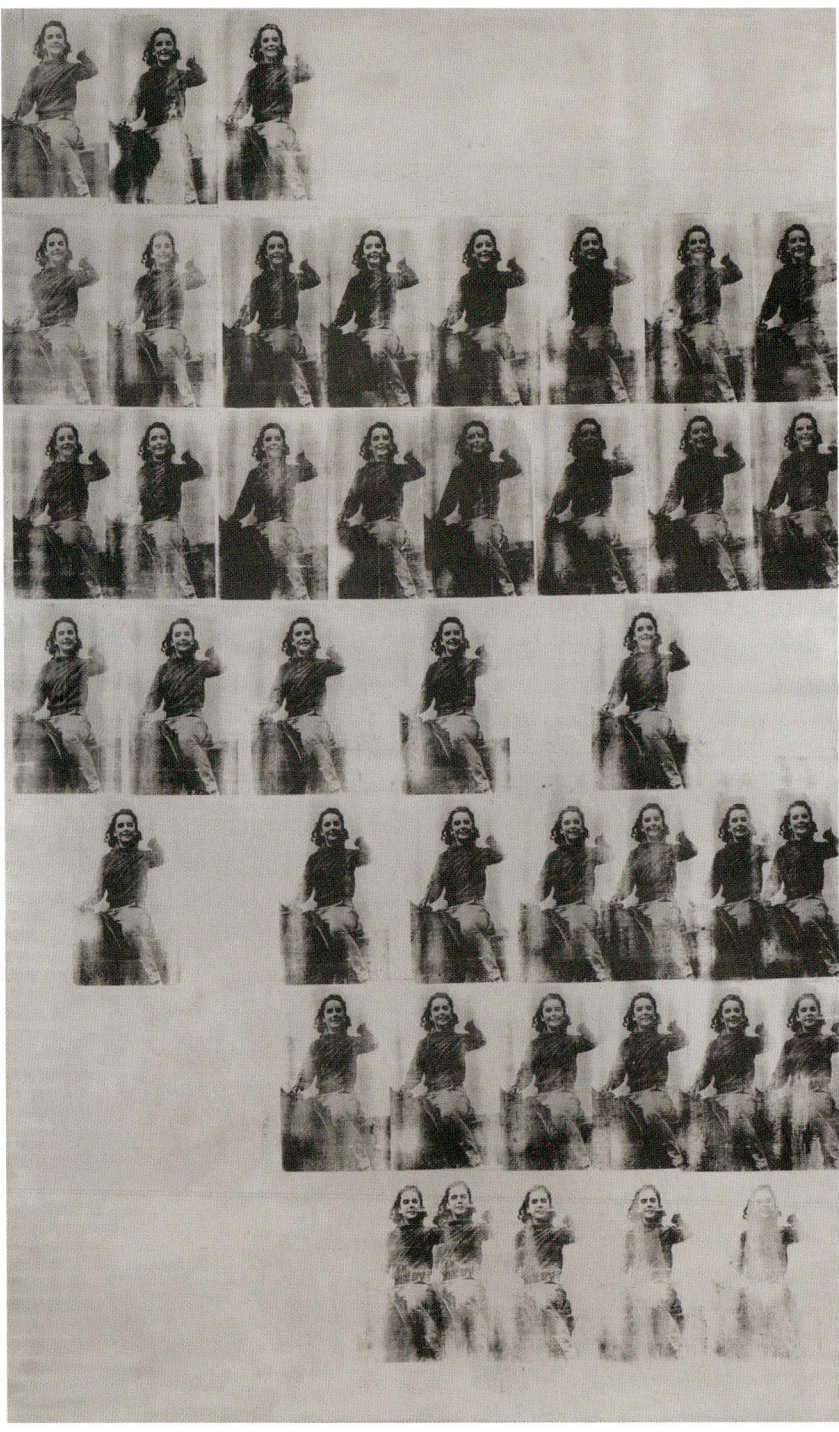

inking again, with irregular spacing, overlapping, and obvious degradations and glitches in the screenprinting.

Before going any further, we need to back up and ask how the still photograph of Taylor from a film got onto the screen mesh in the first place. This will require a quick excursus into the halftone, to describe its production and clarify its role in Warhol's process. The photographs that Warhol incorporated into his work were rasterized as halftones—images broken down into the coarse dot patterns that formed, and continue to form, the backbone of all photographic printing in the twentieth and twenty-first centuries. Halftones make it possible to print photographic imagery on a press, because they turn continuous-tone images into binary patterns that the press can recognize. What I want to emphasize is that halftone patterns, like screenprints, are also made by passing an image through a mesh: the process is optical rather than material, but it too involves screening. For most of the twentieth century, halftones were made by photographing a source image (in this case a film still photograph) through a sheet of glass that had been finely ruled in a diagonal net pattern (FIG. 4.5). This was done with a process camera (a large-format plate camera setup that was a ubiquitous tool of twentieth-century commercial art studios) (FIG. 4.6). As light from the source photograph passed through each tiny aperture in the ruled screen, that aperture worked like a lens, refocusing the light into a point of greater or lesser size. The photograph was essentially refocused into a field of dots. That halftone raster was then enlarged and projected onto a silkscreen coated with photosensitive material. The light areas hardened the emulsion while the dark areas did not. The screen was then washed out, creating a "negative" stencil of the halftone embedded in the screen. When paint was then pushed through the screen, the positive halftone appeared on the canvas.[3]

Warhol's paintings emerge, then, from a process of double screening or straining. Light is strained through the halftone screen in order to make the dot screen stencils, and then ink is strained through those stencils in order to print the halftone on canvas. Warhol directed a whole system of image formation based on forcing the movement of light and matter through tiny apertures, and he borrowed the entire process from the commercial printing world.

Given their direct origins in multiple forms of printing, it's ironic that Warhol's screenprints have been so thoroughly absorbed into—so thoroughly coopted by—the history of painting. Museums characterize, collect, and display Warhol's prints on canvas as "paintings," with the implication being that by having a canvas support they transcend regular screenprinting, perhaps engaging in a radical off-label adaptation or creative misuse of the process. But actually Warhol's paintings can accurately be described as screenprints plain and simple. As we have seen, the practice of commercial screenprinting already included

FIG. 4.5
Illustration of a halftone screen from Julius Verfasser, *The Half-Tone Process: A Practical Manual of Photo-Engraving in Half-Tone on Zinc, Copper, and Brass* (London: Iliffe & Sons, 1904), chapter 2, fig. 7.

FIG. 4.6
Harris & Ewing, *The Levy Process Camera*, 1932 or 1933. Glass negative. Library of Congress, Washington, DC.

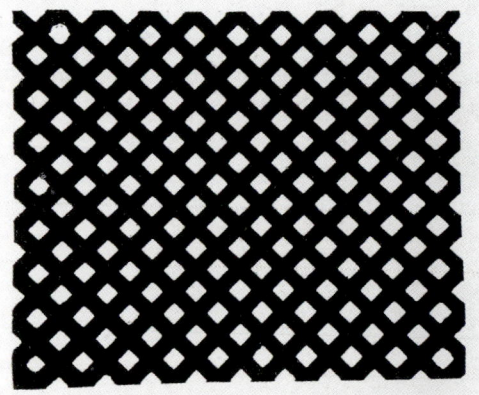

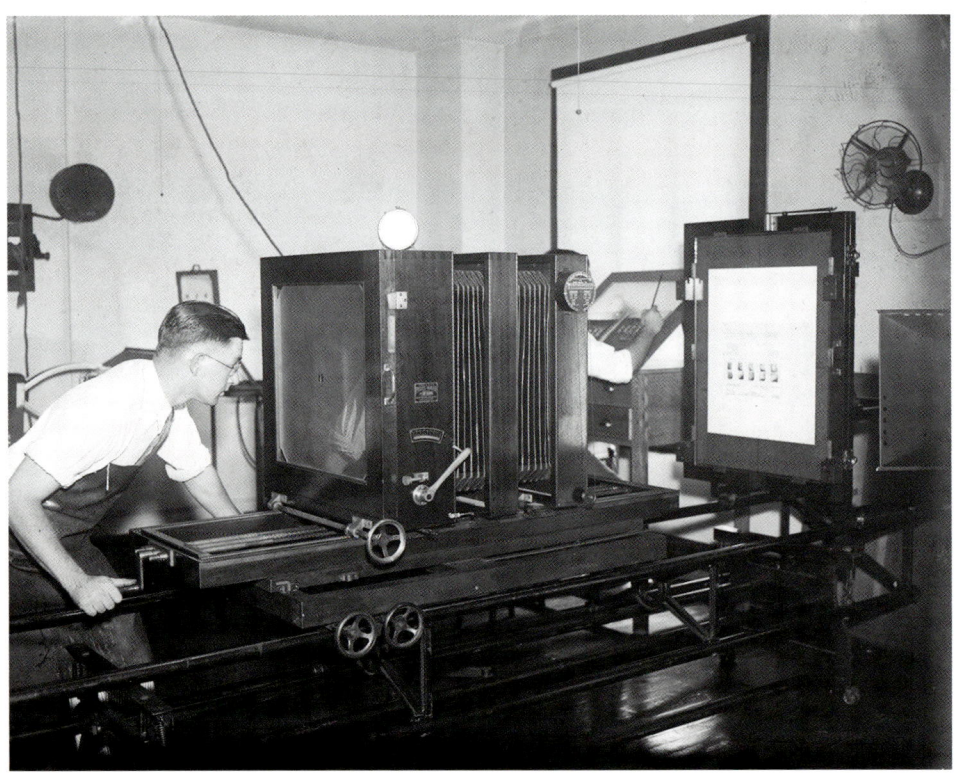

printing on textiles. It was standard practice to print a single screen successively along a bolt of fabric (see fig. 4.3)—a practice repeated verbatim in many of Warhol's most celebrated "paintings." For his exhibition at the Ferus Gallery in 1963, for example, Warhol shipped the work to curator Irving Blum as a single roll of printed canvas (he asked Blum to cut up and stretch sections of the bolt of Elvises at his own discretion) (FIG. 4.7).[4]

Warhol's peers who knew anything about printing were fully aware that these paintings could just as easily be classified as prints. The artist Ed Ruscha noted in an interview that

> they archive them as paintings, although they were strictly silk-screens. . . . Yeah, they were prints on canvas. And that made all the difference in the world and even amused him. He liked that—the very fact that if you put it on a piece of paper, and then take the same image and put it on a canvas, the canvas was worth more.[5]

Why do Warhol's screenprinted canvases need to be paintings to be taken seriously, to be valued? Why not look at Warhol's work as a form of printing that has its own structures of knowledge, skill, and tradition?

One obstacle to recognizing commercial printing as a tradition is that when processes like screenprinting have broken through into the prominent critical narratives of contemporary art, they have tended to be equated with *deskilling*. In the 1960s and 1970s, many artists renounced the skills associated with high art and its academic and economic structures, and turned instead to repetitive, simple, task-based methods. This rebellion against skill happened everywhere from minimalism to conceptual art to performance art. Warhol's adoption of screenprinting is a classic example of deskilling in this sense; in fact, it inspired much of the deskilling language in the critical literature about the art of this period. As the story goes, Warhol replaced centuries of traditional painting knowledge, and all of the elaborate, expressive gesticulations of the bohemian painter, with the simple squirch of the squeegee (FIG. 4.8). This is the value of Warhol's work in the history of painting—that it rejected the history of painting and all of its pieties.[6]

Screenprinting did, in fact, serve this disruptive role in relation to the traditions of painting. But this is only part of the story. The narrative of Warhol's rejection of painting with the squeegee has pushed screenprinting—along with an entire range of other printing processes—into an interpretive corner. If screenprinting is appreciated only as an evacuation of qualities, a removal of expertise, it cannot be logically investigated as a positive process. If it is valued only as a form of deskilling, it becomes invisible as a repository of skills, and there is no

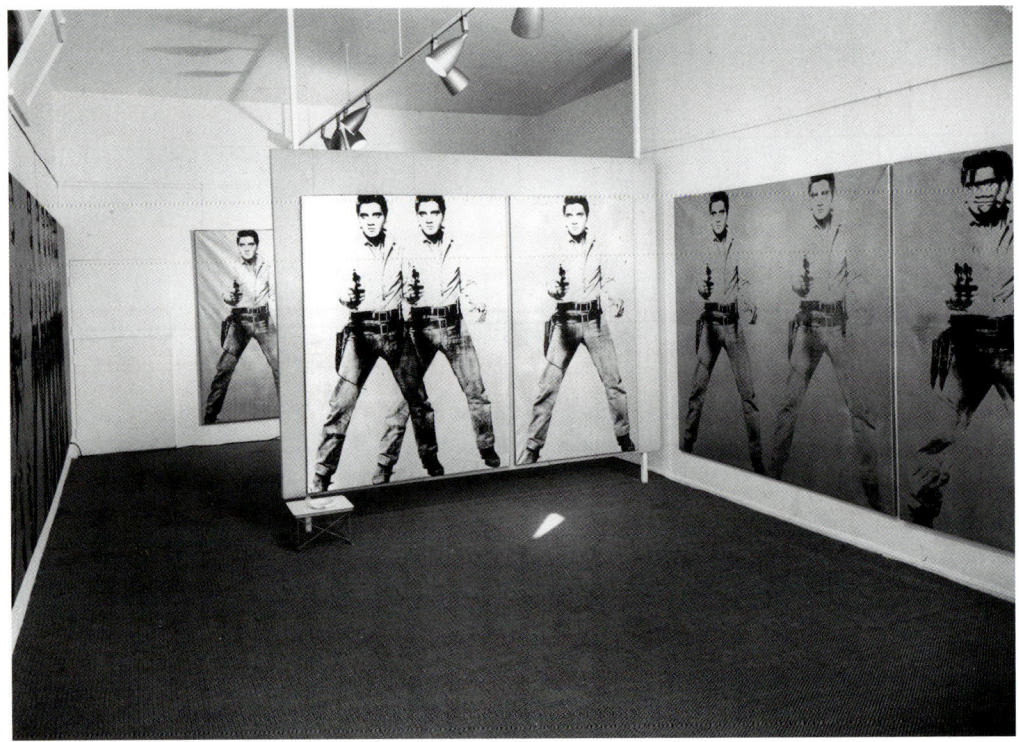

FIG. 4.7

Frank J. Thomas (photographer), installation view of Andy
Warhol's *Elvis 11 Times* at Ferus Gallery, Los Angeles, 1963.

reason to look further into its history. At precisely the moment that screenprinting is acknowledged in the history of the fine arts, it is dismissed as a process that's not worth investigating in any detail. I want to argue that perhaps some artists took up screenprinting not only because it wiped away certain painterly skills and traditions, but also because it added a new set of skills, associations, and traditions in their place. If the squeegee wiped away painting, it also dragged other histories, materials, and skills into the art world.

Granted, it can be difficult to see the facture of those histories in the surface of Warhol's work, because screenprinting has a way of being invisible. Even among screenprinting fans in the world of print studies, the medium tends to be treated as strangely insubstantial, superficial—a medium made of nothing. This is partly due to the quality of the ink deposit that screenprinting produces. The sifting action of the screen mesh distributes the ink evenly across the support,

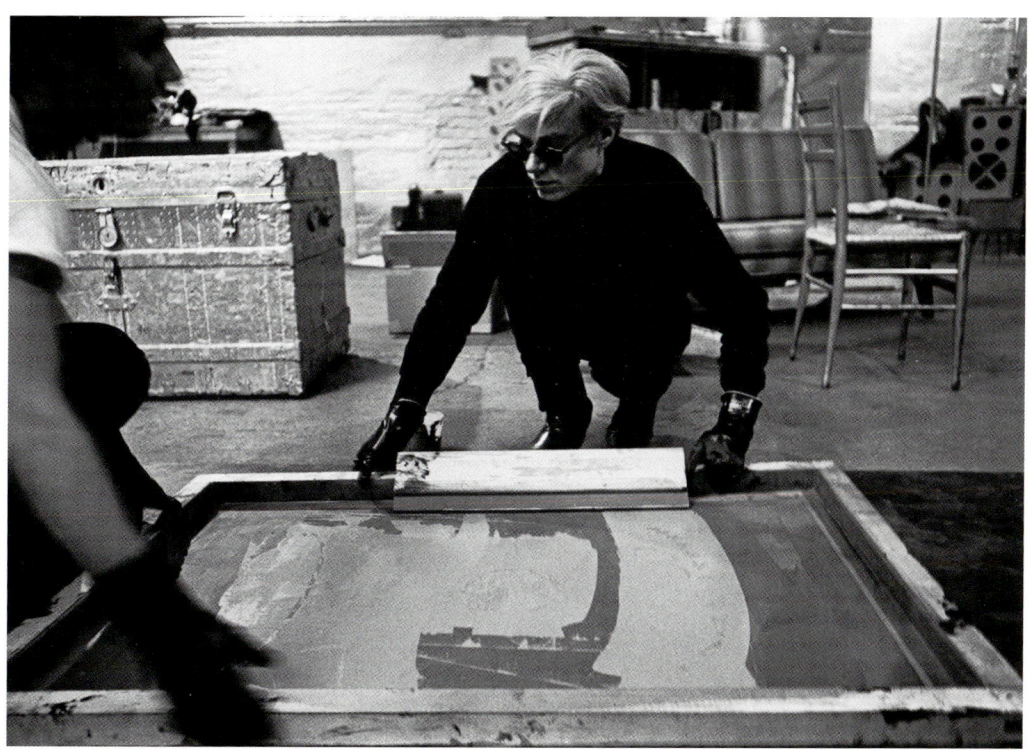

FIG. 4.8
Ugo Mulas, *Andy Warhol and Gerard Malanga Make a Painting*, 1964.
Vintage gelatin silver print. Matthew Marks Gallery, New York.

while also gently aerating it, depositing it in fluffy peaks like so many microscopic dabs of Cool Whip. This produces a uniquely velvety, saturated, unmodulated surface devoid of creative associations. The painter Ad Reinhardt once referred to this as "the ineffable autonomy of the silkscreen deposit" and wished he could achieve the same effect in his paintings. No other printing method—and certainly not painting—can produce quite the same large, evenly distributed areas of rich, thick, bright, perfectly uniform ink.[7]

When the great print curator Richard Field organized an exhibition on screenprinting in Philadelphia in 1971, he emphasized that the process was notable for the way it got out of the way: "The screens of today . . . impose virtually nothing of their own character" on the message they transmit. Here he echoed another foundational print scholar, William Ivins, who had claimed in 1953 that the most "extraordinary step" in the "whole history of human communication" was the development of reproductive technologies whose syntactical marks—line, dot, and so on—retreated "below the threshold of normal human vision." Speaking of both the screenprint and the halftone, Ivins noted that these processes had "no interfering symbolic linear syntax of their own." All this is true enough. I can see the syntax of a line engraving without any special effort, but if I want to see the syntax of a halftone or a screenprint, I need to get out a magnifying glass. But just because something retreats below the range of conscious notice does not mean that it should retreat below the range of critical study or analysis. In fact, it's rather the opposite. It's precisely when a system sinks out of sight that it becomes most powerful, and is most in need of observation.[8]

We might begin by observing a famous example of screenprinting that gets out of the way: the color relation studies of Josef Albers. Albers is known for his theory of relational color—in his paintings, prints, teaching, and seminal 1963 book *The Interaction of Color*, he held that color is not knowable or perceivable intrinsically, but only in relation to the other colors that surround it. In order to make this relationality most clearly evident, he turned to screenprinting. The first edition of *The Interaction of Color* was issued as a two-volume box set, with the color studies presented as a set of meticulously crafted screenprints (FIG. 4.9).[9]

With die cuts, collages, and flaps, these pristine screenprints were the perfect vehicle for the experience of Albers's color relationships, since they permitted highly saturated, flawless color surfaces that did not interfere with pure relational perception. And although Albers produced many of his color compositions as paintings (particularly in the *Homage to the Square* series), his work arguably reached its apogee when it was issued in screenprint form, because the smooth perfection of the color removed any painterly impurities from the system (FIG. 4.10). The screenprints did not seem to have their own syntax, so one could focus only on the syntax of the color.

But the syntax of the screenprints is there when you move closer. When you zoom in on the surfaces, it's evident in the unmistakable imprint of the silkscreen mesh, which left its mark behind as it deposited the ink, then pulled up and away from it. This mesh, we might say, is the structure that allows Albers's color to appear unstructured. But why does it matter? What is it doing? What is the work of this meshwork?

Silkscreen mesh is a weaving, so a good person to ask about this would be Anni Albers. She was a theorist and practitioner of weaving (as well as Josef's spouse). She wrote about weaving as an art that fuses surface values with structural values. A weaving is a soft, pliable surface, associated with the world of the home and of women, with values of tactility and warmth—but these qualities derive from its rigorous structure, its rectilinearity in tension, and its mathematical abstraction (FIG. 4.11). In a weaving, moreover, there is no separation between

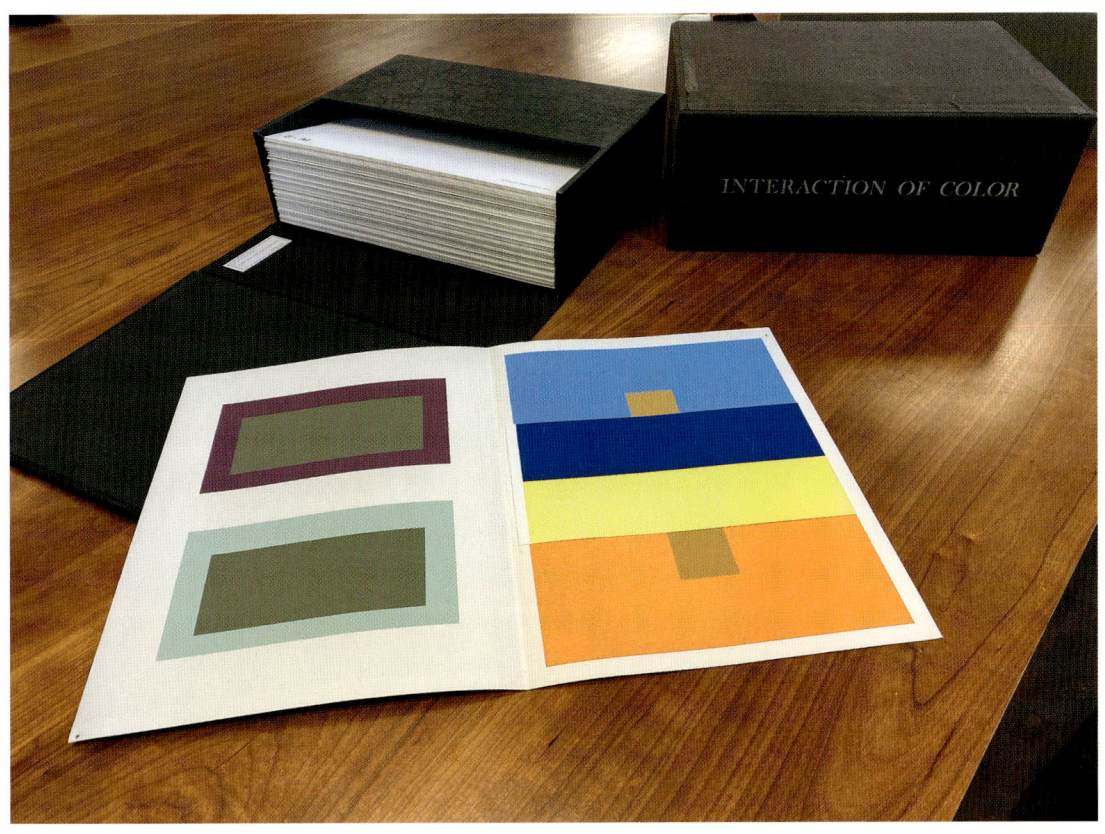

CHAPTER 4

FIG. 4.9
Josef Albers, *The Interaction of Color*, 1st ed. (New Haven, CT: Yale
University Press, 1963). Houghton Library, Harvard University,
Cambridge, MA.

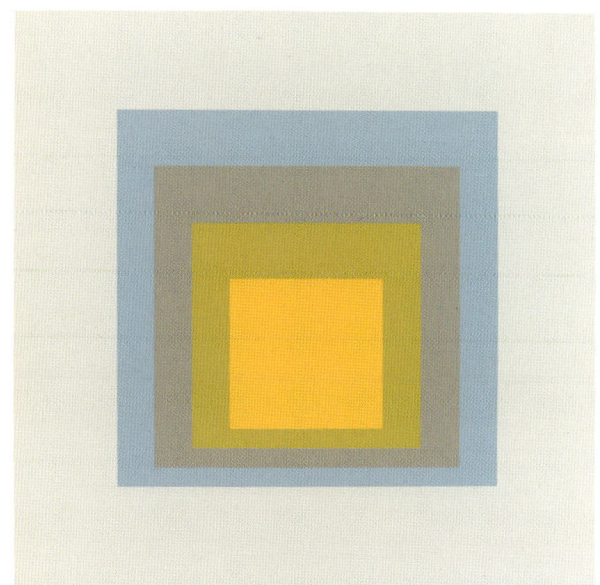

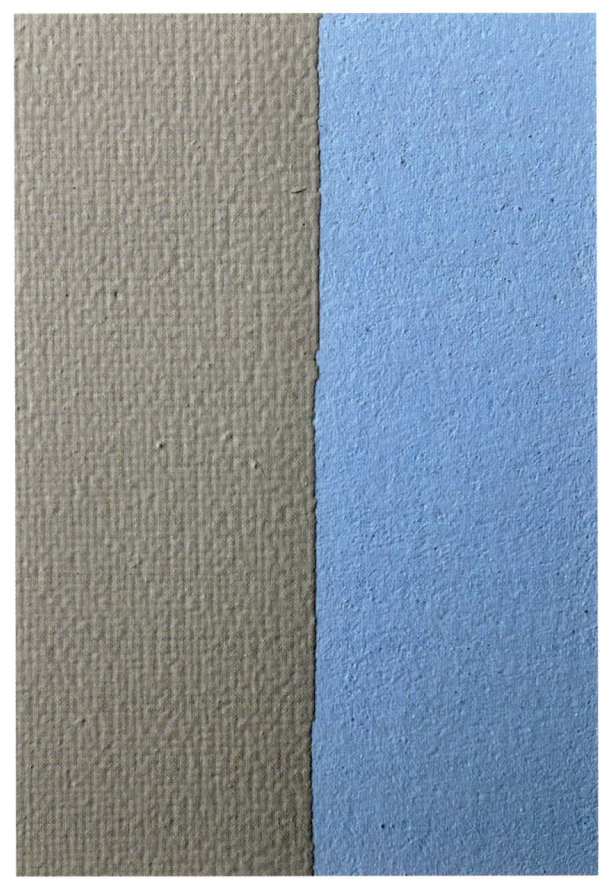

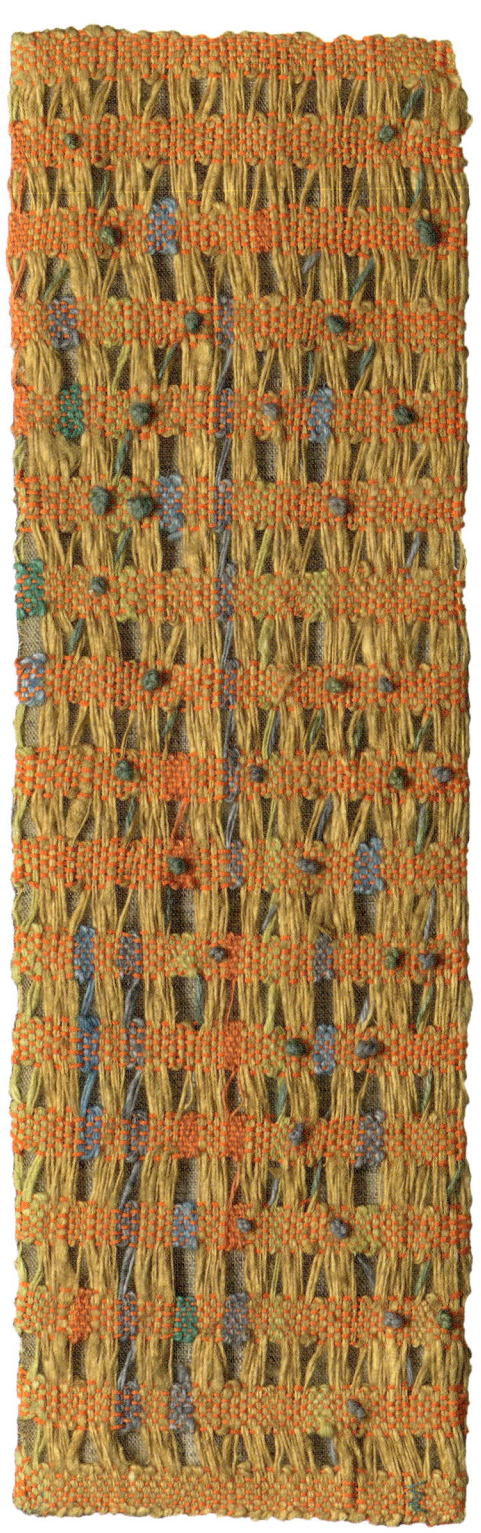

FIG. 4.11
Anni Albers, *Sunny*, 1965.
Weaving. National Gallery of
Art, Washington, DC. Corcoran
Collection. Gift of Olga
Hirshhorn.

idea and matter, between form and vessel, between figure and ground. Weavings are the perfect example of what art historian Carol Armstrong has called "matrixial" media: media that seem to be neutral, superficial, or merely supportive surfaces for the creation of meaning from elsewhere, but that actually generate meaning from within. We are reminded that the word matrix comes from the word for "womb." In both Josef's mesh-made screenprints and Anni's weavings, meshwork actively makes a world. This woven mesh is doing things—even if its soft and pliable structure, like women and women's work, has traditionally seemed ineffable, below the threshold of visibility, below notice.[10]

So the silkscreen mesh is not neutral. It has a peculiar sort of agency, and a history that stretches beyond and before the invention of screenprinting. I suggested earlier that screenprinted images are essentially strained or sifted into being. And indeed, what we might call the primordial origins of screenprinting lie not in printing but in sifting. The fine meshes used for silkscreens were originally made from bolting cloth, a specialized fine-gauge silk gauze that had been perfected in the eighteenth century for sifting flour in the production of white bread (FIGS. 4.12, 4.13). Bolting cloth was hand-loomed by silk weavers in Switzerland up to and through the 1960s.[11]

Screenprinting mesh was not just *inspired* by bolting cloth; it *was* bolting cloth, purchased from Swiss bolting cloth makers. It was literally the same material, its properties ideal both for sifting flour and for sifting images. Although nylon and polyester meshes had begun to replace silk by the 1960s in screenprinting, silk was still considered superior, and the logic of sifting that it brought with it was locked in to the entire process.[12] Indeed, even today, screenprinting remains tied to industrial sifting processes. A quick browse through the website of the Sefar Group, currently the leading manufacturer of "precision fabrics from monofilaments for the screen printing and filtration markets," demonstrates the rich connections between screenprinting and an array of processes in medicine, manufacturing, and engineering that involve filtration and fractionation.[13]

Filtration, fractionation, and flour-sifting may seem strange topics to import into art history. But doing so makes perfect sense from the perspective of the history of technology or the burgeoning field of material studies. In these fields, the adoption of a new technical process (such as screenprinting in art) does not imply an obliteration of cultural and historical complexity. Instead, it implies the productive adoption of complexity from an adjacent realm of technical activity. It involves the taking up of other networks of labor, knowledge, and materials and the merging of those networks with the fine art network.

Bruno Latour, whose work has deeply inspired my own approach, emphasizes that tools and technologies are not so much de-skillers as they are skill-shifters. To take up a technology is to tap into an infinitely complex network

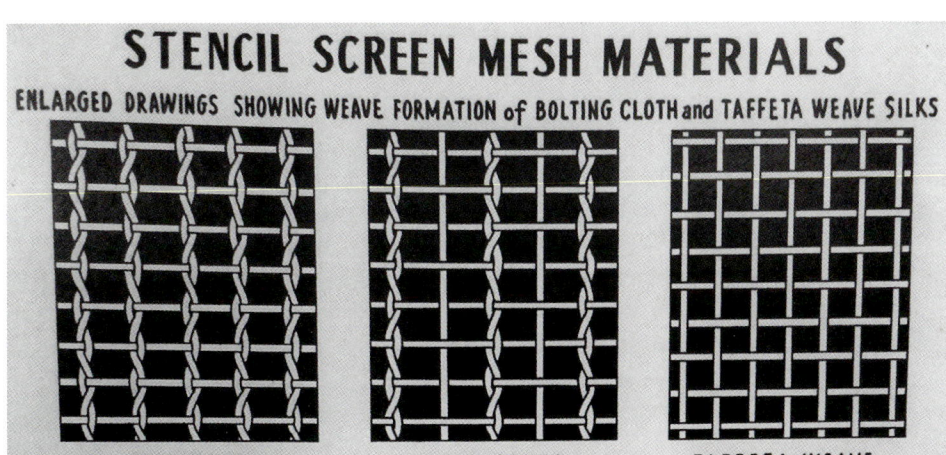

STENCIL SCREEN MESH MATERIALS

ENLARGED DRAWINGS SHOWING WEAVE FORMATION of BOLTING CLOTH and TAFFETA WEAVE SILKS

FULL GAUZE
OR FULL INTERLOCKING WEAVE

HALF GAUZE
OR HALF INTERLOCKING WEAVE

TAFFETA WEAVE
OR OVER AND UNDER WEAVE

FIG. 4.12

Illustration from Harry L. Hiett, *How-To-Do-It Charts on Materials, Equipment, Techniques for Screen Printing* (Cincinnati: Signs of the Times Publishing, 1980).

FIG. 4.13

Jan van Grevenbroeck II, *Bolting Flour*, eighteenth century. Pen and ink and watercolor on paper. Museo Correr Library, Venice. The cylinder was fashioned from bolting cloth so that the flour inside was sifted as the crank was turned.

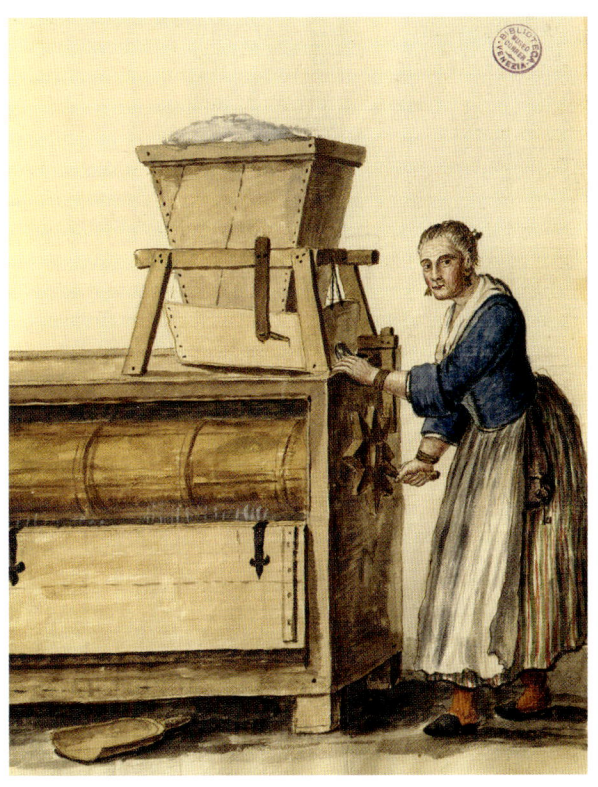

of the skills of other, now-absent actors. It "carries past acts into the present and permits [historical actors] to disappear while also remaining present. Such detours subvert the order of time and space—in a minute I may mobilize forces set into motion hundreds or millions of years ago in faraway places."[14] Following Latour, I want to suggest that with every pull of the screenprinter's squeegee, the old forces and cultures of sifting and straining are partially reactivated. These forces sit at the technical and metaphorical heart of screenprinting, and help us understand the relevance of the process for contemporary art. To explore this procedural link is to help illuminate the peculiarities of the screenprinting process, the nature of its connection to commercial endeavor, and the quality of the engagement with media that it set into play in the period.

The Los Angeles artist Ed Ruscha studied screenprinting as part of his commercial art training. In 1970, he published a portfolio of screenprints titled *News, Mews, Pews, Brews, Stews, & Dues* (FIG. 4.14). For this series, Ruscha claimed that he was exploring the implications of screenprinting not just as a "process" in the usual sense, but as a medium for *processing*. The portfolio of what he called "organic screenprints" was commissioned by the esteemed print studio Editions Alecto in London. What distinguishes it in the history of print is that rather than regular screenprinting inks, Ruscha used foodstuffs like chutney, pie filling, and caviar, creating screenprints that are essentially a series of strained stains. In other words, in these prints Ruscha literally reenacted the historical connection between screenprinting and straining, equating printmaking with food processing.[15]

News is printed with blackcurrant pie filling and red salmon roe. *Mews* has a background of Bolognese sauce and lettering of blackcurrant pie filling over cherry pie filling over unmixed raw egg. *Stews* includes crushed baked beans, caviar, fresh strawberries, cherry pie filling, mango chutney, tomato paste, daffodils, tulips, and leaves (FIG. 4.15). *Pews* has a background of Hershey's chocolate flavor syrup and Camp Coffee and chicory essence, with the lettering in squid ink. *Dues* is just Branston Pickle. *Brews* is axle grease over caviar.[16]

The textures of the foods Ruscha selected interrupted the perfect consistency of the standard screenprint deposit. When blackcurrants or chutney chunks or caviar got jammed in the screen, they created skips and gaps in the print. As the squeegee pressed down, the roughage in the ink blocked the screen and essentially formed a second order stencil, creating a figure or image directly in the material of the ink. In *Brews*, for example, the caviar created the skips in the ink and also left a fine gritty layer behind. The effect is geological, suggesting travertine (FIG. 4.16).

Ruscha's prints announce the work of screening in the screenprinting process. The fact that chunks and large particles become stencils here reminds us

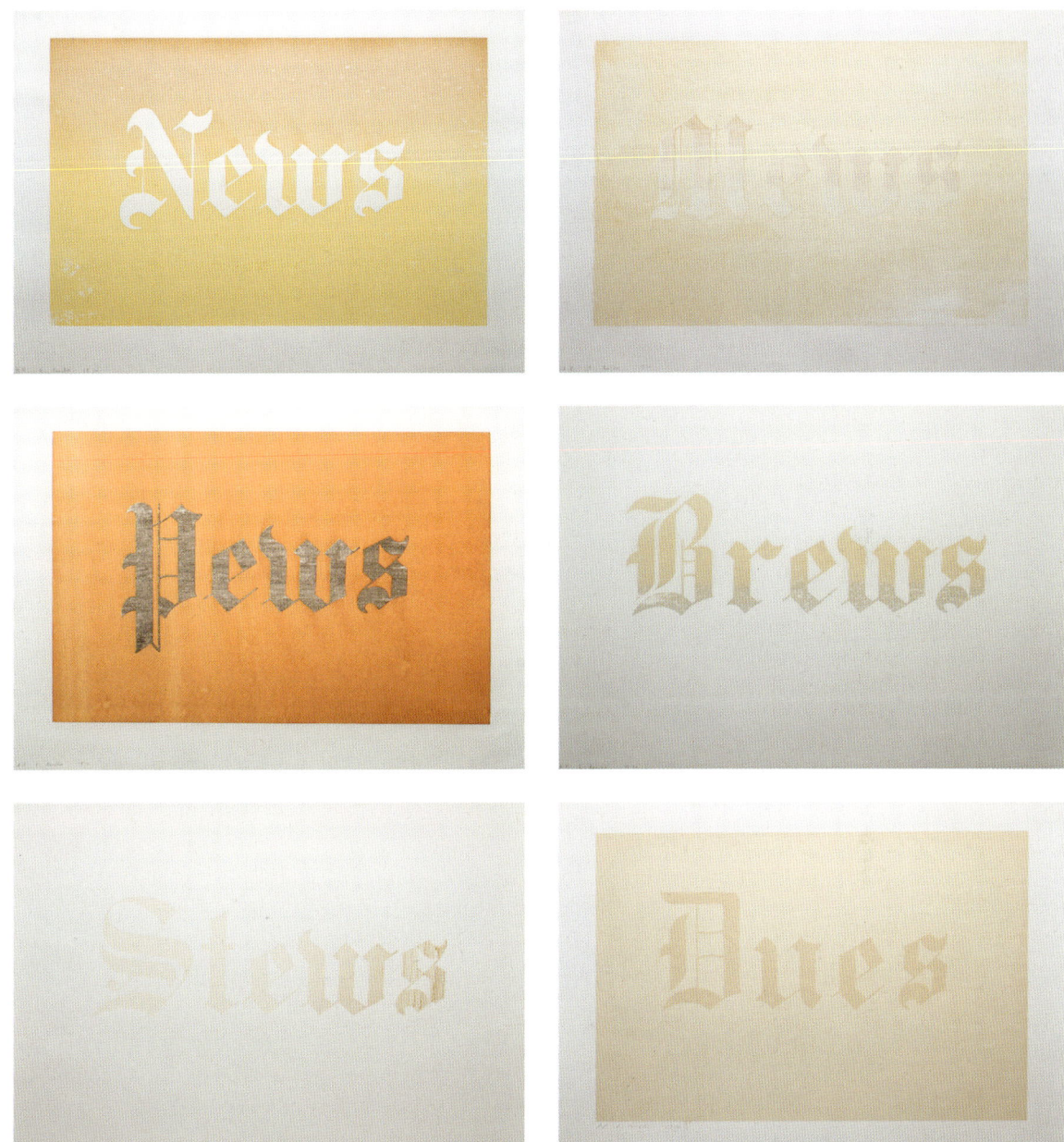

FIG. 4.14

Ed Ruscha, *News, Mews, Pews, Brews, Stews, & Dues*,
1970. Six organic screenprints. Harvard Art Museums/
Fogg Museum, Cambridge, MA. Margaret Fisher Fund.

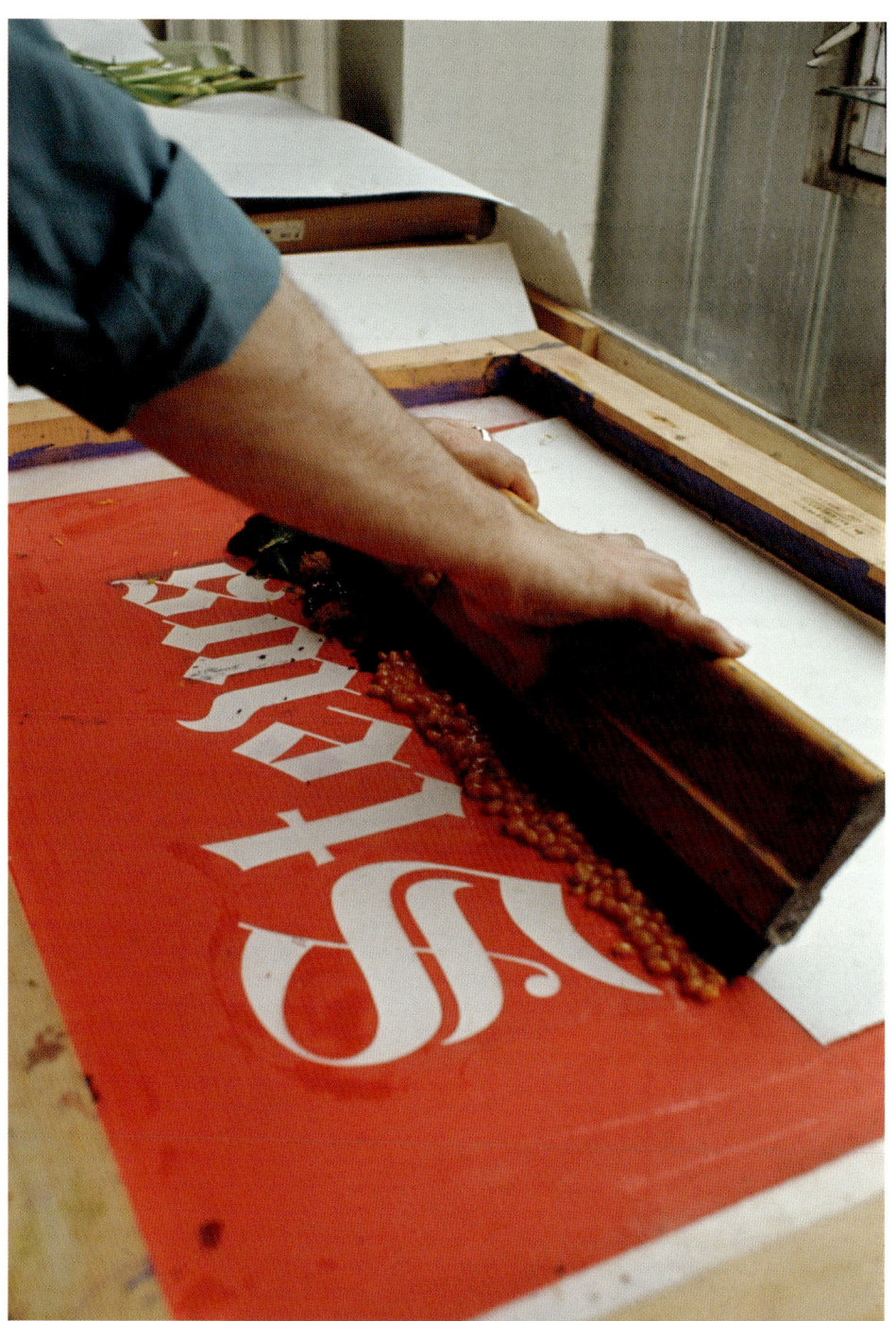

Tony Evans (photographer), Ed Ruscha working on *Stews*, 1970.

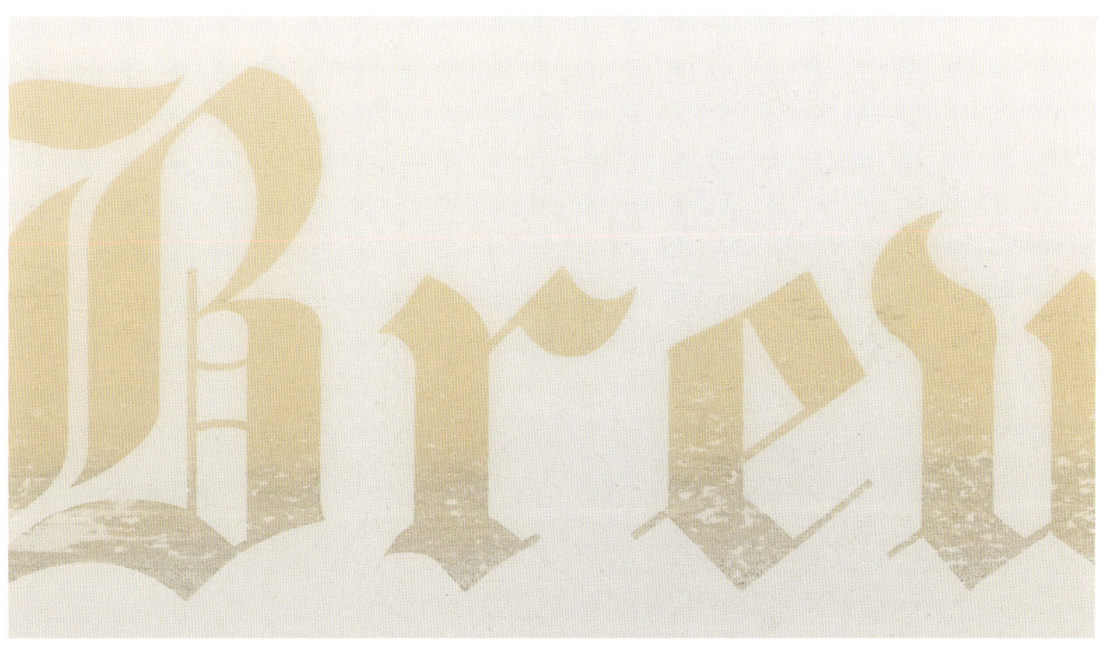

FIG. 4.16

Ed Ruscha, *Brews* (detail), 1970. Organic screenprint. Harvard Art Museums/
Fogg Museum, Cambridge, MA. Margaret Fisher Fund.

that stencils in general work by performing the role of blockage, preventing the flow of ink. The stencil is the bran; the stencil is the roughage. And thus, it dramatizes a truth of all screenprinting: namely, that the image is formed out of the separation of matter that goes through the screen and matter that stays behind. The distinction between refinement and coarseness is the binary system that forms the image in screenprinting.

It's not irrelevant that this exercise in sifting and straining took place in London, where Ruscha stayed for the duration of the project. Editions Alecto, the print studio where these were made, had been establishing an international market for its prints and had also been working to attract well-known American artists to come and work there, luring them with the opportunity to spend time in "Swinging London." Ruscha made this print series into a site-specific project. All of the ink materials were purchased in Covent Garden and the famous Harrods food halls. Most of the foods used as inks—such as blackcurrant pie filling—were common in Britain but not the United States. And the words on the prints, whose stencils were hand-cut by Ruscha into a black Gothic old-English lettering, refer to quintessentially British phenomena.

What to make of this strained Britishness? What does it mean for an American to sift through British products? It can't help but comment on the much longer history of British-American relations, the British empire, and colonial political economies more generally. Consider the mercantile relations that lurked behind the American Revolution in the eighteenth century, in which colonials were made to send raw materials to the metropole to be refined into finished goods. We might think of Ruscha's screenprints as a cheeky reversal of this historical vector. Here, Ruscha, an American, out-refines the refiners, adding another round of processing to quintessentially British-Empire-processed goods like Branston Pickle or chutney. What is exposed in the screenprinting process is actually the lumpiness of British products. The final prints are the processed, refined commodity made by removing the impurities from the British goods. British processed foods become raw materials, Ruscha's prints the finished goods.

His work also has pronounced geopolitical resonances in his own time—this is not just about the eighteenth century. Ruscha's postwar world was a world of new American cultural and economic dominance; Britain was no longer doing the sifting, no longer doing the straining, no longer holding the global screen. Ruscha's humble screenprinting activities speak to nothing less than the succession of empires. So Ruscha's portfolio performs screenprinting as a dramatic binary tension between roughage and refinement.

The look of the screenprint is a product of the inhomogeneities in Ruscha's culinary inks. These create their own figure in the text by clogging the open areas of the weave. Ruscha makes visible the fact that this is an image made by some things getting through and other things getting stuck, getting held back. He reveals something about screenprinting and culture that does not usually rise to the level of conscious awareness on the part of the viewer: the image is made as much by what doesn't get through the screen as by what does. The image is formed by what is kept back, strained out, *restrained*. In dramatizing the glitch or grit or clog as the agent of image formation, Ruscha was picking up on something that was also operative in Warhol's early screenprints and screenprinted paintings.

As I've noted, Warhol began screenprinting onto canvas in 1962. Quickly, over the next year or so, he established a consistent iconography and a consistent aesthetic for these works. His iconography featured movie stars taken from film stills and other forms of popular imagery; in the context of straining, sifting, and refinement, it's worth noting that these were some of the first images to be associated with the new phenomenon of Pop Art in the US. Pop Art emerged into the art world under the sign of vulgarity. It traumatized many tastemakers with its infusion of lowbrow hucksterism into the highbrow world of the fine arts. The critic Max Kozloff wrote in 1962 that "the truth is, the art galleries are being invaded by the pinheaded and contemptible style of gum chewers, bobbysoxers, and worse, delinquents."[17] Alan Solomon lamented in 1963 that

> instead of rejecting the deplorable and grotesque products of the modern commercial industrial world . . . these new artists have turned with relish and excitement to what those of us who know better regard as the wasteland of television commercials, comic strips, hot dog stands, used car lots, juke boxes, slot machines and supermarkets.[18]

Warhol's early screenprint work deals, then, in the tension between refinement and coarseness, highlighting the byproducts, the pictorial roughage of culture, with a medium that performs the relationship between roughage and refinement in its very operation.

Warhol intuited that screenprinting was the perfect medium for producing and performing this very anxiety about the adjacency of the rough and the smooth, the course and the fine. One of the hallmarks of Warhol's work is the grain of the halftone—and here I would ask you to note the resonance of the term "grain" with the theme of flour milling. Warhol's halftones have a coarse appearance (see fig. 4.1). He usually asked for the coarsest possible halftone rasters when getting his screens made. These thematize the concept of the image as formed by an array of grit suspended or trapped in a grid. In many other ways in his screenprint work, Warhol thematizes the screenprint image as an image formed through a sieve. The streaks, gaps, and wide variations that were so striking in his early screenprint work all come about by creating blockages and exploiting irregularities in the passage of ink through the screen.

He would let the squeegee harden with dried ink, which forced ink more roughly through the mesh, creating black streaks. He would pour too much or too little ink into the screen, causing blotches or white streaks and gaps. He would reuse screens multiple times without cleaning them. This would cause the mesh to become clogged with dry ink, creating, as did Ruscha, a second-order stencil that unmistakably announces itself as a form created through blockage. All of these screening glitches, these streaks and hardenings that interrupt the clean work of the intentional stencil, are essentially failures of proper screenprinting hygiene (see fig. 4.4).[19]

Warhol's images also help us to see how the strained-print model relates to the theme of repetition in printing. His work makes it impossible to imagine modern reproductive media as virtual or dematerialized. There are no exactly repeatable pictorial statements in Warhol's work, because each repetition confronts the material remains — the clogs and byproducts — of its previous iteration. Warhol highlights the fact that in all printmaking, the illusion of reproductive perfection is sustained by the invisible labor of hygiene and maintenance in the print studio: cleaning or wiping the matrix between impressions, making a clean slate. Warhol makes that maintenance work visible by showing what happens when it breaks down.

Warhol and Ruscha emphasize screenprinting as a form of straining in which the final product is shaped as much by what is held back or left out than it is by what gets through. And in the rhetoric of clogging that runs throughout their work, they also draw attention to the work of hygiene in the maintenance of these systems. The smooth operation of the system depends upon its constant refreshment and maintenance. I want to finish up with two more contemporary bodies of work that do not explicitly involve screenprinting, but that activate the more general field of the stencil matrix of which the screenprint is a part. Both of them powerfully explore the way that the strain of the stencil can reveal insights about binarization, restraint, visibility, and maintenance.

Glenn Ligon's painting *Prisoner of Love #1* was made with stencils similar to those that Jasper Johns used in his early number and letter paintings (FIG. 4.17). A short sentence is repeated throughout the canvas, top to bottom, without regard for line breaks: "We are the ink that gives the white page a meaning." The sentence is a variation on a passage by Jean Genet about the Black Panthers, from his 1986 posthumous autobiography *Prisoner of Love*. Ligon borrows similar texts throughout his work, and subjects them to a similar repetition process. Another key example is the sentence "I feel most colored when I am thrown against a sharp white background," which was adapted from Zora Neale Hurston's 1928 essay "How It Feels to Be Colored Me."

Glenn Ligon, *Prisoner of Love #1 (Second Version)*, 1992. Oil and gesso on linen. Carnegie Museum of Art, Pittsburgh. Founders Patrons Day Acquisition Fund.

Both of these texts speak to the binarization and sorting we have been discussing, and do so in terms of race. Both argue that the very ideas of blackness and whiteness can exist only by virtue of their context in relation to each other. In particular, they suggest that whiteness needs blackness as the other through which it is defined.[20] The image we have of race, in other words, is sustained by an act of binary, oppositional filtering. White is what you get when you strain out the black, black is what you get when you strain out the white. Here we might remember that our story of the work of straining and sifting and stenciling began with bolting cloth, a processing matrix that was developed in order to refine flour into white bread.

Ligon explores the way the very legibility of race in American culture depends on that opposition. I mean legibility quite literally, because the brilliance of Ligon's text works is that they perform the link between racial binaries and the binaries that are inherent to printing. Ligon uses print against itself, disrupting the operation of its own binary structure. Ligon's paintings are made by forcing paint in the form of oil sticks through the openings of plastic stencils. Oil sticks are enormously sticky; every time he lifts the stencil back off of the canvas after adding some paint, there is paint smudged on the back of the stencil and collected around the edges of the opening. As he makes each painting, Ligon repeats the stenciled text over and over without cleaning off the stencil between returns to the canvas. As the phrases repeat, the sticky paint builds up on the back and edges of the stencil and progressively obliterates the legibility of the text, smudging more heavily with each iteration.

Ligon takes two languages of print—its binary system of articulation and its role as an engine of repetition—and uses them against each other. As with Warhol's paintings, repetition is what breaks down clean legibility, rather than reinforcing it. And the smudging of paint in Ligon's work echoes the themes of straining and sifting that we have been discussing, because his process allows the byproducts of the binary stencil—the smudges of paint left behind, left sticking to the tool—to manifest themselves in the final work, simultaneously announcing the presence of a binary operation and breaking down its effectiveness.

And speaking of byproducts, leftovers, that which is left behind: in the late 1990s, while working with James Baldwin's 1953 essay "The Stranger in the Village," Ligon began adding coal dust to the oil medium (FIG. 4.18). He wanted the material he used to have the same "gravitas" as the text, and he wanted to explore the particular contradictions of this dust. The material is "beautiful, black, and shiny," but it is literally a leftover, a waste product of coal processing. In Ligon's work, these leftovers take over the image, breaking down the ability of the stencil to generate meaning. As a commentary on the fictions and production of race, these accretions of coal dust suggest a refusal to be represented through this

FIG. 4.18
Glenn Ligon, *Sole Nero 5*, 2018. Oil stick, coal dust, and gesso on paper.
Courtesy of the artist, Hauser & Wirth, New York, Regen Projects, Los Angeles,
Thomas Dane Gallery, London, and Galerie Chantal Crousel, Paris.

screen, through the strain, of race relations in America. It is akin to the "right to opacity" that Édouard Glissant has written about in the context of race and empire, and Ligon produces it by putting print under strain.[21]

I will close with a short meditation on an exquisite work on wax paper by Mona Hatoum (FIG. 4.19) that captures all of the dynamics of gender, labor, matter, and strain that I have introduced in this chapter. It is not a screenprint and not (or not quite) a stencil; it is a rubbing. It is one of a series of rubbings of strainers, colanders, and other humble kitchen tools that perform, traditionally in the hands of women, the work of straining and sifting and refining and cleaning in the home. Hatoum began making them in 1996, at a residency at the Sabbathday Lake Shaker community, and continued them in future years while visiting her mother in Lebanon.[22]

A delicate sheet of Japanese wax paper is forced up against a strainer. It can't go through, of course, so instead it preserves the shape of that effort. The wax paper, having undergone the dimensional strain of conforming to the object's concavity, preserves the wrinkles and stresses of the process, the remnants of impact. The wrinkles crackle like sparks, electrical discharges gathering along the folds and crevices of what would otherwise have been invisible labor, making that labor visible, activating it like a form of feminist craquelure. The founder of the Shaker sect in America, Mother Ann Lee, said that "every force evolves a form."[23] And Hatoum's rubbings—prints that capture the action of straining just at its edge, in what it leaves behind—speak to these former forces, making them visible and showing their work.

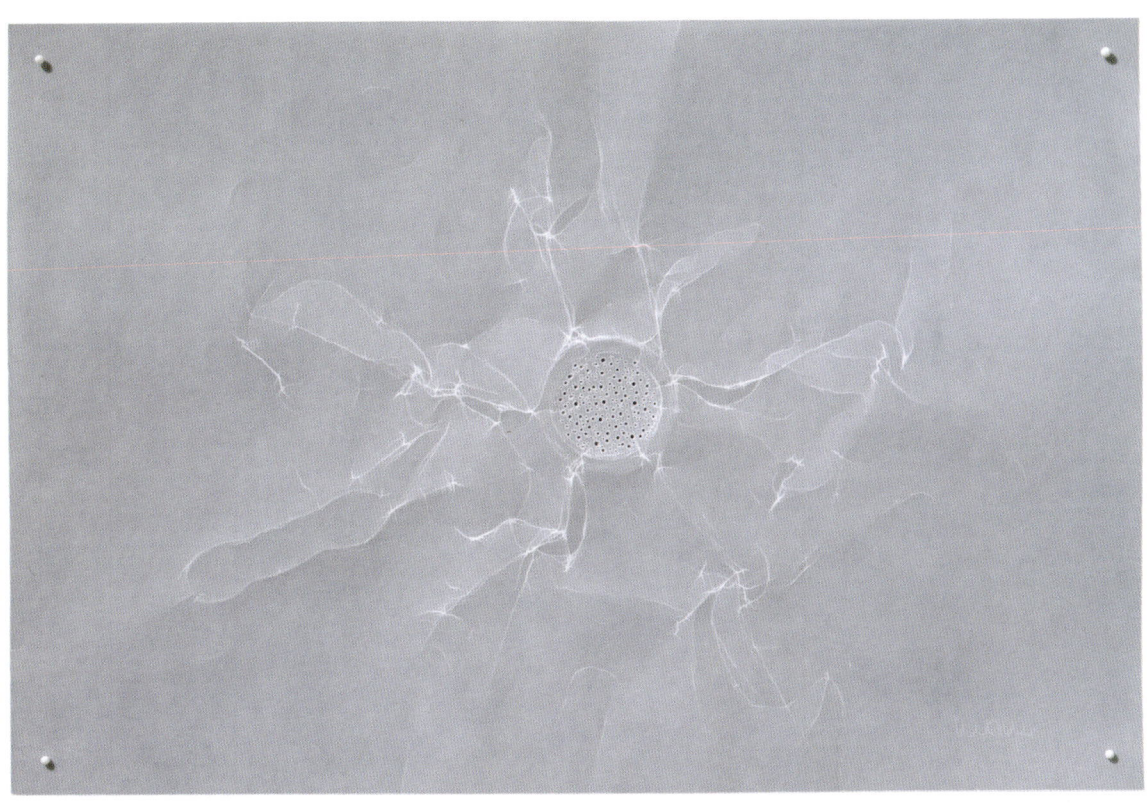

FIG. 4.19
Mona Hatoum, *Untitled (India Strainer)*, 2008.
Japanese wax paper. Property of the artist.

In July of 1969, Robert Rauschenberg was one of a small group of artists invited by NASA to the Kennedy Space Center to observe the launch of Apollo 11 (FIG. 5.1). In response to what he witnessed, he made a series of prints called *Stoned Moon*. While the title of the series could be taken as a reference to drugs (the whiff of such a reference, at least, cannot be definitively ruled out), Rauschenberg actually selected the title to pay homage to stone lithography, the printing process used to create the works. The prints were pulled from enormous limestone matrices, several inches thick and weighing, collectively, hundreds if not thousands of pounds. In fact, two of the prints were the largest that had ever been pulled from a hand-fed stone lithography press. *Sky Garden*, for example, is eighty-nine inches tall. Three separate stones had to be assembled, almost like stacked rocket stages, to launch it into print (FIG. 5.2).[1]

In order to develop this epic meditation on technology, flight, and futurity, then, Rauschenberg chose the most massive and primordial means available. To convey humanity breaking free of the Earth's gravity, Rauschenberg used just about the weightiest possible manner of making a two-dimensional image. Everything about it was heavy, even the ink (each impression of the larger prints required two pounds of it). Moreover, making these lithographs was a technological effort that was commensurate in the print world with the scale of the collective efforts at mission control for the Apollo mission. For two months, the printers at Gemini G.E.L. worked fourteen to sixteen hours a day with Rauschenberg to print the series (FIG. 5.3).

Rauschenberg's work on the *Stoned Moon* project gets at a fundamental paradox of print. It is both light and heavy. In printmaking, images are stretched uncomfortably between their two polar states of materiality and virtuality. On the one hand, printmaking issues forth vast flocks of replications, overcoming the bounds of the singular image-object, entering the strange nongravitational realm of mass-reproductive orbit. But, on the other hand, prints are born under pressure in massive machines from direct physical contact between plates or screens, pulpy paper, and squishy, viscous inks. Moreover, although any given print will usually be lighter than a painting or a sculpture, a single impression of a print represents only a fraction of the mass of the entire edition. A single impression is just a terminal at the tip of what Timothy Morton calls a "hyperobject": the whole network of materials, forces, time, and labor that went into making it.[2] "The print" is really the whole stack of prints that was generated by the matrix, along with all the tools and equipment and people that brought it into being. Prints are made heavily even if they circulate lightly. Rauschenberg recognized that these gravitational paradoxes of print had a kindred sensibility in the Apollo program. For each Apollo launch, the Saturn V rockets delivered over nine million pounds of thrust. All in order to place the spacecraft into a state of weightlessness.[3]

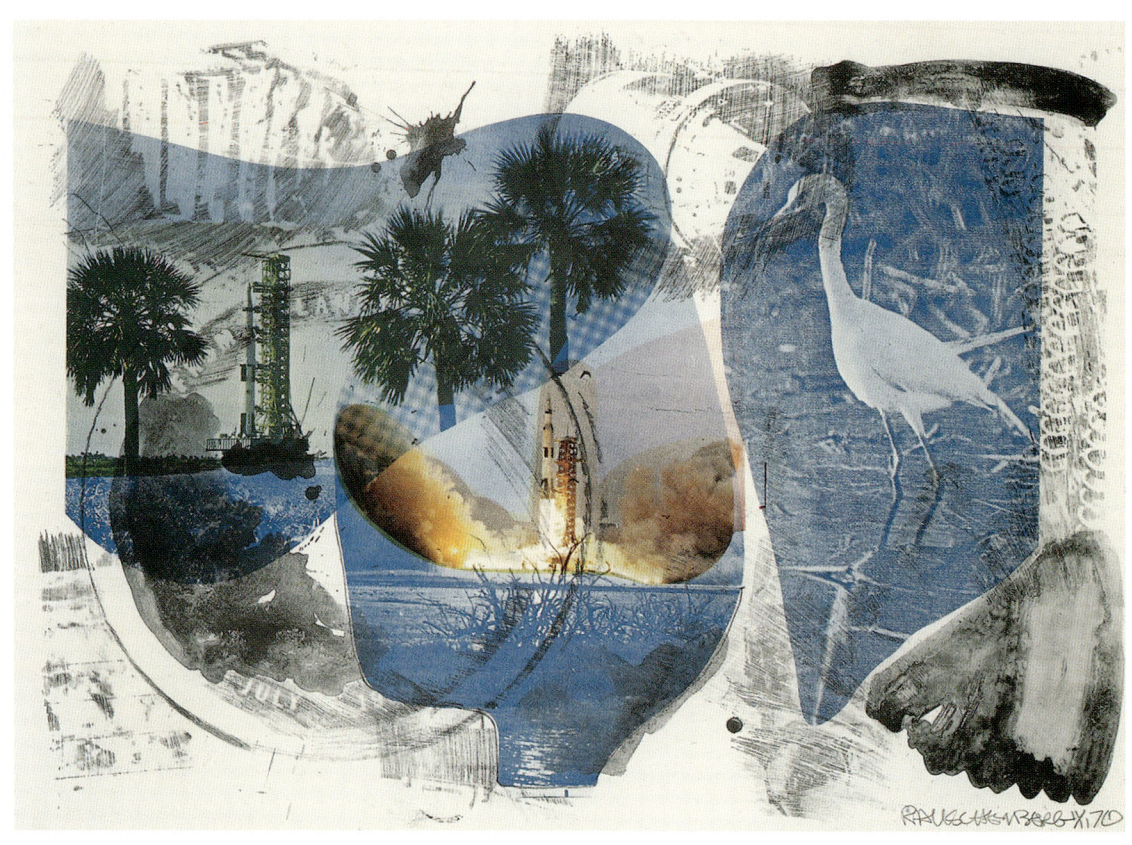

Robert Rauschenberg, *Local Means*, from *Stoned Moon*, 1970. Lithograph
on paper. Moody Center for the Arts, Rice University, Houston.

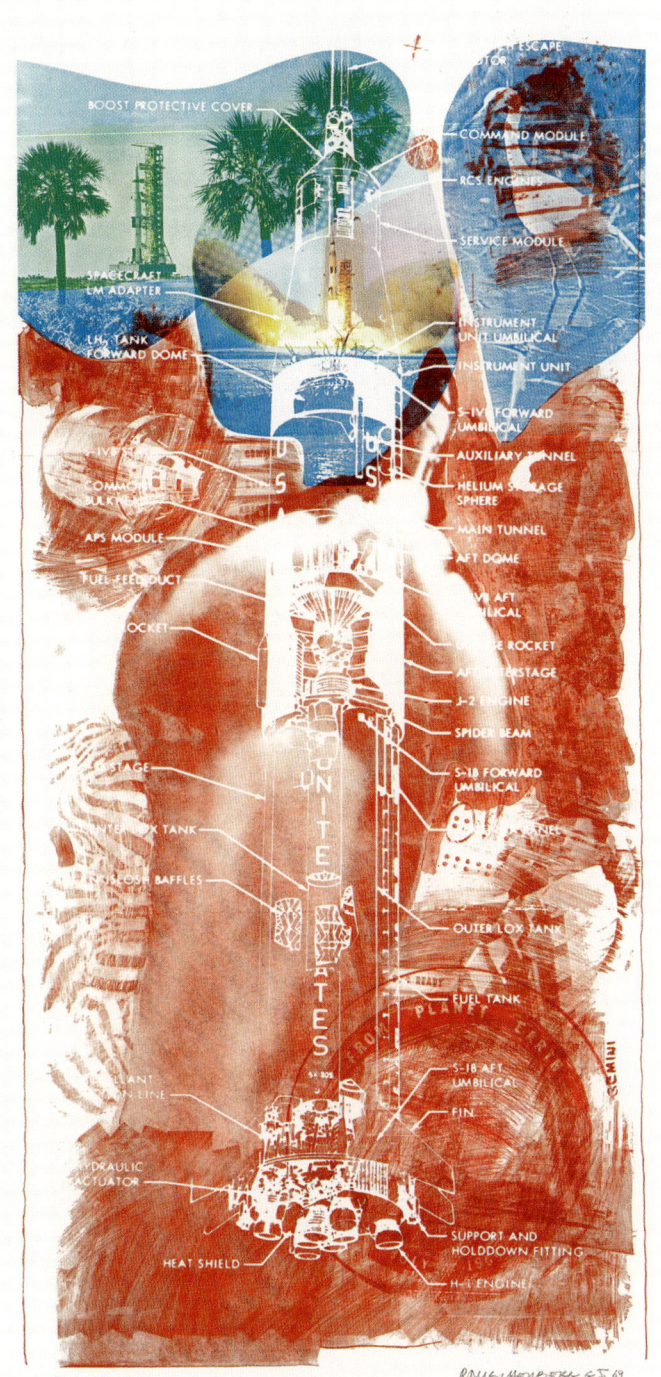

FIG. 5.2

Robert Rauschenberg, *Sky Garden*, from *Stoned Moon*, 1969. Color lithograph and screenprint on Special Arjomari wove paper. National Gallery of Art, Washington, DC. Gift of Gemini G.E.L. and the artist.

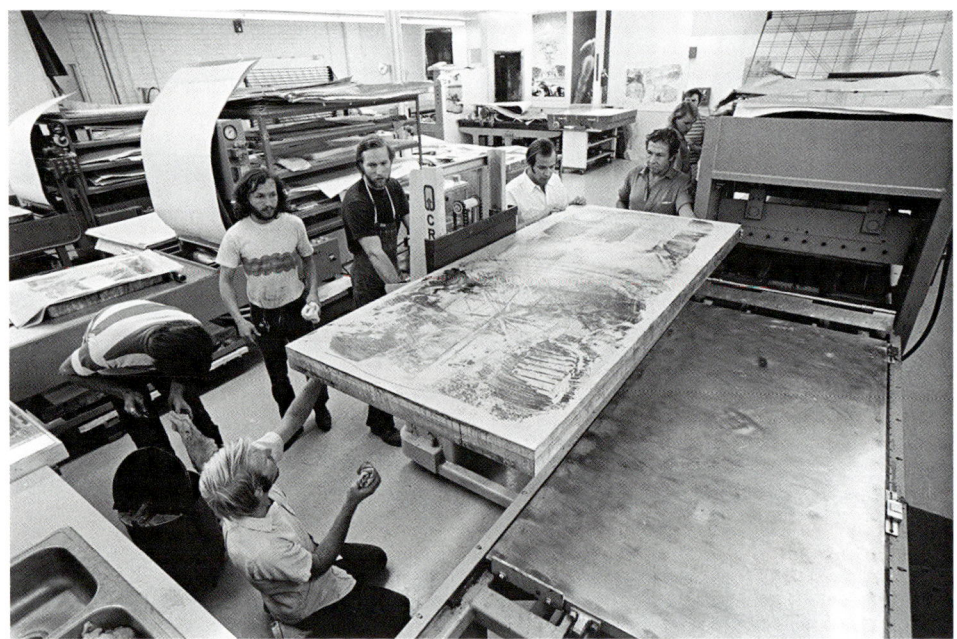

FIG. 5.3
Malcolm Lubliner (photographer), making of the *Stoned Moon* series, 1970. Rauschenberg Foundation, New York.

FIG. 5.4
Malcolm Lubliner (photographer), making of the *Stoned Moon* series, 1970. Rauschenberg Foundation, New York.

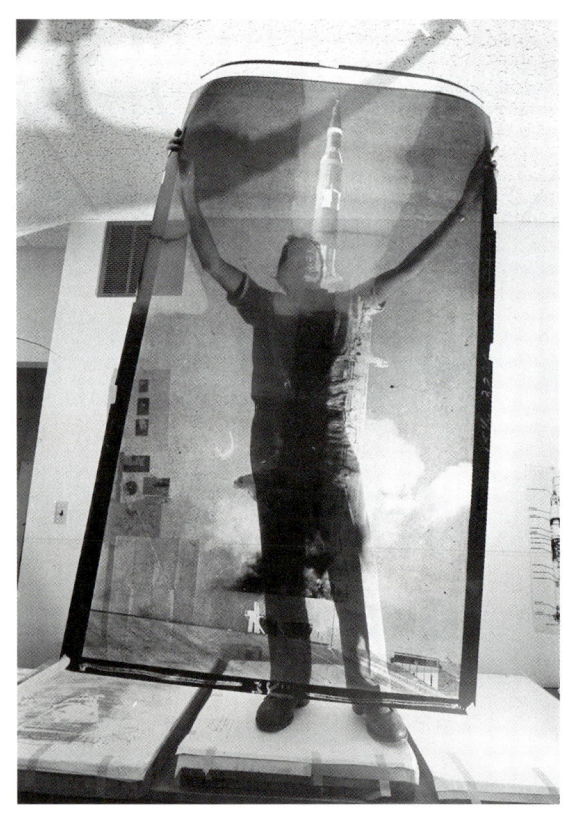

Rauschenberg understood the surface of the lithographic stone as a space of contact, combination, pressure, and release. Just as he had imported photographic imagery into painting through screenprinting earlier in his career, using a print technique to create a new kind of surface that fused painting and photography, he was drawn to lithography because the matrix could accept both transferred media images and hand-drawn elements. It allowed him to bring images together that would otherwise seem incompatible—halftone photographs and technical diagrams; fingerprints and brushstrokes; natural reticulation patterns. The powerful oddity of such assemblies was mirrored in the environment of the moon launch itself, there on the Space Coast, where rocket launches share space with palm trees, shock waves with rippling water, boosters with waterbirds.[4]

As he experimented with lithography in the years leading up to the *Stoned Moon* project, Rauschenberg developed new ways of transferring photographic halftones to the surface of the stone. For many of the *Stoned Moon* prints, he started with large halftone photographs on clear sheets of acetate (FIG. 5.4). He then cut up the acetates and placed them on a lithographic stone that had been treated with a photosensitive material, making a sort of collage out of the transparent images. The stone was then exposed in such a way that the halftone pattern was transferred to the surface as printable chemical trace. Sometimes the transparent acetates overlapped, and when they did, something peculiar happened: a moiré pattern erupted from the interference of the halftone dots. It's just there, behind the palm trees, in both *Local Means* and the larger *Sky Garden*.

As explained in the last chapter, the halftone screen breaks continuous-tone photographs into grid-like arrays of dot patterns. It is the regularity of these patterns that causes interference effects when two or more halftones overlap at a slight angle. Whereas this interference pattern would be considered undesirable by most printmakers (there are many ways of avoiding or minimizing the moiré effect when combining halftones on a print), Rauschenberg decided to cultivate it. Moiré patterning appears prominently in several of the lithographs in the series. In fact, he seems to have relished the formal resonances it created: it echoes the billowing smoke of the rocket and the rippling of the surface of the water in the wetland. And you can almost hear its vibratory pattern, the way you might feel the rumble of a rocket engine. It thickens the space of the print. Rauschenberg later wrote about the visceral experience of the launch: he described "saturated, super-saturated and solidified air with a sound that became your body. For that while everything was the same material."[5]

Interference effects often erupt when images come into contact with each other in the milieu of modern print. Rational patterns can produce irrational effects. These effects can emerge unpredictably and suddenly, like an explosion, a runaway chemical reaction, or a shiver. When images overlap, a flinty pictorial

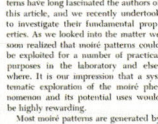
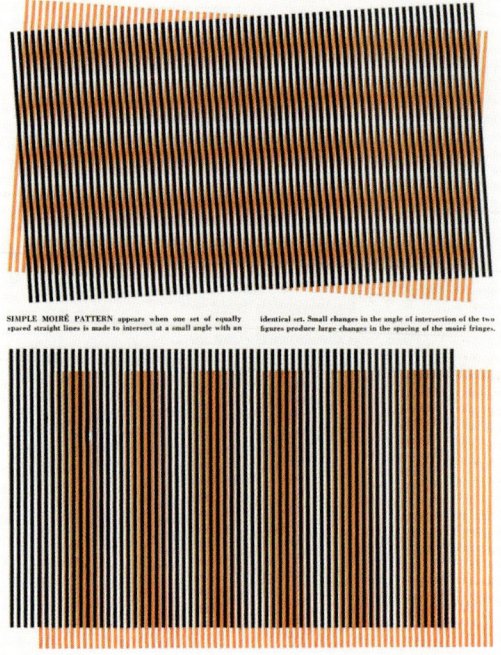

FIG. 5.5
Gerald Oster and Yasunori Nishijima, "Moiré Patterns," *Scientific American* 208, no. 5 (1963): 54–55.

energy can be released that far exceeds the apparent placidity of its elements. And these effects suggest a form of spatial imaginary that is expansive but not optical or illusionistic in the usual sense. This is a form of space triggered by contact and vibration, a kind of atmosphere that owes as much to sound and touch as it does to vision. It is a space of pressure and propagation rather than perspective, one that perhaps resembles outer space more than it does the usual pictorial space.

Moiré or interference effects result from the superimposition, and slight misregistration, of two or more regular patterns (FIG. 5.5). A classic moiré is composed of two sets of parallel lines that overlap at a slight angle. But moiré patterns can also develop out of grids, dot arrays, nested curves, and innumerable other arrangements. The key quality of a moiré pattern is that it emerges in an apparently nonlinear way from its component linear structures—it does not exist in either pattern individually but is generated only in their combination. Depending on the mutual angles, frequencies, and periodicities of the two elements, moiré can crop up in a lot of places: between two picket fences, between two layers of woven fabric, between two window screens, and, as we will see, between any two grid- or mesh-based images. Two layers of a silkscreen, a halftone on a silkscreen, a halftone on a TV camera, a herringbone jacket on a silkscreen, a striped shirt in a digital photograph seen on a monitor.

An interesting aspect of many interference patterns is that although they are born from absolute regularity, they can seem to turn back over into the stochastic world, resembling liquid, woodgrain, or other natural patterns. Moiré patterns that crop up in digital rendering, for example, are often called "woodgrain artifacts." Moiré pulls any image into a field of natural formal associations. It has a quality of dissolving or liquefying patterns and structures that are regular and rational.

The word "moiré" comes from the history of textiles — it is a French term that originally referred to the shimmering quality of what is also known as watered silk (FIG. 5.6). In the traditional making of moiré fabric, a glossy, subtly corded silk is folded over itself, face to face, so that the parallel texture of the two sides of the folded fabric is just slightly misaligned. The two layers are then pressed between heated rollers in a process called calendaring. This generates a moiré pattern from the interference of the two linear arrays. Here we might note that the production of moiré and the practice of printing are closely related from the outset. The making of moiré silk is essentially a form of roller printing in which each side of the fold is used as the matrix for embossing the other side (FIG. 5.7).

There is a kind of miraculous quality about this transformation, and this too links it to themes in the history of printmaking. The moiré pattern develops from a form of self-printing, self-marking, or self-making. The fabric prints itself and generates something that did not previously inhere in it — indeed, an image that seems miraculously excessive, in its swirling, stochastic beauty, compared to the mechanical regularity of the fabric's original structure. Indeed we might think about the moiré image as one of the family of acheiropoetic images — images not made by human hands — that have such a deep connection to the history and philosophy of print, as discussed in chapter 1. The classic example of this in the West, of course, is the Sudarium, the imprint of Christ's face legendarily left on the veil of Veronica (see fig. 1.2). Like the veil, moiré silk is the site of the appearance of a miraculous image in cloth, made without human hands. Like the Sudarium, moiré brings printing, textiles, and nonhuman image production together.

Although moiré emerges independently, it can be cultivated or invited to appear by human intervention. In earlier European printmaking, it was occasionally harnessed in line engraving, where crosshatched arrays of near-parallel arcs and lines could often spark moiré patterns. In the heyday of line engraving,

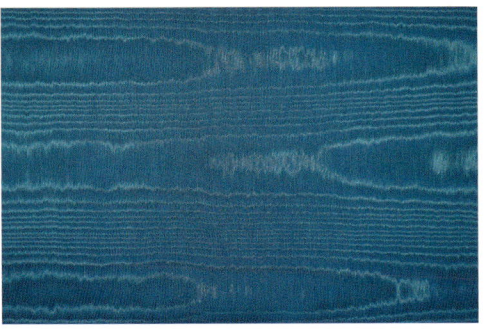

FIG. 5.6
Satin moiré.

FIG. 5.7
Still from *Savoir-Faire: The Art of Moiré Libre* by Dedar Milano, 2023.

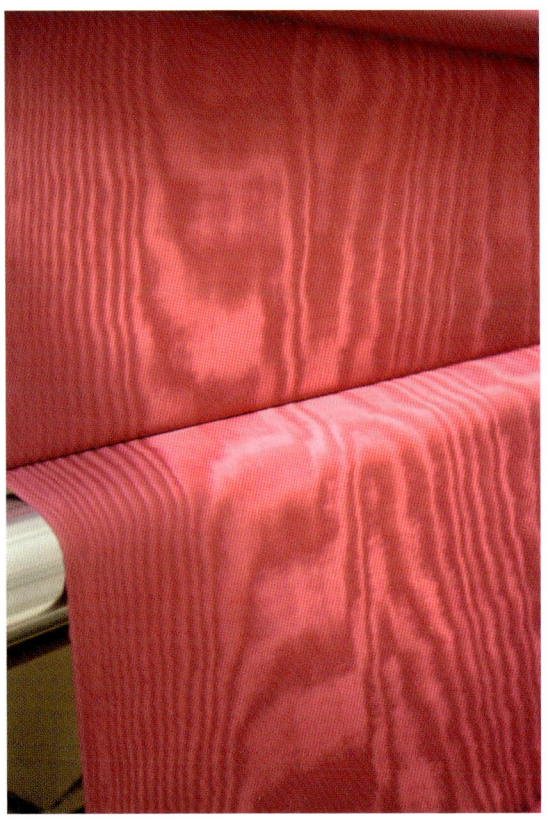

between the sixteenth and eighteenth centuries, engravers often courted moiré in order to generate a dynamic surface effect in their prints; doing so was a sign of the supreme skill of the engraver who was able to invoke and control these unruly patterns. Jan Harmensz Muller's *Arion on a Dolphin (Allegory of Music)*, engraved around 1590, demonstrates not only Muller's technical skill, but also his recognition that, through the interference patterns specific to his medium, he is uniquely able to *perform* the subject matter he depicts (FIG. 5.8). In the ancient Greek fable, the beauty of Arion's music inspires the gods to send dolphins to rescue him at sea. In the moiré patterns in the clouds over Arion's head, Muller generates a direct visual analog for the resonance of sound. The engraving "plays" the story in a way that the source painting could not.

Nested within the scholarly literature about the techniques of early modern line engraving, there is a small but intriguing body of commentary about moiré effects. I say it is intriguing because it often tends to suggest that there is

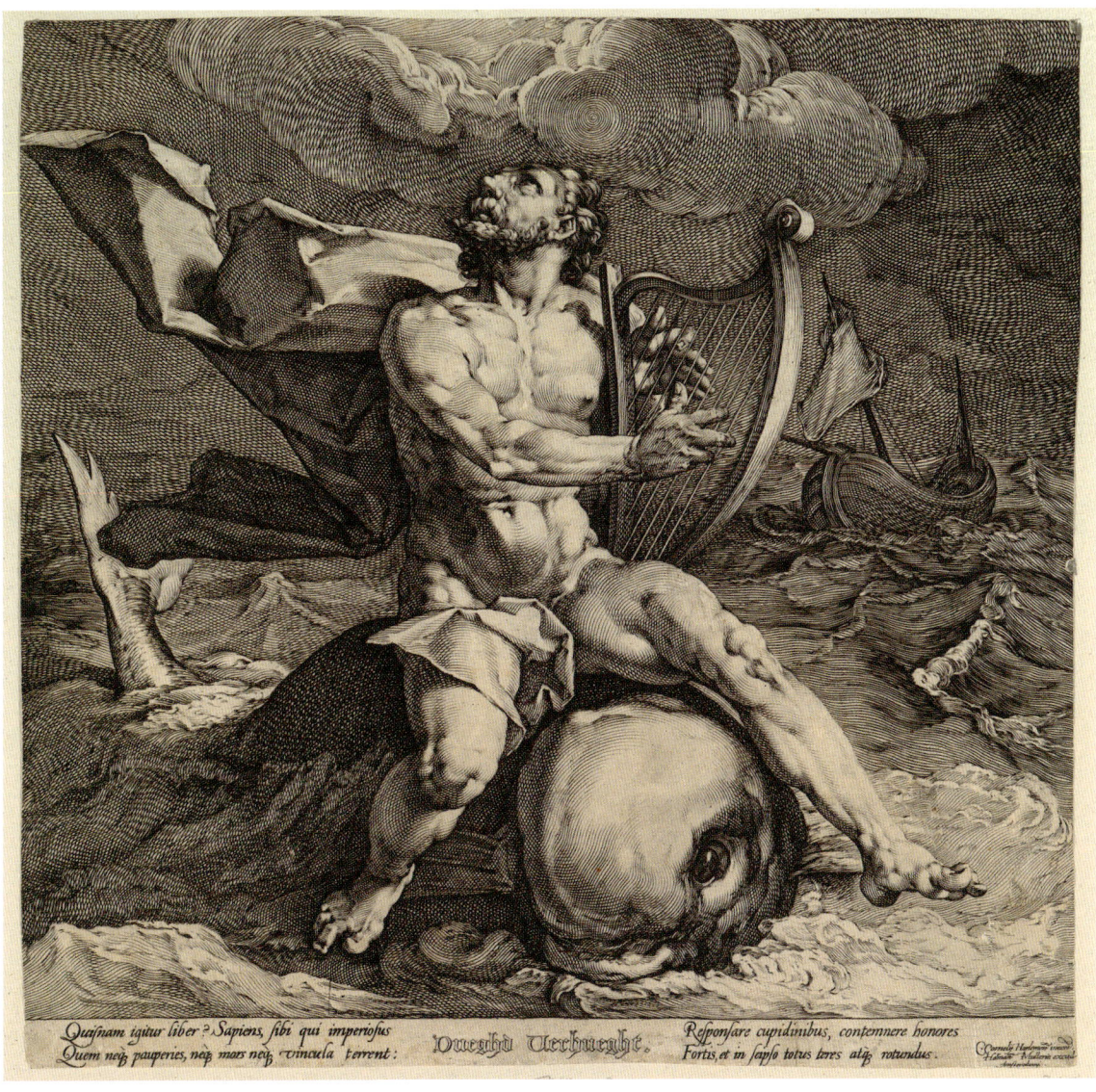

Quifnam igitur liber? Sapiens, fibi qui imperiofus   Dueghú Verhueght.   Refponfare cupidinibus, contemnere honores
Quem neq; pauperes, neq; mors neq; vincula terrent: Fortis, et in feipfo totus teres atq; rotundus.

FIG. 5.8
Jan Harmensz Muller, after Cornelis Cornelisz van Haarlem,
Arion on a Dolphin, c. 1590. Engraving on paper, Filedt Kok's
first state of three. The Metropolitan Museum of Art, New York.
Elisha Whittelsey Collection, The Elisha Whittelsey Fund, 1956.
56.597.5.

something fundamentally improper about moiré. The art historian Martin Kemp, a pioneering scholar of Renaissance art and the intersections between art and science, has been especially sensitive to the apparent contradictions and paradoxes that moiré introduces to the whole project of reproductive printmaking. In his writing, moiré is frequently associated with style over substance, and queerness (I use that term intentionally) over rationality:

> Curved and straight lines in sets of parallels intersect in contrived combinations, not only to create a series of carefully pitched tones but also to form strange patterns which are stylishly assertive in their own right. . . . They are not merely discernible at very close viewing distances, but are openly paraded.[6]

He also notes the intrusion of qualities of fabric and textiles into the world of print. Here's another Jan Muller engraving, after Bartholomeus Spranger's *Venus and Mercury* (FIG. 5.9). Look at the buzzy, vibrational quality, the sense of movement that stretches across the texture of the print. Muller depicts lots of drapery in various states of dynamism, but there is a sense in which the whole page is acting like a piece of moiré silk. Kemp beautifully describes exactly this:

> Throughout the print, moiré patterns are repeated in declamatory fashion, giving a uniformly suave sheen to surfaces of otherwise quite different texture. . . . The net effect is to make the figures look as if they are encased in membranes of diaphanous organza of relative degrees of fineness and translucency.[7]

For Kemp, all of this amounts to a sense of impropriety, even insubordination, on the part of the engraver. William Ivins also writes about moiré as disregarding or neglecting the representational task at hand: for him, "the moiré of engraved lines" amounts to a "forgetfulness of the picture."[8]

Whatever their personal views on the matter, both Kemp and Ivins recognize the power of moiré to disrupt forces of disciplined, rational control from within: diaphanous and decadent effects, "openly paraded," erupt from a series of sharp linear patterns that are supposed to hold an image steady through reproduction. Moiré is related to decadence, luxury, and distraction (even "forgetfulness"), and can be understood as contaminating the proper focus on reproduction and subject matter. And the interference of textile values — the meshiness and messiness of fabric — is always at issue. These are just two of the reasons that there is a very strong potential to study the moiré effect as a "queering" of print.

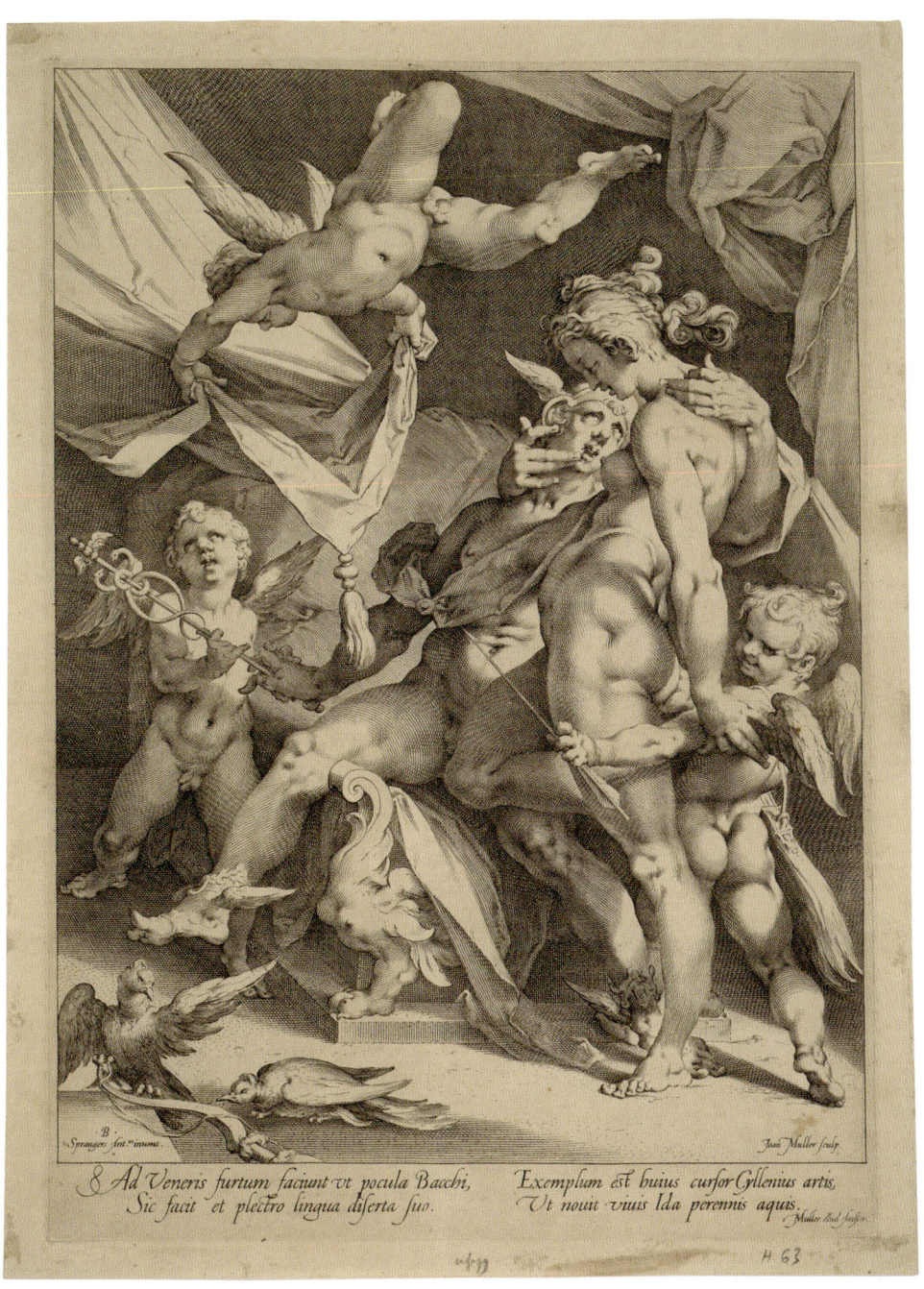

Jan Harmensz Muller, after Bartholomaeus Spranger, *Venus and Mercury*, c. 1600. Engraving on laid paper. National Gallery of Art, Washington, DC. Gift of Ruth Cole Kainen.

What we'll see is that this disruptive power can be, and has been, used critically in modern and contemporary art. Let's pivot now from early line engraving to more recent reproduction technologies. As discussed in chapter 4, the nineteenth and twentieth centuries saw the rise of two new print technologies that transformed the reproduction and dissemination of images: the halftone and the screenprint. Remember that both of these techniques sit close to the world of textiles and weaving that is so central to the history of moiré and interference effects: screenprinting literally uses a textile as the matrix, and the halftone process involves filtering information through a mesh-like veil — although it uses light passing through a grating rather than ink through an actual textile.[9]

With the advent of the halftone and the screenprint, moiré was suddenly everywhere, because they translated all images into a regular, periodic structure, and because they involved transparency, which increased opportunities for layering and superimposition. This may seem strange — these print technologies, with their perfectly regular grids, seem very far removed from the charming old world of watered silk or sixteenth-century line engraving. But, of course, this is the paradox of moiré: it is precisely because of the unrelenting rationality of these image-processing systems that moiré is produced by them. The halftone and the screenprint are the great accelerators of moiré, inviting or enrolling it into the image world at an unprecedented scale. Indeed it became difficult to keep moiré away. Moiré is everywhere in twentieth-century technical literature on printing. And the technical literature reads like a horror story: moiré lurks everywhere, waiting to break out and ruin print jobs. A monstrous, irrational enemy, ready to strike at any time.

Screenprinting manuals are especially Gothic in this respect, especially when discussing the screenprinting of halftones, a process that requires the assembly of two patterned structures: the mesh of the screen and the mesh of the halftone itself. Reading through technical manuals, one is struck by both the ubiquity and the unpredictability of the moiré threat. Moiré can be generated by choosing a twill weave rather than a plain weave screen mesh, or by choosing a screen mesh resolution that is too close to the resolution of the halftone. It can be caused by the artwork itself ("someone in the photograph wearing a tweed jacket is the classic example"), by a screen that is not properly tensioned in its frame and thus sags slightly, by the angle at which the halftone dots line up with mesh threads on the screen, or from the interaction between the halftone pattern and the topography of the surface of the paper or fabric onto which it is being printed. As the commercial printer Bill Stephens puts it: "Moiré is unpredictable. Unfortunately, it often doesn't show up until you're actually looking at a final print."[10]

In many mechanical print processes, moiré is actually unavoidable, and all that one can do is minimize its effects. The halftone color separations that sit

FIG. 5.10
CMYK halftone rosettes.

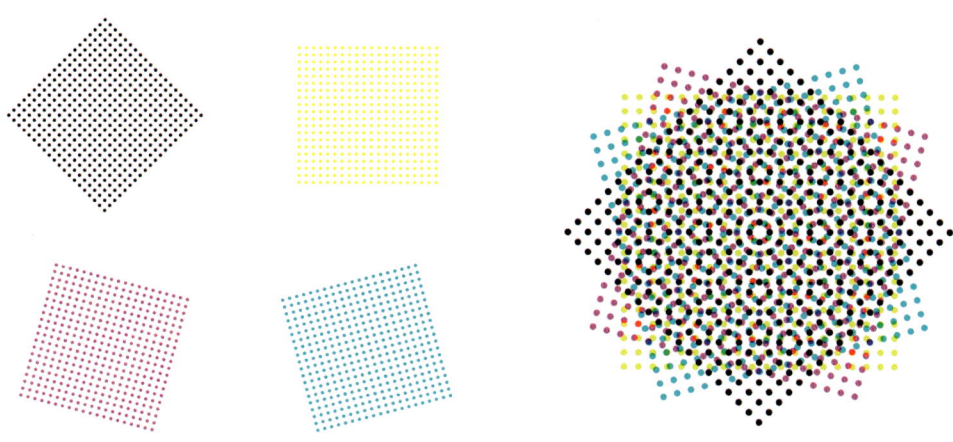

behind most printed color photographs are the best example. As we saw in the chapter on color separation, color printing involves breaking down the original image into four color-separated halftone matrices, then recombining them on a single sheet of paper to reconstitute the image as a print. But this recombination requires that four different periodic patterns be layered on top of each other, and that is impossible to do without generating moiré. Printers must use a formula of offsetting the screens at the proper screen angles to keep the arrays from lining up too closely, but patterning cannot be avoided. Color halftone separations organize themselves into moiré patterns known as rosettes, and they can be reduced but not eliminated (FIG. 5.10).[11]

In short, moiré is what happens when screens and grids and nets and weaves are allowed the power of assembly, and since the twentieth century, information has increasingly been carried by media that rely on different combinations of these mesh-like structures. And while I will not be directly addressing the videographic, telegraphic, or digital life of moiré in this chapter, it is obvious to all of us that this phenomenon continues to inform the transfer of images. Indeed, it is on our screens that most of us encounter moiré, especially (as I have discovered while studying prints) when we are looking at prints on our screens. The regular structures of the print (as in the precisely rendered

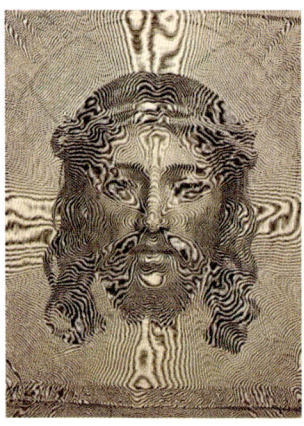 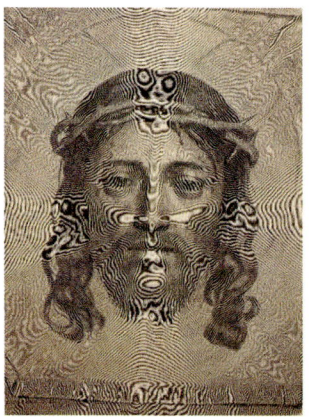 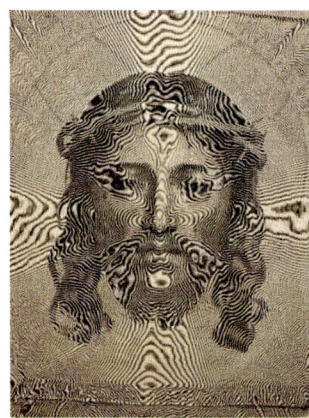

FIG. 5.11
Claude Mellan, *The Sudarium of Saint Veronica*, 1649, as it appeared on three different occasions in a MacBook Pro finder window. See also fig. 1.2.

spiral line that Claude Mellan used to engrave his Sudarium) flare into moiré when they meet the regular structures of our scanners and monitors (FIG. 5.11). Here too we are confronted with the odd doubleness of moiré. On the one hand, we associate it with contemporary digital transmission modalities — utterly rationalized, gridded bits of information passed between advanced devices. But on the other hand, it evokes the primordial world of miracles, water, wood, and silk.

It was in Pop Art of the 1960s that we can see the moiré effect being cultivated again in the same way that it was in early modern line engraving. The most prominent artists associated with Pop had worked directly with commercial print technologies. They tended to be interested in showing and exploring the effects of different kinds of systems meeting, clashing, or interfering. It is in the broad orbit of Pop Art that we find the moiré effect doing its most interesting and consequential work in the period.

Sigmar Polke's *Freundinnen* (FIG. 5.12) and James Rosenquist's *Circles of Confusion* (FIG. 5.13) are just two of many works I could illustrate here to exemplify the prominent role that the moiré effect played in painting as well as print in this period (Gerhard Richter, Ed Ruscha, and Roy Lichtenstein also experimented extensively with interference effects).[12] Polke, in Germany, was known for his "Rasterbilder" (raster pictures): in terms that evoke the capacity of

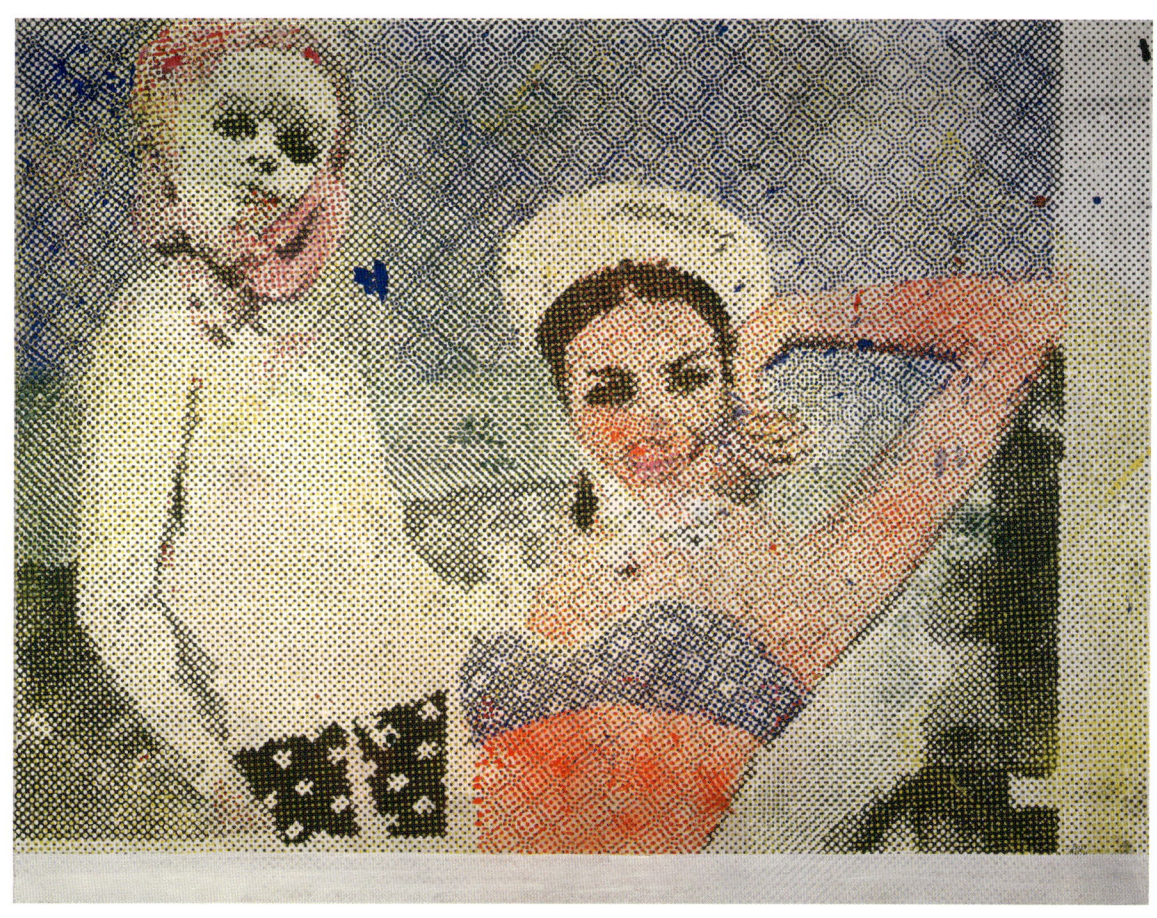

Sigmar Polke, *Freundinnen*, 1965–66. Dispersion paint
on canvas. Estate of Sigmar Polke/ARS/VG Bild-Kunst.

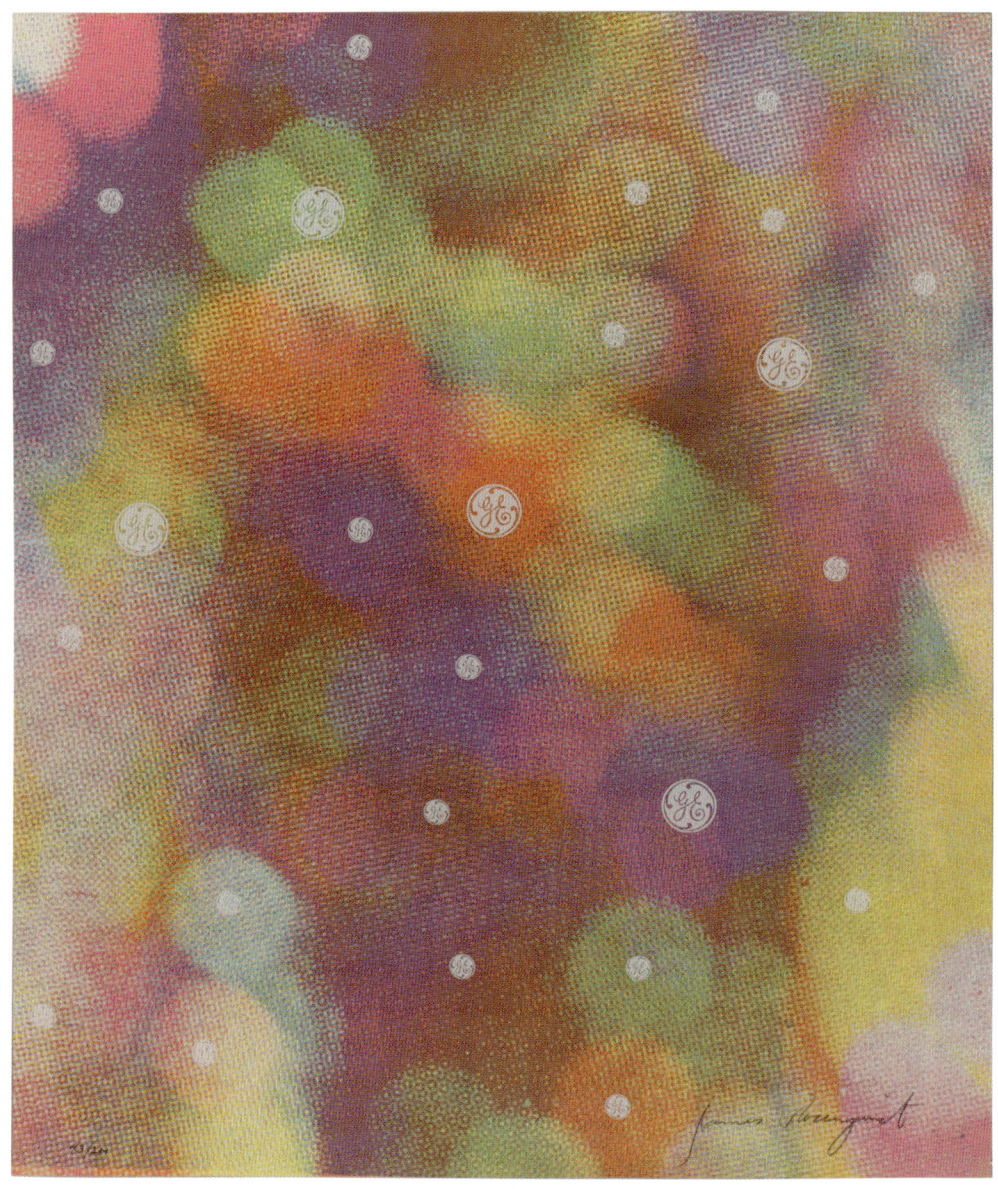

James Rosenquist, *Circles of Confusion*, 1965. Screenprint on paper.
Harvard Art Museums/Fogg Museum, Cambridge, MA. Gift of
Suzanne and Gerald Labiner.

interference effects to shuttle between rationality and ambiguity, he had this to say about his cultivation of moiré:

> For me, the raster is a system, a principle, a method, a structure. It divides, disperses, arranges and makes everything the same. I take pleasure in the blurriness caused by the enlargement, the movement of the dots, the shift between recognizability and non-recognizability of the motif, the indecisiveness and ambiguity of the situation, its remaining open.[13]

Rosenquist's color screenprint features a field of blurry colors interspersed with the General Electric logo. As he explained, "circles of confusion" is the term for colored dappling that appears in the viewfinder when you look through a camera lens into the sun. But it also applies beautifully to the shimmering pattern of the colors as the halftone screens interfere with each other, generating large rosettes that Rosenquist has invited to erupt throughout the image.

Note that in both of these works, the moiré effect conspicuously besets photographs, or photographic phenomena. I want to pause for a moment here to consider what this means for our understanding of photography in the twentieth century, particularly in terms of its relation to print. Our view of photography as *the* mass medium of the twentieth century is so thoroughly entrenched that it is hard to think otherwise, but these interference patterns compel us to recognize that much of the logic of twentieth-century photography is arguably, in the last analysis, really a logic of print. We say that the images in twentieth-century newspapers, magazines, posters, broadsides, billboards, and art history books are "photographs." But they are not, or not only, photographs. This is one of the most important points I want to make in this book, even if it doesn't have an entire chapter devoted to it. These images are printed matter, ink on paper, made on printing presses. They may once have been, say, gelatin silver photographs, but they were translated into a halftone raster and transformed into binary printable surfaces, then printed. You can't efficiently mass produce a photograph with a negative, an enlarger, and a tray of chemicals. You need to print it in ink on paper.

You can't generate the moiré effect from photographs or 35 mm slides. Moiré depends on and announces the gridded patterns of the mass-printed image. What we call "photography" here lives in the world of frequencies generated by the mesh structure of the halftone print. Much of the art and visual culture that we think about in photographic terms has hitched a ride on the back of print, like the Apollo Lunar Module on its rocket and boosters, and if we are truly to understand the mediascape of modern and contemporary culture (particularly its transformations in the digital age) we must work harder to understand the way the logics of print lie beneath it.

In the Polke and Rosenquist works, the moiré patterns manifest themselves at a large scale as they ripple across the surface of the work—a much larger scale than the nearly invisible underlying halftone or screen patterns that generate them. Polke and Rosenquist were seizing on a property of moiré that I will call "critical magnification." This magnification had only recently been systematically explored by scientists and was just beginning to emerge in the popular scientific literature. Gerald Oster, a polymer scientist, biophysicist, and artist, was a pioneering researcher on the moiré effect. A 1963 article he coauthored with Yasunori Nishijima on moiré patterns in *Scientific American* summarized the history of moiré (including its operation in Japanese silks) and explored its instrumental possibilities (see fig. 5.5). In the article, Oster and Nishijima seize upon moiré patterns as powerful magnification devices. They show, counterintuitively, that the smaller the misalignment between two patterns, the greater the magnification. One of their primary examples involves the printing of halftones: if two halftone screens are offset by a large angle of rotation (as at upper left), the moiré is difficult to perceive. But as the two are rotated so that the screens are only slightly misaligned, the magnification of the dot pattern increases drastically (as at lower right). In other words, the smaller the angle of misalignment, the larger the pattern (FIG. 5.14).[14]

Oster and Nishijima suggested many ways of using this magnification technique to test and analyze objects for strain or imperfection. For example, they suggested that by interposing a screen in front of an object printed with a grid, the resulting moiré can project the effects of tiny cracks, strains, deformations, or imperfections at a scale orders of magnitude larger than the primary phenomena. Moiré is a way of testing for flaws and revealing imperfections or misalignments. In particular, it's a tool for revealing things that cannot be seen with the naked eye. In a sense, it is a kind of truth-telling; even today, it is still used for various kinds of document verification and anticounterfeiting.[15]

With Pop Art, the "invisible" image structures of the screenprint mesh and the halftone began to occupy the space of the fine arts. And the way Pop artists drew attention to these structures can perhaps now be understood as a parallel form of critical magnification, forcing these media up into awareness in the same way that scientists thought that the moiré effect could be used to make visible the structural features of patterns below the threshold of vision. Pop Art's rhetoric of critical magnification had many forms. The outsized photoscreens, conspicuous Ben Day dots, intentional silkscreen mishaps, and glaring misregistration of so many Pop works were fundamentally about demonstrating that there were powerful forces pulsing invisibly below the visual threshold in the world of printed

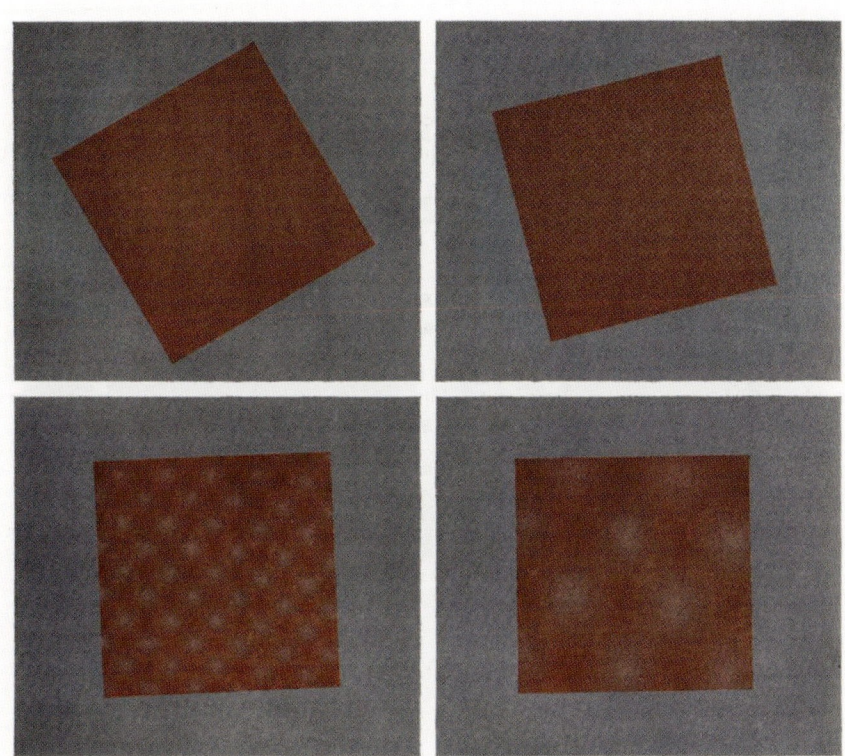

MOIRÉ MAGNIFICATION can be simply demonstrated with the aid of "halftone" screens used by engravers. The photographs in this magazine are reproduced with a screen containing 110 dots to the inch. If two such screens are to be printed one atop the other without producing a moiré, they must intersect at a fairly large angle (*top left*). If the angle is reduced, a moiré of small dots appears (*top right*). As the angle is reduced further, the dot pattern moiré is increasingly magnified, as shown in the two bottom figures.

FIG. 5.14

Illustration from Gerald Oster and Yasunori Nishijima, "Moiré Patterns," *Scientific American* 208, no. 5 (1963): 62.

media. In this context, the adoption of moiré among artists is especially interesting. At precisely the moment when the workings of media retreat beneath the level of perception, moiré becomes articulable as a phenomenon that pulls media syntax back up to the scale of the body, to the level of human perception. And it is a phenomenon in which the media does this to itself.

For an example of how this critical magnification has broad social and political implications, let's return to Rosenquist's *Circles of Confusion*. For Rosenquist, the oversized interference patterns on the print, though referring to halftone rosettes, also suggest other confusions besetting Americans in the Vietnam War era, particularly the increasingly pernicious overlapping of the consumer and the military sectors (FIG. 5.15). Famously, General Electric was a defense contractor as well as a maker of light bulbs. In 1963–64, it reported the highest profits from munitions of any US company. In essence, Rosenquist uses the emergent properties of moiré, a pattern made by the combination of other patterns, to evoke the uncertain new threat of the military industrial complex, an emergent social, political, and economic form that was looming up from the combination of consumer and military systems. The critical moiré here suggests a special form of detective work that reveals hidden aggregations and alliances of power.[16]

The revelatory potential of interference patterns is also explored in a project that Rauschenberg completed soon after finishing his *Stoned Moon* series. In 1970, Rauschenberg went to Malibu while his New York studio was undergoing repair after a fire. At the time, he was struggling to process the enormity of the violence and social unrest that made up the daily news cycle. He was looking for a change of perspective; according to one report, he initially had "the intention of doing a large, peaceful watercolor."[17] He did not produce a watercolor, and he did not produce anything remotely peaceful, but through his engagement with the moiré effect, he did make something with a liquid, wavelike structure. He created a set of collages from articles and advertisements clipped from multiple newspapers from January and February of 1970. These were then transferred to screens and printed in an edition of one hundred (FIG. 5.16). The series was titled *Surface Series* from *Currents*—no doubt playing on the double meaning of the term "currents." The series is printed from three halftone screens, each in one of three inks: white, flat black, and gloss black. But instead of taking the necessary steps to avoid the inevitable moiré effect from the overlay of the color separations, Rauschenberg instead courted it by rotating one of the screens slightly off-register. The entire set of prints is overtaken by moiré. What is the function of the moiré here? Why does Rauschenberg deliberately cultivate it in this current-events context?[18]

I think it is a way of expressing precisely the sense of anxiety and anticipation caused by these events, especially the sense that one can perceive but not

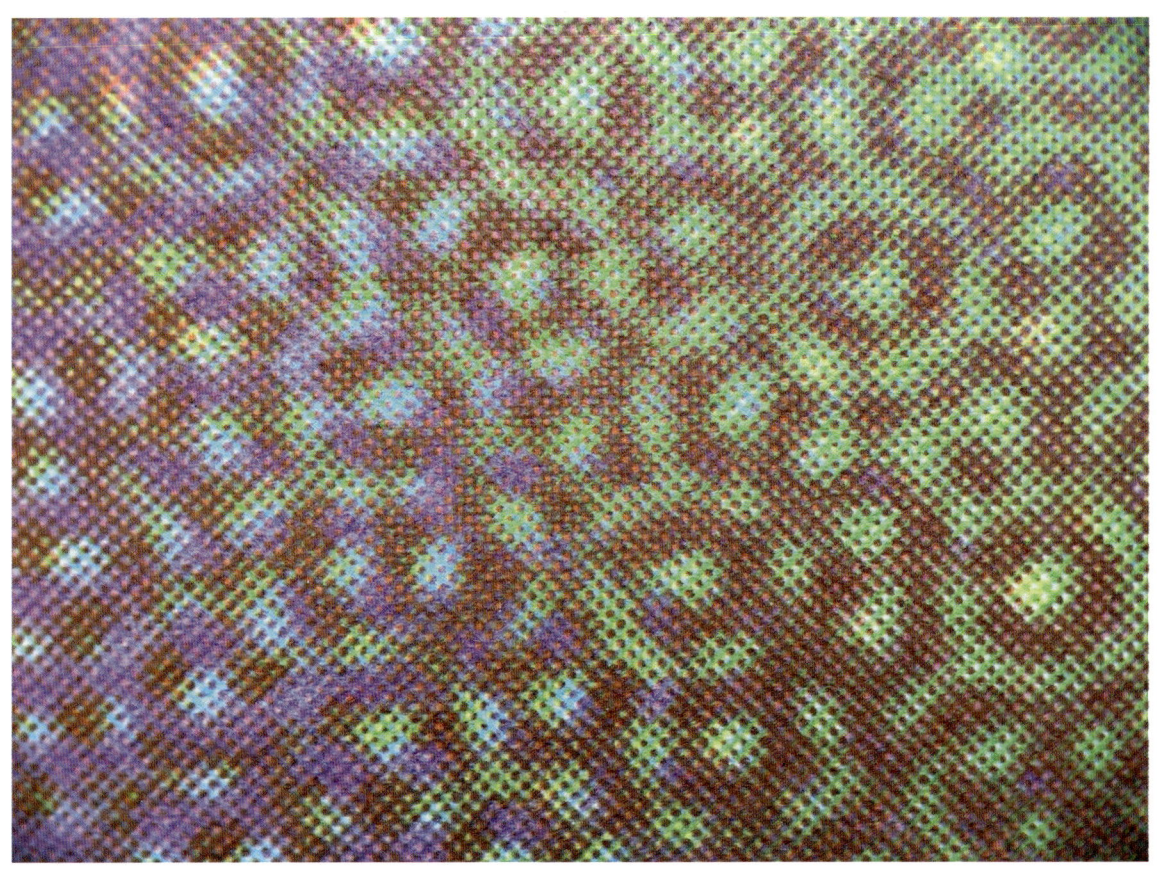

James Rosenquist, *Circles of Confusion* (detail), 1965. Screenprint
on paper. Harvard Art Museums/Fogg Museum, Cambridge, MA.
Gift of Suzanne and Gerald Labiner.

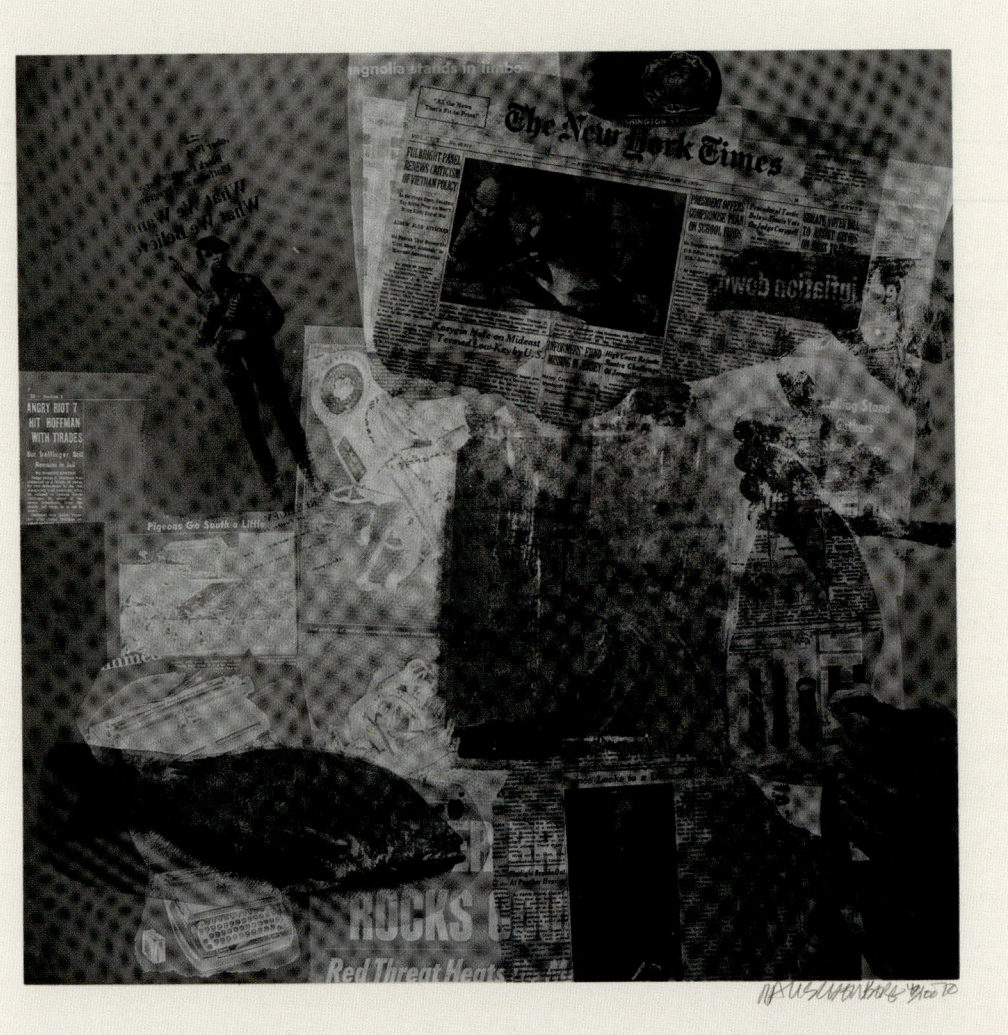

FIG. 5.16
Robert Rauschenberg, *Surface Series 37*, from *Currents*,
1970. Screenprint on paper. The Museum of Modern Art,
New York. Gift of the artist. 307.2008.2.

fully understand their meaning. The interference patterns coursing across the prints, as if hovering above them, seem to convey the shock of these events, as well as recognize that they form some kind of a pattern. That pattern is not resolved, not clear, not visible except as something like a vibration or a noise. It's as if Rauschenberg is giving us an image not so much of a pile of overlapping newspapers but a series of overlapping radio transmissions that are out of phase, and he keeps attempting to tune into the pattern so that it will make sense. I use the term "tune in" and the notion of vibration and noise quite intentionally. There is a powerful link between the interference patterns on these prints and the space of sound and sound media. Moiré is described with terms like frequency, beat, interference, amplitude, and periodicity—as is sound. Rauschenberg was a connoisseur of radio and broadcasting, which informs his work here, but the link between sound and moiré is much older than radio—here, we might recall Muller's use of moiré to evoke sound in the engraving *Arion on a Dolphin* (see fig. 5.8).

If we jump ahead about forty years to a work by Glenn Ligon, we can see this connection between sound, repetition, violence, and interference at work in an explicit way in the present (FIG. 5.17). And since Ligon has played such a large part throughout this book, we can also begin to see how interference effects link up with other printerly themes. This is a work from his series titled *Come Out*. The images are made from layered, overlapping screenprints that repeat the phrase "come out to show them." The phrase is from a sound recording of the 1964 testimony of Daniel Hamm, one of six young men wrongly charged with murder and beaten by police. Denied medical treatment because he had no open wounds to prove his ordeal, he resorted to opening his own bruises so that the blood would come out (to show them).[19]

In layering and repeating the text, Ligon also nods to the musician Steve Reich's 1966 sound work "Come Out," which looped that recording through thirteen minutes of phase shifts and channel splits, releasing Hamm's voice into a multidimensional aural space. There is so much here about body and voice and testimony and endless cycles of racial violence. Is there a way out of these cycles, these structures? Ligon is not clear on this, but he does suggest that these events generate emergent patterns that are difficult to comprehend but need to be perceived. The grid meshes of the screenprint matrix here produce moiré patterns that loom up like bruises or smoke or some extradimensional shadow code that cannot yet be read. They suggest something (to borrow a term from the recording) coming out of the surface. What is that thing? It is not in focus. But it seems to suggest a premonition of a different way of figuring, of imagining, trying to burst out of the trap of the surface, and perhaps of history.

The moiré effect is a form of energy transformation. Like the coal dust in Ligon's paintings in the previous chapter (a form of coal waste that is especially

FIG. 5.17
Glenn Ligon, *Come Out #9*, 2015. Silkscreen on canvas on
panel. Courtesy of the artist, Hauser & Wirth, New York,
Regen Projects, Los Angeles, Thomas Dane Gallery, London,
and Galerie Chantal Crousel, Paris.

dangerous because it can suddenly ignite into a propagative explosion), moiré is a byproduct that can produce sudden, disproportionate change in an image. This is true literally as well as visually. For example, contemporary physicists are currently exploring the remarkable fact that if you stack two layers of graphene (superthin carbon sheets) at a "magic angle," the moiré effects from the interference of their atomic structures will make the material superconductive (FIG.5.18).[20] A whole subfield of "twistronics" is emerging from this realization.

Holding in suspension the issues balanced in Ligon's work — sound, smoke, and the body — I want to conclude by exploring the kind of surface and the kind of space that the moiré effect in print creates. I want to think of this as an emergent surface that evokes a material, or, to borrow Rauschenberg's term from the Apollo launch, a supersaturated space. In the 1960s and 1970s, Rauschenberg and Pop artists experimenting with moiré are doing so in an art world when various different models and philosophies of the picture plane are being hotly debated — the Renaissance windowpane picture plane, Greenberg's modernist picture plane, and especially Leo Steinberg's flatbed picture plane, an enormously productive model that was developed out of Steinberg's encounter with Rauschenberg's work, as I mentioned briefly in chapter 1.[21] But the surface beset by these eruptions of moiré does not quite fit with any one of these models. Artists cultivating the moiré effect are reaching toward a new model of spatial experience and representation. It is made by pressing layers of mediated information into contact, but it does not read as flat. But nor is it the old Renaissance picture plane illusionistic space, opening out to familiar notions of scale, proximity, or atmosphere. The autocatalytic qualities of moiré — the fact that it essentially makes itself — suggest a kind of living or responsive surface that these other models could not capture.

Robert Rauschenberg explored this notion of a live surface response in a set of prints he did in 1969 just before the moon series. *Tides*, *Drifts*, and *Gulf* are three prints that all feature iconographies of bodies and flows (FIG. 5.19). *Tides*, for example, includes a bare torso along with a fireplug, a toilet bowl, and a series of other dimly perceived body parts. The other prints are similar, including some semipornographic imagery. Here, when the photographs overlap, moiré emerges. Rauschenberg actually named these prints *Tides*, *Drifts*, and *Gulf*—watery titles all—because of the watery effect of the moiré.[22]

That this moiré erupts in a carnal context is notable. The pattern, in this realm, suggests goose bumps or blushing or other physiological forms of epidermal sensitivity. There is a libidinal quality to the emergent space suggested by this surface. It's a surface that is not like a window or a tabletop but something more like human skin or a rippling liquid. It is not unrelated to the sense of emergence from the body that we find in the bruising and bleeding in Ligon's work (but with more

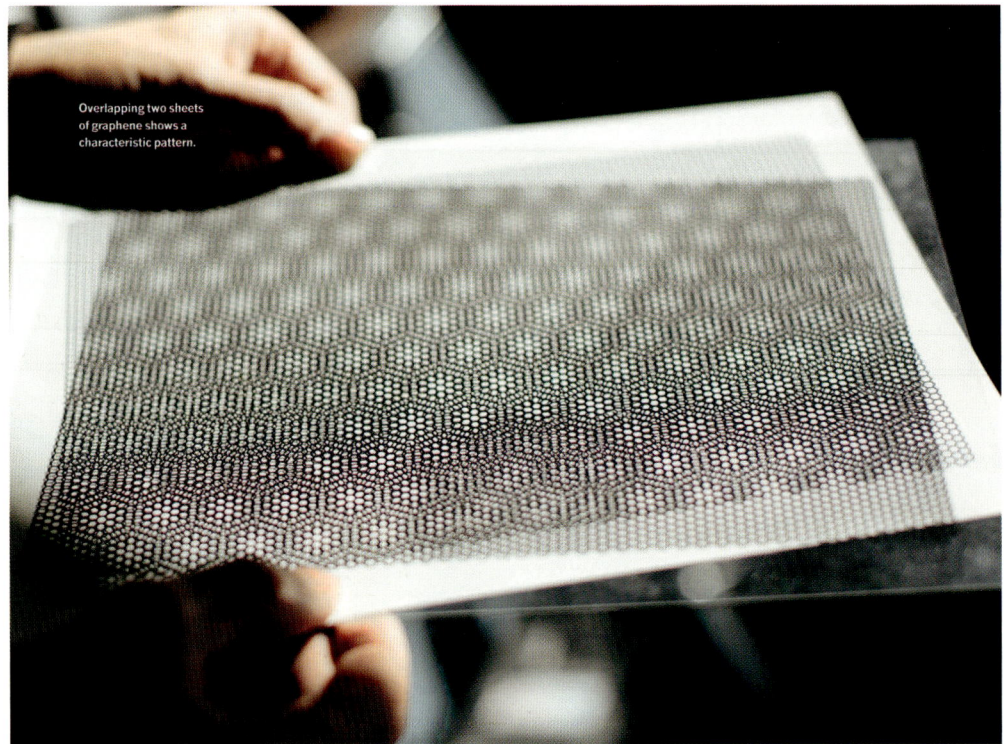

JULIETTE HALSEY FOR NATURE

SUPERCONDUCTIVITY WITH A TWIST

RESEARCHERS ARE SCRAMBLING TO UNDERSTAND CURIOUS BEHAVIOUR IN MISALIGNED STACKS OF GRAPHENE.

BY ELIZABETH GIBNEY

It was the closest that physicist Pablo Jarillo-Herrero had ever come to being a rock star. When he stood up in March to give a talk in Los Angeles, California, he saw scientists packed into every nook of the meeting room. The organizers of the American Physical Society conference had to stream the session to a huge adjacent space, where a standing-room-only crowd had gathered. "I knew we had something very important," he says, "but that was pretty crazy."

The throngs of physicists had come to hear how Jarillo-Herrero's team at the Massachusetts Institute of Technology (MIT) in Cambridge had unearthed exotic behaviour in single-atom-thick layers of carbon, known as graphene. Researchers already knew that this wonder material can conduct electricity at ultra-high speed. But the MIT team had taken a giant leap by turning graphene into a superconductor: a material that allows electricity to flow without resistance. They achieved that feat by placing one sheet of graphene over another, rotating the other sheet to a special orientation, or 'magic angle', and cooling the ensemble to a fraction of a degree above absolute zero. That twist radically changed the bilayer's properties — turning

FIG. 5.18

Elizabeth Gibney, "Superconductivity with a Twist," *Nature* 565 (January 3, 2019): 15.

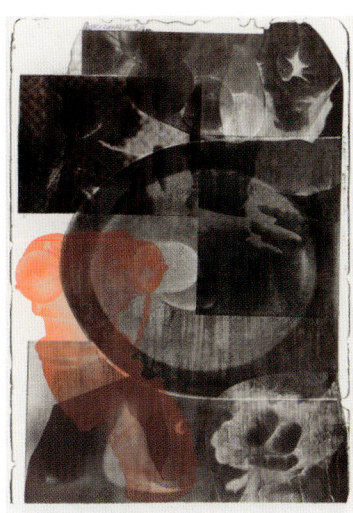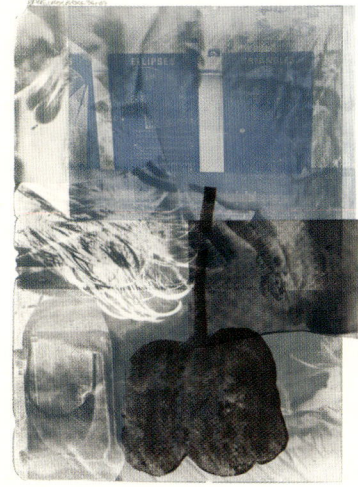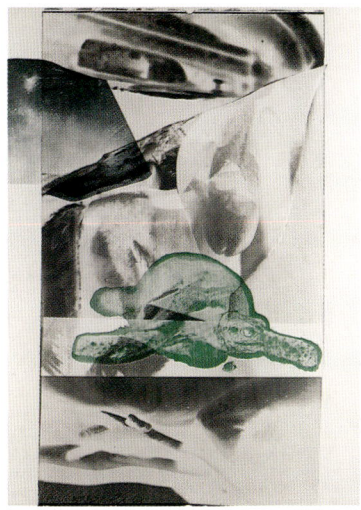

FIG. 5.19

Robert Rauschenberg, *Tides*, 1969. Color lithograph on German
Copperplate wove paper. National Gallery of Art, Washington, DC.
Gift of the Woodward Foundation, Washington, DC.

Robert Rauschenberg, *Drifts*, 1969. Color lithograph on German
Copperplate wove paper. National Gallery of Art, Washington, DC.
Gift of the Woodward Foundation, Washington, DC.

Robert Rauschenberg, *Gulf*, 1969. Lithograph. Rauschenberg
Foundation, New York.

positive connotations). It has a strongly organic quality despite its technological origins. Rauschenberg's *Stoned Moon* series, in a different way, also explores this notion of a space defined and perceived by pressure and contact, a space known by and to the body, rather than standard illusionism that relies on the appeal to the eye. The *Stoned Moon* prints are full of rippling, pulsing surfaces that are occupied by astronauts as if to convey their corporeal experience of off-world space.

I don't think it's an accident that Rauschenberg confronted moiré so intensively in the context of working through the moon launch. Both the moon launch and the moiré effect enter into uncharted forms of spatial experience. The moiré gives the sense that images are beginning to pull away from the gravitational constraints of the Western illusionistic tradition, that they are being launched. Where are they going? What will the space built and experienced by these media look like? Like the extraorbital space between the earth and the moon, it is still a real space, but it will not have the familiar coordinates. The spaces of the Apollo program were largely mapped by radio and other nonoptical wavelengths. They were mapped by sound and pressure, and were experienced in a profoundly defamiliarizing way by the bodies of astronauts. These were zero-gravity spaces reached by thrust, sound, shock, and the propagation of waves. Like the paradox Rauschenberg evoked by using massive lithographic stones as the medium for understanding a zero-gravity mission, the space program raised the problem of imagining a kind of space that was both tactile and expansive, a zone in which mass and space related to each other in ways that could not be approximated in traditional illusionism.

Traditional illusionism in many ways conflicts with print. Every illusionistic print is riven by a conflict between the spaces it evokes visually and the blind crush of pressure that creates it. Moiré, for Rauschenberg, is one way of suggesting a solution to this problem. It emerges from layers of contact, so it is a more palpable kind of space than you could get with something like optical perspective. And moiré is not merely an illusion—it is as real as something can be in our current epistemology. It is created by the literal overlap of structures out of phase (if it were an illusion, you would be hard-pressed to use it to generate superconductivity). And in its relation to sound, to smoke, to shock, to waves of pressure propagating through particles in the air, it evokes ways of connecting, bridging, and defining space that rely on continuities of physical causality.

Following on this, I want to back up from the technical specificities of moiré and think in a more expansive sense about how all this might help us think about print in general. In the first chapter of this book, I insisted on print as a realm of direct physical contact and pressure. Like Rauschenberg's stony orbits, the challenge is to imagine ways that print can evoke and refer to a space beyond its surface, enter as it were a new dimension, without discarding the peculiar physicality of its origins. The challenge is to find a way of rendering the air while always keeping in literal contact with the ground.

Let's return to one of the very first prints I showed in this book—John Cage's *Eninka No. 29*, which was made by setting paper on fire on the press bed and then putting it out by sending it under the roller; extinguishing it, in other words, by printing it (see fig. 1.5). Cage worked from an understanding of smoke as a physical, particulate form of space and light, as something that stretches into wispy patterns that connect the flat space of the press with the air above it. His prints in smoke render that spatiality, that third dimension, in material form. The turbulent patterns of smoke link the flatbed picture plane to the space above materially, rather than illusionistically. Two forms of pressure are brought together here: the variations in air pressure generated by the heat of the fire, which direct the soot into its stochastic patterns, and the pressure of the press, which fixes them at a particular moment of their stochastic evolution. This is "atmospheric perspective" made literal through an atmospheric process. The print is a kind of flat air sculpture or space sculpture, using the dynamics of pressure as the chisel or the mold to produce an imprint on a surface.

The dynamics of moiré I have been tracing link up with all other such artistic practices, practices that attempt to map or evoke spatial experience through matter or pressure rather than optics, whether or not they are technically prints. Often these dynamics are most developed in the work of artists who work with and through sound. Sound, after all, is a picture of space made through beats and frequencies in which one space is connected to another at a distance through pressure and material vibration. Following are two contemporary examples, by artists who are not overtly interested in moiré, or even in print as such, but whose work combines sound, smoke, space, and the body in ways that parallel the impact of interference effects in print.

Consider this print from a portfolio by Dario Robleto, made with Island Press in St. Louis in 2017 (FIG. 5.20). The waveforms you see here and throughout the portfolio come from nineteenth-century cardiographic and pulse recordings, some of the first images made from the living interior of the body. They are palpated images, created by making contact with sounds and vibrations coursing through the flesh, then up and out through the surface of the skin. Many of these waveforms were recorded by scientists tracking responses to sensory or emotional stimuli, and thus they recall the emergent, responsive surface of the skin in Rauschenberg's print. And like the moiré effect, these pulse waves opened a strange new space that could be known only through beats and frequencies transmitted through physical contact.[23]

To make the smoky ground in the prints, Robleto turned each impression upside down and hand-sooted it from below with a burning candle

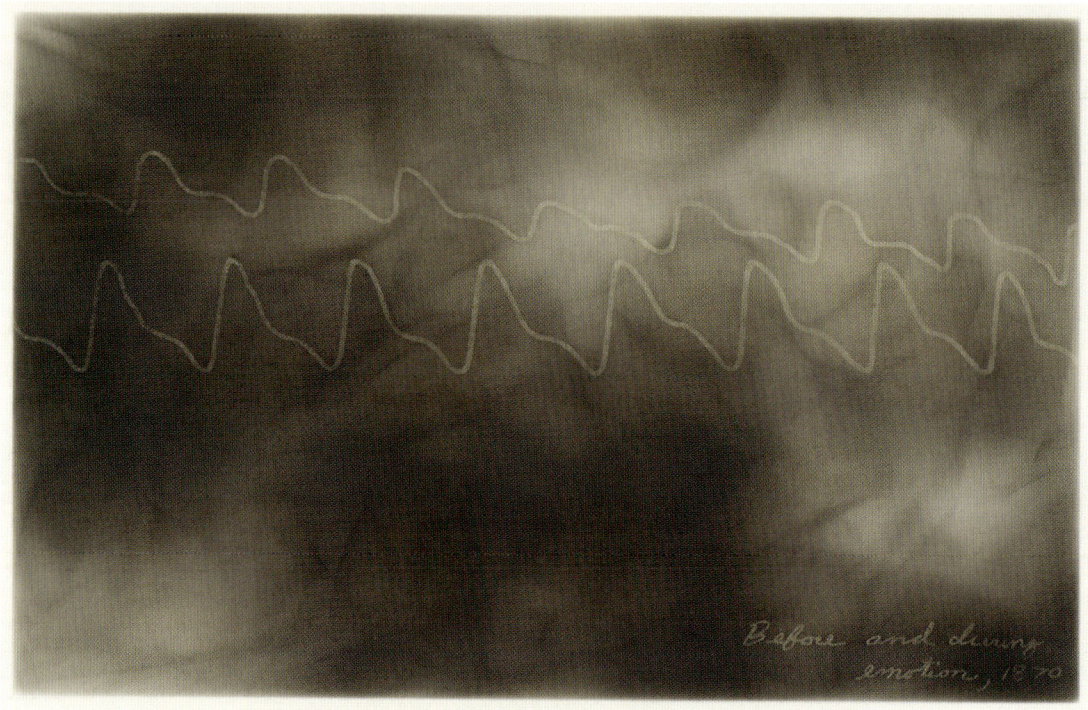

FIG. 5.20

Dario Robleto, *Before and during emotion, 1870*, from *The First Time,
The Heart (A Portrait of Life 1854–1913)*, 2017. Photolithograph
with transparent base ink on hand-flamed and sooted paper; image
brushed with lithotine and lifted from soot, fused in a mild solution
of shellac and denatured alcohol. Harvard Art Museums/Fogg
Museum, Cambridge, MA. Margaret Fisher Fund.

held about an inch away from the surface. This calls back to the original scientific imaging process, in which the vibrations emanating from the body were recorded with instruments that inscribed the delicate waveform into a micro-thin layer of soot on candle-smoked paper. It also recalls Cage's fire prints in the way it evokes space materially. The space seems vast and cosmic, but there is no emptiness here. Sound and smoke cannot travel in a vacuum. This is a space made by material propagation. We might think of Robleto's smoke as a a form of ink that registers its own movement through time and space. But more than anything, in its insistence on palpability, its origins in *feeling* the pulse, it calls back to the way that the space of printed images is built on touch. Like the rubbings I discussed in chapter 1, these prints evoke a space mapped first by touch and only later given over to the eye. And when properly tuned, the contact at the heart of print can pull open forms of space that capture experience beyond the visual realm.

Cai Guo-Qiang is a Chinese artist who works with gunpowder and explosives. This huge drawing—I'd, of course, call it a print—is made by setting off an array of contained explosions; it's a series of fossilized fireworks (FIG. 5.21). He makes works like this by placing high-quality handmade Japanese paper on the floor, arranging gunpowder and fuses over it, covering it with another sheet of paper, then cardboard and stones to weigh it down, and then setting off the explosion. The blast is barely contained by the stones, which leap up from the force of the explosion. (And with those leaping stones, we might see it as an upside-down version of Rauschenberg's stone launch lithographs.)[24]

Evoking the long history of gunpowder and fireworks, both invented in China, the artist describes his work as being based in alchemy and Taoism combined with modern physics. And it also recalls a lot of what I've already said about printmaking—the image is made in a dark, closed space, under pressure, which allows for the transfer of marks between surfaces. After the explosion, Cai usually exhibits both the upper and lower paper surfaces, so that the reversal and reflection of the imprint remains active, composing the final work. The final work may evoke a certain atmospheric visuality, but it was made by blind contact, by shock waves carrying matter and sound. It's an image imprinted by reverberation, as if it were a rubbing of a disturbance in the air. And as in Cage's and Robleto's smoke imprints, it gives us an experience of light, but only in a material, particulate way, as a sooty aftereffect.

And then there is the suddenness of it, the triggering, the way the combination or layering of materials on a flat surface suddenly erupts into something else altogether, something not yet mapped or mappable. Like the way the experience of space transforms in the vicinity of a rocket launch or a war zone, or the way the overlapping repetition of Daniel Hamm's voice billows up and out into

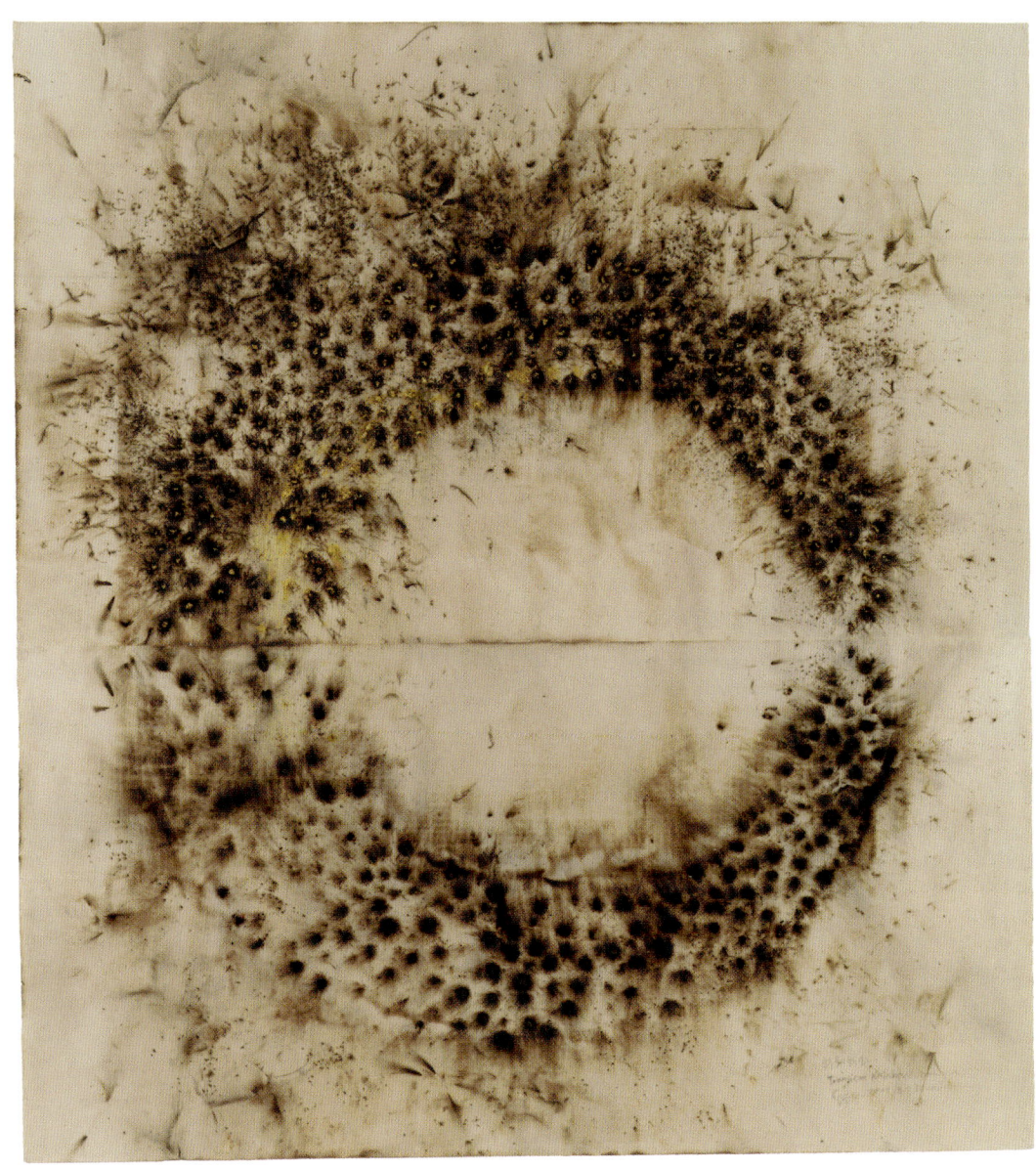

FIG. 5.21
Cai Guo-Qiang, *Drawing for Transient Rainbow*, August 2003.
Gunpowder on two sheets of paper. The Museum of Modern Art,
New York. Gift of Clarissa Alcock Bronfman. 508.2004.a–b.

an explosive pattern of transformational anguish, or the way a goosebump or shimmer or shiver suddenly erupts from a cross-historical crosshatch. Print is a palpation of images, and as it passes them from hand to hand, those contacts have a way of interfering with our habitual ways of being and knowing.

ALIENATION

We finish with alienation. This keyword is not quite like the others, in that it does not appear to capture a physical process—does not appear to get us down into the thick immediacy of printmaking. If anything, it's the opposite—alienation evokes detachment, absence, and loss. I've chosen it because, here at the end of this book about contact, I want to be sure that we're not losing sight of the essential paradox of print: namely, that it is about the pull as well as the press. Printmaking is an embodied art of pressing, touching, and rolling, but also, at the same time and in the same motion, it is an art of letting go.

In this chapter, I'll try to work into this paradox by exploring some of the strange things that happen to time and labor in printmaking. The main question will be: How do we think about the relationship between the all the time and skill that comes together in the making of a print, and the time of the image it generates? (Or: where does all the time go?) We'll explore the misregistration of time in print, especially in terms of the conflicts and convergences between "slow" and "fast" media that are frequently staged in contemporary printmaking.

If you look up the word "alienation" in the dictionary, you'll find that it has three general meanings in the English language, all of which will be coming into play in this discussion. First, it refers to estrangement or the state of being estranged. Second, in legal discourse, it refers to the action of transferring ownership of something from one party to another. Both of these movements, estrangement and transfer, are part of the physical and philosophical adventure of printing. The third meaning is more of a stretch: alienation also denotes mental instability or delirium. I'm not going to be taking this one too literally. I'm not going to say that printmaking is a form of delirium in the pathological sense. But I do want to suggest that printmaking destabilizes us, takes us out of our so-called right minds, and requires us to think differently.

Something that's been hinted at but not overtly expressed in this book is the way printmaking complicates the idea that there can be a direct, plenary relationship between the individual artist and the final work of art. Despite all of the objections that have been raised to this model in art history and theory over the years, it's difficult to do away with the notion that the work and the artist are somehow synonymous, or that the work holds some indivisible kernel of the artist's full and immediate presence that was there in the moment of creation.

Whatever we might say about this model of presence in relation to media like painting or sculpture, it inevitably and definitively collapses as soon as an artist walks into a print studio. It's not that the artist suddenly dissolves away or becomes irrelevant, but instead that they must open themselves out to a series of transfers and estrangements, must accept a certain distributed identity and all the vulnerability that comes with that as the very condition of being there. Consider the fate of an artist's gesture in the production of a print. That gesture is displaced. Even if the artist draws or etches or engraves directly on the matrix, every gesture, every mark, will then be transferred somewhere else. As the art historian Charles Haxthausen put it, "The object to which one does things — the surface on which one makes marks — is not the work of art; the work of art is but an imprint of that surface."[1]

For the same reason, the gesture is deferred. Not only is the mark made elsewhere, but it is made elsewhere at a later time. The time spent on the original gesture does not produce the final imprint; for that, the artist must wait. Jasper Johns described the print shop rhythm of doing and waiting this way: "You do something. Then you have to wait for processing. Then you do something else. And then you wait — like a long-distance call through an overseas operator."[2] And that is because the gesture is delegated. The artist usually relies on the skills of other people in the room, the printers, to move that mark over as faithfully as possible. Even if the artist is working alone in the studio, they still must rely on the press, that alien machine, to make the final, culminating mark on the printing surface.

In most print processes, as we have seen, the gesture is reversed, taken out of the artist's habitual orientation or handedness and returned to them backward, in a defamiliarized way. The gesture is obscured: when the print is actually printed, the mark made, it occurs in an invisible space squeezed between the press and the bed. The artist cannot even witness the delegation of their own gesture. And finally the gesture is often disjointed, as we saw in the chapter on color separation. What would be a fluid or spontaneous series of gestures in painting gets divided up into an array of programmed steps and pieces that bear little relation to the form or logic of the artist's original mark. So: displaced, deferred, delegated, reversed, obscured, disjointed. All forms of printmaking repeatedly stage and enforce the breakup of the artist's continuous presence. They all interrupt the direct connection between the mind and the hand, between the artist and the work. Printmaking is a series of artistic transfers.

Printmaking is a form of distributed intelligence, distributed artistry, and distributed time. The print is suspended among people and materials and machines, and it is suspended in time between moments of action and moments of waiting, moments of call and moments of response, moments of memory and moments of futurity. For most of this chapter, I'll be exploring these dynamics by focusing on a print process that I haven't yet addressed in detail: relief printing. Relief printing produces a particular kind of alienation — a particular estrangement of labor and transfer of time. I'll review it historically, and then look at what it might mean to revive this particular kind of temporal misalignment in the present, by looking closely at the work of contemporary German artist Christiane Baumgartner (FIG. 6.1).

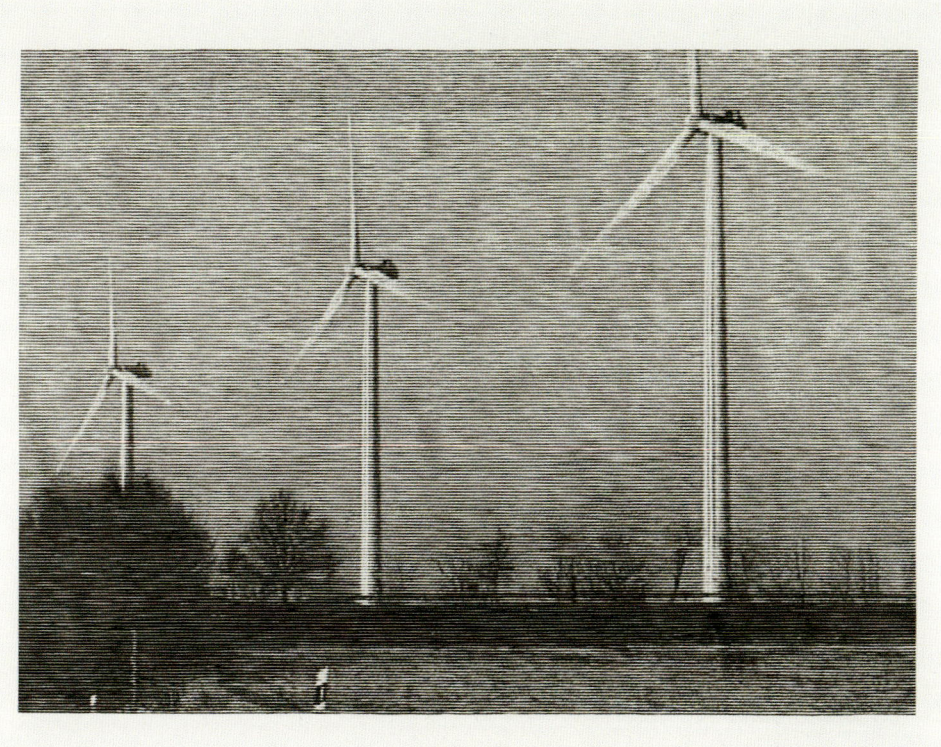

FIG. 6.1
Christiane Baumgartner, *Windräder II*, 2003. Woodcut on Kozo paper. Harvard
Art Museums/Fogg Museum, Cambridge, MA. Margaret Fisher Fund.

Relief printing is defined by a matrix in which the ink sits on surfaces raised above the plane (see fig. 0.5). Relief printing with wood matrices was the first form of printing to be developed on a large scale. As with many modern technologies, the Chinese were the first to develop it. Woodcut was in use by 1420 in Europe, and for centuries it became the preferred vehicle for the widespread dissemination of visual information. Copperplate engraving was also practiced by the fifteenth century, but woodcut was faster and less expensive to print than engraving. And one of its greatest advantages was that it could be combined easily with text. Letterpress is also a relief technology, so you can assemble a woodcut block or blocks together with movable type, and print the whole page together on the same press. Together, woodcut and letterpress generated the early modern information age.

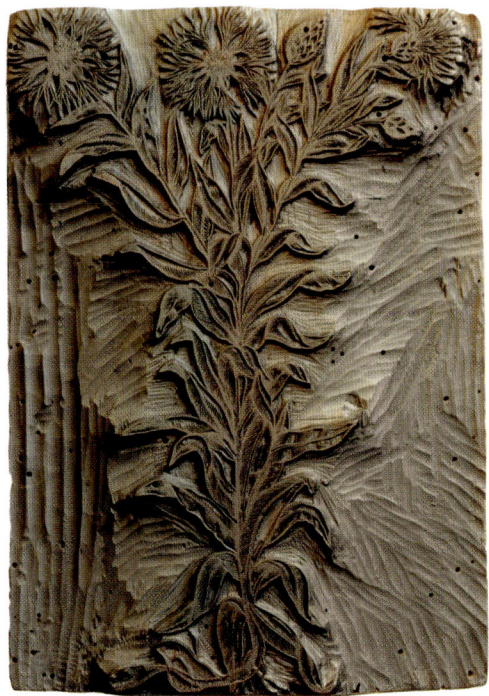
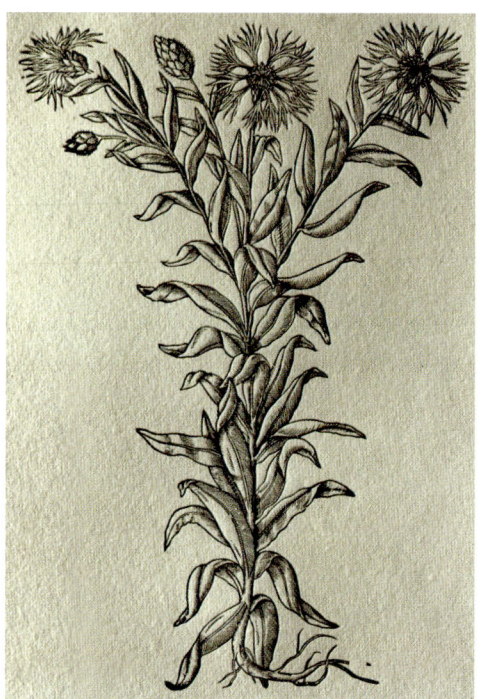

FIG. 6.2
Pietro Andrea Mattioli, woodblock for *Cyanus maior (cornflower)*, 1562.
Carved woodblock.

Pietro Andrea Mattioli (artist); I. M. Imprimit (printer), *Cyanus maior
(cornflower)*, printed 1989. Woodcut on handmade paper. I. M. Imprimit.

The topography of a relief printing block can be quite elaborate.
Woodcut printing is classified, of course, as printing, but it is also a form of sculpture. As Richard Benson has noted, a woodcut is in the last analysis "a visual record of a carving."[3] Consider this sixteenth-century woodblock for a botanical illustration, and a print made from it (FIG. 6.2). This is a highly deliberate relief carving, a fully three-dimensional sculpture that is designed not only to transfer an image from the top surfaces of the design, but also to withstand the effects of pressure. Note that the most deeply carved areas of the block are in the areas that correspond to large swaths of blank space in the print. Expanses of blank space must be deeply gouged on the block, because under the pressure of printing, the paper has a way of buckling into these open areas and picking up any accidental ink that might be lodged there. The block has to be deep enough so that the paper can't get down into the bottom. Notice too that all of the delicate standing lines

cluster together at close range. None of them sit off by themselves in an otherwise empty space, because such a lone line, unsupported by neighbors, might break under the pressure of the press.

But the most important thing to note here is that there is an inverse relationship between the labor expended on the carving of the block and the density of marks on the print. The places where the most muscle has been expended on the block are the places that are blank or empty on the print. The printmaker's efforts on the block are expended in order to disappear. The time spent carving is not directly registered in ink on the print. John Evelyn, in his seventeenth-century printing treatise *Sculptura*, described relief cutting as "a graving much more difficult; because all the work is to be abated and cut hollow, which is to appear white; so that (by a seeming paradox) as the matter diminishes the form increases, and one wastes the other grows perfect."[4]

I'll return to this fundamental inversion of labor in relief printing, but want to move forward a couple centuries to the 1800s, in the midst of the industrial revolution, when some tweaks to traditional woodcut technique allowed relief printing to power another surge in mass media: the rise of illustrated periodicals, books, and the visual news industry. This updated form of woodcut was called "wood engraving." It used boxwood, a much harder, more dense, slow-growing wood with very tight growth rings. This meant that the engraver could render finer, more detailed marks; in fact, the same tools used to engrave copperplates could be used on boxwood. Moreover, the blocks were sawn across rather than with the grain. This meant that the engraver cut into the endgrain of the wood, which reduced the interference of the grain patterns and made the block much stronger and more durable in the press, allowing for higher print runs.[5]

Because it could be combined with letterpress, because it was a high-output printing matrix, and because it allowed such finely detailed engraving, wood engraving lent itself extremely well to the transfer of detailed pictorial information. Wood engraving permitted delicate crosshatches and other Victorian finesses to attain the status of industrial mass media. As an 1884 article in *The Art Amateur* put it, wood engraving was "the process by means of which by far the greatest amount of knowledge, verbal or pictorial, is communicated to the world."[6] Some remarkable reproductive images were generated in wood all the way up to the turn of the twentieth century. Here is a print by Timothy Cole, an important American wood engraver who specialized in the reproduction of paintings (FIG. 6.3); Cole and others like him were instrumental in the birth of narrative art history, because their work made high-quality reproductions of historic art easier to publish with type.[7] Often wood engravings were made after photographs as well: in fact, wood engraving was the most powerful mode of disseminating photographic information in the nineteenth century.

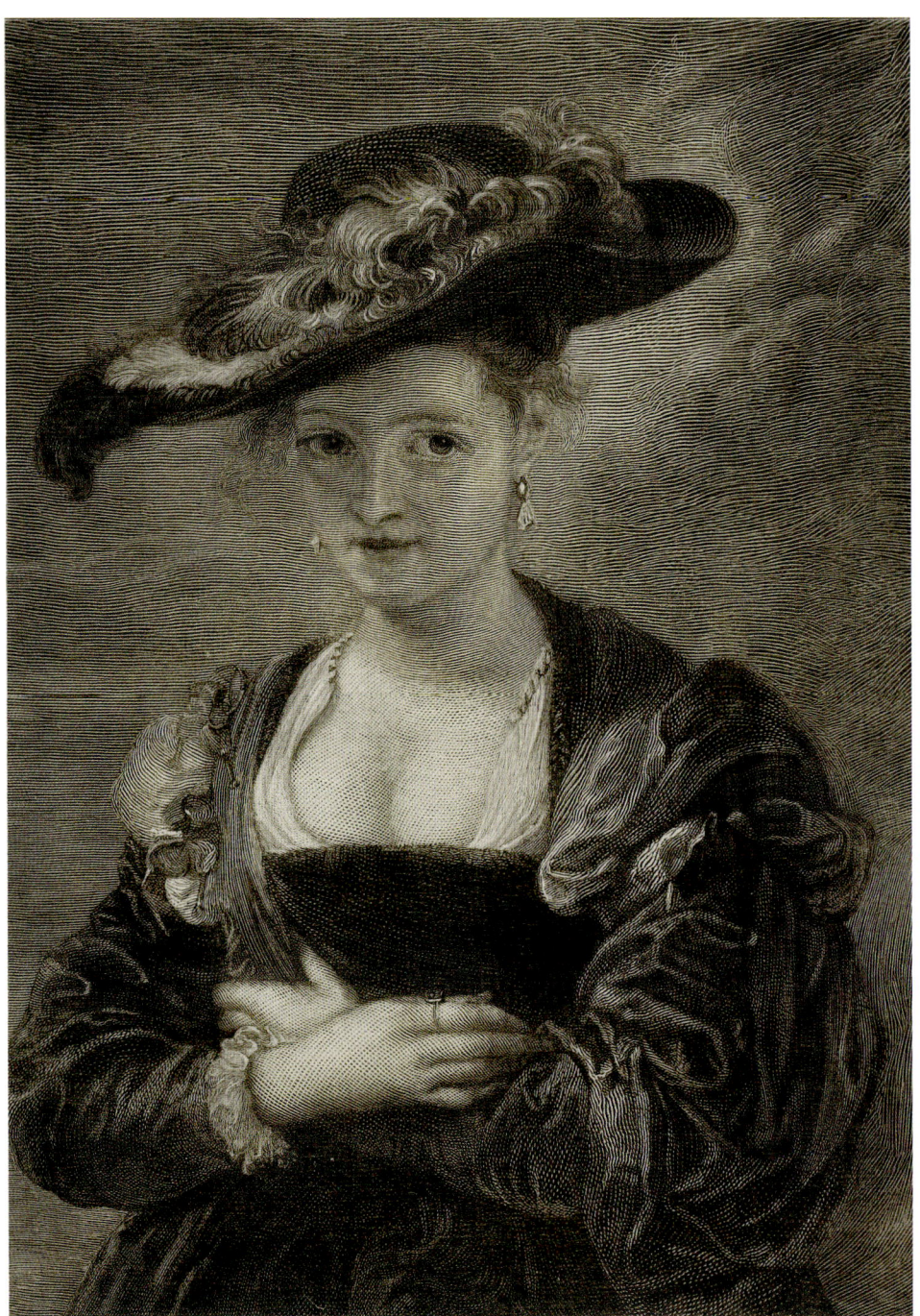

FIG. 6.3
Timothy Cole, after Peter Paul Rubens, *Chapeau de paille*,
nineteenth to twentieth century. Wood engraving, Harvard Art
Museums/Fogg Museum. John Witt Randall Fund.

Remember that photography is not in itself a mass medium in the nineteenth century. It's not feasible to make more than a few hundred copies of a photograph in a darkroom with an enlarger. If a photograph is going to enter the orbit of mass distribution it needs to be translated into a printable surface — preferably a relief surface, so that it can be printed (ideally in a steam press) along with the text. During the heyday of wood engraving, photographs would often be projected onto a boxwood block treated with a photosensitive emulsion. But then that photo-block would have to be hand-carved; the engraver would dig right into the photographic image in order to convey a printable topography to the surface. This is a rare example of a woodblock that was prepared for carving but for some reason was not actually carved (FIG. 6.4). Late nineteenth-century periodical archives are full of what are essentially exquisitely carved photographs like this. But also exquisitely carved drawings, paintings, diagrams — in the nineteenth century, almost every kind of image had to, as it were, go through the wood.[8]

This required a lot of work. A single image was labor enough, but imagine the scale of the operation for a publication like *Harper's Weekly* or *The Illustrated London News*. Tight publication deadlines and ravenous demand for illustrations meant that millions upon millions of images like these had to be carved out of boxwood blocks. Unsurprisingly, a culture of industrial production emerged around wood engraving. There was division of labor among illustrators and an assembly-line approach to completing the work. Any way you slice it, relief printing required a lot of time. So it's worth returning, then, to the paradoxical character of this work, the way the labor of relief printing does not actually show up on the page.[9]

Consider the way a simple line is made in a medium like drawing. It's pretty straightforward. An artist picks up a pen or pencil and makes a gesture — and voilà! There it is on the paper: a mark, a line. The time and effort that went into making that line is directly captured by the line itself. A line is also relatively straightforward to produce in planographic or intaglio printing. In copperplate engraving, for example, the engraver pushes a line into the copper. The incision on the plate will be filled with ink and printed, and although there are many intermediary steps involved, at least the engraver's line eventually translates directly to the mark on the final print. But to make a line in a woodcut or wood engraving, the printmaker does not cut a line; the printmaker has to chip around a line-shaped area, leaving the line standing. The unworked surface of the block becomes the marked surface of the print, and vice versa. This basic inversion at the core of cutting in relief has huge implications, one of which is the disruption or inversion of the relationship between labor and result. The artist's efforts are actively reversed, expended only in order to disappear. The finished print is made

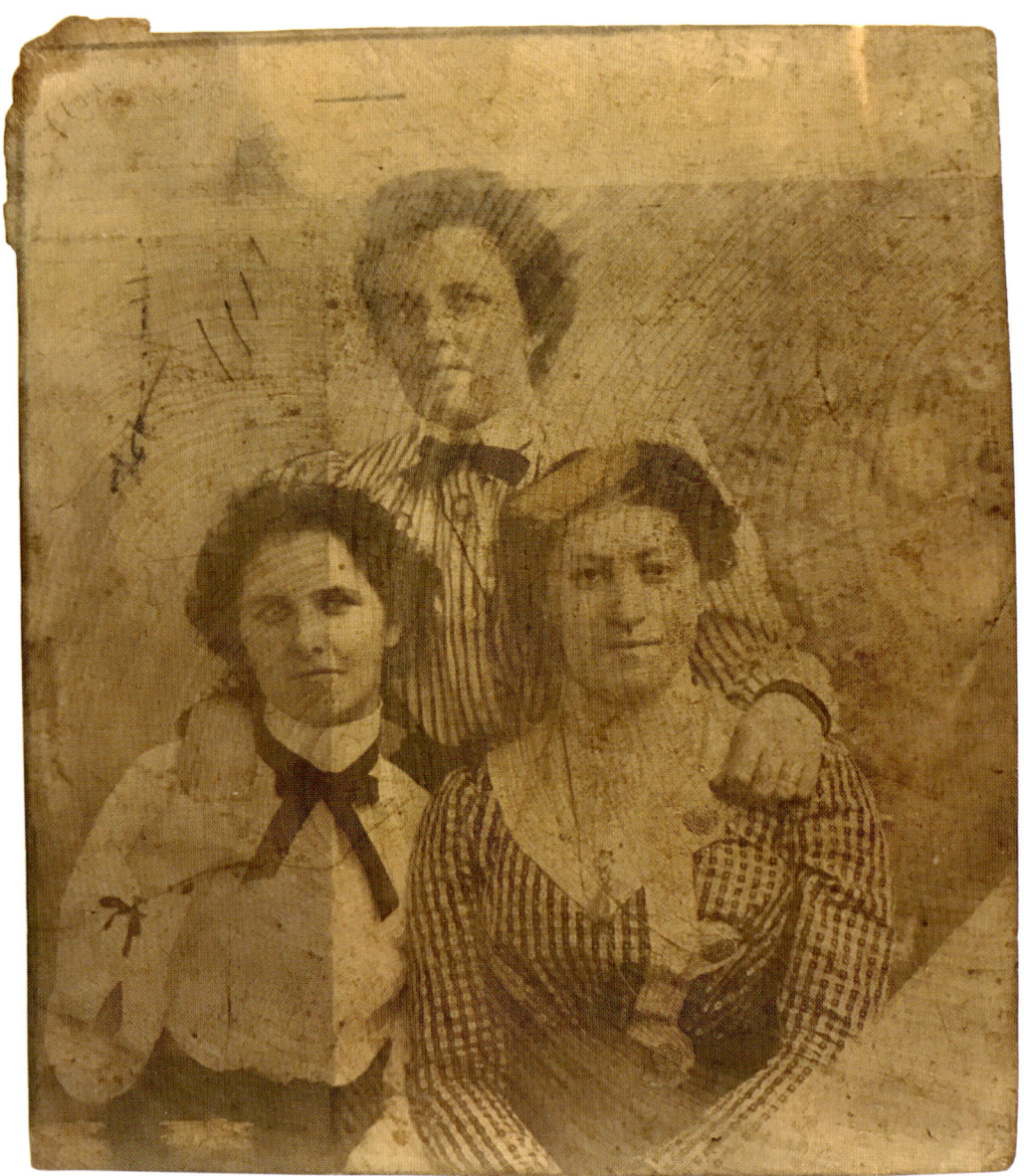

FIG. 6.4
Uncarved photo woodblock, c. late nineteenth century.
Collection of the author.

by the areas the artist does not touch. What does this mean for the millions upon millions of woodcuts and wood engravings circulating throughout the world for centuries? It means that not a single inked mark on any of them was directly carved by a human being.

In the late nineteenth century, as wood engraving became industrialized, writers on art and printmaking began to think seriously about this bizarre situation. And it began to be loosely associated with other forms of the alienation of labor that were being theorized around capitalism. The most insistent and loquacious commentary on this came from the British writer and critic John Ruskin. In his *Ariadne Florentina*, a published series of six lectures on engraving given at Oxford in the 1870s, he made a vivid accounting of the labor economy of wood engraving. The most interesting illustration in that essay is this one—a schematic image of a crosshatch pattern (FIG. 6.5). Crosshatching is a standard way of creating tone out of line in the graphic arts, particularly drawing and engraving. The illustration represents a two-inch square section of a shadow in the background of a scene that had been published in the popular British humor periodical *Punch* (FIG. 6.6). Focusing in on this small section of shadow, Ruskin talked about the difference between the time it took to draw the source image and the time it took for the wood engraver to translate that drawing to the box-wood block.

Ruskin pointed out that whereas the artist drawing the source image was able to make the crosshatch pattern in just a few strokes of the pencil, the wood engraver that transferred the image to the block had to leave all these lines standing, which means he had to chip out all of the interstices between the lines, making thousands of cuts in order to do so. In this "wanton and gratuitous" crosshatching:

> There are about thirty of these columns, with thirty-five interstices each: approximately, 1,050—certainly not fewer—interstices to be deliberately cut clear, to get that two inches square of shadow. Now calculate—or think enough to feel the impossibility of calculating—the number of woodcuts used daily for our popular prints, and how many men are day and night cutting 1,050 holes to the square inch, as the occupation of their manly life. And Mrs. Beecher Stowe and the North Americans fancy they have abolished slavery![10]

Ruskin is so disturbed by the time expended on the holes between crosshatches that he goes so far as to associate relief cutting with slavery—an exaggeration with which we cannot be comfortable, but it is not irrelevant that he is willing to associate wood engraving with the ultimate form of alienated labor.

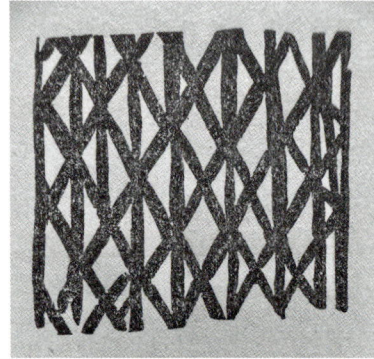

FIG. 6.5
Illustration from John Ruskin, *Ariadne Florentina: Six Lectures on Wood and Metal Engraving* (New York: Charles E. Merrill, 1892).

FIG. 6.6
John Tenniel, *"Astraea Redux!!,"* from *Punch* (November 2, 1872).

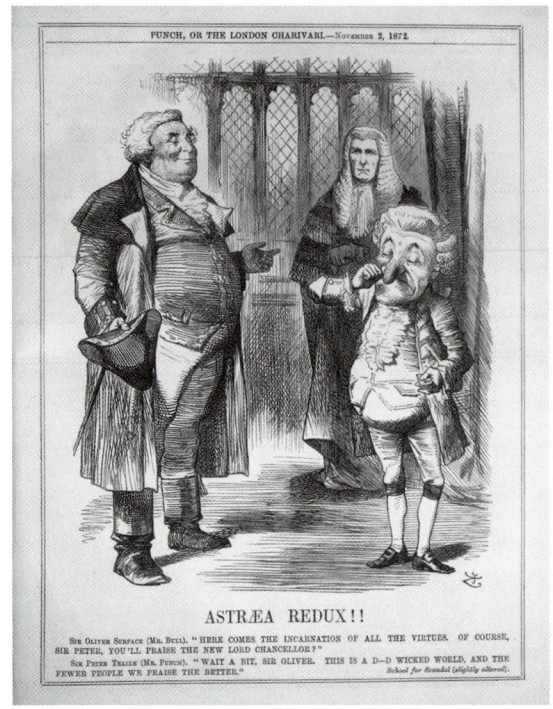

W. J. Linton, an expatriate British engraver working in the United States and probably the most influential writer on wood engraving after Ruskin, simplified the motif but maintained its essential spirit in his manual (FIG. 6.7). He reproduced the simplest possible crosshatch, really more of a tic-tac-toe pattern, and demonstrated that whereas a draftsman could produce this pattern in four strokes, it would take a wood engraver between thirty-two and thirty-six cuts in order to chip away the external edges and interstitial spaces and leave the pattern standing in relief. (Ironically, that is exactly what it took to produce the illustration that illustrates this in his own book, which is a wood engraving set into the text.)[11]

These crosshatching diagrams became something of a standard motif in period commentaries on relief printing. They are diagrams of loss and frustration. For Ruskin, they are a cage; trapping artisanal time and effort behind bars where it wastes away on shadows. For Linton, they suggest (as an incipient grid) the spaces of measurement and accounting, but all that they measure is an account out of balance, where work is expended but never recuperated.

The extremity of the situation in industrial relief printing brought out a truth that is always latent in print but not always so obvious: in printmaking,

FIG. 6.7
Illustration from W. J. Linton, *Wood Engraving: A Manual of Instruction* (London: G. Bell, 1884).

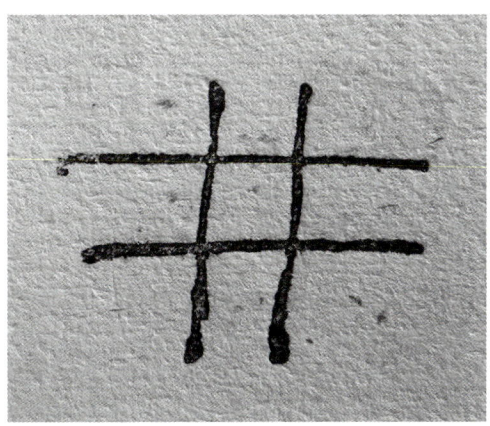

time is always out of joint. Here, in these crosshatches, the alienation of labor and time is a form of failed synchronization. The time it takes to draw the image does not equal the time it takes to carve it. The time it takes to carve the image does not equal the time it takes to consume it.

The time it takes to carve the image is even disjointed within each chip or gouge. Ruskin worried about the speed with which these carvings had to be made, and wrote about his fear that the hand of the artist, the woodcarver, would get ahead of the mind, and the necessary self-conscious presence of the artist would be dismantled. As he said, the hand must be "continually receiving and obeying orders" from the mind as it carves.[12] "The moment it [the hand] moves independently . . . and performs some habitual dexterity of its own, it is base."[13] He goes on to define this habitual dexterity as so wrong as to be sinister—playing on the moral connotations of the dexter/sinister left/right opposition to drive home his point about the dangers of unchecked manual skill.[14] How is one to tell whether one's lines are deliberate instead of habitual, dexter instead of sinister? Ruskin calibrates these qualities in terms of speed. The faster the work, the less chance the mind has to control muscular action. "When the hand moves at the rate of ten lines in a second, it is indeed under the government of the muscles of the wrist and shoulder; but it cannot possibly be under the complete government of the brains."[15] In order to ensure the government of the brains, Ruskin sets a speed limit on carving that he doesn't precisely stipulate but that seems to lie somewhere between two or three seconds for each short line or chip.

So printmaking in this situation is riven throughout by alienation: of the hand from the mind, the draughtsman from the carver, the carver from the print. And this is all expressed in terms of asynchrony, of the loss of some ideal experience of presence and possession of the image.

For all its centrality to the rise of a new culture of mass images, by the mid-1890s, wood engraving as a mass medium was essentially over. What killed it was the development of the halftone, which was able to translate photographs and artwork directly into textured printing surfaces without the sculptural mediation of the wood carver. Turning a flat, continuous-tone image into a printable relief surface — the goal of so much technical energy in these years — could now be done much more quickly, without the peculiar imbalances of the wood engraving process. In 1870, one hundred percent of the images illustrated in the *Illustrated London News* were wood engravings. In 1900, it was two percent.[16]

Relief printing in wood as a mode of mass reproduction virtually disappeared from the scene thereafter. Woodcut did play a role in modern art, but it was as far removed from the industrial wood engraving model as it could possibly be. Instead, it took the form of the rough, often primitivizing, materially immediate forms that emerged in and around German Expressionism. Expressionist woodcuts by artists like Emil Nolde and Ernst Ludwig Kirchner attempted to purvey an image of raw immediacy and presence, with every mark expressing itself and recording each gesture of the carver (FIG. 6.8). These are images that attempt to preserve printmaking as a project of presence; a project of immediacy instead of intermediacy. They can never fully succeed, of course, but they try to minimize the alienation that is at their core as prints.

As we have entered the twenty-first century and the digital age, confronted as we are with so many new difficulties synchronizing ourselves to each other and to our media environments, relief printing from wood is suddenly in a prime position to negotiate these experiences. The German artist Christiane Baumgartner has reengaged with the temporal misalignments of relief cutting, resuscitating its asynchronies and its structure of misregistered labor, all in order to comment on contemporary life.

Baumgartner was born in 1967 in Leipzig, which was part of East Germany at the time, and educated at the Academy for Graphic and Book Arts there. Leipzig is a city famous for its long and vibrant book printing history, and Baumgartner undertook a traditional printmaking education there, in which she spent a lot of time copying prints by Albrecht Dürer. She was thoroughly steeped

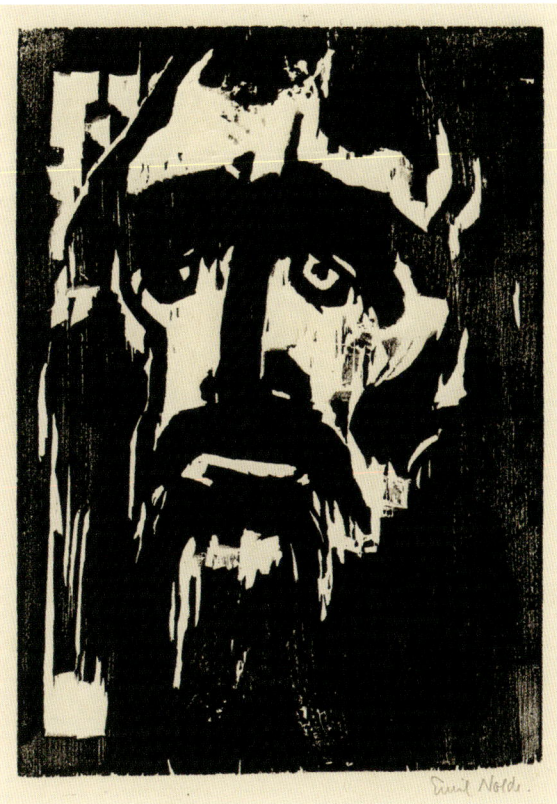

FIG. 6.8
Emil Nolde, *Prophet*, 1912. Woodcut.
National Gallery of Art, Washington,
DC. Rosenwald Collection.

in the German woodcut tradition, from Dürer to Expressionism, and then attended the Royal College of Art in London. She was admitted to the printmaking program, but once there she found herself drawn to what she called the "smooth surfaces" of contemporary media—particularly video. Baumgartner was interested in but frustrated by the distanciation inherent to video: "In a way, the video image is only a formula—it's not really there."[17] In 2000, she returned to Leipzig and began attempting to find a fusion of these two technologies. This was when she hit on the idea of carving video stills as traditional woodcuts. As she has pointed out, this allowed her to combine the earliest popular image reproduction technology (woodcut) with one of the most recent (video).[18]

Baumgartner first selects a still from thousands of video frames. She adjusts the still in Photoshop, translating it into a black-and-white horizontal raster image (this is a kind of halftone, but it's based on lines rather than dots). Then she transfers the rasterized image onto a sheet of poplar plywood and hand-carves it with an adapted cheap kitchen knife (the knife derives from her austere

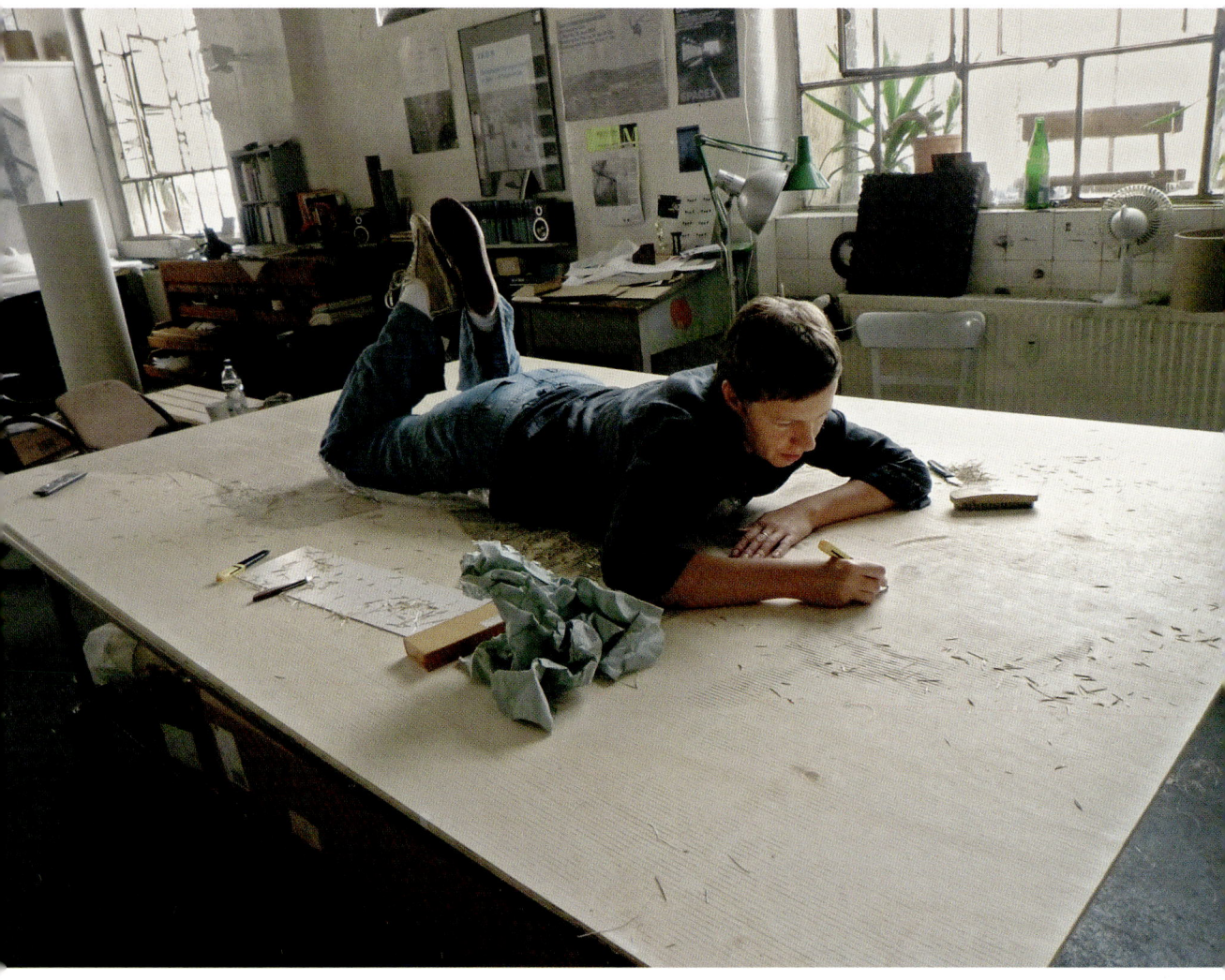

FIG. 6.9
Christiane Baumgartner working on plate for *Ladywood* in her studio in 2010.

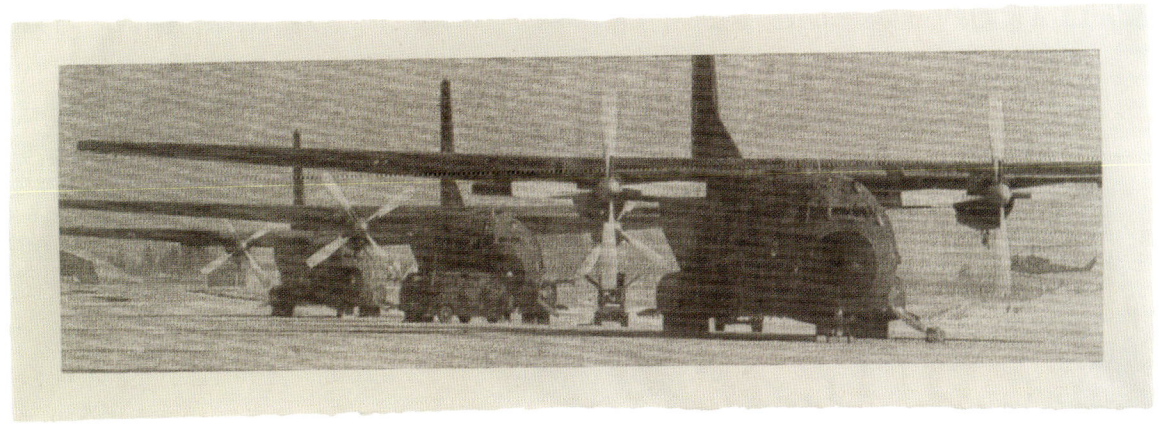

East German training—real carving tools were hard to come by, so printmakers learned to cut down and resharpen common kitchen knives) (FIG. 6.9).

After inking the blocks, she hand-prints them onto handmade kozo paper, usually in small editions of about six. She prints by rubbing the back of the paper with a standard Japanese banana leaf baren, using the edge to get more pressure. Sometimes she uses the armrest of an old armchair if she needs more pressure to print the entire sheet.[19] Her plywood matrices are generally too big for a press, and poplar is too soft for a press, so she always prints by hand. *Transall*, of 2002, is thirteen feet long and four feet high (FIG. 6.10). As Baumgartner said: "Certain images need to be big. . . . the first day [I worked on this print] I cut only three lines and at the end of the day my hands were shaking."[20]

As with *Transall*, she frequently works with images of aircraft. *Manhattan Transfer* features a shot taken of a tourist helicopter in New York (FIG. 6.11). Notice the chain link fence. And the blur of the helicopter rotor blades; her ability to evoke blur in precision-cut wood is remarkable (FIG. 6.12). She has also worked extensively in landscape imagery, and her most recent work (about which more in a moment) explores the effects of reflection, flare, glare, and scatter in sunlight.

The question one has to ask about any project like Baumgartner's is: Why? Why take a video image that was captured in an effortless microsecond and spend months carving it by hand into a sheet of plywood? Why would anyone volunteer to be a twenty-first-century woodcut new media artist? Baumgartner's work suggests that the woodcut printing process offers solutions or insights for contemporary life that are not available otherwise.

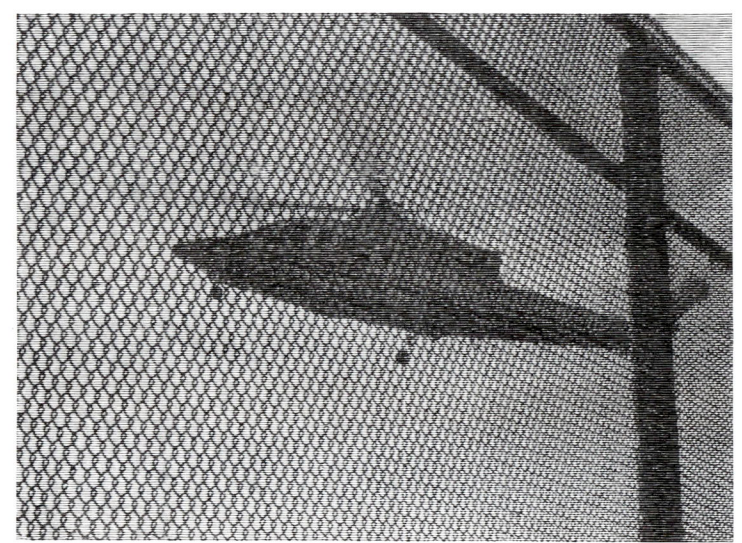

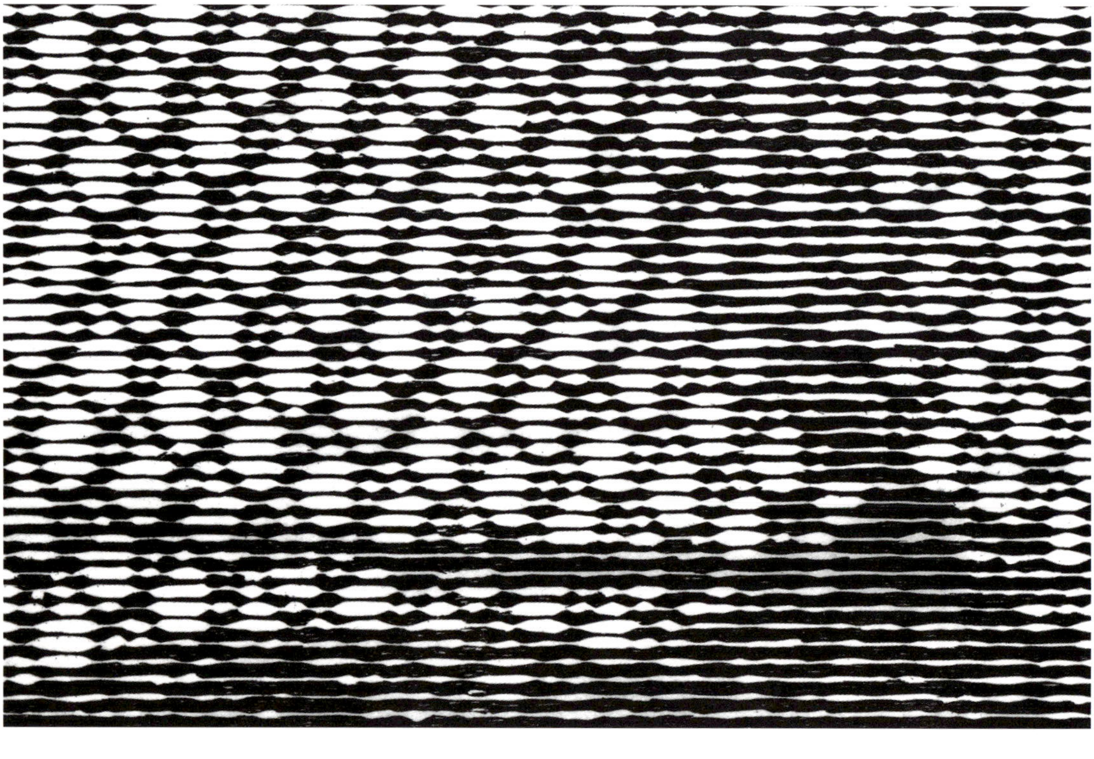

In taking up woodcut as a mode of reproducing an image captured in a faster medium, we might say that Baumgartner has willingly reentered the cage that Ruskin so vividly evoked in the nineteenth century. It is important to her to get into that space of distance, disappearance, and discomfort that Ruskin saw in crosshatch relief carving—important to occupy, to experience, the absurd imbalances of labor between capture and translation. The chain-link fence in *Manhattan Transfer* could easily join the nineteenth-century diagrams by Ruskin and Linton of misaccounted, desynchronized labor. Not only does the fence resemble and reenact the crosshatching in the Ruskin/Punch image, with a line raster meeting a diamond- or lozenge-shaped network, but it's also a section of the print that she fully understood as the most egregiously difficult of all of her laborings. "This one took me the longest time to cut. I had to cut the whole line grid on top of this mesh."[21] It took Baumgartner two years to carve this print.

Baumgartner openly embraces the split between fast and slow that arises between the two media: "Woodcut is such a manual technique, and the body is so intensely involved in it, that it really slows you down. For me it was important to deal with high speed and slowness together."[22] In 2004, Baumgartner completed a twenty-four-part woodcut titled simply *1 Sekunde* (FIG. 6.13). It was based on a single second's worth of video that she shot from a moving car while passing a nondescript woody area. Each print corresponds to a single frame of that video, representing one twenty-fourth of a second. Baumgartner painstakingly carved and printed each frame.

Ruskin had lamented the lost time of the wood engraver, who poured hours of effort into reproducing an image that was sketched in seconds and would be consumed in seconds. Wood engraving, for Ruskin, bumped or jolted the artist out of synchrony: cutting in relief is about *not* being there, *not* being in time—it's about being out of phase. Rather than attempting to recapture some sense of synchrony and presence (as in German Expressionism), Baumgartner actively cultivates that alienated state. She does this by suspending her work between temporal conditions that are inherently nonsynchronous and that lie largely outside of the range of conscious human perception. On the one hand, she works with video, which captures and transmits imagery faster than the human eye can perceive. On the other hand, however, she works so slowly that her progress on the block can barely be measured. And she works with wood, which in its own way represents a structure—a dendrochronology—that eludes human temporal understanding. There is a connection between the long-term, seasonal laying down of differentiated seasonal tissues in the wood, and the laying down of frames in digital video. But neither is really human time—wood is too slow, video is too fast. Baumgartner thus demonstrates a preoccupation with nonhuman perception and posthumanist models of apprehending time. Whether

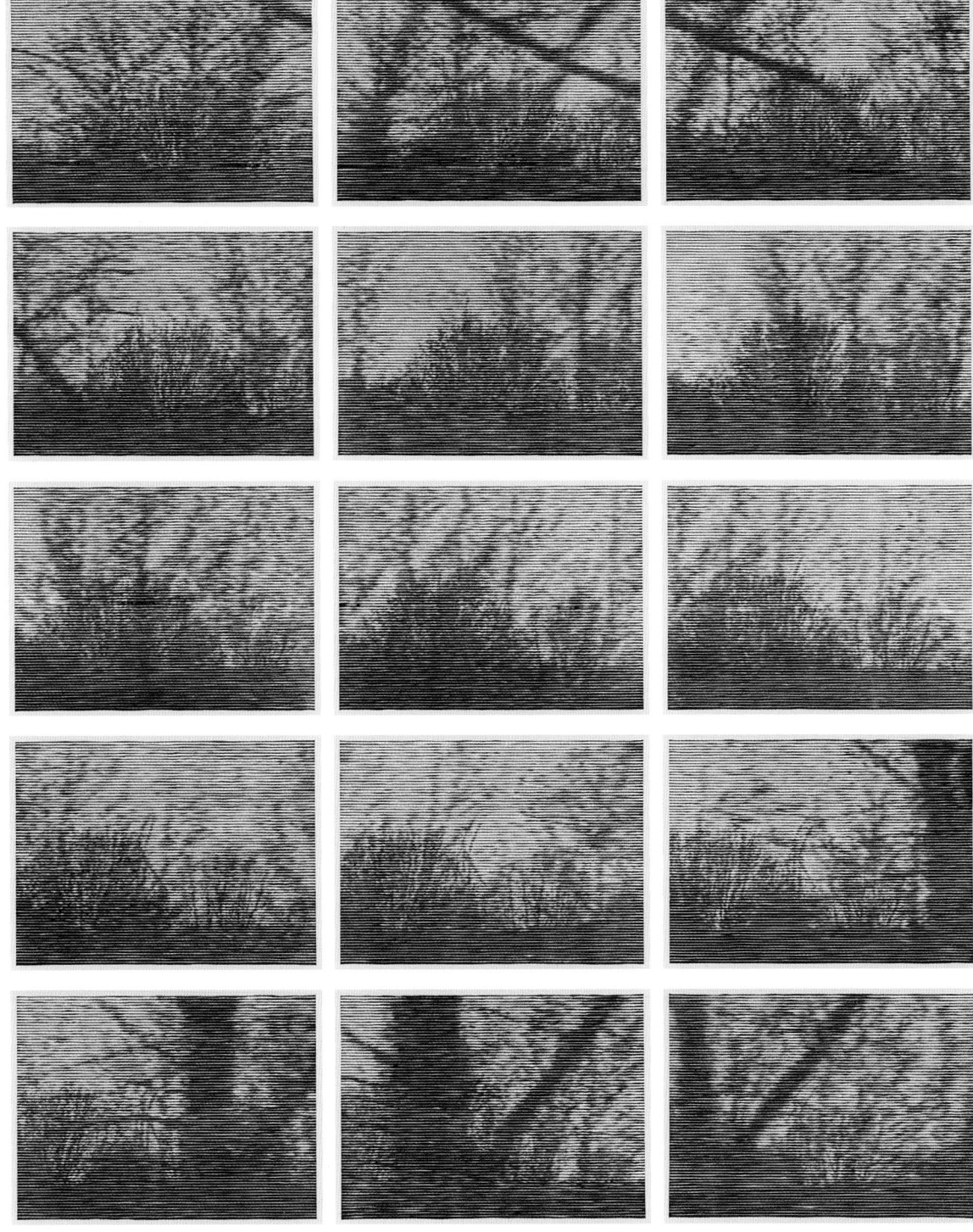

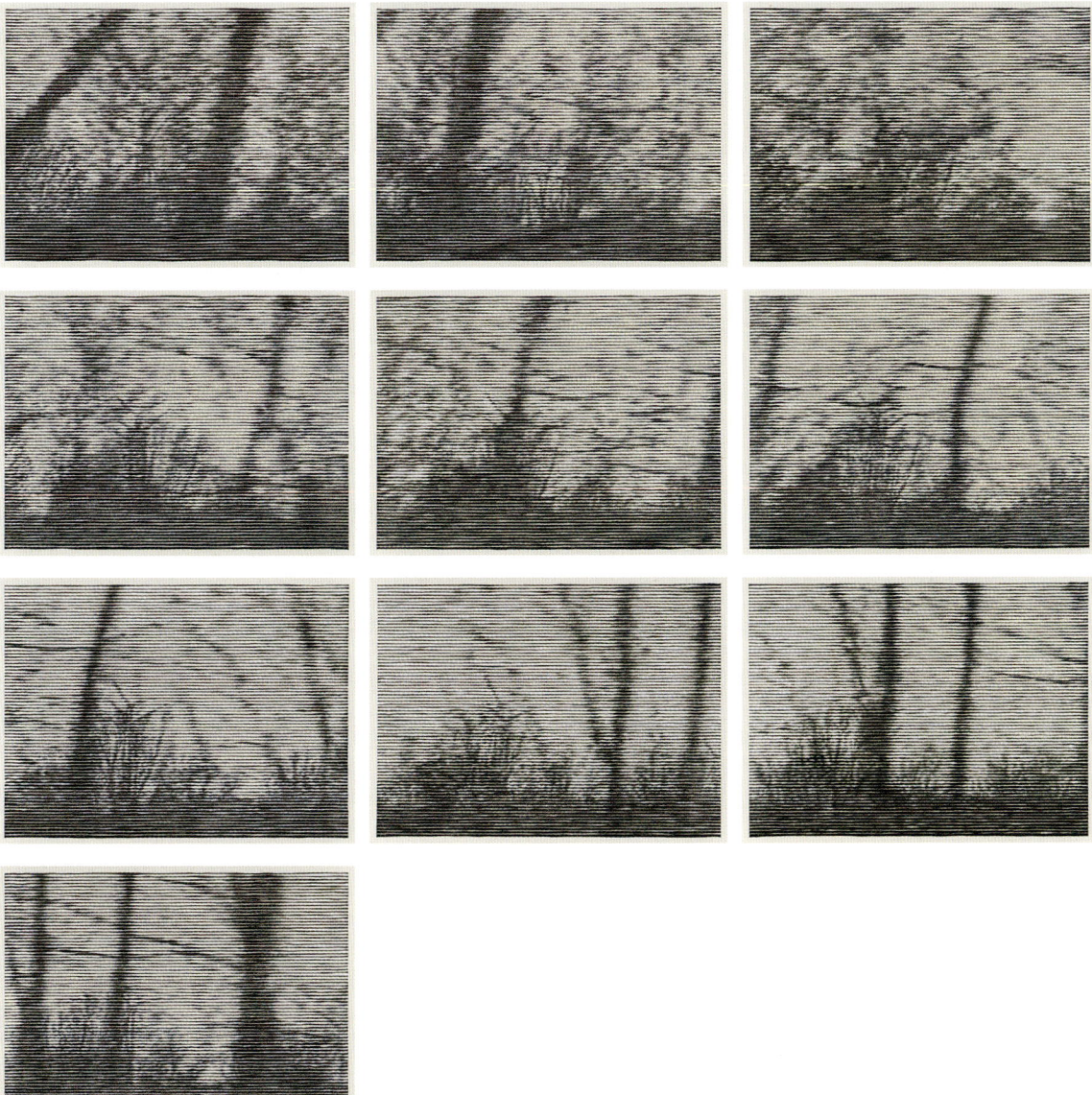

FIG. 6.13

Christiane Baumgartner, *1 Sekunde*, 2004. Woodcuts on
paper. National Gallery of Art, Washington, DC. Gift
of the Collectors Committee.

in the slow time of wood or the fast time of video, we are trapped in the cracks, the spaces, between time scales.

There are a lot of ways to take this observation, but I'd simply note that by working in woodcut, Baumgartner recognizes that the state of being out of phase, the state of alienated time, defines our contemporary lives, where we are all scrambling to adjust ourselves to timescales that exceed us, whether by attempting to keep up with rapid digital technologies or by trying to recognize and respond to the long-term rhythms of global climate change. For Baumgartner, making woodcuts is a way of inhabiting and acknowledging this paradoxical condition.

Baumgartner cuts into the woodblock at regular intervals to create her horizontal rasters. The image is built on a structure of intermittency, with her cut white spaces separating the positive marks that make up the visible image at a specific frequency. It is interesting that so much of her subject matter is similarly concerned with intermittency, with beats and periodicities—representing the division of time and space. I don't think it's an accident that Baumgartner is so drawn to the blades of turbines and propellers—on some level, she seems to recognize the connection between these structures and her own blade, her own cutting tools. Turbines and propellers slice up time and motion; Baumgartner explores the slow frequency of her own blade, cutting apart the block over the course of months, in relation to the blurred, rapid frequency of the propeller blades that are all over her work. Both of them carve up time, though at drastically different rates. Moreover, both her blade and these propellers are used for transfer, for transport, and for translation. They are figures of a kind of in-betweenness, intermediation in themselves.

A few years ago, I saw Baumgartner's retrospective exhibition at the Davis Museum at Wellesley College in Massachusetts. I was fascinated by the most recent work involving light effects and sunsets. This is *Nordlicht — 5:59 pm*, made in 2018 (FIG. 6.14). What most struck me was that it was physically difficult to *see* the new work—much more difficult than in the earlier prints. There is no comfortable distance from which to look at these images. They vibrate optically in an almost aggressive way, refusing to settle down, and I found that I frequently had to look away from them so as not to get a headache. The white suns and flares seemed to sear into the eye. Baumgartner has managed to capture at the level of bodily perception the explosive effects that have been such an important part of her military subject matter. She has talked about how she was almost embarrassed to start doing sunsets because they're such a cliché. But she keeps being drawn to their violence. As she says about them: "I really like how the sun burns into the picture, and burns into your retina."[23]

At the same time that she insists on an immediate bodily sensation caused by the sunset, on its corporeal impact, she also connects the sunset to absence

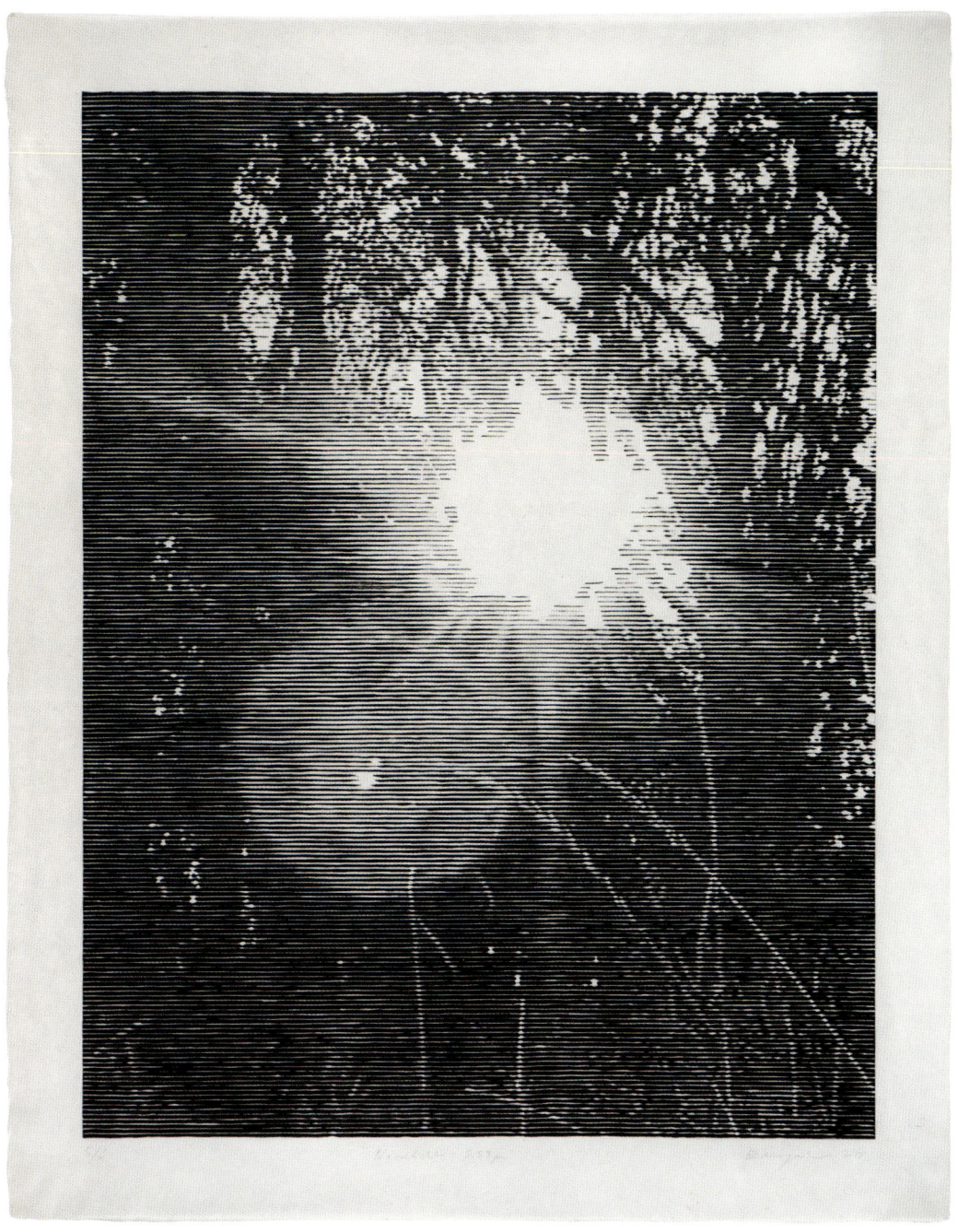

FIG. 6.14
Christiane Baumgartner, *Nordlicht — 5:59 pm*, 2018. Woodcut on
Japanese paper. Harvard Art Museums/Fogg Museum, Cambridge,
MA. Margaret Fisher 1986 Fund.

and distance and that which cannot be reached. She links sunsets to her youthful vacations in East Germany. East Germans were not allowed to travel, so they all had to gather on the Baltic coast for beach vacations. Everyone would gaze into the sunset as it fell into the west, and sometimes, she says, "you could just see, on a very clear day, some distant Danish island."[24] In other words, the sunset for Baumgartner represents a reach across space to some inaccessible elsewhere, in this case the West. This is a print that captures that paradox of press and pull, touch and distance.

Another form of loss or alienation that these sunsets evoke is the lost labor of the printmaking process itself. These are the first prints Baumgartner has made in which she allows a fully blown-out white area to occupy the surface.[25] Keeping in mind the inverted relationship between mark and matrix in relief printing, we can infer that on the block, this white sun is a hole, a crater, that Baumgartner completely cleared from the surface. The sinking sun is a time-sink; a gouged-out space. This sun in this print is somehow both a star and a kind of black hole: the place where all that un-recuperated time goes but cannot get out again. But Baumgartner carves this negative space in such a way that it becomes positive, forcing its way momentarily into the viewer's awareness, like a flare. I like to think of these suns as giving us a way to feel the alienations of Baumgartner's medium and its history, giving those losses a presence without compensating for them; making that loss, that misalignment, that disjointedness perceptible and sensible. As with all of her work, but on a more aggressive perceptual register, these sunsets keep us off guard, between cuts, between times. They keep us in contact with a state of exile.

In the introduction to *Prints and Visual Communication*, William Ivins made the rather curious suggestion that the stars served as the first analog of printed images. He argued that civilizations that developed prior to the advent of print were fatally hampered, because the advancement of useful scientific and technical knowledge required the "exactly repeatable pictorial statements" that printing made possible. Without printed images there could be no meaningful science, he argued, because precise empirical description could not be shared, compared, and compiled across space and time. He did admit that the Greeks had made great strides in astronomy, however, because, as he put it, "every clear night provides the necessary invariant image to all the world."[26] The exactly repeatable stars, then, acted as the first prints. The stars are also a model of visual coordination: two people can look up from two distant points and see essentially the same sky, therefore aligning themselves in a moment of shared experience with a shared image, in the same way that two people looking at the same print in two different cities could be synchronized.

I heartily agree that prints are like the stars, and that printing is an echo of our original relationship to the heavens (FIG. 6.15). But as Baumgartner's

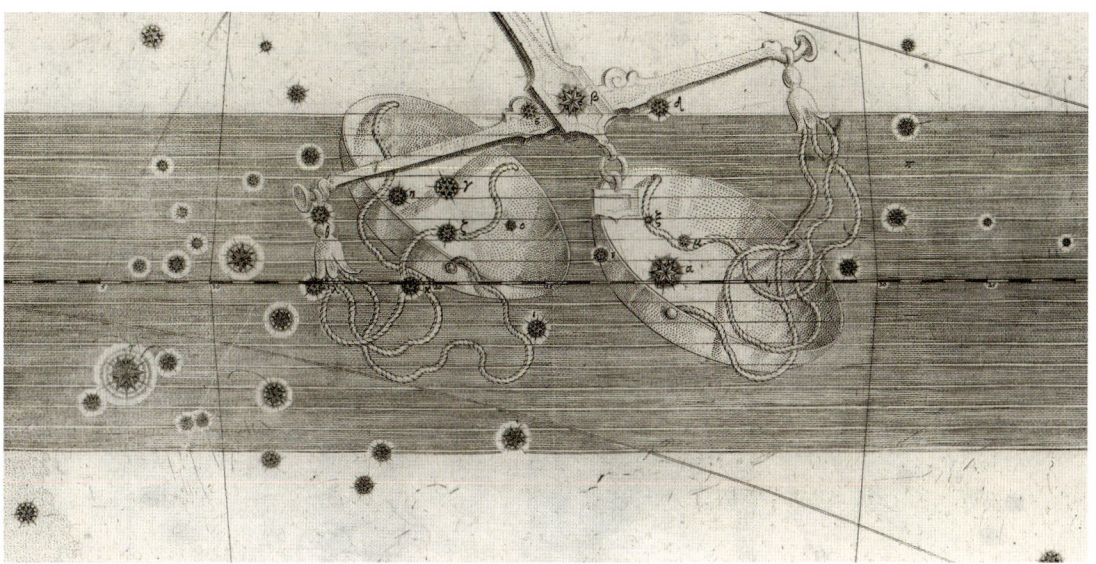

FIG. 6.15
Johann Bayer, *Uranometria: Libra, the Scales* (detail), 1655.
Engraving on paper. David Rumsey Map Collection.

burning, time-ripping sunsets remind us, it is not because the stars are synchronous. It is because the stars are asynchronous. When we look up at the stars, we are seeing light that has traveled thousands or millions or billions of years from its origin. We are looking at the past, at star-fossils. The stars in any given constellation inhabit different times, different distances, and none of them are truly present to us. We can never see a star as it is in the moment; we can never see a star live.

The stars are not synchronous with us or with each other. Contemporary artist Sarah Sze has explored this in a portfolio, titled *Midnight*, that wrestles directly with these questions of time, connection, and asynchrony. The twelve prints in the portfolio combine screenprint, digital print, and laser-engraving (FIGS. 6.16 and 6.17). Each features the front page of a newspaper dated January 1, 2014, from a different city around the world — Santiago, New York, Cairo, Beijing, and so on. The original images printed in the newspapers have been replaced with photographs of the midnight sky above that city. Taken together, the prints appear to deliver to us a form of geosynchrony: the world sharing an instant through this combination of printerly and astronomical synchronization. The common currency of newsprint meeting the common currency of the stars.[27]

FIG. 6.16
Sarah Sze, *Midnight, Santiago*, 2015. Silkscreen and digital pigment
print on laser-engraved paper. Harvard Art Museums/Fogg Museum,
Cambridge, MA. Margaret Fisher Fund.

But with even a moment's consideration, this illusion of synchrony
fails, because, of course, we are actually looking at a series of lapses in time. The
cities of the world do not really celebrate midnight on New Year's Eve simultaneously; in fact, it's on New Year's Eve that we arguably become most aware of
our temporal misalignment. We watch other cities celebrate on different sched-
ules, midnight slowly rolling around the planet, taking its time. The jewellike
printed stars that have taken over the front pages in these prints also speak to that
separation in time and space; no city sees the same midnight sky. Each has its
own divergent heavens as it looks up from the convex surface of the earth. The
stars do not, in fact, present quite the same invariant image to all the world. And,
of course, each star in each image resists synchrony as well; each takes and takes
up its own time.

Speaking of this and similar works, Sze has said that she wanted to
juxtapose the printed structure of current events with images that suggest vast
times and spaces that somehow resist the very notion of an event.[28] She uses the

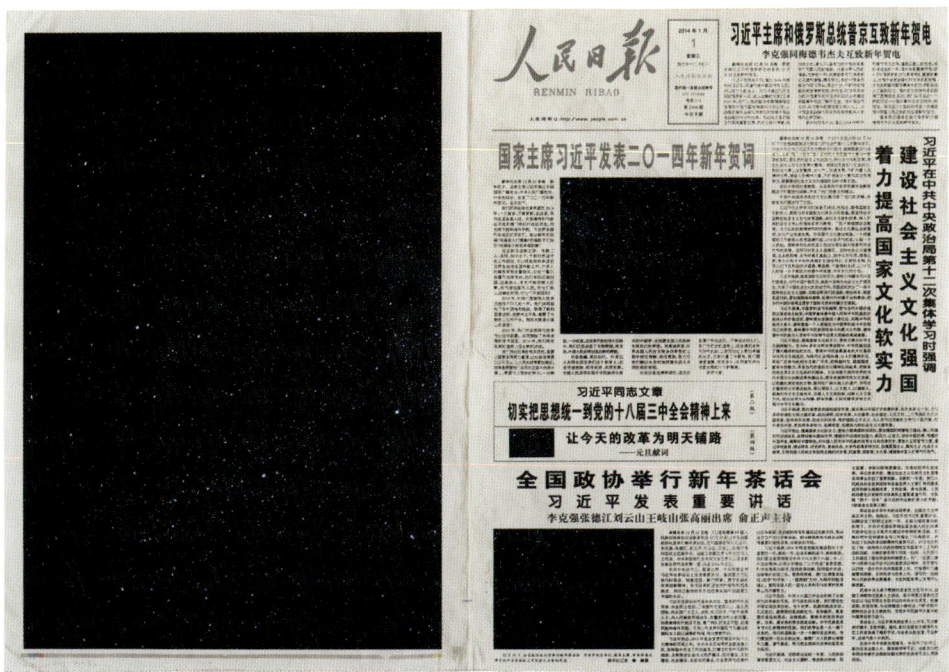

FIG. 6.17
Sarah Sze, *Midnight, Beijing*, 2015. Silkscreen and digital
pigment print on laser-engraved paper. Harvard Art Museums/
Fogg Museum, Cambridge, MA. Margaret Fisher Fund.

stars—again, perhaps the first analog for print—to complicate the newspapers'
appeal to any simple synchronicity. Like Baumgartner's work, which reaches
across timescales so as to make us feel the stretch of our own suspension between
them, Sze helps us see that print shows us our separations as well as our connections; that it can be a vehicle through which we see not sameness but difference
and distance and divergence, and the need for the constant effort it takes to
stretch across these gaps in time and space.

I've come to the end of this book by writing about cosmic distances,
asynchrony, stars, black holes, and alienation. It's starting to sound a little like
science fiction. And on that note, I want to return to the beginning of this project,
or at least to the beginning of the title. Seven or eight years ago, when it began to
dawn on me that my strange project on the physics of print could be a book, I
started playing around with working titles. My first idea was to borrow the title
from the 1999 science fiction film *The Matrix* (FIG. 6.18). I liked it a lot at first.
It would gesture to that generative surface at the heart of printmaking (the

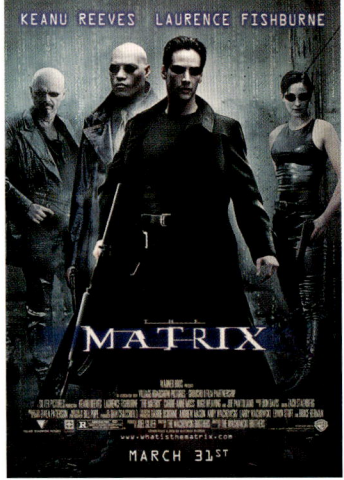

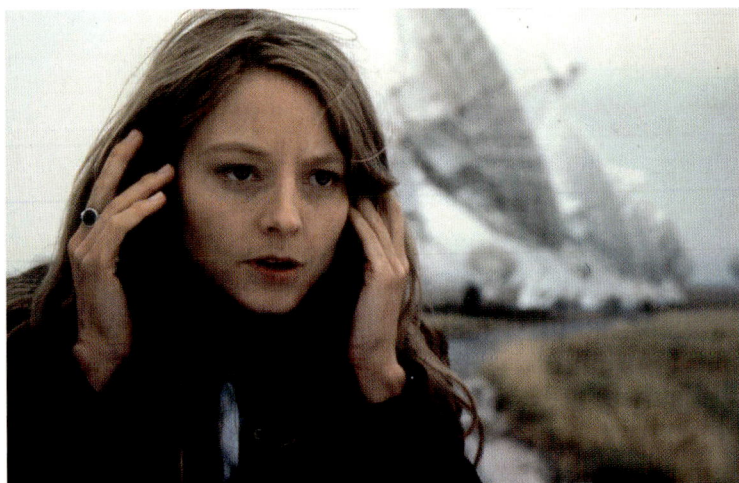

matrix) and all the defamiliarizations that happen there, while also instantly conveying the futurity of printmaking, its relevance to our own lives of technological mediation. I also liked it because it would give printmaking the Gothic air of dark mystique and rebellion that I think it deserves.

But there was something off about the reference, because the dystopian model of the matrix in the film did not match up with the matrices that I encountered in print studios. In *The Matrix*, the matrix puts people to sleep and fills their minds with illusions of normalcy so that their bodies can be literally harvested. The matrix, in other words, is a tool for exploitation, control, and mainline propaganda. It is an eviscerating tool of illusion and false consciousness. This is both too dystopian and too familiar a model—a little too close to the way print is already generally understood as a tool of mass dissemination. So that wasn't the right science fiction movie.

The right science-fiction movie, I decided, was *Contact* (FIG. 6.19)—a 1997 film written by Carl Sagan and Ann Druyan, starring Jodie Foster as a scientist who intercepts a radio signal from an interstellar civilization and has to try to interpret it. In order to decipher the signal, the film's human characters need to adjust themselves to unfamiliar forms of organizing dimensional space, unfamiliar forms of embodiment, unfamiliar forms of extension and compression in time. They need to confront the radical decentering that comes from imagining oneself in reverse: from the perspective of an other looking back across a gap. And unlike the characters in *The Matrix*, whose bodies and minds have been disconnected, the characters in *Contact* need to be awake to the effects of this estrangement, its risks and its potentials, in both body and mind.

This film about fictional contact with aliens gets us closer to the real contact with alienation that I have been trying to evoke here. Alienation is inherent to print. Print forces us outside of ourselves and asks us to attend to this experience. Every print is a transmission from an unfamiliar world: a world of reversal, deferral, disjunction, and darkness. And yet this world can only be made and known through contact; its distance emerges along with its proximity; so that it is both within us and without us. Printmaking is an art of estrangement and dispossession. As such, it can be prone to dystopian results: it can put us in Ruskin's alienated cages, if we lose track of it, if we fall asleep. But if we are awake to it, as artists or scholars or simply as engaged citizens of the contemporary world, we can seize upon its potential for recognizing difference and otherness in all its forms, including our own perpetual otherness in the face of all others. Print can keep us in direct contact with this destabilizing reality.

When I've been talking about contact in this book, this is what I've been reaching for—the way printmaking interrupts normative experience, flips us around, turns us inside out, takes us outside of ourselves. The way it compels us to confront and interpret different forms of orientation, different forms of knowledge, different forms of sensory experience. The way it brings us face to face with otherness—alienness—and makes a space for attending to difference. The way it shows our dependence on the relationships that make up the meshwork of our collective lives. The way it brings us into contact.

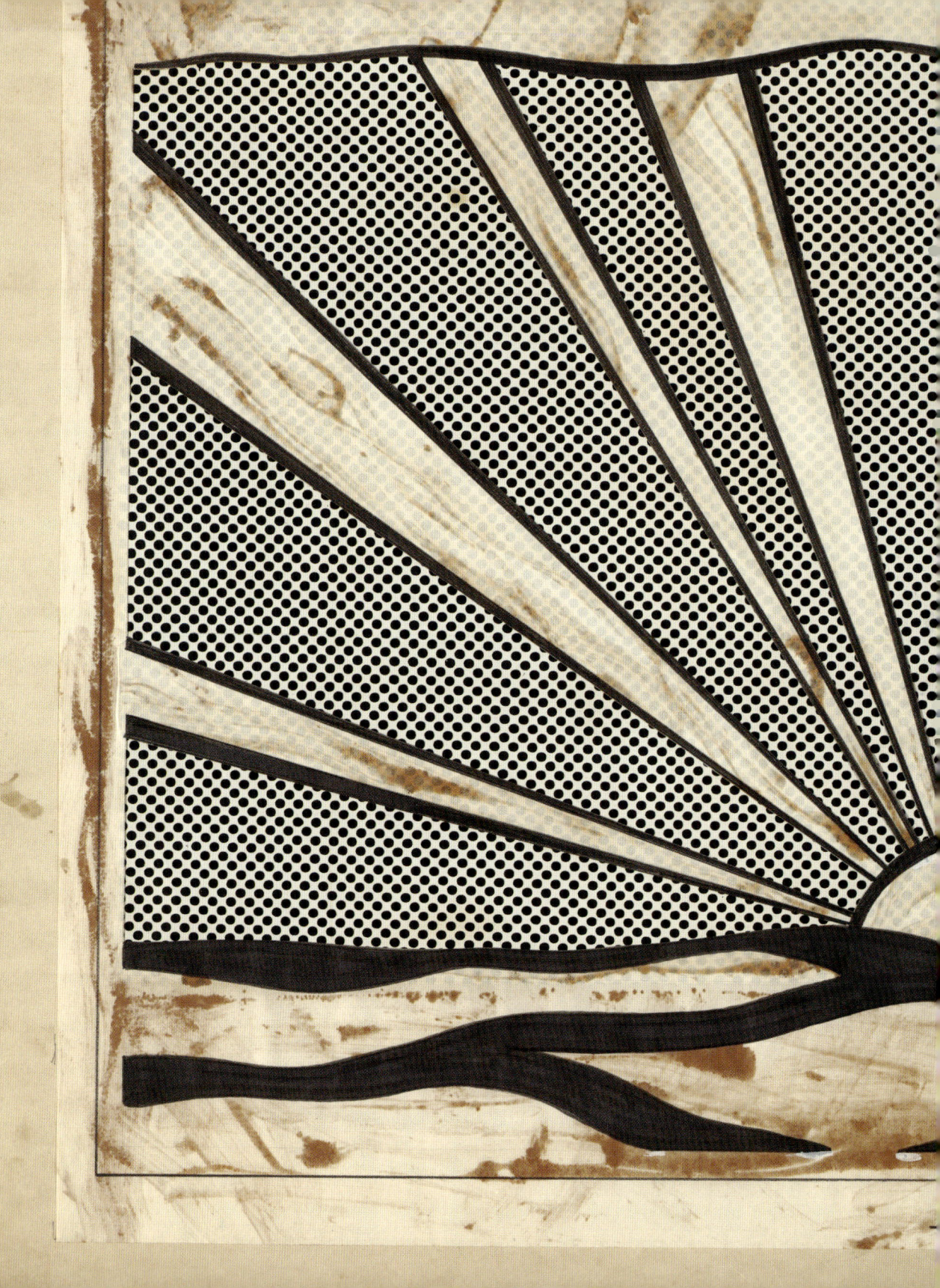

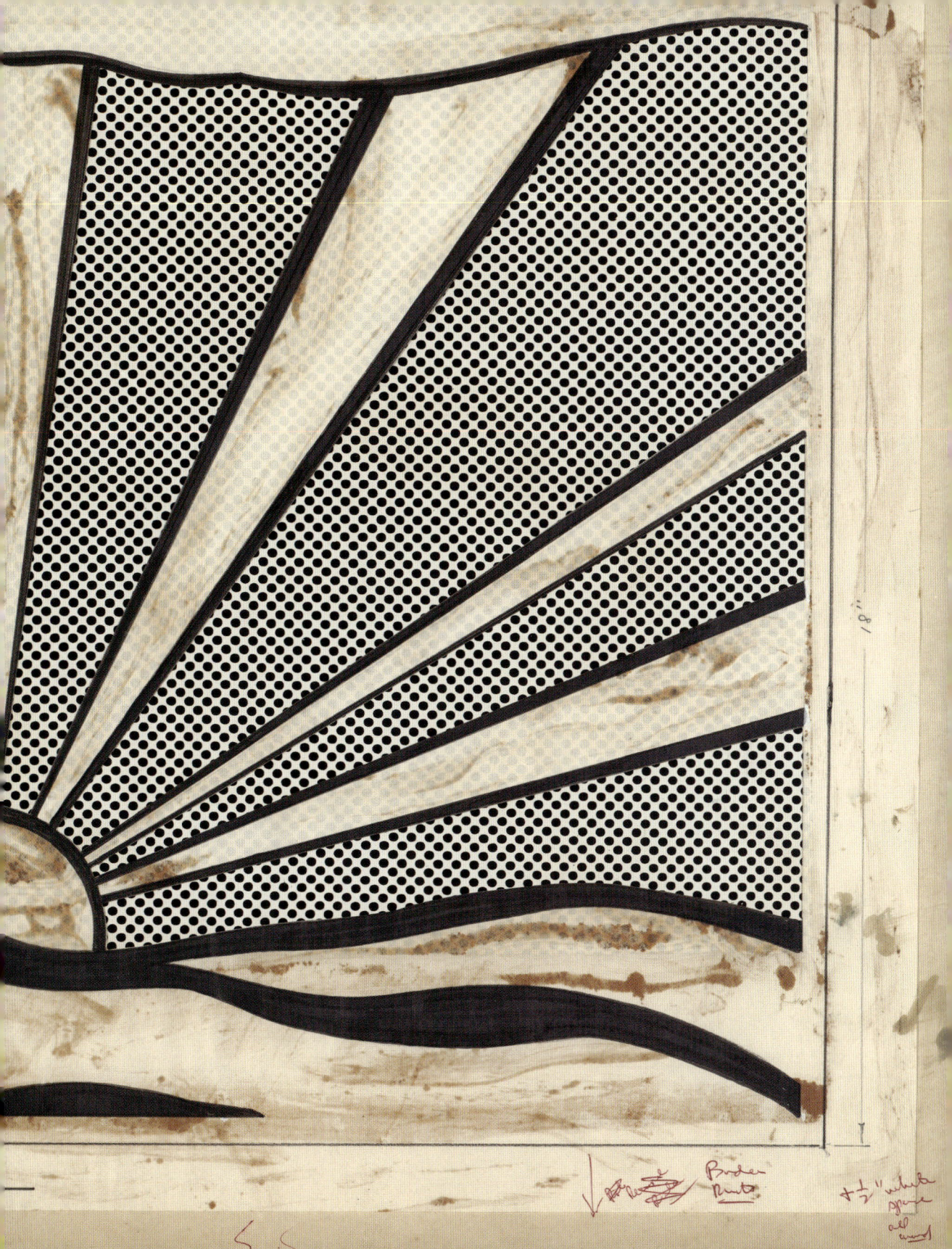

ACKNOWLEDGMENTS

Like any print project, this book has emerged from a network of distributed intelligence and a process of collaborative transfer. I am something of a latecomer to the field of print studies: when I received my PhD in 2000, I knew a lot about painting and sculpture and photography, but I could not have explained the difference between a lithograph and an etching. I had not sought (and had not been expected to seek) knowledge about printmaking as a student of modern and contemporary art history. It was not until I began simultaneously studying early American printed currency and writing about the work of Jasper Johns, a little over a decade ago, that I stumbled into my fanatical interest in print. I would never have been able to transform that interest into this book without the expertise, advice, and generous and generative collaboration of a whole array of artists, printers, curators, and scholars who always knew more than I did.

My first project on Jasper Johns was developed with students at the Harvard Art Museums; it was intended to be a small pocket exhibition based on a single painting, but instead it ballooned into a full-blown show, with a catalog, titled *Jasper Johns / In Press: The Crosshatch Works and the Logic of Print*. I sometimes wonder what would have happened if the curator assigned to serve as the liaison for student projects at the Museums at the time had not just happened to be Susan Dackerman, one of the most brilliant and innovative print curators in the field. Susan became a close friend and collaborator on that and several later projects. She helped introduce me to the (let's face it) rather intimidating world of print specialists, and she taught me most of what I know about the long history of print.

My emphasis on the essential "maneuvers" of print could not have been articulated without years of collaboration with Ethan Lasser, formerly curator of American art at the Harvard Art Museums. Ethan and I developed a series of workshops, funded by the Luce Foundation and the Faculty of Arts and Sciences at Harvard, about artisanal intelligence and its role in the practice of art history. We also co-taught a graduate seminar called "Minding Making." The ideas we hashed out in conversation with each other, with our students, and with dozens of artists and artisans and scientists over the years have indelibly shaped this book.

The most rewarding teaching experience I have had in my twenty years at Harvard has been the "Critical Printing" course I've regularly co-taught with artist Matt Saunders. With three hours of studio printmaking and three hours of historical/theoretical discussion in seminar per week, this course creates a space for intensive pedagogical crossover between the making of, the writing about, and the close study of prints. This book is largely motivated by my desire to capture what I've learned in that remarkable environment and pass it along to future generations of students. Matt's generosity and honesty as a friend and a teacher and a critic has been a constant inspiration, as has his own work as an artist, which has seeped into my thinking about the profundity of print at every level. Another formative co-teaching experience was an introductory course on visual technology that I taught long ago with Robin Kelsey; together, we worked out many of the methods linking art and technical process that I've put to work in this book. Robin is also to thank for introducing me to wood engraving, which hooked me on the whole idea of print as an inverted world that comments on the actual world from its position of critical "reverse intelligence."

Most of my education in the analysis of prints has been conducted in the study rooms of the Harvard Art Museums. I have had the extraordinary good fortune to be able to learn not only from Susan Dackerman but also from her esteemed curatorial predecessor, Marjorie (Jerry) Cohn, and her successor Elizabeth Rudy. Thank you to the entire staff of the museum and the study rooms for so often bending over backward to get me in front of works of art, particularly during the pandemic, when the museum was closed: Christina Taylor, Penley Knipe, Miriam Stewart, Mary Schneider-Enriquez, Makeda Best, Francesca Bewer, Mary Lister, Soyoung Lee, and Director (and print scholar) Martha Tedeschi.

Thanks also to the curatorial and conservation staff at the National Gallery of Art in Washington, for helping me explore and make sense of their extensive collections in the work of Robert Rauschenberg, John Cage, and Jasper Johns: especially Judith Brodie, Adam Greenhalgh, Charles Ritchie, and Julia Burke (thanks too to curator emeritus Peter Parshall for his support and encouragement of this project). Thanks to Jodi Hauptman at the Museum of Modern Art for many stimulating conversations and for inviting me to participate in the programming for her remarkable exhibition on Degas's monotypes. Thanks to Matthew Marks for giving me the opportunity to write the catalogue raisonné of Jasper Johns's monotypes, which helped me commit to the value of thinking about print in nonreproductive contexts.

I have been lucky to have had the opportunity to spend several stretches of time embedded in print studios, both as a (decidedly amateur) printmaker and as a scholar. I cannot possibly express the extent of my gratitude to the printers who have, over the years, taken the time to speak with me about their work: Bill

Goldston of Universal Limited Art Editions, Cole Rogers of Highpoint Editions, John Lund of the Jasper Johns Studio, and Craig Zammiello of Two Palms Press. Thank you to Ann Forbush and Julia Talcott of the Maud Morgan Center in Cambridge for teaching me how to make monotypes and woodcuts, respectively, and Chris Wallace for the many demos in lithography that I think I am just now, finally, beginning to grasp on an intuitive level.

This book argues that printmaking is a way of orienting yourself to the world, one that can be transferred to and cultivated in any other medium. It would have been impossible to articulate this with any specificity if I had not had a chance to learn from artists who do not necessarily identify as "printmakers" but perform this crossover every day in their own work. Every idea in this book has been honed through conversations with the likes of Christiane Baumgartner, Jennifer Bornstein, Bethany Collins, Tomashi Jackson, Andrew Raftery, Michael Zachary, and especially Jasper Johns.

This book was rehearsed in the form of lectures about prints and print-making at many institutions over the past decade, where feedback and questions were invaluable. Thanks to audiences at the University of Chicago, the Blanton Museum, the Smithsonian American Art Museum, the University of Pennsylvania, Northwestern University, the Museum of Modern Art, the Huntington Museum, the University of Minnesota, Columbia University, the Winterthur Museum, the Institute of Fine Arts at NYU, McGill University, Vassar College, Yale University, the Rhode Island School of Design, the Courtauld Institute, the Terra Summer Residency in Giverny, Brown University, and the University of California, Berkeley. An early draft of what would become the Mellon Lectures was delivered in the spring of 2019 at Cambridge University, where I served as the Slade Visiting Professor of Fine Arts. It was a pleasure to meet and learn from Rosalind Blakesley, Alexander Marr, Andrew Chen, Prerona Prasad, Amy Tobin, Carolyn Van Eck, Kirsty Dootson, Sarah Betzer, and Alexander Massouras while I was there.

Some passages of this book have been borrowed or adapted from my previously published academic writing on printmaking (where applicable, the citations to these books and essays are listed in the notes). I gratefully acknowledge the support of the editors and copyeditors who helped me develop those ideas in their earlier form.

Generations of students have contributed to this book through their sharp participation in my courses in and around making, printing, and the arts. Thanks especially to the graduate students who have assisted with research over the years: Layla Bermeo, Jennifer Chuong, Christine Garnier, Jennifer Quick, Sarah Mirseyedi, Rachel Vogel, and Christopher Williams-Wynn.

Thanks to Joseph Koerner, Yukio Lippit, Robin Kelsey, S. Hollis Clayson, Christopher Heuer, Matthew Hunter, Glenn Adamson, Meg Rotzel, and John Kramer, department colleagues and print-adjacent friends from further afield, for many conversations, often random, and not always about print, that reminded me why I am so privileged to work in print as part of the broader realm of material ideas.

For their miraculous work in producing a set of elaborately edited video lectures on a tight schedule in total pandemic isolation, thank you to the incredible team at the National Gallery: Therese O'Malley, David Hammer, Annie Miller, Elise Ferone, and Adam Williams. Kaywin Feldman, Director of the National Gallery, and Steven Nelson, Dean of the Center for Advanced Study in the Visual Arts, both offered crucial support at times when it was most needed. Emily Zoss, Magda Nakassis, Gina Broze, and Christina Wiginton handled the image permissions and acquisition process with great aplomb when it was time to publish the lectures in book form.

And most of all, thanks to Nora Rosengarten, without whose assistance I could not possibly have completed this book. She was a lifesaver during the production of the Mellon Lectures, handling most of the image research and managing the complicated interface with the National Gallery production team. She was so gifted as an executive assistant that I could forget about logistics for days on end, which was essential for my ability to think and write. She handled most of the organizational tasks for this manuscript as well, all while studying for her PhD general exams and beginning her own brilliant dissertation on printmaking. I hesitate to call her my "research assistant" because she has been as valuable to me in talking through ideas as she has been in handling delegated logistical tasks. She has had a true impact on my thinking and I look forward to seeing her own impact on art history in the future.

Thank you to my editor Michelle Komie at Princeton University Press for her confidence in and enthusiasm for this book, and to everyone on the team that helped bring this book together on a tight schedule, especially Annie Miller and Karen Carter.

And finally, to my dear friends Dario Robleto and Anna Von Mertens, who were waiting for me to finish this book so I could turn fully to collaborations with them: thank you for keeping me oriented to the celestial sphere while also reminding me about what matters here on Earth. To my family, Dan and Lottie: thank you for nothing less than everything.

NOTES

INTRODUCTION

1. The disconnect between print studies and the most vital current theoretical activity of the humanities is a common refrain in contemporary printmaking discourse. As Kathryn Reeves has noted about the state of contemporary criticism on print, "Nothing has been looked over and almost everything has been overlooked." Ruth Weisberg notes that "with a few but notable exceptions, critics and curators with powerful venues and easy access to publication have failed to provide printmaking with a theoretical framework." Kathryn Reeves, "The Re-Vision of Printmaking"; Ruth Weisberg, "The Syntax of the Print: In Search of an Aesthetic Conversation," in *Perspectives on Contemporary Printmaking: Critical Writing since 1986*, ed. Ruth Pelzer-Montada (Manchester: Manchester University Press, 2018), 72, 56. There are some exceptions to this rule, of course. One is the early modern European field in art history, in which scholarship on printmaking (at least relative to the modern and contemporary field) is well incorporated into the field and contributes meaningfully to the way the field understands itself. Another is book history/critical bibliography within literary studies, where the study of the material operations of printing text is now having a meaningful impact on the modes of interpreting text. That said, scholars of print in book history and scholars of print in art history are still largely isolated from each other.

2. For readers who would like a vivid and concise general introduction to the processes involved in making printed images, it would be difficult to do better than Richard Benson's outstanding book *The Printed Picture* (New York: Museum of Modern Art, 2008). There are many other excellent surveys that delve into the technical details of printmaking; two of particular note, for starters, include Ad Stijnman, *Etching and Engraving 1400–2000: A History of the Development of Manual Intaglio Printmaking Processes* (London: Archetype Publications, 2012), 287; and Antony Griffiths, *The Print before Photography: An Introduction to European Printmaking, 1550–1820* (London: British Museum, 2016).

3. Clement Greenberg, "Modernist Painting," *Arts Yearbook* 4 (1961).

4. William Mills Ivins, *Prints and Visual Communication* (London: Routledge and Kegan Paul, 1953). Following Ivins, Elizabeth Eisenstein and Chandra Mukerji influentially explored the capacity of print to put standardized images in many hands simultaneously, quickening the pace of gathering, amending, and processing visual knowledge. See Elizabeth Eisenstein, *The Printing Revolution in Early Modern Europe* (Cambridge: Cambridge University Press, 1983); Chandra Mukerji, *From Graven Images: Patterns of Modern Materialism* (New York: Columbia University Press, 1983). Benedict Anderson and other media theorists have equated the reproductive and disseminative capacities of print with the formation of communities and the modern civic sphere. Benedict Anderson, *Imagined Communities: Reflections on the Origin and Spread of Nationalism*, revised ed. (London: Verso, 2016). In contemporary art criticism, printmaking has appeared primarily as a replicative practice that intersects with postmodern themes of iteration and repetition, from Baudrillard's connections between copying and the precession of simulacra to Deleuze's notions of difference in repetition, and psychoanalytic approaches to copying, such as Hal Foster's famous argument that Warhol's screenprints functioned as a Lacanian form of traumatic repetition. Jean Baudrillard, *Simulacra and Simulation* (Ann Arbor: University of Michigan Press, 1994); Gilles Deleuze, *Difference and Repetition* (New York: Columbia University Press, 1994); Hal Foster, "Death in America," *October* 75 (Winter 1996): 36–59.

5. For a study of print that emphasizes its productive ambiguities and material multivalence, see Peter Parshall, S. Hollis Clayson, Christiane Hertel, and Nicholas Penny, *The Darker Side of Light: Arts of Privacy, 1850-*

1900 (Washington, DC: National Gallery of Art, 2009).

6. For a recent study of the role and status of women in printmaking in the twentieth-century United States, one that also serves as a good introduction to the gender politics of the medium more generally, see Christina Weyl, *The Women of Atelier 17: Modernist Printmaking in Midcentury New York* (New Haven, CT: Yale University Press, 2019).

CHAPTER 1: PRESSURE

1. *Oxford English Dictionary Online*, s.v. "print (*n.* and *adj.* 2)," December 2022, https://www.oed.com/.

2. David Summers, *Real Spaces: World Art History and the Rise of Western Modernism* (London: Phaidon, 2003), 35.

3. For more on the Veronica narrative and its evolution from apocryphal sources, see Emma Sidgwick, "At Once Limit and Threshold: How the Early Christian Touch of a Hem (Luke 8.44; Matthew 9.20) Constituted the Medieval Veronica," *Viator* 45, issue 1 (January 2014): 1–24. For the Sudarium in relation to printmaking, see Andrew Gordon, "The Renaissance Footprint: The Material Trace in Print Culture from Dürer to Spenser," *Renaissance Quarterly* 71 (2018): 478–529.

4. On the link between Christ's blood and ink, see Elina Gertsman, "Multiple Impressions: Christ in the Winepress and the Semiotics of the Printed Image," *Art History* 36, no. 2 (April 2013): 310–37.

5. On Cage's fire prints, see Kathan Brown and John Cage, *John Cage: Etchings 1978–1982* (Oakland, CA: Point Publications/Crown Point Press, 1982).

6. On Rauschenberg's *Hoarfrost* prints with Gemini G.E.L., see Adam Greenhalgh, Adam Novak, and Julia M. Burke, "To Print on Air: Robert Rauschenberg's *Hoarfrost Editions*," *Facture* 4 (January 2020): 220–49.

7. Leo Steinberg, "Other Criteria," *Other Criteria: Confrontations with Twentieth-Century Art* (London: Oxford University Press, 1975); David Joselit, "Notes on Surface: Toward a Genealogy of Flatness," *Art History* 23, no. 1 (March 2000): 19–34. There was one influential period model of painterly flatness that came close to the raw reality of Rauschenberg's pressed volume: this was the so-called flatbed picture plane theorized by Leo Steinberg. Steinberg, who had been inspired by Rauschenberg's earlier work to devise the model, argued that the orientation and function of the picture plane had undergone a radical shift at around midcentury. Painters were no longer thinking of the picture plane as a vertical window corresponding to an experience of observing the world upright, but rather as a horizontal surface upon which information could settle and be infinitely reconfigured. But although Steinberg's use of the term "flatbed" made a direct appeal to printing, his model of the flatbed picture plane was more tablelike than presslike; for him, the images in the new modernist paintings were like scraps of pictorial material sitting passively on a horizontal surface and waiting to be shuffled around. Rauschenberg instead takes truly printerly levels of force and pressure to be templates for the picture plane.

8. On rubbings, see Allegra Pesenti, *Apparitions: Frottages and Rubbings from 1960 to Now* (Los Angeles: Hammer Museum, 2015).

9. On Saunders, see Jennifer L. Roberts, "The Back of the Image; the Image of the Back," in *Matt Saunders: Poems of Our Climate*, ed. Deirdre O'Dwyer (New York: Dancing Foxes Press, 2022), 146–50.

10. Saidiya Hartman, *Scenes of Subjection: Terror, Slavery, and Self-Making in Nineteenth-Century America* (New York: Oxford University Press, 1997), 4.

11. On the history of ironing motifs in Cole's work, see Patterson Sims, *Willie Cole's Favorite Brands* (Montclair, NJ: Montclair Art Museum, 2006), 61–68; Wendy Weitman, *New Concepts in Printmaking 2: Willie Cole* (New York: Museum of Modern Art, 1998).

12. For an expanded version of this argument,

see Jennifer L. Roberts, "The Art of Pressure," *Willie Cole: Beauties* (Cambridge, MA: Radcliffe Institute for Advanced Study, Harvard University, 2019), 3–33. Details of the printing process come from the author's interview with Cole Rogers, Zac Adams-Bliss, and Megan Anderson at the Highpoint Center for Printmaking, Minneapolis, November 15–16, 2018.

13. On pressures in printing, see Ad Stijnman, *Etching and Engraving 1400–2000: A History of the Development of Manual Intaglio Printmaking Processes* (London: Archetype Publications, 2012), 287; Antony Griffiths, *The Print before Photography: An Introduction to European Printmaking, 1550–1820* (London: British Museum, 2016), 45. On the platen press, see National Institute of Industrial Research Board, *The Complete Book on Printing Technology* (Delhi: Asia-Pacific Business Press, n.d.), 56; NIIR Board, *Handbook on Printing Technology* (Delhi: Asia-Pacific Business Press, 2017). On lithography, see C. A. Seward, *Metal Plate Lithography — For Artists and Draftsmen* [1931] (Inman Press, 2012); W. D. Richmond, *The Grammar of Lithography* (London: Wyman & Sons, 1880). On the Two Palms hydraulic press: author interview with Craig Zammiello, February 24, 2021.

14. On Bochner's printed-word works, see Mel Bochner and Barry Schwabsky, *Mel Bochner: Words, Words, Words: Monoprints* (New York: Two Palms, 2012); Mel Bochner, *Amazing! Mel Bochner Prints*, with essays by Sienna Brown, Ruth Fine, and Barry Schwabsky, and an interview by Jan Howard (New York: Artbook DAP, in association with the Philbrook Museum of Art and the Jordan D. Schnitzer Family Foundation, 2018).

15. "Printing with Sound," Wyss Institute, August 31, 2018, https://wyss.harvard.edu/news/printing-with-sound/.

16. The photographer Bruce Talamon took an important series of photographs of Hammons assuming these positions as he made the prints. Talamon would not release the rights to his photographs for this project, but they can be consulted in Linda Goode Bryant, Senga Nengudi, Bruce W. Talamon, Laura Hoptman, and David Hammons, *David Hammons:*

Body Prints, 1968–1979, Drawing Papers 144 (New York: The Drawing Center, 2021). On Hammons, see also Joseph E. Young, *Three Graphic Artists: Charles White, David Hammons, Timothy Washington* (Los Angeles: Los Angeles County Museum of Art/Santa Barbara Museum of Art, 1971), 7–8; Bruce Davis and Ebria Feinblatt, *Los Angeles Prints: 1883–1980* (Los Angeles: Los Angeles County Museum of Art, 1981), 26, 81.

17. Kellie Jones, *South of Pico: African American Artists in Los Angeles in the 1960s and 1970s* (Durham, NC: Duke University Press, 2017), 227.

18. Young, *Three Graphic Artists*, 8.

CHAPTER 2: REVERSAL

1. On the topic of reversal and its challenges in printmaking prior to the mid-nineteenth century, see Ad Stijnman, *Etching and Engraving 1400–2000: A History of the Development of Manual Intaglio Printmaking Processes* (London: Archetype Publications, 2012), 160–62; Antony Griffiths, *The Print before Photography: An Introduction to European Printmaking, 1550–1820* (London: British Museum, 2016), 38–42; Peter Parshall, "Albrecht Dürer and the Axis of Meaning," *Allen Memorial Museum Art Bulletin* 1, no. 2 (1997). On Rembrandt's *Lazarus*, see Stijnman, *Etching and Engraving 1400–2000*, 162; Griffiths, *The Print before Photography*, 35.

2. For more on the generative role of print in Johns's oeuvre, see Jennifer L. Roberts, "The Printerly Art of Jasper Johns," *Jasper Johns/In Press: The Crosshatch Works and the Logic of Print* (Cambridge: Harvard Art Museums, 2012), 10–42; Jennifer L. Roberts, "The Metamorphic Press: Jasper Johns and the Monotype," in *Jasper Johns: Catalogue Raisonné of the Monotypes*, ed. Susan Dackerman and Jennifer L. Roberts (New York: Matthew Marks Gallery, 2017).

3. Katrina Martin, "An Interview with Jasper Johns about Screenprinting" [1980], in *Jasper Johns: Writing, Sketchbook Notes, Interviews*, ed. Kirk Varnedoe (New York: The Museum of Modern Art, 1996), 209.

4. Johns interviewed by Christian Geelhaar (1979), reprinted in Varnedoe, ed., *Jasper Johns: Writing, Sketchbook Notes, Interviews*, 195.

5. W. J. Linton, *Wood-Engraving, A Manual of Instruction* (London: G. Bell, 1884), 57–58.

6. Matt Saunders, conversation with the author.

7. Jasper Johns in Martin, "An Interview with Jasper Johns about Screenprinting," 209.

8. Vija Celmins, interviewed by Betsy Sussler, October 18, 2011, Museum of Modern Art Archives, The Oral History Program, New York, 45. For more on Celmins and the desirable difficulty of printmaking, see her interview: Samantha Rippner with Vija Celmins, "A Delicate Balance: An Interview with Vija Celmins," in *The Prints of Vija Celmins* (New York: The Metropolitan Museum of Art, 2002), 12.

9. See, for example, Judith Brodie and Adam Greenhalgh, *Yes, No, Maybe: Artists Working at Crown Point Press* (Washington, DC: National Gallery of Art, 2013), 30–33.

10. Kathryn Reeves, "The Re-Vision of Printmaking," in *Perspectives on Contemporary Printmaking: Critical Writing Since 1986*, ed. Ruth Pelzer-Montada (Manchester: Manchester University Press, 2020), 78.

11. *Oxford English Dictionary Online*, s.v. "proof (*n.* and *adj.*)," accessed January 13, 2023, https://www.oed.com. Leon Battista Alberti, *On Painting*, trans. Cecil Grayson (London: Penguin Books, 1991), 83: book 2, paragraph 46: "I do not know how it is that paintings that are without fault look beautiful in a mirror; and it is remarkable how every defect in a picture appears more unsightly in a mirror. So the things that are taken from Nature should be emended with the advice of a mirror."

12. On chirality, see James P. Riehl, *Mirror-Image Asymmetry: An Introduction to the Origin and Consequences of Chirality* (Hoboken, NJ: Wiley, 2010).

13. Kirk Varnedoe, *Jasper Johns: A Retrospective* (New York: Museum of Modern Art, 1996), 28.

14. Jasper Johns, interviewed by Yoshiaki Tono, "I Want Images to Free Themselves from Me," *Geijutsu Shincho* (Tokyo) 15, no. 8 (August 1964). Reprinted in Varnedoe, ed., *Jasper Johns: Writings, Sketchbook Notes, Interviews*, 100.

15. Jasper Johns, interviewed by Marjorie Welish, "Jasper Johns," *BOMB*, no. 57 (1996): 50.

16. Jennifer L. Roberts, "Backwords: Screenprinting and the Politics of Reversal," in *Corita Kent and the Language of Pop*, ed. Susan Dackerman (Cambridge, MA: Harvard Art Museums, 2015), 61–73.

17. Corita Kent, *Yale Daily News*, March 14, 1966, 6.

18. Matthew Hunter, "The Theory of the Impression According to Robert Hooke," in *Printed Images in Early Modern Britain: Essays in Interpretation*, ed. Michael Hunter (Farnham, UK: Ashgate, 2010), 175.

19. Stijnman, *Etching and Engraving 1400–2000*, 156. For detailed discussions of transfer techniques in early print shops, see Stijnman, 155–59; Griffiths, *The Print before Photography*, 34–42. Griffiths, 35: "Such oiled transfer sheets became very brittle and few survive from before the end of the eighteenth century."

20. Claire Bishop, "Antagonism and Relational Aesthetics," *October* 123 (Winter 2008): 73.

21. Griffiths, *The Print before Photography*, 42: "Whenever artists or engravers tried to do this themselves, they made mistakes in the reversal." Usually, this job was left to a letter engraver. An entire profession of letter engravers developed in the second half of the sixteenth century.

22. Bruce Nauman interview in *Bruce Nauman, Prints 1970–89: A Catalogue Raisonné*, ed. Christopher Cordes with assistance of Debbie Taylor (New York: Castelli Graphics/Lorence-Monk Gallery, 1989), 24.

23. John Yau, "Words and Things: The Prints of Bruce Nauman," in *Bruce Nauman, Prints 1970–89: A Catalogue Raisonné*, ed. Christopher Cordes with assistance of Debbie Taylor (New York: Castelli Graphics/Lorence-Monk Gallery, 1989), 8.

24. Yau, "Words and Things," 17.

25. William S. Smith, with Hock E Aye Vi Edgar Heap of Birds, "In the Studio: Hock E Aye Vi Edgar Heap of Birds," *Art in America*, September 25, 2017, https://www.artnews.com/art-in-america/features/in-the-studio-hock-e-aye-vi-edgar-heap-of-birds-63298/.

CHAPTER 3: SEPARATION

1. Davis Baird, *Thing Knowledge: A Philosophy of Scientific Instruments* (Berkeley: University of California Press, 2004), 8–10.

2. Amy Sillman, "On Color," in *Painting beyond*

Itself: The Medium in the Post-medium Condition, ed. Isabelle Graw and Ewa Lajer-Burcharth (Berlin: Sternberg Press, 2016), 103.

3. On the history of hand-coloring, see Susan M. Dackerman, *Painted Prints: The Revelation of Color in Northern Renaissance and Baroque Engravings, Etchings, and Woodcuts* (Baltimore: Baltimore Museum of Art, 2002).

4. See Bryan F. LeBeau, *Currier & Ives: America Imagined* (Washington, DC: Smithsonian Institution Press, 2001).

5. For the origins of the *disegno e colore* debate, see Giorgio Vasari, *The Lives of the Artists* [1550], trans. Julia Conaway Bondanella and Peter Bondanella (Oxford: Oxford University Press, 1991); Lodovico Dolce, *Aretin, or, A Dialogue on Painting* [1557], trans. W. Brown, (London: I. Dodsley & others, 1970). For an art-historical discussion and historiography of the subject, see David Rosand, *Painting in Sixteenth Century Venice* (Cambridge: Cambridge University Press, 1997), 10–25.

6. For an excellent technical history of color printing in Europe from the sixteenth through the twentieth centuries, see Ad Stijnman, *Etching and Engraving 1400–2000: A History of the Development of Manual Intaglio Printmaking Processes* (London: Archetype Publications, 2012), 360–65.

7. For a video of this process book in action, paging through each layer of color, see "Highpoint Editions — Decade One," Minneapolis Institute of Art, September 27, 2011, YouTube video, 4:00–5:10, https://www.youtube.com/watch?v=GJzujB_kzGI.

8. Julie Mehretu, quoted in Siri Engberg, "Beneath the Surface: Julie Mehretu and Printmaking," *Excavations: The Prints of Julie Mehretu* (Minneapolis, MN: Highpoint Editions, 2009), 10.

9. Statement made by Julie Mehretu to students at San Francisco Art Institute, quoted in Kathan Brown, "Julie Mehretu: The Residual," Julian Page, 2007, https://julianpage.co.uk/artists/34-julie-mehretu/works/201-julie-mehretu-the-residual-2007/.

10. On map engraving, see David Woodward, ed., *Five Centuries of Map Printing* (Chicago: University of Chicago Press, 1975).

11. On Cassatt's color etchings — and *The Bath* in particular — see Nancy Mowll Mathews and Barbara Stern Shapiro, eds., *Mary Cassatt: The Color Prints* (New York: H. N. Abrams in association with Williams College Museum of Art, 1989), 103–11. On French intaglio printmaking in the late nineteenth century, see Phillip Dennis Cate et al., *From Pissarro to Picasso: Color Etching in France; Works from the Bibliothèque Nationale and the Zimmerli Art Museum* (Paris: Flammarion, 1992).

12. Emily York, *Magical Secrets about Aquatint: Spit Bite, Sugar Lift & Other Etched Tones Step-by-Step* (San Francisco: Crown Point Press, 2008), 229–30.

13. I learned this in conversations with master printers John Lund and Bill Goldston, in studio visits on June 30, 2016, and March 3, 2016, respectively.

14. For my understanding of the technical/material challenge of color printing (as well as other technical topics), I have frequently relied on the commercial trade literature. See especially Gordon Pritchard, "Ink Sequence — 4/C Process & Beyond," *The Print Guide* (blog), July 13, 2009, http://the-print-guide.blogspot.com/search/label/Ink%20Sequence.

15. Arthur W. (Arthur Wesley) Dow, *Arthur Wesley Dow, 1857–1922: His Art and His Influence* (New York: Spanierman Gallery, 1999), 11.

16. Douglas Druick, "Jasper Johns: Gray Matters," in James Rondeau, *Jasper Johns: Gray* (Chicago: The Art Institute of Chicago, 2007), 99.

17. Jasper Johns, in *U.S.A. Artists 8: Jasper Johns*, produced and directed by Lane Slate, written by Alan R. Solomon (National Education Television Network and Radio Center, 1966), 16 mm film, transcribed in Varnedoe, ed., *Jasper Johns: Writings, Sketchbook Notes, Interviews*, 125.

18. Chuck Close, quoted in Richard Shiff, "Through a Slow Medium," *Chuck Close Prints: Process and Collaboration* (Princeton, NJ: Princeton University Press, 2003), 27.

19. Sol LeWitt, "Sentences on Contemporary Art," in *Conceptual Art: A Critical Anthology*, ed. Alexander Alberro and Blake Stimson (Cambridge, MA: The MIT Press, 1999), 106–8.

20. For an outstanding (and rare) discussion of Warhol's process, see Marco Livingstone, "Do It

Yourself: Notes on Warhol's Techniques," in *Andy Warhol: A Retrospective*, ed. Kynaston McShine (New York: Museum of Modern Art, 1989), 63–78.

21. Fredric Jameson, *Postmodernism, or, The Cultural Logic of Late Capitalism* (Durham, NC: Duke University Press, 1991), 9.

22. On Bradford's installation, see Evelyn C. Hankins and Stéphane Aquin, *Mark Bradford: Pickett's Charge* (Washington, DC: Hirshhorn Museum and Sculpture Garden, 2018).

23. Mark Bradford, in Carol S. Eliel, "Dynamism and Quiet Whispers: Conversations with Mark Bradford," in *Mark Bradford*, ed. Christopher Bedford (Columbus, OH: Wexner Center for the Arts, 2010), 63.

CHAPTER 4: STRAIN

1. For a thorough and indispensable history of commercial screenprinting, see Guido Lengwiler, *A History of Screen Printing: How an Art Evolved into an Industry* (Cincinnati, OH: ST Media Group International, 2013), especially 62–99. See also J. I. Biegeleisen, *The Complete Book of Silk Screen Printing Production* (New York: Dover Publications, 1963).

2. On the fine-art adventures of screenprinting in the US, particularly in the first half of the twentieth century, see Reba and Dave Williams, *American Screenprints* (New York: National Academy of Design, 1987).

3. On the halftone, see Dusan C. Stultik and Art Kaplan, *Halftone: The Atlas of Analytical Signatures of Photographic Processes* (Los Angeles: Getty Conservation Institute, 2013); Jules Verfasser, *The Half-Tone Process: A Practical Manual of Photo-Engraving in Half-Tone on Zinc, Copper, and Brass* (London: Iliffe & Sons, 1904). On halftone screenprinting, see Albert Kosloff, *Photographic Screen Process Printing* (Cincinnati, OH: Signs of the Times Publishing, 1955).

4. David McCarthy, "Andy Warhol's Silver Elvises: Meaning through Context at the Ferus Gallery in 1963," *The Art Bulletin* 88, no. 2 (2006): 355–56.

5. Siri Engberg, "The Weather of Prints: An Interview with Edward Ruscha" [July 16, 1998], in Edward Ruscha, *Leave any Information at the Signal: Writings, Interviews, Bits, Pages* (Cambridge, MA: MIT Press, 2002), 366.

6. The most nuanced and sensitive discussion of Warhol's screenprinting as a refutation of the techniques and values of painting is Benjamin Buchloh, "Andy Warhol's One-Dimensional Art: 1956–1966," in *Andy Warhol: A Retrospective*, ed. Kynaston McShine (New York: Museum of Modern Art, 1989), 39–57. On deskilling, see the work of John Roberts, especially "Art After Deskilling," *Historical Materialism* 18 (2010): 77–96.

7. Ad Reinhardt, quoted in Richard S. Field, "Silkscreen: The Media Medium," *Artnews* 70, no. 9 (January 1972): 40–43, 75.

8. Field, "Silkscreen," 40; William Mills Ivins, *Prints and Visual Communication* (London: Routledge and Kegan Paul, 1953), 177.

9. Josef Albers, *Interaction of Color* (New Haven, CT: Yale University Press, 1963).

10. Anni Albers, *On Weaving*, expanded ed. (Princeton, NJ: Princeton University Press, 2017); Carol Armstrong, "Seurat's Media, or A Matrix of Materialities," *Grey Room* 58 (Winter 2015).

11. On bolting cloth, see Lengwiler, *A History of Screen Printing*, 52–99.

12. On the continued use of silk bolting cloth through the 1960s, see Biegeleisen, *Complete Book of Silk Screen Printing Production*, 88–92.

13. "Sefar—Filter Technology," Sefar, accessed June 21, 2023, https://www.sefar.us.

14. Bruno Latour, "A Collective of Humans and Nonhumans," *Pandora's Hope: Essays in the Reality of Science Studies* (Cambridge, MA: Harvard University Press, 1999), 189.

15. On the *News . . .* portfolio and Ruscha's views on processing, see Christopher Fox, "Ed Ruscha Discusses His Latest Work with Christopher Fox," *Studio International* 179, no. 923 (June 1970): 281.

16. Ed Ruscha, *News, Mews, Pews, Brews, Stews, & Dues* (London: Editions Electo, 1970), colophon page.

17. Max Kozloff, "'Pop' Culture, Metaphysical Disgust, and the New Vulgarians," *Art International* 7 (March 1962): 36.

18. Alan Solomon, "The New Art" [1963], reprinted in *Artists, Critics, Context: Readings in and Around American Art Since 1945*, ed. Paul F. Fabozzi (Hoboken, NJ: Prentice Hall, 2002), 79.

19. On Warhol's screenprinting methods, see Marco Livingstone, "Do It Yourself: Notes on Warhol's Techniques," in *Andy Warhol: A Retrospective*, ed. Kynaston McShine (New York: Museum of Modern Art, 1989), 63–78.

20. Huey Copeland, "Glenn Ligon and Other Runaway Subjects," *Representations* 113, no. 1 (2011): 73–110. Scott Rothkopf, ed., *Yourself in the World: Selected Writings and Interviews; Glenn Ligon* (New Haven, CT: Yale University Press, 2011), 82, 99.

21. On coal dust, see Rothkopf, ed., *Yourself in the World*, 113. Édouard Glissant, "For Opacity," *Poetics of Relation*, trans. Betsy Wing (Ann Arbor: University of Michigan Press, 1997), 189–94.

22. Janet A. Kaplan, "The Quiet in the Land: Everyday Life, Contemporary Art, and the Shakers; A Conversation with Janet A. Kaplan," *Art Journal* 57, no. 2 (1998): 4–27.

23. Mother Ann Lee, quoted in Guy Brett, "Survey: Itinerary," in *Mona Hatoum* (London: Phaidon Press, 1997), 78.

CHAPTER 5: INTERFERENCE

1. For details on the project, see Jacklyn Babington, *Stoned Moon: Robert Rauschenberg* (Canberra: National Gallery of Australia, 2010).

2. Timothy Morton, *Hyperobjects: Philosophy and Ecology after the End of the World* (Minneapolis: University of Minnesota Press, 2013). Thanks to Sarah Mirseyedi for making this connection.

3. Cliff Lethbridge, "Saturn V Apollo Launch," Spaceline, accessed January 14, 2023, https://www.spaceline.org/cape-canaveral-rocket-missile-program/saturn-v-apollo-fact-sheet/.

4. On Rauschenberg's lithography in the 1960s and 1970s, see Ruth E. Fine, "Writing on Rocks, Rubbing on Silk, Layering on Paper," in *Robert Rauschenberg: A Retrospective*, ed. Susan Davidson and Walter Hopps (New York: Solomon R. Guggenheim Museum, 1997), 376–89; Jay Belloli, *Rauschenberg at Gemini: An Exhibition Organized by the Armory Center for the Arts* (Pasadena, CA: Armory Center for the Arts, 2010); Sienna Brown, "The Lithographs of Robert Rauschenberg" (PhD diss., Emory University, 2010). On photosensitizing stones, see *Robert Rauschenberg: Prints 1948/1970* (Minneapolis: Minneapolis Institute of Arts, 1970), n.p.

5. Rauschenberg, quoted in Babington, *Stoned Moon*, 9.

6. Martin Kemp, "Coming into Line: Graphic Demonstrations of Skill in Renaissance and Baroque Engravings," in *Sight & insight: Essays on Art and Culture in Honour of E. H. Gombrich at 85*, ed. John Onians (London: Phaidon Press, 1994), 232. For a more sanguine view of early modern moiré, see Andrew Raftery, "The Beneficence of the Rule: Decoding Invention in Engraving Technique," in *The Brilliant Line: Following the Early Modern Engraver, 1480–1650*, ed. Emily J. Peters (Providence: Rhode Island School of Design Museum of Art, 2009), 125–41.

7. Kemp, "Coming into Line," 235.

8. William Mills Ivins, *Prints and Visual Communication* (London: Routledge and Kegan Paul, 1953), 100.

9. In 1852, William Henry Fox Talbot patented a textile "halftone" screen made of gauzy fabric — one of the earliest episodes in halftone's history. For more on Talbot and his involvement in the halftone, see Dusan C. Stultik and Art Kaplan, *Halftone: The Atlas of Analytical Signatures of Photographic Processes* (Los Angeles: Getty Conservation Institute, 2013).

10. The technical literature on moiré is too scattered to summarize effectively here. Prior to the 1990s, it tends to be tucked into trade journals and instructional books on photomechanical printing and screenprinting; for example, Albert Kosloff, *Photographic Screen Process Printing* (Cincinnati, OH: Signs of the Times Publishing, 1955), 149–50, 163–64. After the advent of the internet, there is a more conversational literature in blog and forum format. See, for example, the online technical notes of Gordon Pritchard, "Why Use Halftone Screen Angles?" *The Print Guide* (blog), accessed January 15, 2023, http://the-print-guide.blogspot.com/2010/02/why-use-halftone-screen-angles.html; Gordon Pritchard, "Halftone Screen Angles," *The Print Guide* (blog), accessed January 15, 2023, http://the-print-guide.blogspot.com/2009/05/halftone-screen-angles.html. There is also the genre of manuals and troubleshooting documents distributed by companies that make commercial printers:

e.g., *Moiré, Rosettes, and Color Shifts: Technical Information* (Hauppage, NY: Linotype-Hell Company, 1992). There is also relevant research published in physics and engineering journals: see Joseph Shou-Pying Shu et al., "Moiré factors and Visibility in Scanned and Printed Halftone Images," *Optical Engineering* 28, no. 7 (July 1989): 805–12.

11. On screen angles and color CMYK printing, see, for example, Gordon Pritchard, "Rosettes: Everything You Didn't Realize You Needed to Know," *The Print Guide* (blog), accessed January 15, 2023, http://the-print-guide.blogspot.com /2009/04/rosettes-everything-you-didnt-realize .html.

12. See Gerhard Richter, *Elisabeth I*, 1966, offset lithograph, 73.7 x 60.3 cm, Museum of Fine Arts, Boston; Ed Ruscha, *Now Then, As I was About to Say*, 1973, shellac on moiré rayon, 90.8 × 101.6 cm, Museum of Modern Art, New York; and Roy Lichtenstein, *Landscape 2*, 1967, screenprint on board with transparent moiré Rowlux overlay, 30.4 x 45.8 cm, Harvard Art Museums, Cambridge, MA.

13. Sigmar Polke, quoted in Stefan Gronert, *Sigmar Polke: Girlfriends* (London: Afterall Books, 2017), 48.

14. Gerald Oster and Yasunori Nishijima, "Moiré Patterns," *Scientific American* 208, no. 5 (May 1963): 54–63. There is a robust literature in physics, acoustics, and optics on moiré phenomena. See, for example, Isaac Amridor, *The Theory of the Moiré Phenomenon*, vols. 1 and 2, Springer Computational Imaging and Vision Series no. 38 (London: Springer-Verlag, 2009).

15. See for example Isaac Amridor et al., "Moiré Methods for the Protection of Documents and Products: A Short Survey," *Journal of Physics: Conference Series* 77, no. 1 (2007): 1–10; Daniel Post et al., "Moiré Methods for Engineering and Science — Moiré Interferometry and Shadow Moiré," *Photomechanics: Topics in Applied Physics* 77 (2000): 151–96.

16. Taylor Walsh, entry on "Circles of Confusion," in *Corita Kent and the Language of Pop*, ed. Susan Dackerman (Cambridge, MA: Harvard Art Museums, 2015), 100.

17. Mary Lynn Kotz, *Rauschenberg, Art and Life* (New York: Harry N. Abrams, 2004), 180.

18. On the series see Mark Smith, *Image and Word in the Prints of Robert Rauschenberg, 1951–1981* (PhD diss., University of Texas at Austin, 1992), 83–95. For the exhibitions at Dayton's Gallery 12 (April 4–May 2, 1970), Automation House and Castelli Graphics (June 5–June 27, 1970), and Pasadena Art Museum (July 7–September 6, 1970), see John C. Stoller, *Rauschenberg Currents* (Minneapolis: Dayton's Gallery 12, 1970).

19. On Ligon's project, see Ellen Y. Tani, "'Come Out to Show Them': Speech and Ambivalence in the Work of Steve Reich and Glenn Ligon," *Art Journal* 78, no. 4 (2019): 24–37; and Janet Kraynak, "How to Hear What Is Not Heard: Glenn Ligon, Steve Reich, and the Audible Past," *Grey Room* 70 (2018): 54–79.

20. See Elizabeth Gibney, "How 'Magic Angle' Graphene is Stirring up Physics," *Nature* 565 (2019): 15–18.

21. Leo Steinberg, "Other Criteria," *Other Criteria: Confrontations with Twentieth-Century Art* (London: Oxford University Press, 1975); David Joselit, "Notes on Surface: Toward a Genealogy of Flatness," *Art History* 23, no. 1 (March 2000): 19–34.

22. See Brown, "Lithographs of Robert Rauschenberg," 77.

23. See Jennifer L. Roberts, *Dario Robleto: Unknown and Solitary Seas; Dreams and Emotions of the Nineteenth Century* (Cambridge, MA: Harvard Radcliffe Institute, 2019).

24. See Jeffrey Deitch and Rebecca Morse, eds., *Cai Guo-Qiang: Ladder to the Sky* (Munich: Prestel, 2012).

CHAPTER 6: ALIENATION

1. Charles Haxthausen, "Translation and Transformation in Target with Four Faces," in Elizabeth Armstrong et al., *Jasper Johns: Printed Symbol* (Minneapolis, MN: Walker Art Center, 1990), 71.

2. Jasper Johns, in Joseph E. Young, "Jasper Johns: An Appraisal," *Art International* 13 (September 1969), reproduced in Kirk Varnedoe, ed., *Jasper Johns: Writings, Sketchbook Notes, Interviews* (New York: Museum of Modern Art, 1996), 131.

3. Richard Benson, *The Printed Picture* (New York: Museum of Modern Art, 2008), 8.

4. John Evelyn, *Sculptura* [1662], ed. C. F. Bell (Oxford: The Clarendon Press, 1906), 56.

5. On wood engraving, see John Jackson and W. A. Chatto, *A Treatise on Wood Engraving: Historical and Practical*, 2nd ed. (London, 1861).

6. C.M.J., "Lessons in Wood-Engraving," *The Art Amateur* 11, no. 6 (November 1884): 124.

7. See Amy M. Von Lintel, "Wood Engravings, the 'Marvellous Spread of Illustrated Publications,' and the History of Art," *Modernism/Modernity* 19, no. 3 (September 2012): 515–42. See Ann Prentice Wagner, "The Graver, the Brush, and the Ruling Machine: The Training of Late-Nineteenth-Century Wood Engravers," in *The Cultivation of Artists in Nineteenth-Century America*, ed. Georgia Brady Barnhill et al. (Worcester, MA: American Antiquarian Society, 1997), 143–67.

8. See, for example, Robert Hunt, "Application of Photography to Wood-Engraving," *The Art Journal* 47 (November 1858): 335–36.

9. On the industrialization of the process, see Gerry Beegan, "The Mechanization of the Image: Facsimile, Photography, and Fragmentation in Nineteenth-Century Wood Engraving," *Journal of Design History* 8, no. 4 (1995): 257–74.

10. John Ruskin, *Ariadne Florentina: Six Lectures on Wood and Metal Engraving*, vol. 1 (New York: John Wiley and Son, 1874), 74.

11. W. J. Linton, *Wood-Engraving: A Manual of Instruction* (London: G. Bell, 1884), 29.

12. Ruskin, *Ariadne Florentina*, 74.

13. Ruskin, *Ariadne Florentina*, 75.

14. Ruskin, *Ariadne Florentina*, 75.

15. Ruskin, *Ariadne Florentina*, 90.

16. Tom Gretton, "Signs for Labour-Value in Printed Pictures after the Photomechanical Revolution: Mainstream Changes and Extreme Cases around 1900," *Oxford Art Journal* 28, no. 3 (2005): 376.

17. Thomas Marks and Christiane Baumgartner, "'I Don't Call Myself a Printmaker'—An Interview with Christiane Baumgartner," *Apollo*, March 26, 2018.

18. For an excellent introduction to Baumgartner's work, see Lisa Fischman et al., *Christiane Baumgartner: Another Country* (Munich: Hirmer, 2018). For the early work, see especially Jasper Kettner, "Woodcut in Motion:

Time in the Prints of Christiane Baumgartner," *Print Quarterly* 24, no. 1 (March 2007): 21–37.

19. Baumgartner, email to the author, March 17, 2019.

20. Public conversation between Christiane Baumgartner and Paul Coldwell at Chelsea College of Art and Design, London, February 17, 2011, cited in Paul Coldwell, "Christiane Baumgartner Between States," in *Art in Print* 1 no. 1 (May–June 2011): n.p.

21. Christiane Baumgartner, "Davis Museum: Artist Talk Christiane Baumgartner," [lecture on September 20, 2018 in Wellesley, MA], YouTube video, https://www.youtube.com/watch?v=z42A7oyOdz8.

22. Marks and Baumgartner, "'I Don't Call Myself a Printmaker,'" n.p.

23. Baumgartner, "Davis Museum: Artist Talk Christiane Baumgartner."

24. Baumgartner, "Davis Museum: Artist Talk Christiane Baumgartner."

25. Baumgartner, email to the author, March 17, 2019.

26. William Mills Ivins, *Prints and Visual Communication* (London: Routledge and Kegan Paul, 1953), 16.

27. "Sarah Sze / Victoria Miro," Victoria Miro Gallery (London), June 11, 2015, YouTube video, beginning at 2:20, https://www.youtube.com/watch?v=GBZCdu8ywcs.

28. Sarah Sze, "Sarah Sze on How to Make Sense of Your Life," Phaidon, accessed January 15, 2023, https://www.phaidon.com/agenda/art/articles/2015/february/02/sarah-sze-on-how-to-make-sense-of-your-life/.

CREDITS

Alfred Eisenstaedt / The LIFE Picture Collection / Shutterstock, photo: fig. 4.3

© Andrew Raftery: fig. 2.13 (right)

© 2023 The Andy Warhol Foundation for the Visual Arts, Inc. / Licensed by Artists Rights Society (ARS), New York: fig. 0.3, fig. 3.20, fig. 4.1, fig. 4.4, fig. 4.7

© Ann Parker: fig. 1.12

Courtesy artist and Cristea Roberts Gallery, London. Andreas Bode, photo: fig. 6.9

Reproduced with permission of Bedfordshire Archives: fig. 1.19

Ben Blackwell, Courtesy of San Francisco Museum of Modern Art, photo: fig. 4.4

© Birgitte Rubæk; Birgitte Rubæk, photo: fig. 1.4

Bocskai Istvan, photo: fig. 5.10

Boston Public Library, photo: fig. 6.5

Bridgeman Images, photo: fig. 4.13

© British Library Board. All Rights Reserved / Bridgeman Images, photo: fig. 2.12

© 2023 Bruce Nauman / Artists Rights Society (ARS), New York: fig. 2.16, fig. 2.17, fig. 2.18

© Cai Guo-Qiang: fig. 5.21

Cary Markerink, Courtesy Kröller-Müller Museum, photo: fig. 2.18 (right)

Cathy Carver for Hirshhorn Museum and Sculpture Garden, photo: fig. 3.22

CC BY 4.0: fig. 5.18

© 2023 Christiane Baumgartner / Artists Rights Society (ARS), New York / VG Bild-Kunst, Bonn: fig. 6.1, fig. 6.10, fig. 6.11, fig. 6.12, fig. 6.13, fig. 6.14

© Chuck Close Estate: fig. 3.17

© 2023 Corita Art Center / Immaculate Heart Community / Licensed by Artists Rights Society (ARS), New York: fig. 2.10

Courtesy of Cristea Roberts Gallery, photo: fig. 6.11, fig. 6.12

© Daniel B. Freeman: fig. 1.8

© Dario Robleto: fig. 5.20

© David Hammons: fig. 1.20

David Kern, photo: fig. 1.16

© David Lees Photography Archive / Bridgeman Images, photo: fig. 2.4

David Rumsey Map Collection, David Rumsey Map Center, Stanford Libraries, photo: fig. 6.15

© Dedar Milano: fig. 5.7

© Ed Ruscha: fig. 2.15, fig. 4.14, fig. 4.16

FlixPix / Alamy Stock Photo, photo: fig. 6.18

Photograph provided by the Frank J. Thomas Archives: fig. 4.7

Fredrik Nilsen, photo: fig. 2.7

Getty Research Institute, photo: fig. 4.5

© Glenn Ligon; courtesy of the artist, Hauser & Wirth, New York, Regen Projects, Los Angeles, Thomas Dane Gallery, London, and Galerie Chantal Crousel, Paris: fig. 2.6, fig. 2.7, fig. 4.17, fig. 4.18, fig. 5.17

© Gymnastics Art Institute, courtesy of Virgil Abloh Securities: fig. 2.14

Hickey-Robertson, Courtesy The Menil Collection, Houston, photo: fig. 0.1

© Hock E Aye Vi Edgar Heap of Birds: fig. 2.19, fig. 2.20, fig. 2.21

© Ian Mortimer 1989, 2023, photo: fig. 6.2

© Iris Schneider Photographs: fig. 0.4

© 2023 James Rosenquist Foundation / Licensed by Artists Rights Society (ARS), NY. Used by permission. All rights reserved: fig. 5.13, fig. 5.15

© 2023 Jasper Johns / Licensed by VAGA at Artists Rights Society (ARS), NY: fig. 0.1, fig. 2.3, fig. 2.4, fig. 2.9, fig. 3.8, fig. 3.16

© Jennifer Bornstein: fig. 1.11

© Jennifer L. Roberts, photo: fig. 1.9, fig. 1.10 (bottom), fig. 1.15, fig. 1.16, fig. 1.17, fig. 2.1, fig. 2.5, fig. 2.11, fig. 3.1, fig. 3.7, fig. 3.11 (right), fig. 3.19 (bottom), fig. 4.9, fig. 4.10 (bottom), fig. 6.3, fig. 6.4, fig. 6.7

Jennifer L. Roberts and Matt Saunders, photo: fig. 5.11

© John Cage Trust: fig. 1.5

John Kramer Design: fig. 0.5

Jon Sullivan (public domain), Color separation by Jacob Rus (CC BY-SA 4.0), photo: fig. 3.10

© The Josef and Anni Albers Foundation / Artists Rights Society (ARS), New York, 2023: fig. 4.9, fig. 4.10, fig. 4.11

Joshua White, photo: fig. 3.23

INDEX

Evans, Tony: photograph by, **122**
Evelyn, John, 171

False Start I (Johns), 90–91, **91**
Field, Richard S., 113
Field Painting (Johns), 45, **46**
fire, printing with, 16–17, **18**, 161, 163
Five Beauties Rising (Dot) (Cole), 29, **31**
flatness, 19–24, 98, 201n7
*Florentina: Six Lectures on Wood and Metal
   Engraving* (Ruskin), **176**
food: as ink, 120–24
Freeman, Daniel B.: photograph by, **20**
Freundinnen (Polke), 146, **147**, 150

German expressionism, 178, **179**
Ghosthymn (After the Raft) (Mehretu), 78, **81**
Gibney, Elizabeth: article pictured, **158**
Glissant, Édouard, 130
Gray Alphabets (Johns), 5, **6**
Greenberg, Clement, 4, 157
Green Marilyn (Warhol), **9**
Grevenbroeck, Jan van, II: work pictured, **119**
Grosman, Tatyana: pictured, **9**
Gulf (Rauschenberg), 157, **159**

Half-Tone Process, The (Verfasser): illustration
   from, **110**
halftones: and binarization, 109; Bradford's use
   of, 99–101; CMYK color separation process
   and, 80, 144–45, **145**; and decline of wood
   engraving, 178; dots and, 109, 137, 144, 150;
   and interference patterns (moiré), 84, 137–39,
   144–53; Ivins on, 114; and photograph
   conversion, 109, 149; Polke's use of, 146–50;
   and Pop Art, 146–50; rasters and, 109, 125,
   148–50, 180–81 (*see also* rasters);
   Rauschenberg's use of, 92–94, 137–39,
   152–55, 178; Rosenquist's use of, 93, 149, 152;
   and transfer of image for lithography, 137;
   Warhol's use of, 5, 106–9, 125
Hamm, Daniel, 155, 165
Hammons, David, 27, 35–39; work pictured, **38**
*Hand Printing Operation at the de Angeli-Frua
   Plant, Milan, Italy* (Eisenstaedt), **107**
Harris & Ewing, **110**
Hartman, Saidiya, 27
Hatoum, Mona, 130; work pictured, **131**

Haxthausen, Charles, 168
Head of Leda (da Vinci), **23**
Heap of Birds, Hock E Aye Vi Edgar, 66–69;
   pictured working, **68**; works pictured, **67**, **68**,
   69
Hiett, Harry L.: illustration from manual by, **119**
Highpoint Center for Printmaking, 27, 76–78
Hiroshige, Utagawa: work pictured, **85**
Hoarfrost Editions (Rauschenberg), 17, **19**, 19–21,
   22, **23**, 33, 45
Hooke, Robert, 56–57; drawing of ammonites
   (snake stones), **57**
*How-To-Do-It Charts on Materials, Equipment,
   Techniques for Screen Printing* (Hiett):
   illustration from, **119**
hyperobjects, 133

ink: definition of, 13; material properties of, 83;
   Ruscha's use of foods as, 120–24; smoke or
   soot as, 163
inking: and color separation printing (*see* color
   separation); hand-coloring the matrix for
   color printing, 74–75; and screenprinting,
   106–9
intaglio, 11, 28, 30–33, 82–83
Interaction of Color (Albers), 114; illustration
   from, **115**
interference, 3–4. *See also* moiré
Ivins, William, 4, 113–14, 142, 188

Jackie (Warhol), **104**
Jameson, Fredric, 98
Japanese printing technology and techniques: for
   color printing, 83; katagami stencil as, 105,
   106
Jensen, Niels Borch, 17
jigsaw plate printing, 74
Johns, Jasper, 5, 8, 33; on artistic control during
   printing process, 53, 91, 168; and color, 78,
   90–91; pictured, **9**; and printmaking
   background, 43; and reversal, 43–45, 52–53;
   and spatial experience, 52; and subjectivity,
   53–54; works pictured, **6**, **44**, **46**, **53**, **80**, **91**
Jones, Kellie, 37

Kass, Deborah, 62
Kemp, Martin, 142
Kent, Corita, 54–55, 59–60, 68; work pictured, **55**
Khakis (Bornstein), 24, **25**

Jennifer L. Roberts is the Drew Gilpin Faust Professor of the Humanities at Harvard University. She is the author of *Transporting Visions: The Movement of Images in Early America*, *Jasper Johns/In Press: The Crosshatch Works and the Logic of Print*, and *Mirror-Travels: Robert Smithson and History*.

A. W. MELLON LECTURES IN THE FINE ARTS, 1952–2023

1952 Jacques Maritain, *Creative Intuition in Art and Poetry* (published 1953)

1953 Sir Kenneth Clark, *The Nude: A Study of Ideal Art* (published as *The Nude: A Study in Ideal Form*, 1956)

1954 Sir Herbert Read, *The Art of Sculpture* (published 1956)

1955 Étienne Gilson, *Art and Reality* (published as *Painting and Reality*, 1957)

1956 E. H. Gombrich, *The Visible World and the Language of Art* (published as *Art and Illusion: A Study in the Psychology of Pictorial Representation*, 1960)

1957 Sigfried Giedion, *Constancy and Change in Art and Architecture* (published as *The Eternal Present: A Contribution on Constancy and Change*, 1962–64)

1958 Sir Anthony Blunt, *Nicolas Poussin and French Classicism* (published as *Nicolas Poussin*, 1967)

1959 Naum Gabo, *A Sculptor's View of the Fine Arts* (published as *Of Divers Arts*, 1962)

1960 Wilmarth Sheldon Lewis, *Horace Walpole* (published 1960)

1961 André Grabar, *Christian Iconography and the Christian Religion in Antiquity* (published as *Christian Iconography: A Study of Its Origins*, 1968)

1962 Kathleen Raine, *William Blake and Traditional Mythology* (published as *Blake and Antiquity*, 1968)

1963 Sir John Pope-Hennessy, *Artist and Individual: Some Aspects of the Renaissance Portrait* (published as *The Portrait in the Renaissance*, 1966)

1964 Jakob Rosenberg, *On Quality in Art: Criteria of Excellence, Past and Present* (published 1967)

1965 Sir Isaiah Berlin, *Sources of Romantic Thought* (published as *The Roots of Romanticism*, 1999)

1966 Lord David Cecil, *Dreamer or Visionary: A Study of English Romantic Painting* (published as *Visionary and Dreamer: Two Poetic Painters, Samuel Palmer and Edward Burne-Jones*, 1969)

1967 Mario Praz, *On the Parallel of Literature and the Visual Arts* (published as *Mnemosyne: The Parallel between Literature and the Visual Arts*, 1970)

1968 Stephen Spender, *Imaginative Literature and Painting*

1969 Jacob Bronowski, *Art as a Mode of Knowledge* (published as *The Visionary Eye: Essays in the Arts, Literature, and Science*, 1978)

1970 Sir Nikolaus Pevsner, *Some Aspects of Nineteenth-Century Architecture* (published as *A History of Building Types*, 1976)

1971 T. S. R. Boase, *Vasari: The Man and the Book* (published as *Giorgio Vasari: The Man and the Book*, 1979)

1972 Ludwig H. Heydenreich, *Leonardo da Vinci*

1973 Jacques Barzun, *The Use and Abuse of Art* (published 1974)

1974 H. W. Janson, *Nineteenth-Century Sculpture Reconsidered* (published as *The Rise and Fall of the Public Monument*, 1976)

1975 H. C. Robbins Landon, *Music in Europe in the Year 1776*

1976 Peter von Blanckenhagen, *Aspects of Classical Art*

1977 André Chastel, *The Sack of Rome: 1527* (published 1982)

1978 Joseph W. Alsop, *The History of Art Collecting* (published as *The Rare Art Traditions: The History of Art Collecting and Its Linked Phenomena Wherever These Have Appeared*, 1982)

1979 John Rewald, *Cézanne and America* (published as *Cézanne and America: Dealers, Collectors, Artists, and Critics, 1891–1921*, 1989)

1980 Peter Kidson, *Principles of Design in Ancient and Medieval Architecture*

1981 John Harris, *Palladian Architecture in England, 1615–1760*

1982 Leo Steinberg, *The Burden of Michelangelo's Painting*

1983 Vincent Scully, *The Shape of France* (published as *Architecture: The Natural and the Manmade*, 1991)

1984 Richard Wollheim, *Painting as an Art* (published 1987)

1985 James S. Ackerman, *The Villa in History* (published as *The Villa: Form and Ideology of Country Houses*, 1990)

1986 Lukas Foss, *Confessions of a Twentieth-Century Composer*

1987 Jaroslav Pelikan, *Imago Dei: The Byzantine Apologia for Icons* (published 1990)

1988 John Shearman, *Art and the Spectator in the Italian Renaissance* (published as *Only Connect: Art and the Spectator in the Italian Renaissance*, 1992)

1989 Oleg Grabar, *Intermediary Demons: Toward a Theory of Ornament* (published as *The Mediation of Ornament*, 1992)

1990 Jennifer Montagu, *Gold, Silver, and Bronze: Metal Sculpture of the Roman Baroque* (published 1996)

1991 Willibald Sauerländer, *Changing Faces: Art and Physiognomy through the Ages*

1992 Anthony Hecht, *The Laws of the Poetic Art* (published as *On the Laws of the Poetic Art*, 1995)

1993 John Boardman, *The Diffusion of Classical Art in Antiquity* (published 1994)

1994 Jonathan Brown, *Kings and Connoisseurs: Collecting Art in Seventeenth-Century Europe* (published 1995)

1995 Arthur C. Danto, *Contemporary Art and the Pale of History* (published as *After the End of Art: Contemporary Art and the Pale of History*, 1997)

1996 Pierre M. Rosenberg, *From Drawing to Painting: Poussin, Watteau, Fragonard, David, Ingres* (published as *From Drawing to Painting: Poussin, Watteau, Fragonard, David, and Ingres*, 2000)

1997 John Golding, *Paths to the Absolute* (published as *Paths to the Absolute: Mondrian, Malevich, Kandinsky, Pollock, Newman, Rothko, and Still*, 2000)

1998 Lothar Ledderose, *Ten Thousand Things: Module and Mass Production in Chinese Art* (published 2000)

1999 Carlo Bertelli, *Transitions*

2000 Marc Fumaroli, *The Quarrel between the Ancients and the Moderns in the Arts, 1600–1715*

2001 Salvatore Settis, *Giorgione and Caravaggio: Art as Revolution*

2002 Michael Fried, *The Moment of Caravaggio* (published 2010)

2003 Kirk Varnedoe, *Pictures of Nothing: Abstract Art since Pollock* (published 2006)

2004 Irving Lavin, *More than Meets the Eye*

2005 Irene J. Winter, *"Great Work": Terms of Aesthetic Experience in Ancient Mesopotamia*

2006 Simon Schama, *Really Old Masters: Age, Infirmity, and Reinvention*

2007 Helen Vendler, *Last Looks, Last Books: The Binocular Poetry of Death* (published as *Last Looks, Last Books: Stevens, Plath, Lowell, Bishop, Merrill*, 2010)

2008 Joseph Leo Koerner, *Bosch and Bruegel: Parallel Worlds?* (published as *Bosch and Bruegel: From Enemy Painting to Everyday Life*, 2016)

2009 T. J. Clark, *Picasso and Truth* (published as *Picasso and Truth: From Cubism to Guernica*, 2013)

2010 Mary Miller, *Art and Representation in the Ancient New World*

2011 Mary Beard, *The Twelve Caesars: Images of Power from Ancient Rome to Salvador Dalí* (published as *Twelve Caesars: Images of Power from the Ancient World to the Modern*, 2021)

2012 Craig Clunas, *Chinese Painting and Its Audiences* (published 2017)

2013 Barry Bergdoll, *Out of Site in Plain View: A History of Exhibiting Architecture since 1750*

2014 Anthony Grafton, *Past Belief: Visions of Early Christianity in Renaissance and Reformation Europe*

2015 Thomas Crow, *Restoration as Event and Idea: Art in Europe, 1814–1820* (published as *Restoration: The Fall of Napoleon in the Course of European Art, 1812–1820*, 2018)

2016 Vidya Dehejia, *The Thief Who Stole My Heart: The Material Life of Chola Bronzes from South India, c. 855–1280* (published as *The Thief Who Stole My Heart: The Material Life of Sacred Bronzes from Chola India, 855–1280*, 2021)

2017 Alexander Nemerov, *The Forest: America in the 1830s* (published as *The Forest: A Fable of America in the 1830s*, 2023)

2018 Hal Foster, *Positive Barbarism: Brutal Aesthetics in the Postwar Period* (published as *Brutal Aesthetics: Dubuffet, Bataille, Jorn, Paolozzi, Oldenburg*, 2020)

2019 Wu Hung, *End as Beginning: Chinese Art and Dynastic Time* (published as *Chinese Art and Dynastic Time*, 2022)

2021 Jennifer L. Roberts, *Contact: Art and the Pull of Print* (published 2024)

2022 Richard J. Powell, *Colorstruck! Painting, Pigment, Affect* 2

2023 Stephen D. Houston, *Vital Signs: The Visual Cultures of Maya Writing*